AMERICAN GUIDANCE for SENIORS
... and their caregivers

Dedicated to all Senior Citizens — regardless of their race, color, creed, origin of birth, handicap, age or sex — in hopes of making their lives a little better...

KEN SKALA

The intent of this book is to inform the Senior Citizens of our country of the benefits, entitlements and assistance available to them. It is not the intent of either the author or the publisher to provide any legal or financial services. These services should be furnished by either a lawyer, accountant or financial adviser. Consequently, the author and publisher specifically disclaim any liability, loss or risk, personal or otherwise, resulting as a direct or indirect consequence from the reader's use or application of any of the contents of this book.

AMERICAN GUIDANCE FOR SENIORS
... AND THEIR CAREGIVERS

International Standard Book Number: 0-944873-05-7
Library of Congress Catalog Card Number: 93-091571

Printed in the United States of America

Distributed by: G&S
                           P.O. Box 8782
                           Falls Church, VA 22041

AMERICAN GUIDANCE for SENIORS

... and their caregivers

This book tells how our nation, its government, and its people are working to help Senior Americans ensure their financial security and quality of life. It is a book of CARING about others!

Although the terms "older Americans," "Seniors," and "Senior Citizens" are used throughout this book, all lawful permanent residents of the United States are entitled to the benefits and privileges available to American citizens.

Some Special Thoughts . . .

Most writers receive their inspiration to
write because of some event or from
someone that touches their lives in a
profound way. Even though this book is
dedicated to *all* older Americans, one
person, in particular, will always be in
my thoughts for she has continually given
of herself to all those in need with
warmth and understanding.
My very special thoughts and thanks
to my **mother** for being such a fine example
of our older generation in America, and
for teaching me the true meaning of
caring for others.

FROM THE AUTHOR ...

Currently, there are nearly 44 million Americans over the age of 60. Several million more younger Americans care for parents or other Seniors. While many Seniors are financially secure and able to enjoy this period of their lives, too many of them are just barely meeting the costs of daily existence because of their inadequate pensions, the high rate of inflation over the years that has eaten away their savings, the amount of taxes they have paid, and most important, the exorbitant cost of health care. Thousands more will become impoverished because of the enormous costs of a catastrophic illness or long-term nursing home care. Consequently, it is vital that all older Americans and those who care for them be knowledgeable about the many programs of assistance available to them.

While many federal and state agencies and private organizations offer hundreds of programs, services, and benefits to help Seniors, most Americans are either unaware of them or don't know how to take advantage of them. Tragically, millions of dollars in benefits and assistance are lost each year by Seniors and their caregivers. I have written this book to help Seniors and those who care for them learn how to obtain the help they need.

As you read this book, consider it the first stepping stone on the path towards getting the benefits and entitlements available to you or your loved ones. Some are immediately within your reach. Others will require a determined effort to seek out, for they will not come to you automatically. However, as you learned long ago, many of life's rewards require hard work to attain. Do not let any obstacles — or your pride — stand between you and the help you need. Older Americans helped build this great country and are deserving of whatever it can provide for them at this important time of their lives.

A final suggestion: be sure to read the introduction to this book and the summary of the financial perks that follows before proceeding to any other section.

My warmest wishes to you in all of your efforts. I hope **_American Guidance for Seniors_** will help guide you in the right direction of obtaining the assistance that will improve your financial security and quality of life.

... Ken Skala

A SPECIAL NOTE TO CAREGIVERS

Your task of caring for your parents, spouse, or any older person will not always be easy and may require even more of you physically and mentally than raising your children. Try not to despair or become unduly frustrated as you try to cope with the many demands that caregiving has placed upon you. *Help is available!* However, it will take some additional effort and determination to obtain. Much of it can be found right in this book. Take advantage of every element of assistance that you read about.

Above all, remember to take care of **yourself** so that caregiving will not become a burden, or detrimental to your health and well-being. Be assured, that the act of caring for someone you love may require a tremendous amount of effort, but you will reap many personal rewards, as well as the satisfaction of knowing that you have done your best to help someone who needs you.

ACKNOWLEDGEMENTS

A book of this type is never really the work of just one person, but rather that of many individuals who collectively form its basis with their knowledge and information. As the writer, my contribution consisted of gathering and compiling the vast amount of information available and putting it into a form that could be readily understood and used by our older Americans and their families to improve their lives. I alone accept full responsibility for any inadvertent errors, inaccuracies or omissions that may have occurred. I ask that you, the reader, not let the deficiencies, if any, mar your insight into the value of this book.

Throughout my research, preparation and writing of this book and its current edition, I have been fortunate to have had the assistance over the years of many outstanding individuals. Although not listed by name, I want to extend my thanks to them for offering so willingly their suggestions and ideas, as well as their help reviewing my manuscripts.

In addition, my profound respect to those fine organizations and associations mentioned throughout my writing who are dedicated to helping older Americans, and my deepest gratitude for the information and assistance they so generously contributed. Of particular importance is the recognition of the many individuals associated with our federal, state and local governments whose information provided the basis for major portions of this book. I wish to specially acknowledge here certain offices and agencies because of their immense contributions to this book. My sincere thanks to all of the following:

ACTION, Architectural and Transportation Barriers Compliance Board, Department of Agriculture (Food and Nutrition Service), **Department of Commerce** (Bureau of the Census), **Department of Education** (Offices of Information and Resources for the Handicapped, and Special Education and Rehabilitative Services), **Department of Energy**,

Department of Health and Human Services (Administration on Aging, Food and Drug Administration, Health Care Financing Administration, Health Resources and Services Administration, National Center for Health Statistics, National Institute on Aging, National Institutes of Health, Office of Intergovernmental Affairs, Office of Disease Prevention and Health Promotion, Public Health Service), **Social Security Administration**, **Department of Housing and Urban Development**, **Department of the Interior** (Forest Service), **Department of Justice** (Office of Justice Assistance, Research and Statistics), **Department of Labor**, **Department of State** (Bureau of Consular Affairs), **Department of Transportation**, **Department of the Treasury** (Internal Revenue Service), **Federal Trade Commission**, **General Services Administration**, **Legal Services Corporation**, **Library of Congress** (National Library Service for the Blind and Physically Handicapped), **National Archives and Records Administration**, **Office of Consumer Affairs**, **Office of Personnel Management**, **Office of Management and Budget**, **Railroad Retirement Board**, **Senate** (Special Committee on Aging) and the **Veterans Administration**.

Table of Contents

About "800" and "888" Toll-Free Numbers

Like all other long distance numbers, toll-free "800" numbers and the new "888" numbers needed to supplement toll-free "800" calls must be preceded by a "1" in areas where the caller has to dial "1" before any long distance area code (currently, in over 80% of the nation). Think of the "800" or "888" as the number's area code and it should be easy to remember to dial "1" in those regions where it is required. To reach the toll-free information operator, dial 1-800-555-1212.

What This Book Is All About

Every year, thousands of books are published on how to take care of babies, raise children, cope with adolescence, struggle through the early lean years of marriage, succeed at work, and — finally — plan in middle age for eventual retirement into the "golden years" of leisure and the good life. Surprisingly just when they are needed most, few books have appeared to help cope with the changes and challenges of the Senior years. Consequently, these so-called golden years are often already tarnished before they begin.

With the increase in life expectancy, retirement may last from 20 to 40 years — certainly a major portion of an adult's life. But without preparation and knowledge of the assistance available to Seniors, those years will be characterized by struggle and insecurity — hardly a fitting tribute to their efforts during the preceding decades.

Older Americans are entitled to many government and private programs created specifically to help them avoid those struggles. Despite the vast amount of knowledge and experience Seniors acquire through life, many are unaware, or have a limited understanding, of these programs and how they can benefit by them. Without this knowledge, Seniors miss the chance to take advantage of the significant assistance these programs provide.

Recent studies show that:

- More than three-fourths of all Seniors never seek assistance from their local Area Agencies on Aging or any private organizations that offer assistance to Seniors in their communities.

- Less than half of qualified older Americans receive Supplemental Security Income benefits or Food Stamps.

- Less than 30% of eligible Seniors receive any help from Medicaid.

- An average of 42% of those eligible for the Qualified Medicare Beneficiary program are not receiving its assistance.

■ Only one-third of veterans are aware of the many health, pension and burial benefits to which they and their dependents are entitled.

Used often, this book could be the only resource you need to help you obtain this assistance. It provides a clear roadmap to getting the best out of life at a time when you need it most. And, for those who haven't yet reached their "golden years," but who have undertaken the great and rewarding task of caring for a parent or another Senior, this book will also be invaluable in ensuring that that responsibility becomes a joy, and not a burden.

American Guidance for Seniors was written to help Seniors obtain **every** benefit, **every** entitlement, and **all** the assistance they need. Each chapter is self-contained; you can start reading anywhere. However, to gain the most benefit from its contents, take the time at least once to read the book all the way through — from the Table of Contents onward. Of particular note, the listings in each chapter provide a one-step, up-to-the-minute source of addresses and telephone numbers for many of the organizations and agencies who provide the assistance described in *American Guidance.* You may be surprised to discover how the many programs, services, and hints it describes could make these the best years of your life.

American Guidance was written to be as exhaustive as possible. However, it wasn't possible to include every detail of every program and entitlement described. The information included will give you a solid understanding of what entitlements and benefits you can receive, and where to receive them, while the listings provide a convenient reference for reaching those organizations and agencies. This book will set you firmly on the path to getting the utmost assistance you can for yourself, your family, and your friends.

Following this introduction is a summary of many *financial perks* that are described in detail in various chapters of this book — perks designed to help greatly improve your financial security and quality of life. After you've read through the summary, keep your eyes open for further mention of these perks as you proceed through *American Guidance for Seniors.*

Financial Perks To Ease Your Way

The following summary of selected financial perks described in this book can help you, your family, friends, or those you care for. Seniors who have taken advantage of these perks in the past have put literally thousands of dollars into their pockets throughout their retirement years. *So can you!*

The summary does not include the many major federal and state programs described in-depth later in the book. However, **Social Security, Medicare, Railroad Retirement, Medicaid, Supplemental Security Income, Food Stamps, Hill-Burton Free Hospital Care,** the **Qualified Medicare Beneficiary Program,** and **Veterans Benefits** are critically important to many Seniors' well-being and financial security. Therefore, it is also vital that you read the sections in the book devoted to them.

■ *Area Agencies on Aging* (Chapter 10): Over 670 Area Agencies on Aging throughout the U.S. provide the most beneficial perk available to Seniors 60 or over and their caregivers. The Agencies directly provide or contract services and assistance for Senior Americans at a minimal charge or for **free**.

These services include: in-home services such as home-delivered meals, health and personal care, chores, visitation as well as, counseling, rehabilitation services, respite care to relieve caregivers, transportation, outreach programs for needy Seniors, general information and referrals...and many other helpful services. The tremendous help these Agencies provide to Seniors and their caregivers must not be overlooked.

■ *Senior Discounts* (Chapter 11): Senior discounts can save hundreds of dollars for Seniors, some as young as 55. Before you plan your monthly budget, be sure to consider such discounts — they can add up!

Most businesses are keen to attract Senior customers. For this reason, banks and savings institutions in particular now offer tremendous incentives on new accounts opened by older customers, including free checking and fee-free travellers checks.

Other kinds of Senior discounts include reduced admission to public and private recreational facilities, half-fare on public transport, discounted meals at restaurants, discounted movie tickets, and reduced costs for medication at drugstores. Some communities also offer reduced rates to Seniors for local telephone service, gas and electricity.

- *Free Tax Assistance* (Chapter 10): Several community programs provide free help in preparing tax returns. The best-known of these programs is *Tax-Aide*. Started in 1969 by the American Association of Retired Persons (AARP), Tax-Aide has helped millions of Seniors prepare annual federal and state returns. The program's volunteers have been praised by the IRS for the extremely low error rates on returns prepared with their help.

    Other free tax assistance programs include *Community Outreach Tax Assistance* and *Volunteer Income Tax Assistance*, as well as many locally-sponsored tax seminars and clinics — all free to participants.

    Considering that Seniors have the highest rate of tax **overpayment** in the country, free tax assistance could be invaluable in keeping more of their cash — and the interest it could be earning.

- *State and Local Tax Deductions and Exemptions* (Chapter 10): Most American Seniors may reside for many years in the same place, yet never learn about the state and local tax deductions, exemptions, or deferrals to which they are entitled at age 60 or 65 — or even at 55 when they have lower incomes.

    These special deductions and exemptions don't come automatically. You must apply for them! But your state and local tax offices are duty-bound to tell you whatever you want to know about Senior tax savings on income, real estate, and personal property taxes.

- *$125,000 Capital Gains Tax Exclusion* (Chapter 10): The IRS allows Seniors age 55 or older a one-time exclusion from paying up to $125,000 capital gains tax on profits from the sale of their principal home if they have owned and lived in the home for at least three years out of the five year period prior to the date of sale. And, if there are still capital gains remaining, the balance can be applied toward future tax liability by using the money to purchase another residence.

- *Federally-Insured Reverse Mortgages* (Chapter 7): In late 1990, Congress approved 25,000 new government-insured reverse mortgages to help Seniors who are "house rich and cash poor" to tap into the equity in their home without selling or borrowing against it via a standard home-equity loan. This continuing federal program is open to Seniors age 62 or older who own their residence free and clear, or who are very close to paying it off.

  A reverse mortgage is the opposite of a conventional mortgage. Rather than the homeowner paying the bank monthly for the loan, the bank provides the borrower with a monthly payment, lump sum payment or line of credit to be used when needed. With the new federal insurance, homeowners need not be afraid of losing their home or having to pay back the loan unless they (the homeowners) decide to sell the house or they die.

- *Free or Low-Cost Legal Aid* (Chapter 10): Available in almost every community, legal aid and legal service offices provide free legal services to people who cannot afford private lawyers. In addition, other free and reduced-fee legal services are springing up, particularly in areas with a high Senior population. Although the amount of help they provide will vary, the fact that such services can help you save on legal fees does not.

- *Individual Retirement Arrangements (IRAs)* (Chapter 10): Individual Retirement Accounts and Individual Retirement Annuities are two plans for personal retirement savings that offer tremendous advantages. Contributions are deducted from earnings before taxation, and any earnings or gains in the IRA are not taxed until withdrawal.

  Any saver under the age of 70 1/2 with taxable earnings from full- or part-time work should consider an IRA, especially if he or she is not covered by an employer-funded retirement plan.

- *Memorial Societies* (Chapter 8): Numbering over 150 in the U.S. and 25 in Canada, nonprofit memorial societies help plan economical funerals that conform with their members' beliefs and values. The societies arrange contracts and agreements with funeral providers to take care of their members when a death occurs. Generally, society members pay considerably less — up to 50% less — than non-members for funerals and cremation.

- *Senior Community Service Employment Program (SCSEP)* (Chapter 10): Administered by the federal government, with projects sponsored by state/territorial governments and ten national organizations, SCSEP provides part-time jobs in community service to unemployed, low-income Seniors, 55 and older, with poor employment prospects. Participants are paid at least minimum wage or local prevailing rate for similar work. In addition, they receive physical examinations, personal and job counseling, training, and — in some cases — transportation to and from work.

- *Home Energy and Weatherization Programs* (Chapters 1 and 6): These state and local programs provide lower income households with financial assistance, either paid directly or to utility providers, to help meet home heating and cooling needs and provide energy-related crisis intervention and low-cost house weatherization.

- *Elderhostel* (Chapter 11): Adults 60 and over can obtain a unique learning experience that combines education and travel. The inexpensive academic program has sent thousands of Seniors on visits of a week or more to over 1,000 universities in the U.S., Canada, and abroad. No diploma or prior training is required for any of the courses, and the reasonable fees cover tuition, room, and board in on-campus facilities.

- *Golden Age Passport* (Chapter 10): For a one-time fee of *only* $10, any permanent U.S. resident or citizen 62 or older can obtain a lifetime entrance permit to fee-charging federal parks, monuments, and recreation areas. The Golden Age Passport gives the bearer a 50% discount on federal use fees for facilities and services such as campsites, boat launches, cave tours, parking, and many more. Its nicest feature is that it not only covers the bearer, but any companions travelling in his or her vehicle.

- ■ *Senior Centers* (Chapter 11): Almost every community has established at least one Senior Center to serve residents 60 or older. These Centers offer at little or no cost numerous recreational, educational, and social activities. Supported predominantly by public funds, many Centers have full-time professional staffs and host a wide variety of programs, as well as providing lunch (free or for a nominal donation from those who can afford it). Best of all, no one is ever left out of the activities within a Senior Center because of inability to pay (this rule does not apply to off-site excursions).

- ■ *Senior Organizations* (Chapter 11): Many national organizations formed by and for Seniors offer not only enjoyment of locally-sponsored activities and interaction with members who have similar interests, they provide other benefits, such as savings programs, insurance — often at lower costs, discounts on travel, entertainment, accommodation, merchandise, and medication, and much more. Finally, they are a rich source of what every Senior needs: *information* on the many government and private assistance programs that can make Seniors' lives easier.

Elderly Ranks Keep Growing as U.S. Population Reaches 264,023,000!

After releasing final figures from its 1990 census, the U.S. Census Bureau reported that the total population of the United States had increased by nearly 10% since 1980. More significantly, dramatic increases had taken place in all elderly age groups; in particular, the 85 and older group grew by a phenomenal 37.6%, while 75-84 year olds increased their ranks by over 30%!

Census Bureau figures for January 1996 show that the rise in the Senior population continues to outpace growth in any other segment of the U.S. population. Today's Senior population comprises:

- **54,952,000 age 55 and older**

- **43,736,000 age 60 and older**

- **33,725,000 age 65 and older**

- **14,977,000 age 75 and older**

- **3,686,000 age 85 and older**

- **56,000 age 100 and older**

THE AGING SOCIETY

With the median age of the nation's population increasing from 30 in 1980 to 34.5 in 1996 and the 65 and older segment representing almost 13% of the entire population, it is clearly evident that Americans are living much longer and that our society will keep aging well into the middle of the next century.

Chapter 1

The Aging of America

A Senior Boom Just Around The Corner!

Chapter Highlights

A Senior Boom Just Around The Corner!

Over the past 20 years, Americans of all ages have come to realize that our nation's population is aging rapidly. No matter where we go or what we do, we are surrounded by many more older individuals than ever before.

Many factors have influenced this aging trend: societal and environmental changes and improvements; medical advancements against deadly illnesses like heart disease, stroke and cancer; and changes in daily health practices, like improved diet, increased exercise, and cessation of smoking.

However, for millions of Americans, it is still difficult — if not impossible — to accept or even comprehend the aging of our society, and the ever-swelling ranks of the aged in our midst. In particular, the enormous increase in the Senior population that will occur 15 years from now, when the first of the "baby boom" generation (the 75-plus million babies born from 1946-1964) reach age 65. In the year 2011 alone, a whopping 3.5 million of the baby-boomers will turn 65, creating one of the greatest waves of "new" Seniors ever experienced in this country.

The question arises: Is America already in a "Senior boom" or is it simply experiencing the preliminary shock waves of the real explosion . . . just around the corner? This is an extremely important question, because the aging of our society will affect not just older individuals, but the lives of **all** Americans regardless of their ages. It will have a profound impact — economically and sociologically — on the entire nation.

OVERVIEW OF AMERICA'S DEMOGRAPHIC CHANGES — THE AGING SOCIETY

To help answer the question posed about the extent of the growth of our aging society, let us briefly examine some of the characteristics of this aging process as seen by the U.S. Census Bureau and other government sources of demographic information:

- In 1900, only one in 25 Americans reached age 65 or over; today there are over 33 million such individuals: that is, one out of every eight Americans. When the oldest baby-boomers reach 65 early in the next century, one out of every five Americans will be 65 or older.

- In 1985, America's elderly population of 28.6 million persons 65 or older was the **third largest elderly** population in the world, after the People's Republic of China (52.8 million) and India (32.7 million). Though the elderly population is growing tremendously throughout the world, America will still be near the top of the list with its millions of citizens over 65.

- There are currently almost 15 million Americans 75 or older — approximately 45 percent of all those over 65. However, by the turn of the 21st century, more than half of those over 65 will have reached 75.

- In 1900, there were only 123,000 persons aged 85 and over. Currently, there are 3.7 million 85-plus years old. By the year 2000, it is estimated that this number will near 5 million. By 2050, the 85-plus population should have increased seven-fold.

- America ranks **first** in the world for its 80-plus year old population. In 1985, despite the huge population of the People's Republic of China, the United States' population of 6.2 million over 80 exceeded even that of China, whose over-80s numbered 5.7 million, the Soviet Union, with 4.6 million, and India, with 2.9 million. Currently, our over 80 population exceeds 8 million. By 2005, over 30 percent of the elderly population in the U.S. will be age 80 or older — one of the highest proportions in the world. Internationally, the number of people over 80 is expected to skyrocket over the next 40 years — a phenomenon few of us could anticipate.

- More and more people are living past 100 years of age. According to the Social Security Administration's records, there are currently over 50,000 hundred-plus year olds in the U.S. receiving Social Security and Supplemental Security Income (SSI) benefits. If the Census Bureau's projections hold true, by the year 2000 there will be over 100,000 centenarians; before the end of the 21st century this number will approach one million individuals who have reached age 100. Consequently, Americans today have a far greater chance of reaching this ripe old age than ever before.

- The average American's life expectancy has increased by over 28 years since 1900. A baby born in 1900 could only expect to live an average of 47 years. Today, a new born baby can expect to live over 75 years. More significantly, life expectancy at age 65 has also increased dramatically. In 1900, a 65 year old could anticipate living only 12 more years, today a 65 year old can anticipate living at least another 18 years.

Since most Americans are compassionate and caring people who accept their moral responsibility to help society's older members, they will be faced with the extremely difficult task of providing the means for the elderly to continue living meaningful lives — without the many hardships generally associated with aging. While it is clear that our nation is already in the midst of a Senior boom, the near future will see an even greater growth in the elderly population. The aging of America will require many changes in our ways of life, our attitudes, and our approaches to providing for the aged, both socially and medically. Everyone is affected by the aging of America, because we all have one thing in common: unless misfortune occurs, **we all age** . . . and today that means we will become much older than we ever dreamed possible.

MYTHS ABOUT THE ELDERLY

Stereotypes of the elderly — whether negative or positive — are seldom founded in fact since the elderly are not a homogeneous group. In fact, as the elderly age, they manifest more striking differences than individuals in any other adult age group. However, despite knowledge attained in the last decade about the physical and mental characteristics and social and financial needs of older Americans, there are still common misconceptions about the elderly that have grown into accepted beliefs. These "elderly myths" seem to prevail throughout our society. Often, these myths discourage and even prevent us from providing the assistance that millions of elderly need.

Two myths about the elderly seem particularly prevalent in society.

MYTH 1:   Most of the elderly are affluent and don't need any financial assistance.

This is certainly one of the most misleading misconceptions about the elderly as a group. Although the poverty rate among Senior Citizens has been more than halved in the last 25 years, elderly people are still more likely than any other adults to be poor or near-poor. In fact, the vast majority of older Americans have realized no net gain in their standard of living over the last ten years.

What often slants the common perception of the elderly is the tendency to categorize those between ages 50 and 60 as "elderly" even though they are still young compared to the true aged population. These individuals do not depend on Medicare or Social Security, are probably still employed full-time, and have the greatest discretionary income (that is, spending money). Most 50-to-60 year olds would be taken aback if they were classified as elderly. Of course, a significant number of older individuals — like those in any age group — are wealthy, but they hardly constitute the majority of the elderly.

Here was the **true** economic profile of the U.S. elderly population just a few years ago in 1992:

- According to the U.S. Department of Commerce, the poverty rate for the elderly, 65-plus, was 12.4 percent (approximately 3.8 million individuals). However, another 2.3 million were near-poor with incomes between 100 and 200 percent of the federal poverty level. (The federal poverty level for a single person over age 65 was $6,532 and $8,241 for an elderly couple.) This means that over 6 million elderly were either poor or near-poor and barely meeting the costs of housing, food, medical care, utilities and other daily living costs. At only $125-$158 per week average income, many of these individuals were devastated by one unfortunate incident occurring in their lives.

- The elderly were more than **twice** as likely as all other individuals to remain poor if they reach the poverty level because the opportunities to increase their incomes are severely limited.

- The risk of poverty increases with age even among the elderly: approximately 10 percent of those age 65-74 were poor; 15 percent of those age 75-84; and 18 percent of those 85 and older. The 85-plus year olds had significantly lower money incomes than those age 65 to 74, with less than 75 percent of the median cash income of those aged 65-74.

- Elderly women and minorities (both male and female) were the worst off in our society. In fact, nearly three-quarters of the elderly poor were women with a poverty rate of over 15 percent. Elderly Hispanics had a poverty rate of 33.8 percent while over 22.5 percent of elderly blacks were poor.

- Even with Medicare, the elderly paid more than one-fourth of their total health care costs out-of-pocket.

- One catastrophic illness requiring long-term nursing home care or extended home health care was devastating to the elderly bringing them into the ranks of poverty, often resulting in the loss of their dignity and reason for living. Costs in the U.S. for nursing home care ranged from $10,000 per year to as much as $60,000, with the average between $25,000 to $30,000 per year.

A study by the House Select Committee on Aging revealed that:

— After only 13 weeks in a nursing home, seven in ten elderly living alone spent down their income to the poverty level.

— Within one year, over 90 percent of elderly nursing home residents had depleted their incomes, savings and assets and were impoverished.

— For those elderly who had incomes between 125 and 200 percent of the poverty level, it took only six weeks in a nursing home to impoverish them.

— After either spouse in an elderly couple spent only six months in a nursing home, over half of the couples were impoverished.

- Adequate inexpensive housing for the elderly was so rare that millions of Senior Citizens had to choose between food on the table or a roof over their heads. Unfortunately, for other elderly, there wasn't this choice because affordable housing simply was not available in their community.

Although these points may paint a rather bleak picture of the financial state of the elderly, there are, of course, millions of elderly who cannot be classified as poor. However, the elderly as a group cannot and must not be considered affluent: fewer are living a luxurious life or retirement in 1996 than you may think.

MYTH 2: Older individuals are sickly, senile, and unproductive.

If this myth held any merit, older individuals such as former Presidents Carter and Bush (both age 72); Congressmen John Dingell (70), Sam Gibbons (76), Henry Hyde (72); Senators Strom Thurmond (94), Robert Dole (73), Claiborne Pell (78), Ernest Hollings (74), Robert Byrd (79), John Warner (69), and innumerable others in our government who several years ago reached 60, would never have been reelected to these immensely important positions. Nor can we ignore other older individuals who have contributed so much to America and the American way of life for many decades: Hugh Downs, Dr. C. Everett Koop, recently deceased George Burns, Walter Cronkite, Carol Channing, Bob Hope, Lena Horne, Harry Caray, noted columnists Ann Landers and her sister, Abigail Van Buren . . . and I am sure you could think of many more who are just as active and productive, regardless of their years.

Information from the National Center for Health Statistics and the National Institute on Aging further reveals that:

- No more than five percent of the elderly live in nursing homes at any given time. Of these residents, an estimated one percent are between ages 65-74 and only six percent are between 75-84 years of age. Even after age 85, when there is a much greater need for nursing home care, the number increases to only 22 percent.

- The majority of individuals over the age of 65 consider their health as excellent, very good, or good. Only about 11 percent rate their health as poor.

- Almost two-thirds of those over 75 are in good health.

- Over half of those 85 and over have no physical disability which hinders them in their daily activities.

- Very few older individuals are senile — only about five percent of the elderly suffer from severe memory disorders or decrements in mental abilities. In fact, research now shows that decreased mental ability in the aged is frequently caused by loss of vision or hearing, disease like Alzheimer's, or the type and number of different medications taken at one time rather than by age itself. Very few changes actually occur in our brains as we age and those changes that do occur have little or no effect on our mental ability and performance.

- The majority of older individuals live alone and want to be independent for as long as possible.

This information reveals that the vast majority of the elderly are healthy and quite capable of contributing to our society until a very old age.

A MAJOR CHALLENGE FOR CONGRESS: MEETING THE NEEDS OF THE AGING SOCIETY

In 1996, with 43.7 million Americans aged 60 and older and projections that this number will dramatically increase, Congress faces a major challenge: to provide for the social and medical needs of these older Americans. As we have already discussed, a significant number of our Seniors will need help.

With a national debt of $4.7 trillion and constraints imposed by the Gramm-Rudman-Hollings Act of 1985, which required across-the-board reductions in domestic and defense spending, meeting this challenge will not be an easy task! Although the Act did provide some protection for federal programs benefiting the elderly — including Social Security, Supplemental Security Income, Medicaid, Veterans benefits, Railroad Retirement Tier I, and Food Stamps — it is obvious that these programs as well as Medicare and other social service programs must be subject to change and cost reduction.

Unfortunately, very few gains were made by the elderly in legislation passed by the 104th Congress. In fact, this Congress has been one of the least productive in passing laws that we have had in modern history. However, it has set considerable groundwork for future laws.

Our next Congress will have much to do in order to accommodate the major needs currently facing our nation and the elderly. Prominent among these needs are protection against catastrophic long-term in-home or nursing home care, fixing Social Security and Medicare's insolvency problems, job discrimination, the need for elderly housing, and control of the escalating costs of rent, taxes, utilities, home repairs and insurance.

The ability of Congress to meet these needs and provide ways for the elderly to be financially independent is, indeed, one of the most significant challenges it has faced in the history of our country.

BE INFORMED — IT'S IMPORTANT TO YOU!

In several studies of America's Seniors during the past few years some rather disturbing information has been disclosed. Foremost among these findings is that (1) the majority of older Americans are unaware of the many government programs that could help them, and (2) those who may be familiar with certain programs — like Medicaid, Supplemental Security Income and Food Stamps — were unaware of their own eligibility for these programs. Consequently, millions of eligible Senior Citizens never benefit from the very programs designed to help them.

In addition, several studies and surveys indicate that most Seniors are unaware of the various organizations that offer assistance and information to the elderly; in particular, the local Area Agencies on Aging which were founded specifically for older Americans to help them meet their daily living needs.

Almost every study indicates that there is a need for Senior Citizens to become better informed of the various government programs of assistance to them. Without this knowledge, millions of Seniors may never receive the help these programs provide.

In the following section of this chapter, I have tried to describe the major federal programs that provide assistance and benefits for older Americans. It contains invaluable information for you! With it, you will be better informed of the many programs that could one day help you, your family, or friends.

PART II

Federal Programs That Provide Benefits and Assistance to Older Americans

In addition to the federally administered programs providing pension and compensation benefits to veterans of military service and to former federal government and railroad employees, there are several other important federal programs benefiting older Americans. The following overview identifies those programs that provide income and health benefits, assistance to the elderly poor to meet their basic subsistence needs, such as housing and home energy, and the various programs of general benefit which include social, nutritional, legal and employment services. Although many of these programs were not enacted **solely** for the benefit of older individuals, a major portion of their spending is directed towards our nation's elderly.

The programs indicated here are described briefly for easy retention and understanding. Those programs not covered in other sections of this book are discussed in more detail so that you will be aware of the advantages they offer to older individuals.

PROGRAMS PROVIDING RETIREMENT INCOME AND INCOME ASSISTANCE

■ *Social Security*

Established in 1935 at the height of the Great Depression, the Social Security program has become by far the largest and most important income maintenance program in our nation. It is a **national insurance** program providing monthly cash benefits to retired and disabled workers, their dependents and survivors. (Medicare, the health insurance portion of Social Security, is discussed separately in the next section, "Health Programs.") The cash benefits program consists of two portions: Old Age and Survivors

Insurance (OASI) and Disability Insurance (DI). Funding for the Social Security system comes from the taxes paid by employees, employers and self-employed individuals. Approximately 95 percent of the jobs in our country are covered under this program, which is compulsory except for certain special provisions applicable only to a limited number of individuals and their work. The benefits received are an **earned right** regardless of an individual's income from savings, pensions, private insurance or other nonwork related (unearned) income. The program is administered by the Social Security Administration.

■ *Supplemental Security Income (SSI)*

Enacted in 1972, this program was established to ensure the economic security of our country's most needy groups. It is a **cash assistance** program for the low-income aged, blind and disabled individuals who can **demonstrate a need** for income supplementation. The program is financed through general revenues, in contrast to the financing of the Social Security program by payroll taxes, and is not part of the national retirement and disability insurance program commonly referred to as Social Security. It is, however, administered by the Social Security Administration. The cash assistance benefit may be paid either directly to the eligible person or to a representative payee, if the person is incapable of managing benefits.

■ *Veterans Disability Compensation and Pensions*

Administered by the Veterans Administration, there are two major programs which provide income to eligible veterans:

— Veterans **compensation** may be paid to living veterans whose earning power is impaired due to a service-connected disability and to survivors of veterans whose death occurs while on active duty or results from a service-connected disability. Veterans benefits are based on the extent of impairment.

— Veterans **pensions** may be paid to **wartime** veterans who suffer from non-service-connected disabilities which are permanent and total, and which preclude them from engaging in gainful employment.

■ *Food Stamps Program*

The current Food Stamps program was authorized by Congress under the Food Stamp Act of 1964. Since then, the program has been improved and strengthened through various amendments to the Act, particularly by the Food Stamp Act of 1977. This valuable program's purpose is to help low-income households obtain more nutritious diets. Vouchers are provided to help meet the cost of a minimally nutritious diet. The program actually serves as an **income maintenance** program by supplementing available family income. The Food and Nutrition Service office of the Department of Agriculture is responsible for administering and supervising the program and for developing its policies and regulations. At the state and local levels, the program is administered by the state welfare or social services department.

■ *Black Lung Benefits Program*

Originally authorized by the Federal Coal Mine Health and Safety Act of 1969, the Federal Black Lung Benefits program in its current form is authorized by the Black Lung Benefits Reform Act of 1977. The $825 million annual program provides monthly cash benefits to eligible coal miners who are totally disabled by pneumoconiosis ("black lung disease") and to their dependents and survivors. It is divided into two separate programs: Part B and Part C. Part B provides benefits to those who filed claims before July 1973. Its funds are appropriated from general revenues and administered by the Social Security Administration. Part C provides income and medical benefits to those who filed **after** July 1973 or who failed to qualify earlier under Part B. It is funded through taxes on coal producers and loans from the general revenues and is administered by the Department of Labor; however, applications for Part C benefits are accepted by the Social Security Administration and forwarded to the Department of Labor for processing and payment. An application must be filed to entitle a person to black lung benefits. A special form for benefits is available at any Social Security office. It is important to note that black lung benefits are not reduced by any benefits received from Social Security disability insurance or Supplemental Security Income.

HEALTH PROGRAMS

■ *MEDICARE*

In response to our nation's commitment to provide the elderly and disabled individuals with quality health care and protection from the associated costs, Medicare was enacted in 1965 as an amendment to the Social Security Act. This national **insurance** program, which covers virtually all persons aged 65 or older, comprises two portions: (1) A **compulsory** program of hospital insurance (HI); referred to as Part A and (2) a **voluntary** program of supplementary medical insurance (SMI); referred to as Part B. Part A (HI) pays for inpatient hospital care, stays in skilled nursing facilities and home health services. Individuals covered under Social Security contribute payment for Part A through taxation on earnings which is separate from that used to finance the Social Security cash benefits program. Others who are not covered under Social Security may voluntarily enroll and pay the cost of the Hospital Insurance program.

Part B (SMI) pays for all other services covered by Medicare, principally for physician services. All enrolled individuals receiving Social Security benefits pay a monthly premium for the medical insurance program; enrollees who do not receive Social Security benefits pay quarterly. Nearly one out of every nine Americans is insured through Medicare, which is administered by the Health Care Financing Administration within the Department of Health and Human Services.

■ *MEDICAID*

Medicaid is a federal medical **assistance** program enacted by Congress in 1965 to provide matching funds to the states to finance medical care for low-income persons who are aged, blind, disabled or in families with dependent children. Major expenditures of the program are for institutional services, in particular, for long term care in nursing homes. It also includes provisions for supplemental insurance for the needy elderly to provide them with Medicare coverage. All states participate in the program except Arizona. This is considered a joint federal/state program in which each state designs and administers its own program under guidelines set and reviewed by the Health Care Financing Administration within the Department of Health and Human Services.

■ *Veterans Administration Health Care*

The Veterans Administration provides a wide range of health care services to our veterans in VA hospitals, domiciliaries, nursing homes and outpatient clinics and on a contract basis with private and state hospitals and nursing homes. All veterans with service connected disabilities are entitled to VA medical care. Those with non-service-connected conditions are eligible for care if they are unable to defray the cost of care elsewhere.

■ *National Institutes of Health (NIH)*

The National Institutes of Health is the principal biomedical research agency of the federal government. Through its 13 various institutes, it conducts and supports research aimed at improving the health of all Americans. A substantial portion of the NIH's annual budget is allocated to the National Institute on Aging and to research of illnesses affecting many of the elderly, such as Alzheimer's disease, osteoporosis, arthritis, diabetes, hearing disorders, hypertension, arteriosclerosis, strokes and chronic heart conditions.

Of major importance to the elderly is the National Institute on Aging, which is primarily involved in increasing knowledge of the aging process and the associated physical, psychological and social factors resulting from advanced age. Six other Institutes study areas of vital concern to the Nation's older population: The National Cancer Institute, the National Heart, Lung and Blood Institute, the National Institute of Diabetes and Digestive and Kidney Disease, the National Institute of Neurological and Communicative Disorders and Stroke, the National Institute of Arthritis and Musculoskeletal and Skin Diseases, and the National Institute on Deafness and other Communication Disorders (this institute was created in 1988).

PROGRAMS PROVIDING HOUSING AND WEATHERIZATION ASSISTANCE

(The Public Housing, Section 8 and Section 202 housing programs are administered by the Department of Housing and Urban Development)

■ *Public Housing*

Created by the Housing Act of 1937, this is the oldest and most important low-income housing program available to those in need of housing assistance. The Public Housing program provides rental housing for eligible families in projects run by local housing authorities. Government funds are provided for construction, modernization and operating subsidies. Residents must meet low-income guidelines to be eligible for this type of housing. Approximately 40 percent of the 1.4 million public housing units are occupied by the elderly.

■ *Section 8 Housing Program*

This program was created in 1974 to provide rental subsidies to households with low or moderately low incomes so that they could obtain decent housing in the private sector. It also provided long-term obligations of funds to developers for the construction of multi-family housing. More than 60 percent of the units in these new projects are occupied by the elderly. A portion of the program for new construction and substantial rehabilitation was repealed by the Housing Act of 1983. The other portion of this program subsidizing **existing** private housing is still authorized under the Act and continues to provide rental assistance certificates to low income families. Section 8 housing, in conjunction with Section 202 housing, has become one of the major sources of housing assistance to the elderly. Currently, more than 40 percent of all Section 8 existing housing units are occupied by them.

■ *Section 202 Housing Program*

The Section 202 housing program provides direct loans to nonprofit organizations to build and manage housing projects designed specifically for low-income elderly and handicapped individuals. It is the primary federal funding program for constructing subsidized rental housing for elderly persons and works in conjunction with the Section 8 housing assistance payments program. Since the early 70's, approximately 275,000 units have been funded under this program. The elderly and handicapped occupy more than 90 percent of Section 202 housing.

■ *Farmers Home Administration Housing Assistance*

This program, which comes under the Farmers Home Administration within the Department of Agriculture, is vital to residents of rural areas to whom it provides loans and grants to meet their housing needs. Older rural residents benefit from three housing programs. (1) The **Section 502** program provides rural housing loans to low-income persons who reside in rural areas and do not own safe, sanitary or adequate housing. The loans are used to buy, build or improve modest housing. (2) The **Section 504** program makes rural grants available to low-income households in rural areas; in particular, these grants are designed to help the elderly, 62 years of age and older, who do not qualify for conventional loans because of their very low incomes. (3) The **Section 515** program provides loans for the construction of rental or cooperative housing in rural areas for persons with low or moderate incomes and for persons age 62 or older.

■ *Weatherization Assistance Program*

Authorized by Title IV of the Energy Conservation and Production Act of 1976, the Weatherization Assistance program is administered by the Department of Energy. The program was enacted to provide assistance to individuals who do not have sufficient cash or credit to improve the energy efficiency of their homes through the addition of storm windows and doors and other types of insulation. According to federal law, household income must not exceed 125 percent of the federal low-income level for that household to be eligible for assistance. However, the law does allow states to raise their income eligibility levels to 150 percent of the poverty level, while prohibiting them from reducing it to below 125 percent of the poverty level.

The Weatherization Assistance program is designed to give priority to the elderly and handicapped households. The Low Income Home Energy Assistance program and the Weatherization program are basically the only federal programs available to assist the elderly and poor with the escalating costs of heating and cooling their homes.

■ *Low-Income Home Energy Assistance Program (LIHEAP)*

This vital program for home energy assistance to many of the elderly was established by the Omnibus Reconciliation Act (Title XXVI) of 1981. The Act provides grants to the states to assist eligible households in meeting the costs of home energy. Under this program, low-income households may receive funds for heating and cooling costs, and for weatherization expenses and supply shortage emergencies. Priority is given to households with an elderly or handicapped member. Assistance can be provided to households in various ways, such as direct cash payments, vouchers, vendor lines of credit, tax credits, or through public housing operators. It is administered at the federal level by the Department of Health and Human Services.

PROGRAMS OF GENERAL BENEFIT (SOCIAL SERVICES, NUTRITION, EMPLOYMENT AND LEGAL SERVICES)

■ *Older Americans Act*

Enacted in 1965, the Older Americans Act is an invaluable program serving the social service needs of the elderly. The various programs within the Act are designed to assist in the areas of income, health, housing, employment, retirement and community services. More specifically, these programs include transportation assistance, congregate meals, adult day care, outreach, meals-on-wheels, long-term care ombudsman programs and many other essential services for the elderly. The Administration on Aging (AoA) within the Department of Health and Human Services was established by the Older Americans Act and given responsibility for administering the various programs and for developing a network of state and area agencies on aging for implementing these programs. The Older Americans Act contains six titles which define its programs and objectives:

— **Title I: Declaration of Objectives.** This section of the Act is a declaration of its broad social policy goals for improving the lives of older Americans in areas such as: income, health, housing, long-term care and the protection of the elderly from abuse, neglect and exploitation.

— **Title II: Administration on Aging.** Provides for the creation of the Administration on Aging within the Office of the Secretary of the Department of Health and Human Services and established the Federal Council on Aging. The duties of the Council include advising the President on the needs of older Americans, appraising the value and impact of policies and programs affecting older people, serving as a spokesperson for the elderly, informing the public and providing forums on the needs of older persons.

— **Title III Grants for State and Community Programs on Aging.** This extremely important section establishes authority for an "aging network," consisting of state and area agencies on aging, to provide a variety essential social service programs for older persons, especially those with the greatest social or economic needs. The program provides grants to the states which in turn award funds to area agencies for community planning, supportive services, multi-purpose senior centers and nutrition services. It is the largest program under the Act.

— **Title IV Training, Research, and Discretionary Projects and Programs**. This portion of the Act provides for the development and support of training, research and demonstration programs in the field of aging.

— **Title V: Community Service Employment for Older Americans.** Originally funded under the Economic Opportunity Act in 1965, this program was modified considerably until 1978 when it was redesignated as Title V of the Older Americans Act. The program, which has increased considerably in funding and participant enrollment since its inception, provides part-time employment opportunities in various community service activities for unemployed low-income persons, aged 55 and over. It is administered by the Department of Labor which awards funds to nine national service organizations, the U.S. Forest Service and to state agencies on aging. National organizations that receive funds are Green Thumb, National Council on Aging, National Council of Senior Citizens, American Association of Retired Persons, National Center on Black Aged, National Association for the Hispanic Elderly, National Urban League, National Indian Council on Aging and the National Pacific/Asian Resource Center on Aging. Participants work either in services for the general community or in services for the elderly. In addition to wages, participants receive annual physical examinations, personal and job-related counseling and some job training. Participants may work up to 1,300 hours per year or an average of 20 to 25 hours per week. The law requires coordination with state and area agencies on aging on all projects sponsored under this program.

— **Title VI: Grants for Native Americans.** This title provides grants to Indian tribes for the development of supportive and nutritional services for elderly Indians. The 1987 amendments to the Act expanded this title's objective to include authorizing funds for native Hawaiians.

■ *Social Services Block Grant (SSBG)*

Authorized under the Omnibus Budget Reconciliation Act of 1981, this program provides grants, based on population, to the states to enable them to provide a variety of services to low income persons. The states basically determine the services they wish to provide to meet the specific needs of persons in their communities. These services may include programs designed to prevent, reduce, or eliminate dependency on federal assistance, assist low income persons in achieving or maintaining self-sufficiency, prevent neglect and abuse, as well as prevent or reduce inappropriate institutional care. The program is administered by the Department of Health and Human Services. The SSBG supersedes a similar program of social services grants to states, under Title XX of the Social Security Act, which provided assistance to the elderly.

■ *Community Services Block Grant (CSBG)*

This program, also authorized under the Omnibus Budget Reconciliation Act of 1981 and administered by the Department of Health and Human Services, is similar to the Social Services Block

Grant. The Community Services Block Grants provide funds to the states to reduce poverty, promote community development and provide needed emergency assistance. Funds are used by the states in the areas of job training and referral for the elderly, home owner counseling, low income housing construction, transportation, senior centers, energy and weatherization assistance, food and shelter. Although some feel this program duplicates other available programs of assistance, Congress has continued to appropriate funds for these block grants because it feels that cancellation would eliminate several programs on which many communities and their Senior Citizens depend.

■ ACTION — Older Americans Volunteer Programs

This program, administered by ACTION — an independent agency established in 1971 — provides funding for three older American volunteer programs: the Retired Senior Volunteer Program, the Foster Grandparents program and the Senior Companion program. These programs were designed to reduce poverty, help the physically and mentally disabled and serve the local community with the skills and experience of older persons. Compensation varies for volunteers in these programs but may include a minimum hourly stipend, reimbursement for out-of-pocket expenses, transportation assistance, meals while serving as volunteers, annual physical examinations and/or insurance benefits. Since these are volunteer programs, compensation is limited but allows many of these volunteers to obtain some assistance while serving those in need.

■ Legal Services Corporation (LSC)

The Legal Services Corporation was established as a private, nonprofit corporation by legislation enacted in 1974. It consists of an 11-member board of directors, nominated by the President and confirmed by the Senate. The LSC indirectly provides legal services in civil matters for low-income individuals through its funding of local legal aid projects and national legal support centers. The centers are instrumental in developing and providing specialized expertise to legal service attorneys. Senior Citizens may receive legal assistance from local legal aid offices in areas such as government benefits, consumer fraud, pensions, age discrimination, property tax exemptions and assessments, guardianships, nursing home matters and other legal problems unique to older individuals. Approximately 88 percent of the funding for local legal aid projects comes from the federal government. Most of this funding is from Legal Service Corporation grants, with the remaining portion coming from Social Service Block Grants and the Older Americans Act. Other funds come from state and local governments and from private sources.

■ *Job Training Partnership Act (JTPA)*

Enacted in 1982, the Job Training and Partnership Act established a nationwide system of job training programs administered jointly by local governments and private sector planning agencies. Title I of the Act authorized the second major federal program directed towards elderly employment opportunities and assistance needs. JTPA replaced the previous Comprehensive Employment and Training Act programs. There are two major training programs under this Act: (1) The Title II program for economically disadvantaged youths and adults, with no upper age limit, and (2) the Title III program for dislocated workers, including those long-term unemployed older workers for whom age is a barrier to reemployment. Administered by the Department of Labor, allotments are made to each state specifically for the training and placement of older individuals in employment opportunities with private business concerns.

■ *Food Commodities Program*

Under the Food Commodities program of the Department of Agriculture (USDA), there are two programs of primary benefit to the elderly. The Nutrition Program for the Elderly is designed to supplement other nutrition programs authorized under Title III of the Older Americans Act. The Department of Agriculture works with the Department of Health and Human Services by providing to the states either food commodities, cash reimbursement based on the number of meals served, or a combination of both. The Elderly Feeding Pilot program is an important test program which distributes USDA surplus commodities to low-income persons 60 years of age and older through centers in various selected cities. The program currently falls under the larger Commodity Supplemental Food program.

■ *Transportation Programs*

There are several federal programs which help elderly and hand-icapped individuals meet their transportation needs. The major federal transportation programs of assistance are administered by two agencies: the Department of Health and Human Services (DHHS) and the Department of Transportation (DOT).

The programs providing assistance within DHHS are: Title III of the Older Americans Act, the Social Services Block Grant and the Community Services Block Grant. The Medicaid program, to a limited extent, provides assistance by reimbursing the elderly poor for transportation costs to and from medical facilities. These programs are instrumental in providing **specialized** transportation services, such as transporting the elderly and handicapped persons from their homes to community and medical services.

Through its Urban Mass Transportation Administration, the Department of Transportation administers various programs of assistance enacted under the Urban Mass Transit Act of 1964, the National Mass Transportation Assistance Act of 1974, and Transportation Acts of 1978 and 1982. Of particular interest is the requirement in the Transportation Act of 1974 that transit authorities who receive federal grants reduce fares by 50 percent for the elderly and handicapped. DOT's programs, which provide basic funding sources for primary transportation needs of the elderly, have become a major force behind mass transit construction nationwide.

IMPORTANT GOVERNMENT SOURCES OF
INFORMATION AND ASSISTANCE

Obtaining information about our federal government and its many services and programs for older Americans, or simply finding the one government office among thousands that can answer your questions, is an extremely difficult challenge. But take heart. There is assistance and guidance available to you. Despite budget limitations, our federal government continues to help the public obtain the information it needs, and to identify the particular government office or private organization that can provide the requested information.

This assistance comes from several sources that are readily available to **everyone**. Unfortunately, many Americans are not familiar with these important organizations, or with the fact that the only cost for using them is the price of a phone call or a postage stamp.

There are four major programs and centers that can be extremely helpful to you: (1) the **Consumer Information Center** (2) the **Federal Depository Library Program**, (3) the **National Health Information Center** of the Office of Disease Prevention and Health Promotion (ODPHP) and (4) the **Federal Information Center**. The assistance and information provided by each organization — and how it can be obtained — are described below.

■ The Consumer Information Center

The Consumer Information Center, a part of the General Services Administration, was established in 1970 to help federal agencies promote and distribute consumer information useful to the public. A mail order-only operation (the Center does not handle telephone requests), the Consumer Information Center publishes an updated *Consumer Information Catalog* quarterly. From this catalog, individuals may order the publications listed. Numerous topics are covered by the various booklets offered in each catalog, like careers, child care, education, federal benefits and programs, nutrition, health, drugs, housing, money management, small business, travel and hobbies — just to name a few.

The Center is an extremely effective source of information which responds in a very reasonable time to any order placed. Generally, each catalog lists over 200 booklets, of which about half are free and the remaining ones sold at minimal costs — from 50¢ to $2.50. Only a few publications in the catalog cost slightly more.

It costs nothing to request a catalog and see what publications may be of interest to you — many of them free. There is no fee if you order only one booklet. When you order two or more free booklets, there is a charge of $1.00 to help defray costs. The Center allows individuals to order up to 25 booklets at one time, so you and your friends can place an order together. To receive the latest free Consumer Information Catalog, write to:

> Consumer Information Center
> Catalog Request Department
> P.O. Box 100
> Pueblo, CO 81002

■ *The Federal Depository Library Program*

Established by Congress in the early 1800s to allow the public free access to government publications, the Federal Depository Library Program has become a major information link between the federal government and the American people. The program has expanded considerably since its inception and currently provides government publications to more than 1,370 designated libraries throughout the United States. A central core of 50 selected regional libraries receives and retains at least one copy of nearly every unclassified federal government publication. The regional libraries retain the material they receive permanently, on paper or microfiche, for inter-library loans among the depository libraries within their regions, and provide reference services.

Each year, the depository libraries select titles from more than 25,000 new publications issued by the federal government. In addition to information on the government itself — such as the federal budget — the publications include information on subjects like nutrition, environment, weather, business, health care, energy, education, science and technology, and hundreds of others.

Using this program is very simple, since a Depository librarian will help you obtain the publications you may be interested in. To find the Depository Library in your area, contact any library or write to the Superintendent of Documents, Washington, DC

20402. As with the many other services provided by our nation's libraries, there is no charge associated with obtaining the government publications. However, some publications cannot be checked out. Your librarian will explain the policy for publications whose use is limited to the library reading room.

■ *ODPHP National Health Information Center*

The National Health Information Center of the Office of Disease Prevention and Health Promotion (ODPHP) was created in 1979 to help both consumers and health professionals locate information on health-related subjects. The specific objectives of the Center are:

— to identify health information resources through an established database;
— to channel requests for information to these resources;
— to develop publications that provide information on health related topics of widespread interest.

The National Health Information Center is one of our country's most useful sources for obtaining up-to-the-minute health information — some of it unpublished or extremely hard to find. It can help locate information on specific diseases, health statistics, health education material, health promotion programs, nutrition, exercise and a variety of other general health topics. However, it does not diagnose diseases, recommend health care providers or perform in-depth research. In addition, the Center has a special component called the National Information Center for Orphan Drugs and Rare Diseases (NICODARD) which responds to inquiries on rare diseases and orphan drugs (medicines not widely researched or available). The Center's library of medical and health reference books, directories and books on health promotion is open to the public.

When the Center receives an inquiry, either by telephone or letter, a referral specialist searches the Health Information Center's database to match the question with the organization(s) that can best respond to it. The caller is then referred to that organization(s).

Any individual may write, call or visit the Center. However, if you decide to visit the Center, call in advance for an appointment, Monday through Friday between 9 a.m. and 5 p.m. (EST). There is no charge for any service provided by the Health Information Center.

Direct telephone inquiries to:
  In Maryland, call: (301) 565-4167
  Outside of Maryland, call toll-free: 800-336-4797

Address correspondence to:
ODPHP National Health Information Center
P.O. Box 1133
Washington, DC 20013-1133

■ *Federal Information Center*

If you have a question or problem about the federal government, the Federal Information Center can be a one-stop source of information. The Center's staff can usually answer your question, or give you the name and current telephone number of the office that can provide the answer or assistance you need.

The Federal Information Center answers millions of inquiries each year about Social Security, veteran's benefits, patents, copyrights, discrimination laws, immigration and naturalization, federal jobs, selling to or buying from the federal government and many other topics.

The Center has a large collection of reference materials on government agencies, programs and services for use in research. The primary resource at the Center is a directory of available services indexed by keywords to expedite access to information and minimize the time spent on telephone inquiries. The Federal Information Center's staff is both courteous and extremely well trained to help you get the information you need from the more than 125 agencies and departments in the federal government.

To answer your questions about the federal government, you may call the Center's nationwide toll-free number between the hours of 8:00 a.m. and 8:00 p.m. (EST): 800-688-9889.

Users of Telecommunication Devices for the Deaf may call the following nationwide toll-free number: 800-326-2996 (TDD/TTY).

If you prefer, you can write to: Federal Information, P.O. Box 600, Cumberland, MD 21501-0600.

1996 COST-OF-LIVING ADJUSTMENTS (COLAS) AND PAY RAISES

Although certain changes approved by Congress for 1996 will take money out of your pocket, several increases in benefits and pay should help cover some of those additional outlays. These cost-of-living increases and pay raises are:

- Social Security beneficiaries received a **2.6%** increase on January 1, 1996.

- Effective March 1st, military retirees received a **2.6%** increase in April.

- In January, railroad retirees received a **2.6%** increase in Tier I benefits and a **0.8%** increase in Tier II benefits.

- In January, uniformed military personnel received a **2.4%** increase in basic pay and basic allowance for subsistence (BAS). They also received a **5.2%** increase in their basic allowance for quarters (BAQ) and variable housing allowance (VHA).

- Federal and postal retirees received a delayed cost-of-living increase in April. Those retired under the old Civil Service Retirement System (CSRS) received a **2.6%** increase. Retirees age 62 and older who retired under the Federal Employees Retirement System (FERS) received a **2.0%** increase.

- Federal white-collar workers received a **2.0%** national pay raise in January plus varying locality pay adjustments. They were effective with the first full pay period beginning on or after January 1, 1996.

- Special rate employees - those in hard-to-fill positions such as medical personnel, engineers, and scientists, as well as clerical workers in high-cost regions - received a **2.0%** national pay raise plus *for some* a locality adjustment (geographic differential raise) depending on the amount of their current differential.

- Retired federal and postal employees receiving monthly compensation benefits under the Federal Employees Compensation Act (FECA) received an increase in their benefits in April of **2.0%**.

- In January, wartime service veterans and their dependents who receive benefits from the VA Improved Pension received an increase of **2.6%** retroactive to December 1, 1995. Deceased veterans' parents who receive Dependency and Indemnity Compensation (DIC) payments also received the **2.6%** increase.

- Veterans with service-related disabilities who receive VA Disability Compensation benefits received an increase of **2.6%** retroactive to December 1, 1995. Compensation benefits for widows and children of veterans who died of service-related disabilities will reflect the same **2.6%** increase.

IMPORTANT LEGISLATION AFFECTING BOTH YOUNG AND OLD ALIKE

Here are some recent Congressional Acts that are milestones in the history of our nation:

- *Passage of the Americans with Disabilities Act:* In 1990, Congress passed the *Americans with Disabilities Act*, which President Bush signed into law without modification. Overwhelmingly approved by the both House of Representatives and the Senate, this emotionally charged legislation extended the provisions of the acclaimed Civil Rights Act of 1964 to over 43 million Americans with physical and mental handicaps. Compromises were reached by both houses so that the legislation would not protect users of illegal drugs and will contain provisions for exemptions for small businesses with less than 15 employees.

- *Passage of the Older Workers Benefit Protection Act:* In a move to protect older employees from losing earned benefits, the 102nd Congress passed this act in 1991. The Act prohibits discrimination in an employee benefit plan except when age-based reductions in such plans are justified by significant cost considerations.

- *Family Leave Act Signed:* Twice vetoed by President Bush, the *Family and Medical Leave Act* became the first bill to clear the 103rd Congress. President Clinton signed it into law in February 1993. The new law requires employers with 50 or more workers to provide unpaid time off for the birth or adoption of a child or to care for a seriously ill child, spouse or parent. The Act also provides unpaid time off for an employee's own illness.

PART III

Caregivers — Their Numbers Keep On Growing In Our Aging Society

In the face of the Senior boom, society must begin to adjust to the dramatic growth in the Senior population. Numbering almost 34 million today — more than the entire population of Canada — the U.S. over-65 population is projected to reach 40 million by the year 2000 and more than 52 million by 2020. With nursing-home and medical costs increasing at a staggering rate, the care and well-being of America's vast number of Seniors will rest primarily in the hands . . . and hearts . . . of their families.

It is estimated that seven to ten million Americans between ages 45 and 60 care for a dependent relative or older adult. With the projected growth of the Senior population, and the increased lifespan of most Seniors, the number of caregivers will double or even quadruple in the next ten years. Recent studies show that about 65% of *all* American caregivers are under age 65; over 40% hold full-time jobs.

Millions of Americans who aren't yet Seniors themselves, or who are just entering the "golden years," are responsible for their parents or older family members. Some are also still raising their children, adding another demand on their time, finances, and emotional resources. Most often, it is the women of the family who take on the bulk of these responsibilities. According to a House of Representatives Committee on Aging report, today's average woman can expect to spend 17 years taking care of her children and over **18 years** taking care of her or her husband's parents.

CAREGIVERS NEED ALL THE HELP THEY CAN GET!

Although caring for a parent or Senior relative can be rewarding, it may also seem like a tremendous burden physically, mentally, and financially. However, there is help available — albeit, limited — to caregivers. Here are a few steps caregivers should take to help cope with their responsibilities:

- Learn all you can about the many government and private programs, benefits and assistance available to Seniors and make sure those in your care are receiving all their entitlements.

- Contact your local Area Agency on Aging to get on their mailing list for newsletters and other mailings. Find out what resources in your community are available to help Seniors and caregivers.

- Be sure your loved ones get proper medical care. Learn about any illnesses they have so you can cope with any problems the illness may cause. Use the listing in the health chapter to obtain as much current information as possible.

- Contact your local Senior Center to find out what activities they sponsor. Attend their lectures and discussions on problems affecting Seniors.

- Review your relative's insurance and financial situation so you are completely aware of his/her resources. If financial assistance is needed from other family members, don't be reluctant to ask for help.

- If possible, join a local support group for caregivers. Such groups give you a chance to communicate with others who have the same responsibilities and difficulties. If you can't find a group in your community, you may want to start your own — or at least ally yourself with a sympathetic neighbor or co-workers who you can rely on for moral support.

- Find as many activities as possible for the Senior you are caring for at home. Contact your local library for ideas, especially if the Senior is confined totally to the home.

- Join — or have your loved one join — one or more organizations mentioned in Chapter 11 and participate in their local activities. Their magazines and other publications will keep you updated on the services, benefits and help available to Seniors.

- Take care of **yourself**! Spend time on your own or with your spouse, **away** from the Senior you care for. Take advantage of any respite care you can find in your community. Contact your local Area Agency on Aging for guidance. Request relief on a regular basis from family members or friends who are willing to help. You can't do it alone. The time you devote to yourself will make you an even better caregiver . . . and a happier person.

MILES APART . . . THE DILEMMA OF
MANY CAREGIVERS

Millions of caregivers are faced with one of the most difficult dilemmas of their lives: how to provide for the care and well-being of parents or aging loved ones who live far away. Frequently referred to as "long-distance caregivers", their numbers are increasing almost as fast as our society is aging.

Naturally, these caregivers worry about their loved ones' medical care and medications, proper nutrition, shopping and transportation, as well as whether there is someone to regularly check on their well-being. Any caregiver who is faced with trying to provide care from a distant city or town needs all the help he or she can possibly find. The following sources of information and services can be invaluable to them.

■ Before seeking help elsewhere, long-distance caregivers should contact the Area Agency on Aging in their loved one's community. It can provide considerable information on many services and assistance available there. However, due to the Agency's heavy workload, it cannot always devote its full time and attention to one individual. Consequently, you may want to use the services of a geriatric-care manager — a social worker with special training in the care of older individuals. Geriatric care management services are usually low-cost, especially considering the peace-of-mind they can provide.

   There are two national organizations that provide help locating such social workers: (1) the *National Association of Private Geriatric-Care Managers* and (2) the *Aging Network Services*. The first will provide a **free** listing of its members in a specific area of the country who are state licensed or certified. Aging Network Services has a national network of over 300 geriatric social workers that provide innumerable direct services. The addresses and phone numbers for these organizations are:

National Association of
Private Geriatric-Care Managers
1604 N. Country Club Rd.
Tucson, AZ 85716
Tel: (602) 881-8008

Aging Network Services, Inc.
4400 East-West Hwy, Ste. 907
Bethesda, MD 20814
Tel: (301) 657-4329

- Another fine organization which helps long-distance caregivers is the *Elder Support Network*, a service of the Association of Jewish Family and Children's Agencies. The Network acts as a link between you and your Senior loved one through the Jewish Family Service Agency nearest his or her home. Contact the network by calling toll-free **800-634-7346**.

- The *American Association of Retired Persons (AARP)* has published several pamphlets which can be of considerable assistance to all caregivers . . . and they are **free** for the asking! The following five are highly recommended:

    — *A Path for Caregivers (D12957)*
    — *A Handbook about Care in the Home (D955)*
    — *Coping and Caring: Living with Alzheimer's Disease (D12441)*
    — *Miles Away and Still Caring: Guide for Long-Distance Caregivers (D12748)*
    — *A Checklist of Concerns/Resources for Caregivers (D12895)*

To order single copies of any or all of them, send your request listing the title and order number shown next to them to: AARP Fulfillment Section, Box 2400, Long Beach, CA 90801.

- An outstanding organization which every caregiver should be aware of is the *Children of Aging Parents (CAPS)*. It not only serves as a national clearinghouse for caregivers, but has developed and maintains caregiver support groups, and publishes a national newsletter, with vital, up-to-date information for caregivers. Write today for further information on becoming a member: CAPS, 2761 Trenton Road, Levittown, PA 19056.

- *Family Service America* (FSA) provides valuable assistance to caregivers. This non-profit association, comprising nearly 300 member agencies nationwide, provides a variety of aid and services to caregivers, such as counseling, information, and support groups. To obtain the location of an FSA agency in your area, write or call: Family Service America, 11700 West Lake Park Drive, Milwaukee, WI 53224 Tel: (414) 359-1040.

- Urinary incontinence is extremely common in older people, and thus presents one of the most difficult problems a caregiver may face. Unfortunately, many health care professionals ignore urinary incontinence, failing to provide adequate diagnosis and treatment despite the fact that most cases of urinary incontinence can be cured or mitigated. *The Simon Foundation for Continence* and the *National Association for Continence* organization provide education and assistance to incontinence sufferers, their families, and professionals responsible for their care.

For further information, contact either of these outstanding organizations:

The Simon Foundation
  for Continence
P.O. Box 815
Wilmette, IL 60091
Toll Free: 800-237-4666
	National Association
	  for Continence
	P.O. Box 8310
	Spartanburg, SC 29305
	Toll Free: 800-252-3337

NATIONAL ELDERCARE LOCATOR SERVICE !

In a joint effort of the National Association of Area Agencies on Aging, the Administration on Aging, and the National Association of State Units on Aging, a new service called the *Eldercare Locator* was established in 1991 as a demonstration program in the states of Connecticut, Maine, Massachusetts, New Hampshire, Rhode Island, and Vermont. Because of its immediate success, the toll-free telephone service was expanded two years ago as a nationwide information and referral service to identify resources and services available for older persons.

The service helps toll-free callers find information about community services available throughout the nation. Information specialists help callers identify the most appropriate source of information anywhere in the country, based on the Senior's city or zip code. This service is extremely helpful to caregivers interested in locating Senior services such as day care, home health care providers, legal assistance, financial aid, meals-on-wheels, and nursing homes.

Anyone in the United States, Puerto Rico and the Virgin Islands can use the *Eldercare Locator* by calling toll-free **800-677-1116** between the hours of 9:00 A.M. and 8:00 P.M. (EST).

TO CAREGIVERS OF THE TERMINALLY ILL...

For those of you who are faced with providing home care for a loved one who may have less than a year to live, be certain to seek the help of a hospice within your community. Hospices are there to provide not only the highest quality of care possible for the patient but also to give caregivers the guidance and support they need during this difficult period of caregiving. Without the dedicated and caring help of a hospice, many caregivers would never have been able to provide the special care needed by their loved ones.

Hospices will ensure that the proper medicine and supplies are available to relieve pain and provide the utmost comfort to the patient as well as loving attention by nurses, nursing assistants, therapists, social workers, chaplains and trained volunteers. As explained in Chapter 4, Medicare will cover nearly all of the costs of hospice care. Contact your local hospice today — it will mean so much to you and your loved one.

ADULT DAY CARE CENTERS

Although a vast majority of caregivers are unaware of adult day care centers or of the tremendous assistance provided by them, there are over 3,000 of these special centers in the United States. Non-profit organizations and local governments operate adult day care centers in almost every community. The centers not only offer meals but also a variety of social, recreational and health care services during the day for mentally or physically impaired adults. Above all, they offer a much needed respite for caregivers.

Since care is given in a group setting, the costs are generally quite reasonable especially when compared to the costs of individual home care and that of a nursing home. Costs vary depending on the geographical area of the country and the support by local governments and organizations. Although Medicare and most private health insurance policies do not cover any of their costs, you can sometimes obtain assistance from Medicaid, the Veterans Administration and some of the private organizations within your community. Call your local Area Agency on Aging to find out if there is an adult day care center available to help you.

YOUR DIRECTORY OF IMPORTANT ASSISTANCE

The following telephone numbers shoud be filled in as soon as possible so that they are readily available when you seek assistance or information concerning benefits and entitlements for Seniors. In many cases, several regions or counties within your state are served by the same office and may not be close to your home. **Be sure to obtain the telephone number of those offices which serve your county or local area.** If you have any difficulty in obtaining these numbers, contact the telephone directory assistance operator to get the number of your local Human Services Information and Referral Service or Area Agency on Aging. They will provide you with the necessary assistance to complete this list.

Organization or Agency	Telephone Number
Human Services Information & Referral	_____
Area Agency on Aging	_____
District Social Security Office	_____
County Department of Social Services/Welfare Services	_____
Veterans Administration Regional Office	_____
County Health Department	
Public Health Assistance Office	_____
Legal Aid/Legal Services Office	_____
County Housing Authority Office	_____
District Railroad Retirement Office	_____
Job Service Office/Senior Citizens Employment Services	_____
Adult Protective Services	_____
Community Vocational & Rehabilitation Office	_____

Chapter 2

Social Security

Touching the Lives of Almost Every American

Chapter Highlights

Due to the length of this chapter and the numerous topics contained within it, a special Topic Index, which immediately follows the Introduction, has been prepared to assist in locating items that are of particular interest to the reader.

Social Security's Nationwide Toll-Free Telephone Service
800-SSA-1213 (800-772-1213)

Call the toll-free number indicated to order Social Security publications or to ask questions on Social Security, and Supplemental Security Income, as well as questions on general enrollment and coverage in Medicare. Service on the toll-free number is available weekdays from 7:00 A.M. to 7:00 P.M.

Social Security

Touching the Lives of Almost Every American

Since its inception at the height of the Great Depression, Social Security has become one of the finest pieces of social legislation ever enacted by Congress. When President Franklin D. Roosevelt signed the Social Security Act into law on August 14, 1935 as a modest retirement plan providing financial assistance to a limited number of retired workers who had been employed in nonagricultural industry and commerce, he and members of Congress could not have envisioned that it would eventually be expanded to provide coverage for almost every American. Today Social Security is the most important income maintenance and health insurance program in the United States, covering approximately 95 percent of the total American work force.

In 1995, Social Security's coverage of workers and their families reached unprecedented heights: over 141 million employees earned protection under Social Security; 44 million persons (one out of every six) in the country received Social Security checks; and over 32 million people 65 and older, and another four million-plus disabled Americans under 65, received health insurance under its Medicare program.

Although no other program has a greater impact on the lives of the American people, many people do not fully understand Social Security and the many benefits it may provide when earnings stop or diminish because of retirement, disability or death. Simply defined, Social Security is a national insurance program which workers pay for through payment of premiums in the form of taxes. Its benefits are an **earned right**, regardless of an individual's income from savings, pensions, private insurance policies, or any other form of non-work income. The Social Security Act does not require insured workers and their families to prove financial need before receiving its benefits.

There are basically four kinds of insurance provided under Social Security:

- **Retirement insurance** — Referred to as the "Old Age Insurance" portion of Social Security, it provides monthly cash benefits to workers and their families to help replace part of the income that is !ost at retirement. Monthly benefits do not replace all employment earnings and were never intended to do so. However, they do provide a solid base that one can build on with savings, a pension plan, investments and other insurance.

- **Disability insurance** — An invaluable portion of Social Security that provides monthly income to workers when a severe physical or mental impairment prevents them from working for at least a year, or when the condition is expected to result in death. In some cases, benefits may also be payable to a worker's spouse and children.

- **Survivor's insurance** — When a worker dies, surviving dependents may receive a lump-sum death payment and monthly benefits. Over the years, the total benefits can become a substantial amount. This portion of Social Security is actually a **life insurance** policy providing the financial support that a spouse or children will need when the worker is no longer there to take care of them.

- **Health insurance** — When a worker is 65 or older or has been receiving disability payments for 24 months, Medicare helps pay for hospital and medical expenses. It also provides Medicare coverage for spouses at age 65 or other family members who receive disability payments for 24 months. Of major importance is Medicare's coverage of a large percentage of the costs of dialysis treatment or kidney transplant surgery for a worker or dependent of any age.

There is not an insurance policy available in the private sector of our economy that provides the same coverage that Social Security does for similar costs. Many insurance actuaries have calculated the financial protection of Social Security, excluding health coverage, for people of all ages. Most of them have determined that protection comparable to Social Security's would be almost impossible for a private sector insurance company to offer. In fact, if such a policy were available it would be so costly that practically no one could afford it.

An attempt has been made in this chapter, and in Chapter 4 on "Medicare," to explain complicated programs of Social Security in a manner that can be easily understood. In some cases, it was necessary to leave intact the wording used by the Social Security Administration in order to preserve the intended meaning, and to avoid any misinterpretation of a particular requirement.

This chapter is divided into nine general topics. Each section, except the first one, discusses specific facets of the Social Security program and their application to workers and dependents. The first section presents a basic explanation of the program's provisions and some particulars that provide for a better understanding of the entire program.

Frequently in a discussion like this, concerning a subject with so many complex rules, eligibility requirements and limitations, it is more helpful to repeat some items rather than refer the reader back to another section for clarification. While repetition has been kept to a minimum, you will find that it does occur. Hopefully, it will enhance your understanding of the topic.

It is advisable to look over the topic index of this chapter's contents following this discussion, so you can easily find those items of interest to you or your family. However, since this chapter could not possibly contain all details of the various rules and regulations concerning Social Security benefits, you should seek further information and clarification of these benefits from your nearest Social Security office.

Of Interest to Many . . .

Out of the 44 million individuals receiving Social Security benefits in 1995, 30.7 million were retired workers; 5.9 million were workers with disability and their children; and 7.4 million were survivors of deceased workers.

Topic Index

Of Interest to Many . . .

According to the Social Security Administration, monthly Social Security benefits in the past few years have made up more than half of the total income of 59% of recipients. For a quarter (24%) of recipients, their monthly benefits made up more than 90% of their total income, and for 13% of recipients, Social Security benefits made up 100% of their income— their only source of income!

SECTION 1

How Social Security Works

As mentioned in the Introduction, Social Security is really an insurance program providing retirement, disability, survivor and health benefits to you and your family. This section explains how this invaluable insurance program works by answering several questions frequently asked about Social Security. Most of these questions, which cover the essential basic provisions of the program, are generally the same questions individuals ask about their own private insurance policies.

A few selected items of general information, that are not discussed in detail elsewhere but are important to you as a beneficiary, are included at the end of this section. Also, a summary of Social Security tax and benefits changes that occur on an annual basis is provided to help clarify some points that may be of particular interest to you. Although certain answers to the various questions presented are general in nature, specifics concerning the questions and other facets of the program are explained in detail in the remaining portions of this chapter.

WHO ADMINISTERS SOCIAL SECURITY?

The Social Security Administration, with over 65,000 employees (down 15,000 from the staffing level of 1985) located in 1,300 offices throughout the country, is responsible for administering the Old Age, Survivors and Disability Insurance (OASDI) portion of Social Security and for providing the assistance and information needed by individuals covered under Social Security. Technically, the Health Insurance (HI) portion, Medicare, is administered by the Health Care Financing Administration (HCFA), but Social Security personnel take applications for Medicare, complete claim forms and, in general, answer most questions an individual has concerning the Medicare program. Previously under the Secretary of the Department of Health and Human Services, the Social Security Administration became an independent agency on March 31, 1995.

The Internal Revenue Service of the Department of the Treasury, however, has responsibility for collecting the Social Security contributions which workers, employers and self-employed persons are required to pay on covered wages and earnings. The Department of the Treasury also issues and mails the monthly Social Security benefit checks. The benefit amounts determined by the Social Security Administration are forwarded to the Department of the Treasury for processing. If any problem arises with the receipt of a benefit check, its loss, or any changes that occur in the normal check amount, the Social Security Administration should be contacted. The Department of the Treasury does not deal directly with Social Security beneficiaries in these matters.

WHO DETERMINES WHAT BENEFITS AN INDIVIDUAL CAN RECEIVE?

In all cases, the amount of benefits payable and the individual's rights to these benefits are clearly defined under Social Security law. Consequently, even though the Social Security personnel are responsible for evaluating each applicant's eligibility for benefits and calculating the amount that should be paid monthly, their determinations must be made in strict accordance with the requirements, procedures and calculations set by law for all beneficiaries. In other words, the latitude for individual judgments or discretionary decisions by Social Security personnel is limited.

If ever you disagree with an unfavorable decision or determination concerning your Social Security benefits, you have the **right to appeal** — a right which the law provides to everyone.

HOW IS THE PROGRAM FINANCED?

Social Security is a program that operates on a "pay-as-you-go" basis. That is, Social Security payments, in the form of taxes paid by today's workers, finance the current benefits being paid to beneficiaries. Workers, employees and self-employed individuals pay taxes on earnings up to an annual taxable maximum which is automatically adjusted each year as wages rise (if there is also a benefit increase in the same year).

In 1996, the maximum amount of annual earnings covered by Social Security is **$62,700**; however, the wage base for Medicare Hospital Insurance is higher than for the Social Security tax portion. **All** wages and salaries will be subject to the Medicare tax portion. For the self employed, the tax of 2.9 percent applies to all of their earnings. The tax rate that both employees and employers pay in 1996 is 6.20 percent for the Old Age, Survivors and Disability insurance (OASDI) and 1.45 percent for Medicare Hospital insurance (HI). The total for both cash benefits (the OASDI portion) and hospital insurance (the Medicare portion) is 7.65 percent. Future Social Security tax rates already scheduled by law are as follows:

Years	For Cash Benefits: (OASDI)	For Hospital Insurance: (HI)	Total: (Percent)
1990 and after	6.20	1.45	7.65

Self-employed persons pay taxes at a rate twice the employee rate. However, since 1990, self-employed individuals can take two deductions to help reduce their Social Security tax liability. These deductions are designed to tax the self-employed in much the same way as employers/employees for Social Security and federal income tax.

First, net earnings from self-employment are reduced by an amount equal to half the total self-employment tax. Second, half of the self-employment tax can now be deducted as a business expense.

The following indicates the tax rates scheduled by law for self-employed individuals:

Years	For Cash Benefits: (OASDI)	For Hospital Insurance: (HI)	Total: (Percent)
1990 and after	12.40	2.90	15.30

The taxes that are paid into Social Security are deposited into three separate trust funds: (1) the OASI (Old Age and Survivors Insurance) trust fund, (2) the DI (Disability Insurance) trust fund, and (3) the HI (Hospital Insurance) trust fund. The money received by the trust funds can only be used to pay for benefits and administrative costs to operate the programs. Any money not used for these purposes is invested in interest-bearing securities guaranteed by the government. The hospital insurance fund is separate from the first two funds since it goes towards Medicare costs; consequently, when discussing Social Security benefits and financing, only the OASI and DI funds are considered.

The taxes paid into the OASDI programs account for almost 95 percent of the program's revenue. The other 5 percent comes from various sources: interest earned from the trust funds, investments, money from the federal government as the employer of certain federal employees covered under Social Security, and revenues obtained from the federal taxation of some Social Security benefits.

HOW SOLVENT IS SOCIAL SECURITY? —
WILL IT STILL BE AROUND WHEN IT'S TIME TO COLLECT BENEFITS?

In the late '70s and early '80s, most of you were aware that the financial status of the Social Security trust funds, which pays your benefits, had rapidly deteriorated. This was due in part to the high levels of inflation in our economy, slow wage growth, and the recession of 1974-75 which raised unemployment rates, thus reducing payroll tax income. Additionally, of utmost importance, a major technical error created by Congress in its 1972 legislation led to "over-indexing" of benefits for some new retirees and created an unexpected additional drain on trust funds reserves.

Recognizing the vulnerable status of Social Security, Congress reacted by passing Social Security amendments in 1977. These amendments increased payroll taxes beginning in 1979 and resolved the technical problems in the method of computing benefit amounts. However, due to the poor performance of our economy, the trust fund's long-term deficit still remained. Consequently, President Reagan appointed a bipartisan National Commission on Social Security Reform to study the situation and make recommendations that would restore both short and long-term solvency to Social Security. The commission was highly successful, and in 1983 Congress passed into law Social Security amendments which closely followed the Commission's recommendations. These amendments have had a major impact on restoring the solvency of the Social Security trust funds.

The changes enacted by these amendments were basically in the area of expanded Social Security coverage of federal employees hired after January 1, 1984 and of certain employees of private, nonprofit, tax-exempt organizations; annual adjustment of benefits in which cost-of-living adjustments (COLAs) were shifted to a calendar year basis with the July 1983 COLA delayed to January 1984; acceleration of previously scheduled payroll tax rate increases plus an increase in self-employment tax rates; federal income taxation of some Social Security benefits; and an increase in the retirement age from 65 to 67 gradually phased in between the years 2000 and 2022.

The 1995 annual report to Congress from the Board of Trustees of the Social Security Trust Funds stated that Social Security is financially adequate over the next decade and for several years thereafter until at least 2030. Since that report, the current Advisory Council on Social Security and Medicare to Congress and the President was given the task to develop specific recommendations that would assure Social Security's long-term solvency past 2030. You can be certain that Congress and the President will take whatever measures are needed to maintain Social Security's solvency just as they did in the early 80's.

Consequently, Social Security will be there at the time of your retirement, disability or death, when the benefits you earned are needed by you and your family!

WHO IS INCLUDED IN THE COVERAGE PROVIDED BY SOCIAL SECURITY?

Social Security is, for all practical purposes, universal in its coverage of workers and their families — almost everyone in our country is protected by it. The relatively few workers within our population who are not covered by Social Security include: railroad workers covered under the Railroad Retirement System (which is actually coordinated with Social Security), federal employees hired before January 1,1984 who are covered by their own Civil Service Retirement System, certain employees of state and local governments who have retained their own retirement programs, individuals, such as household workers, farm workers and self-employed people, who may not earn enough to be covered, and a very small group of individuals whose work does not meet the requirements established by Social Security law for coverage such as occurs in family employment of children or parents. Effective July 1, 1991, almost two million state and local government employees — with some exceptions — were covered by Social Security and Medicare.

As a worker and family provider, you are most justified in your concern as to whether your dependents will be fully covered by Social

Security if you are disabled or die. Except in those particular circumstances, like when a dependent child does not meet the applicable age criteria or a parent is not considered financially dependent on the worker, you may be assured that your dependents will receive Social Security benefits as provided for them by Social Security law if they meet the established eligibility requirements.

The following summary indicates which individuals may be eligible for monthly Social Security benefits. The eligibility criteria for each type of benefit are discussed in the various sections of this chapter.

SUMMARY OF INDIVIDUALS ELIGIBLE FOR MONTHLY SOCIAL SECURITY BENEFITS

In addition to the monthly benefits paid to a **retired insured worker at age 62 or over** or to a **disabled insured worker under age 65**, certain dependent family members of an insured worker may also be eligible for monthly Social Security benefits. The following individuals are generally considered eligible for Social Security payments:

Dependents of a retired or disabled worker
- Spouse, age 62 or over
- Spouse under 62, if caring for a child under 16 (or disabled) who is getting a benefit based on the retired or disabled workers' earnings
- Unmarried children under 18, or under 19 if they are full-time high school students
- Unmarried children, 18 or over, who were severely disabled before age 22 and who continue to be disabled.

Dependents who are survivors of a deceased worker
- Widow or widower, 60 years of age or older
- Widow or widower, or surviving divorced spouse, if caring for a worker's child under 16 (or disabled) who is getting a benefit based on the earnings of the deceased worker
- Widow or widower, 50 or older, who becomes disabled not later than seven years after the worker's death, or who becomes disabled not later than seven years after becoming entitled to benefits on the worker's earnings record
- Parents, 62 or older, of the deceased worker, who were dependent on the support they received from their child

- Unmarried children (of the worker), 18 or over, who were severely disabled before age 22 and who continue to be disabled.
- Unmarried children under 18 years of age, or under 19 if they are full-time high school students.

Individuals with special eligibility

- There are two groups of individuals who, even though not considered to be members of the worker's family, may be eligible for monthly payments based on a worker's Social Security record. These include: (1) divorced spouses, at or beyond age 62, who have been divorced for at least two years; and (2) a disabled divorced spouse, age 50 or older, if the marriage lasted 10 years or more.
- Certain grandchildren may be eligible for benefits based on a grandparent's or great-grandparent's earnings if the child lived with the grandparent, who provided at least one-half of the child's support.
- Certain individuals who reached age 72 before 1972 and are not insured for regular monthly benefits may receive a special monthly payment. This provision is known as the "Prouty Benefit".

HOW MUCH ARE BENEFITS WORTH?

Once you become eligible for benefits by having sufficient work credits, the amount of your benefit check will depend entirely on your age and your earnings over a period of years. In calculating these benefits, your actual earnings over the past years are adjusted to take into account the changes in average wages since 1951. These adjusted earnings are then averaged together and a formula is applied to the average to obtain the rate upon which your benefits are based.

After the initial benefit amount is established, your benefit rate will be increased annually by cost-of-living adjustments which are based on the upward changes in the economy. For individuals who continue to work after receiving Social Security benefits, payments will be somewhat reduced if their earnings exceed certain annual exempt amounts.

When Social Security began paying benefits in 1940, it expended $35 million to almost 222,500 individuals. Since that time, both expenditures for benefits and the number of beneficiaries have increased dramatically, at a rate far outpacing the economy and expectations. In 1996, Social Security is expected to pay out over $381 billion to more than 44 million beneficiaries of Old Age, Survivors and Disability insurance benefits. The average benefit payments have also increased considerably over the years. In 1996, a single retired worker can expect average monthly benefits of $720, a retired worker and an aged spouse $1,215 per month, an aged widow or widower could anticipate receiving $680 while a disabled worker and spouse with one or more children could receive $1,148. These are all average benefit amounts, with many individuals receiving considerably more depending on their past earnings.

The cash benefits provided to you and your family during retirement, disability or death are of tremendous worth. Beyond a doubt, Social Security is truly a successful program that touches the lives of nearly every American. Although it has changed substantially over the more than 50 years since its inception, its basic principles are unchanged. It remains our nation's most important program providing for the needs of our people — both young and old — during old age, periods of disability, even to death!

ITEMS OF GENERAL INFORMATION

As with any in-depth explanation of a complex program such as Social Security, there are at times some items which may not have been mentioned or discussed in detail even though they are important or of interest to many individuals. I hope the following items will provide information that is useful in furthering your understanding of certain aspects, services and provisions of Social Security which may apply to you.

YOUR SOCIAL SECURITY CARD

Your Social Security number is the key to identifying your lifetime earnings, from covered employment or self-employment, on which your benefits are based. The same number is used throughout your lifetime and must be recorded by each employer. If you ever get more than one Social Security number, you should notify any Social Security office about the error.

If your Social Security card is lost or stolen, you should apply for a replacement card as soon as possible. You should also contact Social Security to apply for a corrected card if you change your name. This will ensure that all of your earnings are applied properly to your earnings record. Evidence that identifies you under both your old and new names will be required when applying for the corrected card. One document will be acceptable if it shows both your old and new names, or multiple documents if each shows only one name. If the name change is due to marriage or divorce, a marriage certificate or divorce decree that shows both your previous and new name is usually sufficient.

APPLYING FOR A SOCIAL SECURITY CARD

Whether you are applying for an original, replacement or a corrected Social Security card, you must provide evidence of your age, identity and U.S. citizenship. If you are a naturalized U.S. citizen, or you were previously but are not presently a U.S. citizen, you must also provide evidence of your current citizenship or immigrant status. The documents that are required must be originals or certified copies; uncertified or notarized photocopies are not usually acceptable.

If you have never had a card before or are a citizen of another country whose immigration documents should not be mailed, you must apply in person. Others may apply either by mail or in person. Contact your nearest Social Security office for the necessary application form (Form SS-5) and any additional information you may need for processing your application. If you have any difficulty obtaining the required documentation to support your application, the personnel at the Social Security office will assist you. It takes approximately two weeks after you have made application to get a new Social Security card or replacement.

The evidence you must submit will depend on your particular circumstances. Generally, if you are a U.S. citizen, born either within or outside the U.S., you will need only two documents: one showing evidence of your age and citizenship and one showing evidence of your identity.

The preferred document for proof of age and U.S. citizenship is a public birth certificate, or foreign birth certificate, that shows the date and place of birth recorded before age five. Other documents include church records, certificates of naturalization, hospital records of birth, U.S. consular reports of birth and U.S. passports.

For evidence of your identity, a document should be provided that shows your name, signature, photograph, or other identifying information. Documents that can be used to establish identity include driver's license, state identity cards, U.S. passport or citizen ID cards, school records, marriage licenses, divorce decrees, military or draft records and voters' registration cards.

Individuals who are **not** U.S. citizens and were born outside the U.S. must also present evidence of their lawful alien status when applying for Social Security numbers. Any document issued by the U.S. Immigration and Naturalization Service (INS) can be used to verify their status. These individuals must be authorized to work by the INS before they can be issued a Social Security number. If a lawfully admitted alien is not permitted to work but has a valid need for a Social Security number other than for work, a Social Security card will be issued. However, the card will show that it may only be used for non-work purposes. If the individual uses the number in employment, the Social Security Administration is required to notify the Immigration and Naturalization Service about the individual's unauthorized work.

DIRECT DEPOSIT OF YOUR BENEFIT CHECKS

Social Security benefit checks may be sent directly to a bank or other financial institution for deposit into a checking or savings account. For recipients of monthly benefit checks, direct deposit has several advantages:

- Their checks will not be stolen or lost.

- Their money is always available, even if they are away from home for an extended period of time.

- There is no need to cash or deposit the check into an account.

- It is much safer than cashing the check and carrying a considerable amount of cash or keeping it at home.

More than a third of all Social Security and Supplemental Security Income beneficiaries now utilize direct deposit for their benefit checks. To arrange for direct deposit, you choose the financial institution where you prefer your checks to be sent. It can be a commercial bank, savings bank, savings and loan association, federal or state credit union, or other similar financial institution. You will be required to complete a direct deposit form, SF-1199, which is available at your financial institution. Bring along your most recent benefit check since it contains all of the information that is needed to complete the form. Your financial institution will forward your completed SF-1199 to Social Security. Processing takes about 90 days after Social Security gets the form from your financial institution. Your checks will continue to be sent to your home address until the processing is completed.

If for any reason you want to change to another financial institution, you simply fill out another Form SF-l199 at the new institution. Your checks will be sent to the old organization until the new form is processed by Social Security.

Financial institutions are required to notify direct deposit beneficiaries that their monthly payments have or have not been received. In addition, the law requires all financial institutions to credit the benefit payment to the beneficiary's account on the same day it is received.

The direct deposit program only applies to where the monthly benefit check is sent; all other notices or information from Social Security are sent to the beneficiary's home address. If you change your home address, be sure to notify Social Security.

INTERNATIONAL SOCIAL SECURITY AGREEMENTS

If you have worked or may work outside the United States, be aware that special Social Security Agreements with several countries improve Social Security protection for people who work or have worked in both countries. These agreements are called "International Totalization Agreements" and provide specifically for coordination of our Social Security system with the systems of certain other countries. These agreements benefit both workers and employers by eliminating dual coverage and contributions for the same work under the Social Security systems of both countries. Currently, the U.S. has bilateral agreements with eleven countries: Belgium, Canada, Germany, France, Italy, Netherlands, Norway, Portugal, Spain, Sweden, Switzerland and the United Kingdom.

In general, these agreements help many people who were not eligible for monthly retirement, disability, or survivors' benefits under one or both country's Social Security systems, as well as those people who are now paying Social Security taxes to both countries, by eliminating double taxation and permitting individuals, under certain circumstances, to use their work under both systems to qualify for benefits. These agreements cover Social Security taxes and retirement, disability, and survivors' insurance entitlement, including death benefits; however, they do not include the U.S. Medicare program, Supplemental Security Income (SSI) program or any special payments to certain uninsured people age 72 or older.

Special booklets have been prepared by the Social Security Administration covering agreements the U.S. has with each particular country. These booklets explain in detail how an individual's work in those countries can affect his or her Social Security coverage in the U.S. The pamphlets may be requested from any Social Security office.

YOUR BENEFIT PAYMENTS WHILE OUTSIDE THE U.S.

Recipients of Social Security benefits should be aware that there are special rules which may affect their right to receive payments if they go outside the U.S. for extended periods of time or to reside permanently. Being outside the U.S. means that you are not in one of the 50 states, the District of Columbia, Puerto Rico, the U.S. Virgin Islands, Guam or American Samoa.

If you are a U.S. citizen, you do not have to be concerned since generally your benefit checks will keep coming regardless of where you reside, so long as you are eligible for benefits, except for those few countries to which the U.S.Treasury Department cannot send benefit checks. Currently, regulations prohibit sending these funds to Albania, Cuba, Cambodia, Iran, North Korea and Vietnam. As a U.S. citizen you can receive any checks that are withheld while you are in one of these countries once you return to the U.S. or go to another country where checks can be sent. However, if you are not a U.S. citizen, you cannot receive any checks for the months in which you live in one of these countries, even after you leave it.

If you are not a U.S. citizen, your benefit checks will cease after you have been outside the United States for six months unless you meet one of the exceptions specified by law. Your local Social Security office will provide information about these exceptions. However, regardless of the various restrictions imposed on individuals who are not U.S. citizens, benefit payments will continue if nonpayment of benefits to these individuals would be contrary to a treaty obligation of the United States **or** if they are citizens or residents of a country with which the U.S. has an international Social Security (totalization) agreement.

Also, there are special residency requirements which may affect benefit payments for non-U.S. citizens who were first eligible for benefits after 1984 as a dependent or survivor of a worker. The requirements state that these individuals must have resided in the U.S. for five years and had, during that time, a family relationship to the worker on whose record their benefits are based.

This residency requirement does not apply to individuals entitled to benefits on the record of a worker who died while in the U.S. military service or as a result of a service-connected disease or injury. Nor does it apply to those cases where the U.S. has a treaty obligation or international Social Security agreement.

All individuals, whether U.S. citizens or aliens, who intend to leave the U.S. for an extended period of time should contact the Social Security office well in advance of their departure. They should provide the agency with forwarding address instructions for their benefit checks and seek guidance regarding any further requirements that may apply to them.

BENEFICIARIES IMPRISONED FOR CONVICTION OF A FELONY

Of particular importance to older individuals who are financially dependent on their spouses or adult children convicted of a crime and imprisoned, are the following Social Security rules regarding payments of Social Security benefits to imprisoned beneficiaries and their dependents.

BENEFITS PAYABLE TO IMPRISONED BENEFICIARIES AND PERSONS CONFINED IN PUBLIC INSTITUTIONS

Recent legislation has expanded the ban on providing Social Security benefits to prisoners. As of February 1995, **no** benefit payments will be made to individuals convicted of a criminal offense punishable by more than one year's imprisonment—*regardless of the actual sentence imposed.*

Benefits will not be paid for months a person is imprisoned for a criminal conviction. The new rule also prohibits benefits for individuals confined by court order in an institution at public expense if they have been found:

- Guilty but insane *or*

- Not guilty by reason of insanity or similar factors (such as mental disease, mental defect, or mental incompetence) *or*

- Incompetent to stand trial.

BENEFITS PAYABLE TO A SPOUSE OR DEPENDENT OF A PRISONER

Social Security law permits continuation of benefit payments that a spouse or other family members were entitled to based on the imprisoned beneficiary's earnings record. Social Security will adjust the benefit amounts that currently are paid and arrange to send the adjusted payments directly to the spouse or other dependents who are entitled to these benefits. Social Security should be notified immediately to ensure that dependents' benefits are not suspended when the imprisoned beneficiary's payments are and to make any other arrangements required to assure that payments are properly received.

IMPORTANT TIMES TO CONTACT YOUR SOCIAL SECURITY OFFICE

Regardless of your age, it is extremely important that you contact your Social Security office whenever any of the following events or needs occur:

- If you wish to seek employment and have never had a Social Security card, you must obtain one before you begin working. It is important that your Social Security account reflects all your employment credits.

- When you lose your Social Security card, or if it is stolen, contact the office to obtain a replacement card.

- If you wish to obtain your Social Security retirement benefits, apply at least three months before you reach retirement age; 62 for reduced benefits, 65 for full benefit payments.

- Upon the death of a family member, such as your spouse or a parent, contact the office to apply for survivor or death benefits to which you may be entitled.

- If you become disabled, contact the office to make application for disability benefits.

- When you change your name used in employment because of marriage, divorce or any other reason, contact the office to ensure that all future wages will be properly recorded by Social Security.

- When you have a change of address, even if your Social Security checks are sent directly to your bank or financial institution for deposit, it is necessary to contact Social Security so that all notices of information concerning your benefits — which are not sent to your bank — are forwarded to your new address.

- Contact Social Security at any time you have a change that would affect your monthly benefits.

- Contact the office whenever you have a question concerning Social Security or need assistance in resolving a discrepancy or problem with your benefits.

- Check your Social Security earnings record at least every **three years** throughout your employment years to make certain your earnings have been correctly reported by your employer and correctly recorded by Social Security.

Becoming Insured: Work Credit Requirements

THE IMPORTANCE OF WORK CREDITS (QUARTERS OF COVERAGE)

In order to qualify for retirement or disability Social Security bene-fits, workers must earn a certain number of work credits. These credits are also necessary to establish eligibility for spouses and dependents to receive benefits based on the workers' earnings record.

A work credit is also called a "quarter of coverage". This becomes somewhat confusing to many individuals since they believe that work credited to their earnings record must have accrued in a calendar quarter of the year such as January through March, April through June, and so forth. Prior to 1978, this was true: credits were called quarters of coverage because they were based on money earned during a calendar quarter of the year. However, since 1978, work credits (quarters of coverage) are based on an individual's yearly earnings. You will find that frequently the terms are used interchangeably.

The amount of covered earnings needed for a work credit is raised each year to conform with the increases in average wage levels. For the years **before** 1978, workers earned one quarter of coverage for any three month calendar quarter in which they were paid covered wages of $50 or more. Self-employed individuals were credited with four quarters of coverage for any taxable year prior to 1978 in which they had $400 or more in self-employment income. Since 1978, indi-viduals, both wage earners and self-employed individuals, earned one work credit (quarter of coverage) for the following established amounts of covered annual earnings:

1978 — $250	1979 — $260	1980 — $290	1981 — $310
1982 — $340	1983 — $370	1984 — $390	1985 — $410
1986 — $440	1987 — $460	1988 — $470	1989 — $500
1990 — $520	1991 — $540	1992 — $570	1993 — $590
1994 — $620	1995 — $630	1996 — $640	

In general, self-employed individuals must have net earnings of at least $400 before receiving any Social Security earnings credits; however, in some cases, net earnings of less than $400 may count for future Social Security credits. Although, yearly net earnings of at least $400 count in determining the amount of your future Social Security benefits, you need net earnings of $640 in 1996 to gain 1 earning credit.

No more than four work credits can be earned for any year, regardless of total earnings. The number of Social Security work credits needed for retirement, survivors and disability benefits depends on the worker's age as explained in the following synopsis of requirements for each type of benefit.

WORK CREDITS REQUIRED FOR RETIREMENT BENEFITS

The following tables show the amount of credit needed for individuals to be eligible for retirement benefits. The first table depicts credit requirements for all workers **except** for some individuals who work for certain mandatorily covered nonprofit organizations which are indicated in the second table.

For Most Workers

If you reach age 62 in:	Years you need of credit:	Equivalent number of work credits:
1983	8	32
1984	$8\frac{1}{4}$	33
1985	$8\frac{1}{2}$	34
1986	$8\frac{3}{4}$	35
1987	9	36
1988	$9\frac{1}{4}$	37
1989	$9\frac{1}{2}$	38
1990	$9\frac{3}{4}$	39
1991 or later	10	40

For certain individuals who work for a nonprofit organization that was mandatorily covered by the Social Security Amendments of 1983, with coverage beginning in 1984, fewer work credits may be needed to obtain retirement benefits. The work credits must be earned after

January 1, 1984. Furthermore, for an individual to qualify under this ruling, he or she must have been **both** 55 or older and an employee of the organization on January 1, 1984. The following table shows the work credit requirements for these individuals:

For Certain Nonprofit Organization Employees

Worker's age on January 1, 1984:	Years of credit needed:	Equivalent number of work credits:
55 or 56	5	20
57	4	16
58	3	12
59	2	8
60 or older	1$^1/_2$	6

Work Credit provisions for nonprofit organization employees are not applicable to individuals who declined Social Security coverage when it was offered by the employer.

WORK CREDITS REQUIRED FOR SURVIVORS' BENEFITS

Once an individual reaches age 62, the number of work credits needed for survivors' benefits is the same as those needed for retirement benefits. However, if the deceased worker earned fewer credits than the number required for retirement benefits, survivors' benefits will still be paid under the following circumstances:

- If born before 1930, the deceased worker must have earned one credit for each year between 1950 and the year of death.

- If born in 1930 or later, the deceased worker must have earned one credit for each year he/she lived after reaching the age of 21.

Regardless of the year the worker was born, benefits may be paid to the worker's surviving dependent children if the worker had earned six work credits (1$^1/_2$ years of work) in the three years before the death occurred. A widow or widower may also be eligible for benefits if caring for disabled children or children under 16 who are entitled to benefits based on the deceased's earnings.

WORK CREDITS REQUIRED FOR DISABILITY BENEFITS

The number of work credits needed for disability benefits depends on the age at which you become disabled and when the credits were earned:

For Older Workers

■ *Disabled at age 31 or older* — Generally, a worker must have earned at least five years of work credit in the 10 years immediately before becoming disabled, in accordance with the work credit requirements shown in the following table:

Born after 1929, become disabled age:	Born before 1930, become disabled before age 62 in year:	Years of work credit needed:	Equivalent number of at work credits:
31 thru 42		5	20
44		$5\frac{1}{2}$	22
46		6	24
48		$6\frac{1}{2}$	26
50		7	28
52	1981	$7\frac{1}{2}$	30
53	1982	$7\frac{3}{4}$	31
54	1983	8	32
55	1984	$8\frac{1}{4}$	33
56	1985	$8\frac{1}{2}$	34
57	1986	$8\frac{3}{4}$	35
58	1987	9	36
59	1988	$9\frac{1}{4}$	37
60	1989	$9\frac{1}{2}$	38
62 or older	1991 or later	10	40

For Younger Workers

■ *Disabled at age 24 through 30* — A worker needs credit for having worked half the time between age 21 and the time the worker becomes disabled.

■ *Disabled before age 24* — A worker needs credit for $1\frac{1}{2}$ years of work (six work credits) in the three-year period ending when the disability started.

Additionally, workers who become disabled before the age of 31, recover, and then become disabled again at age 31 or older generally do not need 20 work credits to be eligible for benefits. They will need credits for half of the time between age 21 and the second time they became disabled. The period in which they were previously disabled does not count.

There is a special exception for anyone disabled by blindness: **no recent work credit** is needed to qualify for disability benefits. Benefits can be paid to those disabled by blindness if (1) a minimum of six work credits (1½ years) was earned, and (2) one credit was earned for each year since 1950, or for each year between age 21 and the time the worker becomes blind.

"FULLY INSURED" OR "CURRENTLY INSURED" STATUS

Since Social Security regulations frequently refer to a worker being either "fully insured" or "currently insured," it may prove helpful to discuss the meaning of these terms. Due to the many factors involved in the actual determination of a worker's status as either fully or currently insured, the following gives only the basic meaning of each term. The Social Security people will help you further interpret them if the need arises when you apply for benefits.

■ *Fully Insured Status* — Individuals are considered "fully insured" if they have been credited with a required number of quarters of coverage (work credits) on their Social Security earnings records. More specifically, to be "fully insured," an individual must be covered for a number of quarters equal to or exceeding the number of years from his/her 21st birthday to: (1) his/her 62nd birthday, (2) his/her disability, or (3) his/her death (whichever comes first). An individual whose 21st birthday occurred before 1936 — the year of the Social Security Act — should begin counting credit quarters from 1936, **not** from his 21st birthday. Although most types of benefits can be paid to workers who are fully insured, being "fully insured" does not assure eligibility for all types of benefits, since there are other requirements which must be taken into consideration. Regardless of age, anyone who has 40 work credits is considered to be fully insured for life.

■ *Currently Insured Status* — Individuals are considered "currently insured" if they have at least six quarters of coverage (work credits) during the full 13-quarter period ending with the calendar quarter in which they either.(1) died, or (2) most recently became entitled to disability insurance benefits, or (3) became entitled to retirement insurance benefits. A currently insured status is sufficient for payment of several types of benefits, such as the lump sum death payment to survivors or benefits payable to a widow or widower (or divorced spouse) caring for the worker's child and the child is either disabled or under the age of 16.

SECTION 3

Your Earnings and the Amount of Your Benefits

YOUR EARNINGS RECORD

Since your Social Security earnings record is the basis for determining your eligibility for Social Security benefits, Medicare protection, and how much your monthly benefit will be, it is critical for you to check the accuracy of your earnings record at least every three years. This is particularly important to those who have worked under different names, changed jobs frequently, were employed by more than one employer in the same year, or performed only part-time or seasonal work. Mistakes can occur in the process of recording the millions of wage and tax statements that the Social Security Administration receives each year. These mistakes will probably not be corrected unless an individual reports an inaccuracy shown in the report of his or her earnings record.

You may obtain a copy of your earnings record by requesting it from your local Social Security office. They will send you, at no cost, Form SSA7004 "Request for Earnings and Benefit Estimate Statement", which you fill in and send to the processing center indicated. Generally, it takes from four to six weeks to process your request. At the same time,you may request an estimate of your future retirement benefit.

If your earnings were properly reported each year and no errors have been made in recording them, the earnings statement you receive should show all of your earnings covered by Social Security since 1937 and the number of work credits (quarters of coverage) you have earned. If you requested an estimate of your future retirement benefit, this too will be shown on your statement. Although benefits are based on earnings covered by Social Security and not on the amount of taxes paid, the statement also includes a summary of the total amount of Social Security taxes you have paid.

MAXIMUM AMOUNT OF COVERED YEARLY EARNINGS

The maximum taxable wage base covered by Social Security rises each year to keep pace with increases in average wage levels. If amounts above the maximum for a year were reported in your earnings record, they may appear on your earnings statement, but only the maximum amount of yearly earnings is used to figure benefits. The maximum is the combined amount of wages and self-employment income for a single taxable year. When individuals find that they paid Social Security taxes on more than the maximum allowable amount because they worked for more than one employer in the year, they should apply for a refund of the excess (Social Security) taxes withheld on their income tax return for that year. If a person worked for only one employer who overwithheld the Social Security taxes, he or she must apply to the employer for a refund. The Internal Revenue Service will be able to respond to questions concerning overwithholding of Social Security taxes and refund procedures. The table on the following page shows the maximum amounts of covered yearly earnings allowable for each year from 1937 through 1996.

ERRORS OR DISCREPANCIES IN YOUR EARNINGS STATEMENT

Whenever you find any errors or discrepancies in your statement, you should immediately contact the Social Security office. If you report a problem more than three years after the year in which it occurs, a correction may not always be possible. In most cases, it will be necessary for you to provide evidence to verify any errors recorded. This evidence could include wage and tax statements (Form W-2), pay slips, other proof of wages earned, cancelled checks showing payment of Social Security taxes for self-employment or copies of your tax returns for the year(s) in question. It may take considerable effort to locate the necessary documents or proof needed to verify errors. However, correction of such errors can be beneficial to individuals in the eventual determination of the actual amount of their Social Security benefits.

Maximum Amounts of Covered Yearly Earnings

Annual Maximum:	For Each Year:
$ 3,000	1937 through 1950
$ 3,600	1951 through 1954
$ 4,200	1955 through 1958
$ 4,800	1959 through 1965
$ 6,600	1966 and 1967
$ 7,800	1968 through 1971
$ 9,000	1972
$10,800	1973
$13,200	1974
$14,100	1975
$15,300	1976
$16,500	1977
$17,700	1978
$22,900	1979
$25,900	1980
$29,700	1981
$32,400	1982
$35,700	1983
$37,800	1984
$39,600	1985
$42,000	1986
$43,800	1987
$45,000	1988
$48,000	1989
$51,300	1990
$53,400	1991
$55,500	1992
$57,600	1993
$60,600	1994
$61,200	1995
$62,700	1996

THE AMOUNT OF YOUR SOCIAL SECURITY BENEFITS

Generally speaking, the amount of your Social Security benefits will be based on your average covered earnings computed over a period of time you could have been reasonably expected to work in covered employment. This period of time, generally from age 21 to age 62, is frequently referred to as your "work life" or "working lifetime". The number of years in the average "work life" are calculated as follows:

- If you turned 21 before 1950, your work life is five years less than the number of years between 1950 and your 62nd birthday, disability, or death — whichever comes first.

- If you turned 21 after 1950, your work life is five years less than the number of years between your 21st birthday and 62nd birthday, disability, or death — whichever comes first.

For those individuals who reached age 62, became disabled or died **before** 1979, the **actual** dollar amount of their covered earnings is used in the computation which determines the worker's average monthly earnings. All other workers who reach age 62, become disabled, or die after 1978 have their actual monthly earnings **indexed**, which means they are adjusted to reflect increases in average wage levels in the economy. This adjustment is important because average wages in our economy can change considerably over an individual's working lifetime of a 30 or 40-year period.

After an individual's average monthly earnings (AME) or the average indexed monthly earnings (AIME) has been determined, a benefit formula is applied to determine the amount on which **all** Social Security benefits related to a worker's earnings are based. This amount is called a worker's primary insurance amount, or simply "PIA".

The formula used to determine benefits is weighted in favor of low earning individuals. Since January 1982, there is no longer a fixed minimum benefit amount, as previously granted, for workers who reach 62, become disabled, or die after December 1981 except for members of religious orders who have taken a vow of poverty and only if they first become eligible for benefits before 1992.

MAXIMUM BENEFITS

In general, the maximum monthly benefit is payable to a worker who had earnings at or above the maximum taxable wage base for contribution and benefit purposes each year. If a worker retires at age 65 in 1996 after making maximum contributions throughout his or her working lifetime, the worker's Social Security monthly benefit maybe as much as $1,248. If the same person takes a reduced benefit at age 62 (approximately 20 percent less), the monthly retirement may be as much as $998. Reduced benefits for people who retire early take into account the longer period of time that they will receive payments.

MAXIMUM FAMILY PAYMENT

Social Security law places a ceiling, referred to as the "maximum family payment", on the total amount of monthly benefit payments that can be paid to a family on a worker's earnings record. If the maximum amount is exceeded, each person's benefit, **other than the worker's**, is reduced until the total of payments are below the maximum limit. In turn, if a family member who is receiving benefits becomes no longer eligible, for whatever reason, the other family members' benefits may be increased up to the total maximum allowed.

Special provision for divorced spouses — Divorced spouses who are eligible for benefits solely on the basis of age have their benefits computed separately from other family members. This provision is also applicable to divorced spouses who are eligible for benefits based on the care of the worker's child. Consequently, divorced spouses' benefits will not reduce payments to other present family members receiving benefits. In some cases because of this provision, payments to divorced spouses may cause total payments on a worker's record to exceed the established family maximum limit.

ANNUAL COST-OF-LIVING INCREASES

In 1972 Congress passed a law which indexed Social Security retirement benefits to the Consumer Price Index (CPI). The law provided for annual cost-of-living adjustments (COLAs) for Social Security recipients when the inflation rate for the previous fiscal year was three percent or more. This meant that any year the CPI rose less than three percent there would be no increase. The legislation also provided that if an adjustment was not made, neither the maximum wage base on which Social Security taxes are levied, nor the Medicare premiums for Part B insurance, would be increased.

Every year since the law was passed an increase has been given. In January 1987 Social Security beneficiaries and federal and military retirees received a 1.3 percent increase after the 99th Congress mandated that increases be given **whenever** the CPI increases, thus abolishing the three percent cutoff. The adjustment, which became effective in January, 1990, was the largest in several years. In January 1996, Social Security beneficiaries, federal and military retirees' benefits increased by 2.6 percent.

ESTIMATING YOUR RETIREMENT BENEFITS

In 1977, Congress approved a new formula for calculating Social Security benefits for those born after 1921, which affects the majority of future retirees. (If you were born before 1917, your benefits continue to be calculated using the pre-1977 formula; a third transition formula was devised for those individuals born between 1917 and 1921 who are commonly referred to as "notch" individuals or "notch babies.")

Estimating your future retirement benefits isn't easy, particularly using the 1977 formula, which entails numerous calculations. To help future beneficiaries, Social Security will calculate the estimate for you at no charge as many times as you request it.

In 1990, Social Security implemented a new program for providing estimates that more accurately account for future earnings and are easier to understand. The new calculations are based on a worker's past and current earnings, **and** the worker's own estimate of his/her future average yearly earnings up to the date he/she plans to retire.

When you request an estimate from Social Security, your future benefits are calculated as follows:

1) Starting in 1951, each year's total earnings covered by Social Security are listed.

2) Each year's earnings until you reach(ed) age 60 are adjusted (indexed) to reflect the percentage of change in average earnings since that year. For example, average earnings for 1989 are 5 times greater than average earnings were for 1958. To make 1958 earnings comparable with current earnings, they are multiplied by 5. Earnings are indexed for each year up to the year you reach age 60. The indexing factor becomes smaller the closer you get to the present. Actual earnings you have after age 60 are used.

3) The indexed earnings in your highest paid 35 years (420 months) are selected. If you didn't work for 35 years, Social Security adds years of "zero" earnings to bring the total years worked up to 35.

4) Your average monthly income is calculated by dividing your total earnings for 35 years by 420 months.

5) A three-level formula is applied to your average monthly earnings to arrive at an actual benefit rate. For example, for people born in 1928: The first $356 of your monthly income from Step 4 is multiplied by 90%. The second $1,789 is multiplied by 32%. The remainder (if any) is multiplied by 15%. The three products are totalled, then rounded down to the next lower dime. The result equals your basic full benefit at retirement age (currently age 65).

Each year, Social Security uses a new formula to calculate benefits for people turning 62 in that year. The percentages in Step 5 remain constant, but the dollar amounts change. Be aware that government employees who did not pay Social Security taxes will have their retirement benefits calculated using a different formula.

For an estimate of your future Social Security benefit, call Social Security's toll-free number—**1-800-772-1213**—and ask for SSA Form 7004, *Request for Earnings and Benefit Estimate Statement.* Once you complete this form and return it to Social Security, they will have all the information they need to prepare your estimate.

ADJUSTMENTS NOT FIGURED IN YOUR ESTIMATE

The estimate of future benefits that you request from the Social Security Administration will not take into consideration any individual circumstances that may reduce or increase your benefit when you actually retire. Also, by law, individuals who qualify for benefit checks on both their own and their spouse's work records can only receive one benefit check. This check will equal the larger of the two entitled benefit amounts. Most circumstances which could reduce or increase your benefits are discussed throughout this chapter. A few are summarized here to emphasize their importance when you review the benefit estimate you receive from Social Security or when you calculate your own estimate.

- Any special credits that are applied if you delay collecting benefits until after the age of 65
- Increases you will receive from Colas (cost-of-living adjustments) each January
- Any reduction because you also receive a pension based on work that was not covered by Social Security
- Reduction due to the Government Pension Offset when you also receive a pension based on your work in federal, state or local government employment not covered by Social Security
- Any reduction because you also receive a disability benefit paid by a federal, state or local government program.

Important Reminder ! — Questions about your estimate of future benefits, your earnings record, or about any reduction or increase that may affect your benefit should be directed to Social Security. Do not delay contacting Social Security if you notice any discrepancy in your earnings record, or if the benefit estimate prepared by Social Security appears to be too low either compared with the estimate you calculate yourself or with the amount you anticipated for any other reason. These discrepancies should be clarified **before** your actual benefit is determined at the time of retirement.

THE "NOTCH" CONTROVERSY
(Affecting Those Born Between 1917 and 1921)

Since almost 12 million beneficiaries are affected by this controversial calculation of benefits, a brief explanation of it may be helpful. The controversy began in 1983 when newspaper columnist Abigail Van Buren ("Dear Abby") published in her column a letter from an individual complaining about a cut in her Social Security benefits simply because she was born in the period 1917-1921. The phrase "notch babies" was coined in the column and has since been used by many people when referring to the individuals born during that five year period.

Briefly, "the notch" describes the situation wherein the benefits for workers born between 1917 and 1921 are determined under a special formula provided in the 1977 amendments. The benefits derived from this formula are, in some cases, significantly lower than the benefits payable to workers with identical earnings retiring at the same time who, because they were born before 1917, have their benefits computed under the pre-1977 formula. The difference in benefit amounts becomes quite substantial for those in the highest benefit levels who defer retirement until age 65. This became particularly noticeable in 1982 when individuals born in 1917 became age 65.

The problem stems from a series of changes that Congress made in the Social Security benefit formula several years earlier. In 1972 Congress enacted automatic annual indexing both in the formula to compute initial benefits at retirement and of benefit amounts after retirement. The basic intent was to fix benefit levels in relation to the economy. The concept was good; however, the method of indexing the formula was flawed because initial benefits were being indexed twice — for increases in both prices and wages — a critical over-adjustment. Consequently, without further changes to the benefit formula, individuals retiring around the year 2000 would have received more in monthly benefits than they were earning prior to retirement. It became apparent that with this system of calculating benefits Social Security eventually would be faced with a financing crisis verging on bankruptcy.

In 1977 Congress acted to resolve the situation by phasing in a new benefit formula over a five-year transition period. The new benefit formula was to be applied to the benefit calculations for all workers born after 1916. Special computations were included in the amendments for people born from 1917 through 1921 to ease the transition from the old formula to the new formula.

It is important for those born in the transitional or "notch" period to have their benefits calculated under **both** the new benefit formula and the transitional provisions. These individuals are paid the higher of the amounts determined under both formulas. For some, the benefits received are somewhat more than they would have had under the new formula but not as much as they would have received under the old (pre-1977) formula, *especially* if they retire at age 65.

In response to the many complaints received from beneficiaries caught in the transitional period, as well as by those individuals born between 1921 and 1926, a special bipartisan Commission on the Social Security Notch Issue was appointed. In late December 1994, the Commission reported to Congress that they had reached a conclusion that the benefits paid to those in the "notch" years are equitable and that no remedial legislation was in order. Consequently, it is evident that Congress will take *no further action* concerning "notch" benefits.

ANNUAL EARNINGS LIMITS FOR BENEFICIARIES

If you retire and continue to work, your earnings may affect your Social Security benefit checks. However, this does not mean that you should not consider working on a limited basis to supplement your retirement income. It does mean though that if you exceed the maximum earnings established by the Social Security Administration, you will lose some of your benefits.

The measure of income used by Social Security to determine whether benefits are to be reduced or stopped is called the "earnings test." This test refers to an established limit of total annual earnings an individual may earn from a job or self-employment while receiving Social Security benefits. One should be aware that, at times, some people refer to the "earnings test" as the "retirement test". However, this particular term — "retirement test" — really is meant to be used when referring to **all** of the various eligibility conditions, including earnings limits, that a worker must meet before obtaining retirement benefits. Throughout this discussion, the term "earnings test" is used since it is more appropriate and frequently applicable.

The annual earnings limits, which are based on age, **apply** to **everyone** who gets Social Security benefit checks except those who are 70 years of age or older. This includes beneficiaries whose monthly payments are based on the Social Security earnings record of a retired, disabled or deceased worker. In other words, if you get checks as a retired worker, total family benefits may be affected because of your earnings. Consequently, your benefit payments may be withheld as well as those payable to your family. However, for individuals who get checks as a wife, husband, widow, widower, or other dependent or survivor, work will affect **only** their own check.

In general, you will receive all Social Security benefits due if your earnings do not exceed the following limits in 1996:

- For people under the age of 65, the limit is **$8,280**.

- For people age 65 through 69, the limit is **$12,500**.

The annual limits increase each year with increases in general wage levels. If your earnings exceed the annual amount, Social Security currently deducts $1 from your benefit check for each $2 you earn above the exempt amount. For people 65 and over, $1 in benefits will be withheld for each $3 in earnings above the limit. Also, starting in the year 2000, the age at which full benefits can be paid (now age 65) will be gradually increased until it reaches 67. The age at which the withholding rate applies will also increase. The following table shows the age at which **full** retirement benefits will be paid in future years.

Retirement Age for Full Retirement Benefits
(After the Year 2000)

If you were born in:	Retirement age will be:
1938	65 yrs and 2 months
1939	65 yrs and 4 months
1940	65 yrs and 6 months
1941	65 yrs and 8 months
1942	65 yrs and 10 months
1943-1954	66 years old
1955	66 yrs and 2 months
1956	66 yrs and 4 months
1957	66 yrs and 6 months
1958	66 yrs and 8 months
1959	66 yrs and 10 months
1960 and after	67 years old

SPECIAL RETIREMENT EARNINGS RULE

During the first year of retirement, there is a special rule that allows people who retire in that period to receive unreduced benefits for the remainder of the year, regardless of their earnings before retirement. Under this rule you can get a full benefit payment for any month your wages do not exceed the monthly exempt amount and you do not perform "substantial services" in self-employment.

Social Security decides whether services by a self-employed person should be considered *substantial* based on several factors, such as the amount of time devoted to a business, the kind of services performed, and how the services compare with what the individual did in the past. In general, the services of individuals who work more than 45 hours in a month will be considered substantial; anything under 45 hours will not be considered substantial.

To clarify this special rule for new retires, the following *current* information should be helpful: (1) In 1996, if monthly earnings are limited to $690, a person under 65 is considered retired; for those aged 65-69, the monthly limit is $960. (2) When earnings for a particular month exceed these monthly limits, that month is subject to benefit withholding based on your total earnings for the year. The $1-for-$2 and $1-for-$3 rules cannot be applied in connection with the monthly test. Thus, a whole month's Social Security benefit could be withheld if your earnings exceed the monthly limit by even $1. After the first year of retirement, benefits are always paid based on *annual* earnings.

BENEFICIARIES WHO WORK OUTSIDE THE U.S.

If you work or own a business outside of the U.S. and you are under age 70, your earnings can also affect your retirement benefits in the same manner as they do for those who work within the U.S. Failure to report your work to the nearest U.S. Embassy, Consulate or Social Security office could result in a penalty against you which could cause the loss of benefits. The following "work tests" are used for individuals working outside the U.S.:

■ *The "Foreign Work Test"* — Under this test, a monthly benefit is withheld for each month in which a beneficiary under the age of 70 works more than 45 hours outside the U.S. in employment or self-employment which is not subject to U.S. Social Security provisions. It does not matter how much was earned or how many hours were worked each day.

- *The "Annual Retirement Test" or "Earnings Test"* — Under this test, if a beneficiary's work outside the U.S. is covered by our Social Security program, the same annual retirement test on earnings that applies to people in the U.S. will apply to a beneficiary working outside of the United States.

WHAT SHOULD YOU CONSIDER AS EARNINGS?

Some of the most frequently asked questions of the Social Security personnel concern the items of income that should be counted in the earnings test. Because of their importance in accurately determining your total annual earnings for Social Security purposes, the following items summarize what is counted as earnings and other types of income that generally are not counted as earnings in applying the earnings test.

INCOME THAT COUNTS IN YOUR EARNINGS TEST

- Gross wages you earn from work as an employee — not just take home pay: wages paid after a year has ended must be included in the total earnings for the year in which the work was done;
- Any net earning from self-employment: (if self-employed, count your net-profit or loss from any enterprise in which you are a sole owner or a partner);
- Income in the form of bonuses, commissions, fees, vacation pay, pay in lieu of vacation and severance pay;
- Cash tips amounting to $20 or more in a month from your work for one employer;
- Payment from an employer in some form other than cash: such as meals or living quarters. *Exception:* Domestic employees and farm workers count **only** cash wages;
- Fees paid to you as a director of a corporation.

OTHER INCOME THAT DOES NOT COUNT IN AN EARNINGS TEST

- Investment income in the form of dividends from stock you own, unless you deal in securities;
- Interest on savings accounts;
- Income from Social Security benefits, pensions, other retirement pay, or Veterans Administration benefits;

- Income from annuities;
- Gain (or loss) from the sale of capital assets;
- Gifts or inheritances;
- Rental income from real estate you own, unless:
  — you are a real estate dealer, **or**
  — you rent out a farm, and under your rental arrangement you participate materially in the production or management of farm commodities on your land;
- Royalties you receive in or after the year you become 65 from patents or copyrights that were obtained before that year;
- If you are a retired partner, retirement payments you receive from the partnership if:
  — the retirement payments are to continue for life under a written agreement which provides for payments to all the partners (or to a class or classes of them), **and**
  — your share of the partnership capital was paid to you in full before the end of the partnership's taxable year and there is no obligation from the partnership to you except to make retirement payments;
- Income from a limited partnership; this is considered investment income rather than self-employment income;
- Income from self-employment received in a year after the year you become entitled to benefits; this income cannot be attributable to services performed after the month of entitlement
- Also, under certain conditions, the following do not count as wages: payments from certain trust funds, payments from certain annuity plans, sick pay received after the sixth full calendar month after the employee last worked or was paid upon termination of employment, loans from employers unless repaid by work, moving expenses, travel expenses, and pay for jury duty.

OTHER CONDITIONS UNDER WHICH YOUR SOCIAL SECURITY BENEFITS MAY BE REDUCED

If you are receiving or are about to receive Social Security benefits, it is important to know that certain incomes you might have from other sources could reduce your benefits. In addition to earnings from employment or self-employment, under the Social Security law, three conditions, or rulings, may reduce your benefits. They are categorized as follows:

(1) Reduction by the "government pension offset" ruling
(2) Reduction due to receipt of a pension from work not covered under Social Security
(3) Reduction in disability benefits due to receipt of workers' compensation payments or other public disability payments.

Each of these conditions contains its limitations, special exceptions and various methods for determining whether your anticipated benefits will be affected. They are discussed separately here so that you are aware of their basic provisions and potential effects. Contact your Social Security office for further information concerning each ruling, for assistance in explaining the methods of reduction and to determine the amount of reduction, if any, to your benefits.

REDUCTION BY THE GOVERNMENT PENSION OFFSET

This provision, called the "government pension offset" or "public pension offset," applies only to Social Security benefits for a spouse or surviving spouse. It does not apply to Social Security retirement or disability benefits based on a person's **own** work covered by the program even if the person also receives a government pension.

The government pension offset was enacted to eliminate additional benefit payments to retired government workers who have their own pensions (from a federal, state, or local government job **not covered** by Social Security) and who would also receive Social Security benefits as a spouse. The offset reduces the amount of the Social Security check normally received as a spouse in much the same way that benefits are reduced when a person is entitled to more than one type of Social Security benefit. However, the amount of the government pension that will be used in figuring the offset depends on when you first became eligible for the pension (not when you actually apply for it):

- *If you were first eligible before July 1983* — All of your pension will be used to offset any benefits payable for the months before December 1984. Effective in and after December 1984, the offset amount is two-thirds of your pension.

- *If you are first eligible in July 1983 or later* — Two-thirds of your pension will be used.

When the government pension offset does not apply — Benefits to spouses who meet the requirements in any of the following three categories generally will **not be adversely affected** by the government pension offset.

■ *When both of the following requirements are met:*

(1) You began to receive or were eligible to receive your federal, state, or local government pension before December 1982. This means you must have met the age and length-of-service requirements for your pension before December 1982 even though you did not apply for your pension before then.

(2) You meet all requirements in effect in January 1977 for Social Security spouse's benefits. At that time, a divorced woman's marriage must have lasted at least 20 years, rather than the 10 years as required today. Also, a husband or widower must have received at least one half of his support from his wife.

■ *When both of the following requirements are met for Social Security benefits initially payable in December 1982:*

(l) You received or were eligible to receive your federal, state, or local government pension before July 1, 1983.

(2) You were receiving at least one-half support from your spouse. If you met all of the requirements for your government pension in November 1982 or June 1983 but were not eligible to start receiving it until the following month — which would be after the deadlines mentioned above — you can still qualify for this exemption, effective from December 1984.

■ *When any of the following is applicable to you:*

(1) The government job upon which your pension is based is covered by Social Security on the last day of employment — generally, the official termination date shown on your separation papers.

(2) You are entitled to Social Security benefits as a spouse based on an application filed before December 1977.

(3) The government pension you are receiving is not based on your own earnings.

(4) You are covered under the new Federal Employees Retirement System (FERS).

REDUCTION DUE TO RECEIPT OF A PENSION FROM WORK NOT COVERED BY SOCIAL SECURITY (WINDFALL BENEFIT PROVISION)

This provision, which was established by a 1983 change in the Social Security law and effective in 1986, affects only those people who became eligible after 1985 for **both** a Social Security benefit as a retired or disabled worker and a pension from work not covered under Social Security. Under this ruling, a different Social Security benefit formula is used to figure the benefit amount (resulting in a lower benefit).

It is important to know that the pension received from work not covered by Social Security is not reduced by this provision nor are any Social Security survivor benefits. Additionally, the law provides a guarantee designed to protect workers with relatively low pensions. The guarantee states that the reduction in the Social Security benefit cannot exceed one half of that part of the pension attributable-to earnings after 1956 that were not covered by Social Security. Only those workers who meet **both** of the following criteria will have their benefits reduced by the special benefit formula:

(1) They must reach 62 or become disabled **after** 1985, and
(2) They must first become eligible **after** 1985 for a pension based (at least in part) on work not covered by Social Security. Be aware that if you were eligible before January 1986 to receive a pension (from work not covered by Social Security) but continued to work any entitled Social Security benefits will **not** be reduced by the windfall formula.

However, there are several groups of people who, though they meet both of these conditions, will not have their benefits reduced. Special groups exempted from the windfall formula include:

(1) Federal workers who were newly covered under Social Security on January 1, 1984;
(2) Employees of nonprofit organizations that were mandatorily covered under Social Security for the first time on January 1, 1984;
(3) People whose only pension is based solely on railroad employment;
(4) People whose only pensionable employment not covered by Social Security was performed before 1957;

(5) People who receive a military pension based on military service before 1957 if this is the only pension the person receives that is based on service not covered by Social Security;

(6) Workers who have 30 or more years of coverage under Social Security.

Recent Legislative Change — Congress has approved legislation to allow retirees who receive pensions from work not covered by Social Security but who have between 20 and 29 years of Social Security coverage, to receive **more** Social Security benefits than the windfall reduction formula normally allows. The new ruling reduces the windfall's maximum allowable benefits (approximately 90% of Social Security benefits) by only five percent for each year the individual is shy of 30 years of Social Security coverage. For example, individuals with 25 years of Social Security coverage would get an estimated 90% minus (5 [years] x 5%)= 25% — or 65% of their entitled benefits under the windfall formula (rather than the approximately 40% received in the past). Individuals with less than 20 years of coverage do not benefit from this change.

REDUCTION DUE TO RECEIPT OF WORKERS' COMPENSATION AND PUBLIC DISABILITY PAYMENTS

Under this provision of the Social Security law, if you receive benefits from workers' compensation or public disability programs, your Social Security disability check will be reduced if the combined amount of (1) your Social Security monthly disability benefits, plus (2) the Social Security benefits payable to your dependents, plus (3) your workers' compensation payment (or public disability payment) is more than 80 percent of what is called your "average current earnings." The amount by which this sum exceeds 80 percent of your average current earnings (see definition below) will be deducted from your Social Security disability benefit. In other words, you cannot earn more from combined Social Security and disability than you did from full employment. However, the amount of the combined benefit paid to you and your family will **never** be less than the original sum of both your Social Security benefits and those of your family's. Reductions due to receipt of workers' compensation and/or public disability payments remain in effect until you reach 65 or until the month such payments stop.

"Average current earnings" are defined by Social Security as the **highest** of the following:

- The average monthly earnings amount used to figure your Social Security disability benefits or

- The average monthly earnings from your work or self-employment covered by Social Security during the five successive years after 1950 in which you had the highest earnings; or

- The average monthly earnings in your most lucrative year of work or self-employment covered by Social Security during the five year period just before you became disabled, or in the year you became disabled.

Workers' compensation payments are payments made to a worker because of a job-related injury or illness. They are paid by the federal or state workers' compensation agencies, insurance companies or employers. Public disability payments are different in that the workers' disability need not be job-related. Public disability payments are required by a federal, state or local government law or plan and can be paid by one of the governments, an insurance company or an employer.

Receipt of the following payments **does not reduce** your Social Security benefits: Veterans Administration benefits, federal benefits based on work covered by Social Security, state and local benefits based on state and local government work covered by Social Security, private pensions or insurance benefits, Supplemental Security Income (SSI).

SECTION 4

It's the Law — Appeal Rights and Taxation of Benefits

YOUR RIGHT TO APPEAL SOCIAL SECURITY DECISIONS

Of utmost importance is the right you have to appeal any unfavorable decisions or determinations concerning your Social Security benefits. Under Social Security law, four steps are required to make an appeal. They are:

■ *Reconsideration* — This is an independent review of your case to determine whether the original decision was correct.

■ *Hearing* — If you disagree with the reconsideration decision, you may request a hearing before an Administrative Law Judge (ALJ). These judges are employees of the Office of Hearings and Appeals of the Social Security Administration who are specially qualified through education and experience to hear cases concerning Social Security benefit decisions. The ALJ will not have taken part in any of the earlier decisions in your case.

■ *Review by an Appeals Council* — If the Administrative Law Judge's decision is unfavorable to you, the decision may be reviewed by an Appeals Council. However, the Council may decline a review of your case or return the case to an Administrative Law Judge for further action, which could include a supplemental hearing and a new decision.

■ *Appeal through a Federal Court* — If the Appeals Council has declined a review, or if you disagree with the outcome of a review or supplemental hearing, you may take civil action in the U.S. District Court for the judicial district where you live.

Certain rules and procedures which apply to all forms of appeals:

■ You generally have only **60 days** to appeal after receiving notice of a decision. The time limit for filing an appeal will be extended only if there is a good reason for missing the deadline.

■ A special form to file an appeal is required. This form can be obtained from your Social Security office.

■ You may be represented by a qualified person of your choice if you feel you can not handle your appeal alone. The individual you select can be an attorney or any other qualified person you choose as a representative. However, you cannot appoint any individual who has been suspended or prohibited by the Social Security Administration from representing claimants nor can you select someone who has been otherwise prohibited by law from acting as a representative.

— You must appoint your representative in writing by using Form SSA 1696-U3, "Appointment of Representative."
— You are responsible for paying the fees charged by your representative; however, the Social Security Administration must always approve any fees charged. Only the Social Security Administration can decide the maximum fee a representative

can charge. A contract for a fee in excess of that approved by the Social Security Administration is not considered binding.

— You may attend an Administrative Law Judge hearing either alone or with your representative.

— If an Administrative Law Judge hearing is scheduled at a location a considerable distance from your home (over 75 miles away), reasonable travel and meal expenses may be paid by the Social Security Administration for yourself, your representative and any witnesses that are necessary to present your case.

TAXATION OF SOCIAL SECURITY BENEFITS

Though only about 10 percent of upper income beneficiaries are affected by the 1983 law concerning taxation of Social Security benefits, you may be one whose benefits are partially subject to federal income tax. The law states that up to one half of your benefits are subject to federal income tax when the sum of (1) your adjusted gross income for federal tax purposes, plus (2) nontaxable interest income, plus (3) one half of your Social Security benefits exceeds a base amount.

The established base amount is **$25,000** for an individual; **$32,000** for a couple filing jointly; and **$0** (zero) for a couple filing separately if they lived together during any part of the year. If your total income does not exceed these base amounts, your Social Security benefits are **not** taxable.

Important tax rate change: For taxable years after 1993, the tax rate for some beneficiaries will be increased to **85** percent of their Social Security benefits if (1) as an individual his/her income exceeds **$34,000** or (2) as a couple filing jointly their combined income is more than **$44,000**.

When determining the total amount of Social Security benefits you received, you must include all benefits received in addition to your monthly check, such as: any Medicare medical insurance premiums that have been deducted from your check, any overpayments that you did not repay in the year you received them, any lump-sum payment of monthly benefits received, and any workers' compensation benefits which caused a reduction in your Social Security disability checks. Since lump-sum payments that include payment for periods in earlier tax years may be prorated, ask your Social Security or Internal Revenue Service office about the method used to prorate these payments.

The amount of your benefit subject to tax will be the **smaller** of:

(1) One half of your benefits, **or**

(2) One half of the amount by which the sum of (1) your adjusted gross income, plus (2) tax-exempt interest, plus (3) one half of your Social Security benefits, exceeds the base amount.

The following example may help clarify the amount that is subject to federal income tax for an individual whose income does not exceed the $34,000 threshold but does exceed the $25,000 threshold for a single individual:

Tom Peters, who files as a single individual, has an adjusted gross income of $22,000 plus $5,000 in tax-exempt interest for a combined subtotal of **$27,000**. Since Tom also received a total of $8,000 in Social Security benefits, he adds one half of these benefits (**$4,000**) to his subtotal of $27,000 for a total of **$31,000**. Since the base amount for a single individual is $25,000, Tom's total income exceeds the base amount by **$6,000** ($31,000 minus the base of $25,000). The amount that is subject to tax is: (1) one half of Tom's total Social Security benefits, which is **$4,000** — or — (2) one half of the amount by which Tom's total exceeds the established base amount, which is **$3,000**. Since the lesser of these two amounts is **$3,000**, this will be the amount subject to tax.

Every year, before the end of January you will receive a Social Security Benefits Statement (Form SSA-1099) showing the amount of benefits you received during the previous year and a work-sheet from the Internal Revenue Service (IRS Notice 703) which will help you determine whether any of your Social Security benefits are taxable. If you receive two Social Security Benefit Statements because you receive benefit checks on two different Social Security earnings records, you should combine the benefit amounts from both forms when figuring any taxation of benefits.

Since both the Social Security Administration and the Internal Revenue Service (IRS) are responsible for implementing the taxation of Social Security benefits, you should direct your questions to, or request assistance from, the agency (either IRS or Social Security) which issued the form. In those cases where a verified error was made in the Social Security Benefit Statement, an amendment will be issued by the Social Security Administration.

SECTION 5

Retirement and Survivor Benefits

WHEN SHOULD YOU RETIRE?

Since almost 75 percent of those who are eligible to retire do so before the age of 65, 65 can no longer be considered the standard retirement age. However, age 65 is still the age at which **full** retirement benefits are paid under Social Security. Before deciding whether to retire early at age 62 with reduced benefits, at age 65 with full benefits, or to delay your retirement past 65, you should carefully consider the various factors that could influence your decision. These factors may include your health, personal dissatisfaction with your job, the earnings limits imposed when you take Social Security benefits before age 70 and how they reduce your benefits, or possible tax liability on your Social Security benefits if your retirement, savings or other income exceed prescribed limits. You should also be aware of the advantages and disadvantages of an early or delayed retirement.

■ *Retirement Before 65 ("Early" Retirement)* — In addition to your own personal reasons, there are four important items to consider before deciding whether to retire early with reduced benefits or to wait until you are eligible for full benefits at age 65:

(1) Reductions in benefits due to early retirement are **permanent**. Although you will not always receive the same benefit payment because of cost-of-living adjustments and other general increases, you will always receive a lower payment than you would have received if you had waited to retire at age 65.

(2) Benefits are reduced by a percentage for each month you are under age 65. This can result in a 20 percent reduction at age 62; 13 percent reduction at 63; and 7 percent reduction at 64. Consequently, the longer you wait past age 62 to take retirement benefits, the higher your benefit payments will be.

(3) If you anticipate receiving higher earnings from your work between ages 62 and 65, these three years of higher earnings will replace three years of lower earnings and raise your average earnings, resulting in a **higher basic benefit** at age 65.

(4) One advantage of retiring **before** age 65 with reduced benefits is that you will receive several thousand dollars in benefits before reaching age 65. According to actuarial estimates, generally it takes an individual who defers retirement to age 65 between 12 to 14 years to catch up on the amount of benefits that could have been received during early retirement. The actual number of years that it would take to recover these payments depends on several factors, such as the age before 65 that retirement benefits are taken and the amount of basic benefits due at age 62 versus the amount due at age 65.

■ *Delaying Retirement Past 65* — If you delay retirement and continue to work past 65, you will receive a special credit. This credit, which is a percentage added to your Social Security benefit, varies depending on your date of birth. For people turning 65 in 1996, the rate is 5 percent per year. That rate gradually increases in future years, until it reaches 8 percent per year for people turning 65 in 2008 or later.

WHEN TO APPLY FOR BENEFITS

Since benefits are not generally payable for any months before the month you apply for them, it is important for those people who want to retire before age 65 to apply no later than the last day of the month they want benefits to begin. Understand too that benefits can be paid only for months in which an individual is eligible throughout the entire month. There is an exception made for widows and widowers. They can apply for benefits in the month after their spouse's death and get a benefit payment for the month in which their spouse died. Also, individuals who retire at age 65 or older can apply for retirement or survivors' benefits at any time and receive back payments for up to six months before the month in which they apply.

Social Security allows individuals to apply for benefits up to three months before the month they want their benefits to begin. Consequently, it is advisable to apply early to be certain your benefits begin as you have planned. This is particularly important when you apply for Medicare coverage, even if you do not intend to retire at age 65. Since your Medicare coverage may begin in the month in which you reach 65, you should apply **three months before your birthday month**. This will assure that your coverage begins in the month you reach 65. As explained in Chapter 4, which discusses Medicare, individuals who are not eligible for Social Security benefits can enroll in Medicare (both the hospital and medical portions) by paying the required monthly premiums. These individuals should also apply three months before their birthday months so that this important protection is available as soon as they are eligible.

WHEN A BENEFICIARY DIES

When your spouse or family member who has been receiving Social Security benefits dies, the following actions should be taken:

- The Social Security office should be immediately notified of the death.

- Any Social Security benefit check received for the month of death must be returned since a Social Security benefit is not payable for that month even if the beneficiary dies on the last day of the month.

- Application should be made for any survivor's benefits for which a family member may be eligible.

- Application should be made for "lump-sum death payment."

LUMP-SUM DEATH PAYMENT

Social Security provides a one-time lump-sum death payment of **$255** for a worker who dies either fully or currently-insured. An application for this payment must be filed within the two-year period ending with the second anniversary of the insured person's death. However, a widow or widower does not need to apply if he or she is entitled to the spouse's benefits on the deceased person's Social Security record for the month just before the month in which the spouse died. The lump sum payment is payable in the following order of priority:

(1) To the spouse who was living in the same household as the worker when the worker died;

(2) To a spouse *not* living with the deceased worker at the time of death providing he or she was entitled to or eligible for benefits based on the deceased's record for the month the worker died;

(3) *If there is no spouse to whom the lump-sum can be paid*: to a child or children of the deceased worker who were entitled to or eligible for benefits in the month the worker died. In the case of several children, each one is eligible for an equal share of the lump-sum. Each child must apply for his/her share.

The lump-sum payment cannot be paid to a divorced spouse or anyone other than the parties noted above.

INFORMATION YOU NEED TO APPLY FOR RETIREMENT AND SURVIVORS' BENEFITS.

As soon as you are eligible for Social Security benefits, either as a worker or family member eligible for benefits based on a deceased worker's record, you should contact your local Social Security office to apply for these benefits. They will **not** come automatically to you without application. You may apply in person or by phone.

Certain information and documents are required at the time of application; however, if you have difficulty obtaining any of the needed items, you should ask the Social Security personnel for assistance so that there will be no delay in filing your claim.

When you apply for these benefits, you must have the Social Security number of each family member who may be applying and proof of each applicant's age. The best proof of age is an original or certified copy of a birth certificate or religious record (such as a baptismal certificate) issued before age five. As explained in Section 1 of this chapter, "Applying for a Social Security Card," other documents can be substituted if you do not have a birth certificate or religious record.

Depending on the basis of your eligibility for benefits, there may be other documents which are needed to complete your application:

- If you are applying for wife's, husband's, widow's, or widower's benefits, you must present your marriage certificate.

- If you are applying for benefits based on the record of a former spouse, you must have been married for at least 10 years and you must present your divorce decree.

- If you are applying as the dependent parent of a deceased child, you must present evidence that you received at least one half of your support from that child.

- If you are applying for survivor's benefits, you must present proof of the deceased worker's death, such as a death certificate.

- If you had any military service or railroad employment, you must present your dates of service or employment.

- If you are already receiving or plan to receive other benefits, you must supply information about these benefits.

SECTION 6

Disability Benefits

IF YOU BECOME DISABLED OR BLIND

An important feature of Social Security is its protection for workers and their families against loss of earnings due to disability or blindness. There are now over four million recipients of Social Security disability benefits. Without these benefits, a vast majority of these people would not be able to meet their daily living expenses.

Requirements for Social Security disability benefits are very strict. Also, once a claim for benefits has been approved, payments can be made only so long as the person's impairment has not medically improved and continues to prevent the beneficiary from engaging in substantial gainful work. Although its requirements are strict and permit few exceptions, the disability program can provide assistance to a variety of beneficiaries. In addition to disabled workers under 65 and their families, benefits may be paid to unmarried people disabled before age 22, disabled widows and widowers and, in some cases, disabled divorced wives and husbands of workers who were insured at death (see the summary of individuals eligible for Social Security benefits in Section 1 of this chapter).

The determination of disability for widows and widowers is considerably more restrictive than for disabled workers. The survivor's disability determinations are based on the person's level of impairment without regard to age, education or work experience which are considered in the determination of a disabled worker's claim.

ELIGIBILITY REQUIREMENTS FOR A DISABLED
OR BLIND WORKER

■ *The basic eligibility requirements for disabled workers are:*
  (1) The individual has worked long enough **and** recently enough
      under Social Security to be insured. This means that a required
      number of work credits must have been earned within spec-
      ified time limits based on the worker's age when the disability
      is certified. (Work credit requirements are explained in detail
      in Section 2 of this chapter.)

  (2) The individual has a physical or mental condition which:

      • Precludes doing any substantial gainful work.
                              and
      • The condition is expected to last — or has lasted — for at
        least 12 months, or is expected to result in death.

If an individual cannot continue his or her job, but can do other
work that is considered to be substantial and gainful, the individual
will generally **not** be considered disabled by Social Security.

■ *The requirements for blind people are*:
  (1) The individual must have earned enough work credits to be
      insured.

  (2) The individual must have vision, with corrective lenses, that
      is no better than 20/200 in the better eye, **or** must have a
      visual field of 20 degrees or less.

Blind individuals who have worked long enough to be insured
and either are not working or have earnings within specifically established limits may receive monthly disability benefits (there are several
special provisions for blind people who work which are explained
later in this section).

SUBSTANTIAL GAINFUL WORK
(also called Substantial Gainful Activity)

Since this term is a key element in awarding disability benefits to a
disabled worker, it is essential that you understand what constitutes
"substantial gainful work" under Social Security law.

In general, "substantial" means work that is significant and productive, physically or mentally, while "gainful" means that the work is
done (or is intended to be done) for pay or profit. Work can be "substantial" even if it is part-time, or even if the worker is paid less or has
less responsibility than before. Work can be "gainful" even if there
is no profit, as sometimes occurs with self-employment. The rules
explained below, differ, depending on whether you are employed
or self-employed.

- *For Employees* — If your monthly wages average over $500
  (after allowable deductions), your work generally is considered
  substantial and gainful. Average monthly earnings between $300
  and $500 may be substantial gainful activity if the amount and
  quality of your work is about the same as that of non-disabled
  workers performing similar functions. Work with average monthly
  wages of less than $200 is **not** generally considered substantial
  gainful activity but should be reported.

  If your earnings are subsidized (meaning you are paid more than
  the value of your work), the subsidy part of your pay is not
  considered earnings.

- *For Self-Employed Individuals* — Usually, Social Security offi-
  cials are less concerned with how much a self-employed workers
  earns than with (1) the extent of the worker's business activities
  and (2) the worker's supervisory, managerial, or advisory services.
  This attitude prevails because earnings or losses from the business may result from factors like the country's current economic
  situation or the services of other people. In other words, more
  consideration may be given to the kind and value of the self-employed
  person's work — the "substantial" element — rather than the
  amount of income it generates (the "gainful" element).

SPECIAL PROVISIONS FOR BLIND WORKERS

Under Social Security law, the following special provisions are applicable to blind individuals who work as employees or who are self-
employed:

- Though you must have earned sufficient work credits to be
  insured, depending on your age and when you became blind,

there is no **time** constraint on when a blind worker's work credits must have been earned.

■ You can earn up to $960 a month in 1996 before your earnings are considered substantial gainful work.

■ If you are 55 to 65, monthly benefits continue if you cannot do the regular (or similar) work you did before you reached age 55 or became blind, whichever is later. Checks will not be issued, however, for any month in which you actually perform substantial gainful work.

■ If your earnings are too high to allow disability benefits, you are still eligible for a disability "freeze". This means that your future benefit checks, which are figured from your average earnings, will not be reduced because of relatively lower earnings in those years when you are blind.

APPROVAL OR DISAPPROVAL OF CLAIMS FOR DISABILITY BENEFITS

If you meet all of the basic requirements discussed, your application (claim) will be sent by Social Security to a Disability Determination Services (DDS) office located within your state. Several trained experts, physicians and disability evaluation specialists in the DDS office will review all the facts of your particular case. They will request medical information and evidence from your doctors and from any hospital, clinic or institution in which you have been treated, in order to properly evaluate your condition. Sometimes, when additional information is needed, it may be necessary for them to request that you take a special examination or test.

When a decision which generally takes two or three months is made on your claim, you will be notified in writing by the Social Security Administration. A notice of approval will indicate the monthly benefit amount and the date the payments will start. Monthly checks for a disabled worker or a disabled widow or widower generally start in the sixth full month of disability. If the first disability check is issued after that date, it may include some back payments. If the claim is denied, the notice will give the reason for denial.

Appealing a Denial of Your Disability Claim — Your right to appeal any unfavorable decision made by Social Security regarding your claims or benefits includes appealing a disallowed claim for disability bene-fits. All four appeal steps, explained in Section 4 "Your Right To Appeal," are available to you. They include: (1) reconsideration, (2) hearing by an Administrative Law Judge, (3) review by an Appeals Council, and (4) filing a suit in federal court. The first of these appeals, reconsider-ation, is very important because it gives you the immediate opportu-nity to present any new evidence on your behalf If you need to appeal, promptly request the aid of the local Social Security office since you must usually file within 60 days of receiving the negative ruling notice.

DISABILITY REVIEWS

Social Security law requires that those who receive disability benefits must have their eligibility reviewed periodically to ensure that they have not medically improved enough to perform substantial gainful work. In these reviews, if medical evidence of continued impairment is required, a beneficiary may be asked to undergo additional examinations or tests.

For several years, the disability review process was sharply crit-icized. Disparate application of the procedures throughout the country frequently resulted in unfairness to some beneficiaries. Congress reacted by passing the Social Security Disability Benefits Reform Act of 1984 which mandated suspension of reviews until new rules could be developed. The revised process of review was finally formulated and approved in late 1986. It is a much better process, affording consid-erably more uniformity than before.

Major changes in the review process include: (1) maintenance of benefits, unless there is substantial evidence of **both** medical improve-ment and ability to work, (2) use of more realistic rules in determining a mentally impaired beneficiary's ability to work, and, (3) most impor-tant, beneficiaries who appeal a decision will continue to receive their disability payments until the adverse decision is upheld by an Admin-istrative Law Judge.

The frequency of reviews depends on the severity of the impair-ment and its potential for medical improvement. A case may be reviewed as early as six months after the initial approval of disability benefits or as late as seven years after entitlement. Due to the backlog of disability claims incurred while the new rules were being prepared, the scheduling and frequency of reviews will vary considerably from case to case. Currently, priority is given to those cases for which benefits were terminated under the old system of review.

DISABLED INDIVIDUALS WHO WANT TO RETURN TO WORK

Since most disabled individuals would prefer to work, Social Security law provides several special provisions to assist those who want to return to work even though they may still be disabled. These provisions include:

- *A trial work period* in which individuals can continue receiving full disability checks while testing their ability to work. The trial period may encompass up to nine months, which need not be consecutive. The amount of monthly earnings that currently triggers a "trial work period" is $200; 40 hours of self-employment. When the trial work period ends, a decision will be made on the individual's ability to perform substantial gainful work. If your earnings are $500 or less a month, benefits will generally continue. If earnings average more than $500 a month, benefits will continue for a 3-month grace period before they stop.

- *A reinstatement of benefits* provision which allows a special protection for 36 months after an individual completes a nine-month trial work period. During this 36-month period, benefits can be paid for each month in which the individual continues to be disabled and does not perform any substantial gainful work. When individuals inform Social Security that disability recurred within the reinstatement period, benefit checks are issued covering the term of disability.

- *A continuation of Medicare* will continue for 39 months beyond the trial work period. If your Medicare coverage stops because of your work, you may purchase it for a monthly premium.

OTHER RULES AND PROVISIONS AFFECTING DISABILITY BENEFICIARIES

If you are approved to receive Social Security disability benefits, there are several rules which may affect the amount you receive and various provisions under which your benefits could be extended or disclaimed. Also, there are special provisions to ensure that your medical needs are met, and that you receive assistance in the form of vocational rehabilitation services. Some of these rules, which are discussed in subsequent sections of this chapter, apply to other Social Security beneficiaries as well as to those receiving disability benefits. The rules and provisions are outlined below:

- *Medicare Coverage* — All individuals who have been entitled to monthly disability checks for 24 months are covered by Medicare hospital insurance (Part A). These months need not be sequential or in the same period of disability. Since these individuals are eligible for Medicare hospital insurance, they also may participate in the medical insurance portion of Medicare.

- *Vocational Rehabilitation Services* — All individuals who apply for disability benefits, whether their claims are approved or not, are considered eligible for services provided by their state's vocational rehabilitation agency. These agencies offer programs of counseling and guidance, medical and surgical help, job training and placement. If an individual refuses these vocational rehabilitative services without good reason, monthly benefit checks cannot be issued. Acceptance of these services does not prevent individuals from receiving disability payments if their claims are approved.

- *When a Medical Impairment Improves* — If your medical condition improves and you are able to do substantial gainful work, unless an exception is determined by Social Security to be applicable in your case, your monthly disability payments will stop. Payments will continue over a three-month adjustment period, which includes the last month of disability.

- *Becoming Disabled Again After an Improvement Period* — This extremely important provision affects those individuals whose impairments improved to the point that they were able to resume work, but became again unable to sustain any substantial gainful activity. The law provides for restoration of disability benefits without a one-month waiting period to individuals who become disabled a second time within five years after payments ceased. This provision also applies to a disabled widow or widower, or to individuals who were disabled before age 22 and become disabled again within seven years after disability benefits had ended.

■ *Taxation of Benefits* — Some of your disability benefits may be subject to federal income tax just as other Social Security benefits may be taxable. The amount by which your adjusted gross income, plus any nontaxable interest income, plus half of your Social Security benefits, exceeds an established base amount is taxable. Information concerning this taxation is covered under Taxation of Social Security Benefits" in Section 4 of this chapter.

■ *Receipt of Another Social Security Check* — Social Security law prohibits the payment of a disability benefit in addition to other Social Security income. If you are entitled to more than one monthly check, you will receive only the larger of the two amounts. Frequently, the amount of your disability check may be higher than the other benefit check you received before becoming disabled; consequently, it behooves you, if eligible, to apply for disability benefits even if you are already receiving Social Security benefits.

■ *Reduction of Benefits by the Government Pension Offset* — Your Social Security disability payments may be reduced if you are a disabled widow/widower, or the spouse of a disabled worker and become eligible for a federal, state or local government pension based on your own work not covered by Social Security. The amount of any benefits you receive based on your spouse's Social Security earnings record may be reduced by two-thirds of the amount of your government pension. This reduction is called the Government Pension Offset and is covered in Section 3.

■ *Reduction of Benefits Due to Receipt of a Pension from Work not Covered by Social Security* — Individuals who become disabled and are entitled **after** 1985 to a Social Security benefit **and** also to a monthly pension based, in whole or in part, on work not covered by Social Security, will have the amount of their disability payments calculated by a different formula. This will result in a smaller benefit payment for certain individuals. This reduction of Social Security benefits is discussed in detail in Section 3.

INFORMATION YOU NEED TO APPLY FOR DISABILITY BENEFITS

The Social Security Administration is required to obtain considerable information and authenticating documentation in order to approve an application for disability benefits. If you are a disabled worker or a disabled spouse, widow, widower or dependent of an insured worker, you can expect that the following information, or other documentation, will be requested to substantiate the claim. Furnish this information as promptly as possible so as not to delay the application process, which generally takes two or three months to complete.

- Social Security number and proof of age for each person, spouse or other dependents eligible for payments
- Date the medical condition started
- Names, addresses, and phone numbers of doctors, hospitals, clinics, and institutions that treated you for the disabling condition
- Dates of medical visits and type of treatments or tests administered
- Hospital, clinic, or Medicaid patient number
- Claim number for any other benefit payment check you receive or expect to receive because of your disability
- Medicines now taken (names, dosages and frequency)
- Any restrictions your doctor advised
- Work history and daily activities (specify how your condition keeps you from working, the date you stopped working, information concerning your current work, and name of your employer)
- Copy of your W-2 forms (Wage and Tax Statement) or, if you are self-employed, your federal tax returns for the past year
- Dates of any military service.

Additional Information Required for Certain Applicants:
- Dates of any prior marriages if your spouse is applying
- Worker's death certificate and proof of marriage if applying for checks as a disabled widow or widower
- Information concerning the medical condition of a child disabled before age 22 if applying for a disabled child's entitlement (this is particularly important to a dependent child who is receiving Social Security benefits that may end at age 18; if the child is disabled, benefit checks may continue on the basis of disability)

■ Medical information concerning the disability of a widow or widower age 50 to 60, if applying for disability benefits based on the deceased spouse's earnings record

■ Medical documentation of disability, divorce decree and proof that a marriage lasted 10 years (marriage certificate) if applying for benefits as a disabled divorced wife or husband.

SECTION 7

Special Benefits and Assistance

ASSISTANCE FOR PEOPLE WHO ARE BLIND, HANDI-CAPPED OR HAVE HEARING IMPAIRMENTS

For people who are blind, handicapped, deaf or have hearing impairments, special assistance is available for obtaining information on Social Security and its many programs. For hearing-impaired individuals, arrangements may be made with the Social Security office for an interpreter to assist them in conducting their Social Security business. However, arrangements for interpreter Services must be made in advance of any visits to a Social Security office. If there is not an available qualified employee or trained volunteer to assist during your visit, Social Security may hire an interpreter.

Additionally, the Social Security Administration provides a nationwide toll-free telephone number with teletype service for deaf or hearing impaired individuals who have general inquiries about Social Security. The toll-free telephone number to use for these inquiries is **800-325-0778**; for those in Missouri, call **800-392-0812**. The telephone service is primarily for use by organizations that work with the deaf and by individuals who have the special teletype (TDD or TTY) equipment necessary to use this service.

For those individuals who are blind or handicapped, the Social Security Administration, in conjunction with the Library of Congress, has produced an updated recording of Social Security information. The recording, a 9-inch, 8 RPM, flexible disc record, is played on a special phonograph. Both the phonograph and the record can be borrowed, free of charge, from any library affiliated with the Library of Congress. Contents of the recording include the publications: *Your Social Security*, which is a general description of all aspects of the Social Security program; *SSI for Aged, Disabled, and Blind People;* and *Basic Facts About Medicare and Other Health Insurance*. This Social Security recording is one of the many free library services that the Library of Congress provides to people who are unable to read or use standard printed materials because of visual or physical impairments. A discussion of these special services by the Library of Congress appears in Chapter 10.

REPRESENTATIVE PAYEES

When individuals who are entitled to Social Security benefits are not capable of managing their own funds, arrangements can be made with the Social Security Administration to send their benefits checks to a relative or other person willing to act on behalf of the beneficiary. This person, who is called a "representative payee," assumes an important responsibility for ensuring that all payments received are used properly for the benefit and well-being of the beneficiary.

Representative payees are required to report to the Social Security Administration: (1) how the funds were disbursed, (2) changes in the beneficiary's physical status which would include improvement of the disabled person's condition, (3) whether the beneficiary moves, or enters or leaves an institution, (4) changes in the beneficiary's financial status such as a change in the amount of benefits received or the receipt of another benefit. The representative must also advise the Social Security Administration in advance if he or she no longer intends to act as payee.

The Social Security office has pamphlets available which give a detailed explanation of the duties of a representative payee and the rights and responsibilities of a beneficiary. It is advisable to obtain this information before agreeing to act as a representative payee since the many duties and responsibilities involved are critical to the well-being of the beneficiary.

BENEFIT PAYMENTS TO A DECEASED WORKER'S PARENTS

Many parents who were dependent on their son's or daughter's financial assistance may be eligible to receive Social Security benefits based on their deceased child's work record. Eligibility for these benefits is based on several conditions which must be met in full before any payments can be made. It is important that the parent file an application for these benefits within the established time period.

Conditions for receipt of Social Security parental benefits are as follows:

- The insured person (their child) was fully insured by Social Security at the time of death.
- The parent has reached age 62 (benefits are paid at this age; however, an application should be made at any age for future payments).
- The parent was receiving at least one half of his or her support from the insured person and evidence of this support has been adequately demonstrated to the Social Security people within the established time limit. Filing of the application with evidence of support must be accomplished within **two years after the date of death**, even if the parent has not reached the age of 62. This period may be extended for good cause.
- The parent is not entitled to a retirement insurance benefit that is equal to or larger than the amount of the parent's unadjusted insurance benefit.
- The parent has not remarried since the insured person's death.
- **One** of the following conditions is met:
  (1) The parent would be eligible under the law of the state of the worker's domicile to share in the intestate personal property of the worker (where the worker did not make a will) as the worker's father or mother, **or**
  (2) The parent had legally adopted the insured person before the child reached the age of 16, **or**
  (3) The person claiming benefits became the deceased's stepparent by a marriage entered into before the child had reached the age of 16.

SPECIAL BENEFIT PROVISION FOR A DEPENDENT GRANDCHILD

Those of you who have had to assume the care of your grandchild due to the death of your adult child or other unfortunate circumstances should be aware that your grandchild may qualify for benefits based on your Social Security earnings record as a grandparent at the time you become eligible for benefits.

The primary consideration used in determining eligibility of a grandchild for these benefits is that the child is **dependent** on the grandparent. In order for a grandchild to be considered as a dependent by Social Security, he or she must meet the following conditions:

■ The grandchild must have begun living with the grandparent before becoming 18 years old.

and

■ The grandchild lived with the grandparent in the U.S. and received at least one half support from the grandparent throughout either of the following periods:

(1) For one year before the month the grandparent became entitled to retirement or disability insurance benefits, or died;

or

(2) For one year immediately before the month in which a period of disability began if the grandparent had a period of disability that lasted until he or she became entitled to benefits.

In those cases where a grandchild may have been born during the one-year period described, it is necessary for the grandparent to have lived with the child and provided at least one half of the grandchild's support for the entire period from the child's birth to the month indicated above.

In addition to the primary condition that a grandchild must be dependent upon the grandparent for support, there are other requirements which must be met before the grandchild may qualify for benefits. These requirements are somewhat complex but, in general, a grandchild will qualify for benefits under either of the following conditions:

■ The grandchild's natural (or adoptive) parents are deceased or disabled at the time the grandparent becomes entitled to Social Security benefits or dies. Once again there are special provisions when the grandparent has a period of disability which eventually qualifies for disability benefits or ends in death; **or**

- In those cases where the grandchild's natural (or adoptive) parents are not deceased or disabled at the time the grandparent dies, the grandchild will qualify if he or she was legally adopted by the grandparent's surviving spouse. However, the regulations stipulate that in this particular case, the grandchild's natural (or adoptive) parents must not have been living in the same household and must not have been making regular contributions to the child's support at the time the grandparent died.

If a child in your care meets these described criteria, you should contact your local Social Security office promptly for assistance. The provisions discussed here are also applicable to a step-grandchild or great-grandchild.

SECTION 8

Of Particular Importance to Women

AS A WORKING WOMAN, WIFE, WIDOW OR DIVORCEE

Since so many older women fall into the ranks of America's "poorest of the poor," it is imperative that all women be aware of the Social Security benefits to which they may be entitled as a single woman, wife, widow or divorcee.

The tendency for a woman to receive Social Security benefits only as a dependent of her spouse is changing, with many women today being insured for benefits in their own right. Nevertheless, because women's average earnings over the years are still much lower than those of men, benefits received on their own work records are frequently lower than what they may receive on their husband's record.

The following is a synopsis of the benefits a woman may be entitled to as a working woman, a wife, a widow or a divorcee . Many of the items are discussed in other sections of this chapter. (Even though this synopsis has been written with women in mind, it is also applicable to men because gender distinction has been virtually eliminated from the Social Security law. However, since the regulations limit the amount a recipient can earn and still receive benefits, the majority of men, because of their higher earnings, are often excluded from certain benefits as a spouse, widower or divorcee.)

As a Working Woman

- A woman may become eligible for reduced retirement benefits at age **62** or for full Social Security benefits at age 65. If she stops work before earning enough Social Security credits, no benefits will be paid on her own work record. However, credits earned will always stay on her record so that she can go back to work and accumulate sufficient credits for retirement benefits. Also, if her earnings were low throughout her employment and she had several years of unpaid or non-covered work — such as that of a housewife — which does not count towards her average earnings, Social Security benefits based on her own earnings record generally will be quite low.

- If a woman becomes disabled at age 31 or later, she will need a required number of work credits depending upon the date of her birth and the age at which she becomes disabled. In addition, she must have five years of work credit out of the 10 years immediately before becoming disabled. If she does not meet this requirement, she will not be eligible for disability benefits.

As a Wife

- A woman can receive benefits as early as age 62 when her husband retires or becomes disabled; however, her benefits will be lower than if she waited to age 65 at which time her full benefit amount would be 50 percent of her husband's benefit. Consequently, a couple under these circumstances could receive 150 percent of the benefits due the husband.

- A wife can receive a benefit at any age if she is caring for her husband's child who is under 16 or disabled and entitled to benefits.

As a Widow

- A widow can receive benefits at any age if she is caring for her husband's child who is under 16 or disabled and entitled to benefits.

- She can receive a widow's reduced benefit beginning at age 60 and full benefits at age 65. These benefits range from $71\frac{1}{2}$ percent of the deceased husband's benefit amount if they begin at age 60, to 100 percent if they begin at age 65.

■ If disabled, she can get widow's benefits as early as age 50. The widow's benefit amount approximates 71^1/2 percent of the deceased husband's benefits.

■ If a widow remarries, she generally loses her Social Security benefits; however, she may continue receiving benefits, without reduction, if she remarries after age 60. If she is disabled, she may remarry after age 50 without losing her benefits.

If a woman receives a pension based on her own work in public employment not covered by Social Security and expects to get a Social Security benefit as the wife or widow of a worker covered by Social Security, she should be aware that the "government pension offset," which is explained earlier in Section 3 of this chapter, may reduce her Social Security benefit.

As a Divorcee

■ Under a rule that became effective in January 1985, a woman who has been divorced for at least two years after at least 10 years of marriage can receive benefits at age 62, based on her ex-husband's work record if he is eligible for Social Security benefits, whether or not her ex-husband receives them, or whether or not he has remarried. However, she may lose her rights to benefits if she remarries. In order to receive these benefits, she must not be entitled to a retirement or disability benefit based on her own earnings, which equals or exceeds one half of her ex-husband's full benefit amount.

Special conditions of the above rule: (1) In general, a marriage must have lasted at least one year before dependents of a retired or disabled worker can receive monthly benefits. Survivors can get benefits usually if the marriage lasted at least nine months. (2) There is a family maximum payment, explained in Section 3 of this chapter, that limits the amount that can be paid to members of the same family based on a worker's record.

WOMEN AND MEDICARE — A VITAL CONSIDERATION

Women entitled to monthly Social Security benefits, either based on their own record or on their husband's, become eligible for Medicare's hospital insurance (Part A) protection at age 65. If they are not entitled to monthly Social Security benefits, they must have worked long enough under Social Security or in covered federal employment to have Medicare's hospital insurance without paying a monthly premium ($289 in 1996). To obtain Medicare's medical insurance (Part B), an individual must enroll for it and pay the required monthly premium which is, for most individuals, $42.50 in 1996.

As a widow, you are eligible for Medicare at age 65 if your husband was or would have been entitled to Social Security monthly benefits before his death. You may also be eligible for Medicare, if your husband had worked long enough in covered federal employment before his death. Widows who are 50 or older, and become disabled while getting benefit checks because they have young children in their care, may be eligible for Medicare if they have been disabled for 24 months or longer. They may apply for the Medicare coverage even if they haven't filed a claim for payments based on the disability.

SECTION 9

Special Rules and Requirements Affecting Certain Work Categories

Due to the complexity of our Social Security system and the coverage it provides for almost all workers in our country, there are many rules and provisions that govern participation by beneficiaries engaged in specific types of work. This section summarizes the rules and provisions that apply only to the various groups of workers or individuals that do not fall under the typical universal coverage rules for the general population. Those who might be directly affected at one time or another by these special rules should be aware of the basic elements that distinguish these groups or individuals and the regulations that affect their Social Security benefits or coverage.

Your local Social Security office can help determine and clarify the impact of these rules on your own particular circumstances. In many cases, pamphlets or booklets are available which will help explain these provisions and rules in more detail. It is important to remember that the amount of your future Social Security benefits depends on the amount of earnings you have on your Social Security record; whereas work credits only determine eligibility for benefits. Therefore, it is always to your advantage to report **all** of your earnings to ensure that they are counted when your benefit payment is determined.

SELF-EMPLOYED INDIVIDUALS

Almost all self-employment is covered by Social Security. Individuals are considered as self-employed if they engage in a trade, business, or profession either by themselves or as partners. They will receive Social Security earnings credit from their self-employment if their net earnings amount to $400 or more in a year. Additionally, there is a provision for self-employed individuals whose net earnings are less than $400 to receive credit for their earnings by using an optional method of determination for coverage if their gross earnings are $600 or more or when their net profit is less than $1,600. Individuals who qualify to use the optional method should contact their Social Security office for further explanation on how to use this method to calculate their earnings credit.

All individuals with net earnings of $400 or more in a year will receive Social Security earnings credit up to the maximum amount covered by Social Security. In 1996, the self-employment tax rate is 15.3% on earnings up to $62,700 and 2.9% on **all** earnings above $62,700 for Medicare Hospital Insurance (Part A). Previous tax credits allowed have been replaced by two new deductions which result in treating the self-employed in much the same manner as employers and employees are treated for Social Security and income tax purposes. Net earnings from self-employment are reduced by an amount equal to half of your total self-employment tax and you can deduct half of your self-employment taxes as a business expense.

Individuals who do not owe any income tax must still report their earnings and pay self-employment Social Security taxes if their net earnings from self-employment amount to $400 or more in a year. This rule also applies to individuals who are already receiving Social Security benefits. To report self-employment earnings, the following Internal Revenue Service forms are used:

- Form 1040 (U.S. Individual Income Tax Return)
- Schedule C (Profit or Loss from Business or Profession)
- Schedule SE (Computation of Social Security Self-Employment Tax)

For each calendar year, tax returns, schedules and self-employment taxes must be filed on or before April 15 of the following year. If, for any year, an individual expects to owe $100 or more in income taxes and self-employment tax, that person may have to file a declaration of estimated tax on Form 1040-ES and pay the estimated tax or the first installment.

If any individual has wages as well as self-employment earnings, the wages count **first** for payment of Social Security taxes. When the wages plus self-employment net earnings **exceed** the Social Security maximum covered amount, the worker pays the self-employment tax **only** on the difference between the wages earned and the Social Security maximum covered amount. If wages plus self-employment net earnings are **less** than the Social Security maximum covered amount, the worker pays self-employment tax (after paying the regular Social Security tax on wages) on the total of the self-employment net earnings.

Special Rules and Provisions

There are special rules and provisions concerning Social Security coverage applicable to the following individuals who are treated as self-employed:

- Those who operate a family business together either as partners or as a joint venture
- Members of the clergy who report their earnings in the ministry as self-employment income
- U.S. citizens who work in this country for a foreign government, an international organization, or an instrumentality wholly owned

by a foreign government and who must report their earnings from these employers as though they were self-employed.

Further information about these rules and provisions can be obtained at any Social Security or Internal Revenue Service office.

INDIVIDUALS WHO WORK FOR FAMILY MEMBERS

Some individuals hire their parents or other family members who lack sufficient work credits to qualify for Social Security benefits, thus enabling these family members to earn the additional work credits needed to establish their eligibility for benefits. It is, therefore, important to know that some types of family employment are not covered by Social Security law. These include: (1) work done by a child under 18 for a parent, and in certain cases (2) parents who do domestic work in the private home of their son or daughter. However, work performed by parents in connection with their son's or daughter's business is covered by Social Security. As of January 1, 1988, a new provision in Social Security law now provides coverage for spouses who are employed in their husband's or wife's business. Formerly, the law prohibited this type of coverage.

Special Exception

Domestic work by a parent for the son or daughter in the private home of the son or daughter may be covered by Social Security if the following conditions are met:

- There is a genuine employment relationship between parent and son or daughter, **and**
- The son or daughter who employs the parent has, living in his or her private home, a child who is under age 18, or an older child with a mental or physical condition that requires the personal care or supervision of an adult for at least four continuous weeks in the calendar quarter in which the domestic work is performed, **and**
- The employer (son or daughter) is a widow or widower, or divorced and has not remarried, or has a spouse living in the home who has a physical or mental condition that renders him or her incapable of taking care of the child for at least four continuous weeks in the calendar quarter in which the parent performs the domestic work.

INDIVIDUALS WHO WORK FOR NONPROFIT ORGANIZATIONS AND CHURCHES

Tax-exempt, nonprofit organizations were mandatorily covered under Social Security as a result of the 1983 amendments to the Social Security Act. Prior to January 1, 1984, religious, charitable, and educational nonprofit organizations were excluded from mandatory Social Security coverage because of their tax-exempt status.

Most employees of nonprofit organizations are covered by Social Security if they are paid $100 or more in a year. In addition, employees 55 or older on January 1, 1984 working for nonprofit organizations newly covered by Social Security, are generally considered fully insured for retirement, survivors, and disability benefits with fewer credits than would otherwise be required. Further discussion of the credit requirements for these individuals appears in the section on "Work Credits" found earlier in this chapter.

EMPLOYEES OF CHURCHES AND CHURCH-CONTROLLED ORGANIZATIONS

Under the 1984 Deficit Reduction Act, a church or church-controlled organization which is opposed, for religious reasons, to payment of taxes can elect exemption from Social Security taxes. Employees of such organizations are covered by Social Security but are considered self-employed persons even if their earnings are less than $400. They need to earn only $100 in a year from the church or church-controlled organization to have their earnings count for Social Security coverage. However, these individuals are not permitted to deduct business expenses from their earnings for tax purposes as do other self-employed people.

MEMBERS OF THE CLERGY

As with other church employees, there are special provisions covering members of the clergy whose earnings from the ministry are automatically covered by Social Security. In general, members of the clergy must report their earnings from the ministry as self-employed income unless their ministry has been exempted from Social Security coverage by the Internal Revenue Service.

SPECIAL ENACTED PROVISIONS

In mid-1987, the Internal Revenue Service announced that a provision of the 1986 Tax Reform Act enabled those churches and church controlled organizations which elected exemption in 1984 from Social Security taxes to revoke those elections if they now prefer to be covered by Social Security.

Under the new provisions, these churches and organizations may revoke their elections, starting with any calendar quarter after December 31, 1986, by filing Form 941, "Employer's Quarterly Tax Return," accompanied by full payment of the Social Security taxes. If, contrary to its election, a church or church-controlled organization had paid all employment taxes from the stated effective date of its election through December 31, 1986, the election will be treated as though it had never been made.

INDIVIDUALS WHO RECEIVE TIPS FOR THEIR WORK

Special rules apply to those who receive cash and/or non-cash tips as a substantial portion of their income. These rules ensure that tips earned count toward Social Security coverage. Unlike regular wages, the employee — not the employer — is responsible for reporting and paying Social Security tax on tips.

The employee reports tip income using Internal Revenue Service Form 4070 or any other form containing the following information: worker's name, address, and Social Security number; employer's name and address; total tips and the period in which the tips were earned. If the tips made in one month working for one employer are less than $20, the employee need only include them in the calculation of his/her gross income. If, however, the employee's monthly tips with one employer **exceed** $20 — the amount which qualifies the income for Social Security coverage — the employee must give his/her tax form to the employer within 10 days of the end of the month in which the tips were earned. In addition, the employee must keep a daily record or other evidence to substantiate the amount of tip income reported on the tax form. Entries in this record should be made on or immediately after the day the tips were received.

The employer collects the taxes due on the reported tips either by deducting them from regular wages paid or by receiving money for this purpose directly from the employee. In 1996, the Social Security tax rate for employees is 7.65 percent of each dollar earned in tips.

A change in law over a year ago requires employers to pay the matching Social Security (7.65 percent) on the full amount of tips received by their employees, as they do with the employee's other earnings (under prior law, employers paid the matching tax only on the amount of tips considered wages for purposes of meeting the federal minimum wage requirements). Further information on paying taxes and the forms required can be obtained from the nearest Internal Revenue Service office.

HOUSEHOLD (DOMESTIC) EMPLOYEES

Since 1994, any individual employed in your household in the capacity of cook, maid, gardener, cleaning person, companion or someone who assists in the care of an individual, must have his/her wages reported **only** if they were paid $1,000 or more during the year. No Social Security taxes are due if earnings are under $1,000. Workers under the age of 18, including babysitters, are exempt from the law.

An exception to this rule applies when the individual works in a rooming house, boarding house, hotel or motel. In this case, **all** wages paid to the employee must be reported.

In most situations, the employer and employee share responsibility for the required Social Security and Medicare taxes. However, some employers pay the entire tax to assist the employees or because of the workers' objection to paying the tax themselves. Regardless of who pays the required taxes, the employer must file a report of wages paid during the calendar year on or before April 15 of the following year. Filing is not required if wages paid are less than $1,000. In addition, the employer must give the worker a Form W-2 ("Wage and Tax Statement") by January 31 after the year in which the wages were paid.

Employers should contact either the Social Security office or the Internal Revenue Service office for further information concerning the hiring of a domestic worker, the proper reporting of wages and the payment of required taxes.

FARM EMPLOYEES

Since farm work is often irregular and part-time, special rules control how such work is credited towards Social Security. In general, only cash payments for farm work are counted as wages for determining work credits. For Social Security purposes, the definition of a "farm" includes stock, dairy, poultry, and fur-bearing animal farms, as well as plantations, ranches, nurseries, ranges and orchards. The term is further defined to include greenhouses, except those used primarily for display, storage purpose or for making wreaths or bouquets, and any other structure which is used primarily for raising agricultural or horticultural commodities.

Currently, farm workers (including domestic workers on a farm) working for an employer who spends **more** than $2,499 per year for agricultural labor, receive Social Security credit for their cash wages, regardless of the amount of wages earned or how many days they work. If an employer spends **less** than $2,500 for agricultural labor, a farm worker is still covered by Social Security if he or she is paid at least $150 during the year by the employer. An alternate Social Security coverage test which covered individuals who worked for a farmer on at least 20 days during the year for cash pay figured on hours of work, or other time basis, was eliminated in December 1987.

Work payments are credited as wages for Social Security purposes when the wages are paid. For example, if an employee worked in 1994 and 1995 but was paid $150 in 1995, the entire $150 is counted as 1995 wages even though part (or all) of the work was done in 1994.

Several other important rules govern Social Security coverage for farm work performed in the cultivating, raising, harvesting, processing or packaging of any agricultural or horticultural commodity. Questions on how coverage for such work is applied to your Social Security earnings record can be clarified by Social Security.

FORMER AND CURRENT MILITARY MEMBERS

Members of the U.S. military have been covered by Social Security since December 31, 1956. They earn Social Security benefits in the same way as civilian employees. Only basic pay received while on active duty or active duty for training counts.

Of particular interest to older individuals is that they may also receive **additional earnings credits** for their military service if they or their family need them to qualify for benefits or if the additional credits would result in a higher benefit amount. Additional earnings credits may be granted as follows:

- *For military service from September 16, 1940 through December 31, 1956 (World War II and post-World War II periods)* — Individuals may receive **earnings credits** of $160 a month for active military service under these conditions:

  (1) The veteran was discharged or released from active service under conditions other than dishonorable, either after active service of 90 days (or more) or after less than 90 days service by reason of a disability or injury incurred or aggravated in the line of duty, **or**
  (2) The veteran is still in active service, **or**
  (3) The veteran died while in the active military service.

  The $160 a month credits are not automatically posted by Social Security on a veteran's record. Only when benefits are claimed on a veteran's Social Security record are the earnings credits considered by the Social Security personnel. It is imperative that individuals who could benefit from these additional credits inform the Social Security people of any military service performed during this period of time.

- *For military service in 1957 through 1977* — Individuals may receive an additional **earnings credits** of $300 for each calendar quarter in which they had any active duty basic pay.

- *For military service in 1978 and later* — Individuals may receive an additional **earnings credits** of $100 for each $300 of their active duty basic pay, up to a maximum of $1,200 in earnings credits for each year.

FEDERAL EMPLOYEES

Since 1986, there are two federal civilian employees' retirement plans: (1) the Civil Service Retirement System which is the oldest and most widely known and (2) the Federal Employees Retirement System, enacted in 1986, which includes coverage by Social Security as one of its benefits. Each of these plans is discussed briefly to help you understand who is covered by each plan and more specifically, the participants' coverage by Social Security.

Of particular importance to older individuals who lack sufficient Social Security work credits in order to qualify for Social Security benefits, is that these individuals may now consider part-time or full-time government employment under the Federal Employees Retirement System to fulfill their needed work credit requirements — a significant feature of this new plan.

CIVIL SERVICE RETIREMENT SYSTEM

All full-time permanent employees hired before January 1, 1984 were covered by the Civil Service Retirement System (CSRS). They are not covered by Social Security **except** for coverage provided since January 1983 under the Medicare hospital insurance program (Part A). Federal employees contribute the same tax rate (in 1996, 1.45% of covered earnings) as do non-federal employees for the Medicare hospital insurance. Further information concerning the coverage provided by Medicare for these employees is discussed in Chapter 4, "Medicare".

However, some federal employees hired before January 1, 1984, mostly part-time and temporary, were not covered by the federal retirement system (CSRS). Since 1950, these individuals have been covered by the full Social Security program which includes the Old Age, Survivors' and Disability insurance as well as the Medicare hospital insurance.

A special provision in the legislation which created the new Federal Employees Retirement System provided that federal employees under the Civil Service Retirement System would have the option to transfer into the new retirement plan during a scheduled open season, from July 1 to December 31, 1987. Any employee who decided to join the Federal Employees Retirement System cannot go back to the old system since the decision is irrevocable under the legislation's provisions.

FEDERAL EMPLOYEES RETIREMENT SYSTEM

Federal civilian employees hired after December 31, 1983 are covered by the Federal Employees Retirement System, which is referred to as "FERS". This new retirement plan began with legislation enacted in

1983 which provided that federal employees hired after December 31, 1983 would be fully covered for benefits by both Social Security and the old Civil Service Retirement System during a transitional period (from January 1, 1984 to December 31, 1986) until a plan could be fully developed by Congress. In December 1986, legislation was passed establishing the Federal Employees Retirement System with an effective date of January 1, 1987.

FERS includes employees hired after December 31, 1983, individuals with previous periods of federal service who had a break in service lasting more than 365 days, those federal employees under the old system who choose to transfer to the Federal Employees Retirement System, and other current employees including: the President and Vice President, members of Congress, congressional staff employees, federal judges, political appointees, foreign service employees, fire fighters, law enforcement officers, air traffic controllers and military reserve technicians.

The Federal Employees Retirement System is a three-tiered retirement plan. Its three components, each of which provides benefits independent of the other components, are *Social Security, a basic retirement annuity,* and a special *savings plan.* Under the Social Security component, all FERS participants pay the full Social Security tax on their salary up to the maximum taxable wage base. They are, therefore, covered under Social Security by both the Old Age, Survivors and Disability insurance (OASDI) and the Medicare hospital insurance (HI) program. The federal government, as the employer, pays an equal amount. The tax rate that each pays is the same as all other Social Security participants pay.

Social Security provides benefits to FERS participants and their dependents who qualify for benefits, in the same way it pays all other workers who are covered by Social Security. There are **no special Social Security rules** for FERS participants, including those who transferred to FERS. Consequently, individuals who transferred to FERS with less than 10 years remaining until retirement may not have sufficient Social Security work credits (quarters of coverage) to qualify for Social Security cash benefits. In general, as indicated previously in the discussion on work credit requirements, it requires 40 work credits or 10 years of covered earnings under Social Security to be fully insured and eligible for most benefits. Unless those individuals who transferred have earned prior Social Security work credits or intend to work after their government retirement in order to obtain sufficient work credits, they may not be eligible to receive the Social Security benefits of this new retirement system.

Any questions that an individual may have concerning the Social Security coverage and the earning of work credits under this new retirement plan should be directed to Social Security; additional information concerning the plan itself may be obtained from any federal agency's personnel office.

RECENT LEGISLATIVE CHANGES

Several important changes to Social Security coverage have been made in the past few months. These changes will affect millions of beneficiaries both on the retired and disability roles. Since these changes may have an effect on your Social Security coverage or that of a family member, it is vital that you be aware of them.

(1) *SS Coverage for State and Local Government Workers:* On July 2, 1991, per the mandate of Congress, approximately 2.3 million employees who were not members of a state or local retirement program acquired Social Security protection. This is the largest remaining group of Americans workers who were not covered mandatorily by Social Security.

(2) *New Changes to Disability Provisions:* Two provisions of the Omnibus Reconciliation Act of 1990 affect those who receive Social Security Benefits based on a disability. The changes became effective in late 1991 and early 1992. They are:

■ *Trial Work Period* — Starting in January 1992, disability beneficiaries who return to work will be considered to be in a trial period for up to nine non-consecutive months out of a consecutive 60-month period. Reentitled workers with disabilities will be eligible for the same trial period.

The trial period will give beneficiaries with disabilities some time to test their ability to work without losing benefits. Beneficiaries who find they are unable to continue work, but who try again at a later date, will always have a five-year period with another nine-month trial.

For example, if the first attempt to return to work occurs during the first year of disability, the next attempt is made during year three, and the subsequent effort is made during year five, the amount of time worked during year one will not be considered during year six as long as the nine months have not been used up during the consecutive 60-month (five-year) period.

■ *Extension of Benefits to Recovered Non-State VR Participants* — Starting with benefits payable in November 1991, disability beneficiaries who recover while participating in an approved non-state vocational rehabilitation (VR) program will continue to receive Social Security and Supplemental Security Income. This provision extends coverage from state-only VR programs, as long as Social Security has approved the non-state program, and has determined that completing or continuing the program will increase the beneficiary's likelihood of leaving the benefit rolls permanently.

(3) Representative Payee Changes: Representative payees are individuals or groups (relatives or non-relatives) who volunteer to oversee the financial management of monthly payments to those who have been judged unable to do so on their own behalves. To protect beneficiaries from unscrupulous representative payees, Congress in 1990 instructed the Social Security Administration (SSA) to ensure that current and future representative payee applicants meet more stringent eligibility standards, and that they will be more thoroughly investigated than past applicants. The law requires SSA to develop a centralized file of beneficiary and representative payee data so that an applicant's past performance as a payee can be evaluated to determine if that individual should be reappointed a payee.

Congress has provided further protection to those who need representative payees by generally limiting to one month the deferral or suspension of direct benefit payment while a payee is being selected.

(4) Benefits to Deemed Spouses: Under a new law, both a legal spouse and a deemed spouse may now be entitled to benefits on the same worker's record. In the past, *deemed spouses* — those who entered into an invalid ceremonial marriage in good faith — were unable to collect benefits if a legal spouse was entitled to those benefits, or had previously been entitled, and still was considered the legal spouse. Although the provision applies to spouses and widow(er)s of all ages, it requires that the deemed spouse must be living in the same household as the worker at the time of the claimant's initial application or at the time of the worker's death. In cases where a deemed spouse has been divorced from the wage earner, the ten year duration-of-marriage requirement may be met by a deemed marriage. Under this requirement, a divorced spouse aged 62 or older may be eligible to receive benefits based on the former spouse's record if the marriage lasted at least ten years and the applicant has not remarried.

(5) *Two-Year Rule Change for Older Divorced Beneficiaries:* Prior to a provision passed last year by Congress, a divorced woman had to wait two years after a divorce before she was eligible to receive benefits based on her former husband's Social Security work record. This two-year rule has now been changed but **only** for those individuals whose divorces occur after Social Security benefits have already begun. These spousal benefits can continue even if the former husband re-enters the work force and earns above the annual earnings limitation.

(6) *Special Minimum Benefit Formula Change:* Per Congressional action last year, a change has been made which will increase Social Security benefits for workers who have many years of work at low wages. The new law lowers the amount of earnings a worker needs to earn a year of coverage towards a special Social Security minimum benefit.

(7) *Change in Definition of Widows with Disabilities:* About 8,000 widows with disabilities will now receive benefits because of a change in the definition of *disabled widows* eligible to receive Social Security benefits. Now the ability of a widow with disabilities to perform work will be a major factor in determining her disability. In the past, only medical factors were used in this determination, thus prohibiting many from receiving these benefits.

SUMMARY OF MAJOR SOCIAL SECURITY TAX AND BENEFITS — 1996

Wage Base on Which Social Security Taxes and Benefits are Based: (Maximum amount of annual earnings on which Social Security taxes are paid. Also the *maximum* amount on which benefits will be paid.)	**$62,700 (OASDI)** (Old Age, Survivors, Disability Insurance) **All earnings above $62,700 (HI)** (Hospital Insurance/ Medicare Part A)
Social Security Tax Rate: (Percentage of the Wage Base) (1) *Employees Pay*	**6.2%** (OASDI) on $62,700 earnings **1.45%** - (HI) on all earnings above $62,700 (Total of 7.65% on first $62,700 in earnings)
(2) *Employers Pay*	Same as employees pay
(3) *Self-Employed Individuals Pay* (Two deductions apply for the self-employed: Self-employed individuals can reduce their self-employment income by 7.65% before calculating their SS tax, and deduct half of that tax on their income tax form.)	**15.3%** on first $62,700 earnings **2.9%** on all earnings over $62,700
Earnings Test for Beneficiaries: (Maximum amount an individual can earn *annually* without having Social Security benefits withheld.) (1) *Under age 65* (Benefits reduced $1 for every $2 of earnings over this amount.) (2) *Age 65-69* (Benefits reduced $1 for every $3 of earnings over this amount.) (3) *After age 70* (Can earn *any* amount and *not* lose Social Security benefits.)	$ 8,280 $ 12,500 No limit
Amount of Earnings Needed for Social Security Credits: Minimum amount of earnings required to receive one quarter of coverage. A maximum of 4 quarters of coverage can be earned in one year.)	$ 640

SUMMARY OF MAJOR SOCIAL SECURITY TAX AND BENEFITS — 1996
(continued)

Cost-of-Living Increase (percent): (Based on the rise in the Consumer Price Index from the 3rd quarter of one year through the corresponding period of the next year.)	**2.6%**
Delayed Retirement Credits: **(For People Turning 65 in 1996)** (This credit, which is a percentage added to the Social Security benefit, is given for each month that a person over 65 continues to work and delays retirement. These credits are applied to a person's full age 65 benefit rate.)	**5.0%**
Lump-Sum Death Payment: (Payable only to a surviving spouse or eligible child/children.)	$ 255
Monthly Payments: Maximum Social Security benefits for a worker retiring at age 65.	**$ 1,248**

Monthly Payments:
 	
Average amount of benefits for:
    (1) *All retired workers (per person)*
 	
    (2) *Aged couple, both receiving benefits*
 	
    (3) *Widowed mother and two children*
 	
    (4) *Aged widow (or widower) alone*
 	
    (5) *Disabled worker, spouse and children*
 	
    (6) *All disabled workers (per person)*
	
	$ 720
	
	$ 1,215
	
	$ 1,407
	
	$ 680
	
	$ 1,148
	
	$ 682

Chapter 3

Railroad Retirement

An Overview of Its Benefits and Its Tie-In to Social Security

Chapter Highlights

Railroad Retirement

An Overview of Its Benefits and Its Tie-In to Social Security

The Railroad Retirement System is a federally managed $8 billion-a-year program providing retirement, disability and survivor benefits to nearly a million active and retired railroad employees and their families, as well as providing benefits to individuals employed by certain companies, associations and labor organizations closely associated with the railroad industry. It is a separate system from Social Security; however, all railroad workers are covered by Medicare on the same basis as are individuals covered under Social Security.

Administered by the Railroad Retirement Board, an independent agency of our federal government's executive branch, the Railroad Retirement System is the **only** remaining federally administered pension program for a private industry.

Railroad employment reached a peak in 1945 with almost 1.7 million employees. The work force then declined steadily for a number of years. It appears now to have stabilized at approximately 165,000 active employees, with about 800,000 beneficiaries receiving Railroad Retirement benefits at mid-year.

The original Railroad Retirement System was created in 1934 (just before the enactment of Social Security) in response to the demands of the then enormous railroad industry for a separate federally managed retirement system which would provide annuities to railroad retirees based on their earnings and length of service with the railroad. Since its inception, the Railroad Retirement System has undergone several major changes through various legislative amendments intended to expand benefit coverage and, later, to bring the system more closely in alignment with Social Security.

RAILROAD RETIREMENT ACT OF 1974

Under the Railroad Retirement Act of 1974, followed by important legislative amendments enacted in 1981 and 1983, the Railroad Retirement System was more or less tied in to Social Security by mandating that most of the rules which had been applicable to Social Security were to be applicable to Railroad Retirement benefits. Another provision stipulated that all railroad workers who have less than 10 years of creditable railroad service would have their railroad earnings transferred to Social Security and counted towards their eligibility for Social Security benefits. Currently, the basic requirement for a regular Railroad Retirement annuity is 10 years (120 months) of creditable railroad service.

The Railroad Retirement Act of 1974 fundamentally reorganized the Railroad Retirement System and established the basic provisions of its present-day organization. A major change was that Railroad Retirement annuities would be calculated under a two-tier formula. The first tier (**Tier I**) approximates a Social Security benefit and is based on Railroad Retirement credits and any non-railroad credits covered by Social Security that a worker has earned. The second tier (**Tier II**) is comparable to a private pension and is based only on earned railroad service credits.

EMPLOYEE CONTRIBUTIONS

Since benefits of the Railroad Retirement System (except for vested dual benefits) are financed through a combination of employer and employee contributions to a trust fund, railroad employees and employers pay taxes on both Tier I and Tier II. Tier I taxes are the same as those paid by individuals covered under Social Security and are increased whenever Social Security taxes rise. In 1996, the Tier I tax rate for employees and employers is 7.65 percent on a maximum wage base of $62,700. However, the maximum compensation subject to the Medicare Hospital Insurance (HI) tax of 1.45 percent was increased to include all earnings over $62,700; consequently, all Tier I earnings over $62,700 will be taxed with the additional 1.45 percent (HI tax).

Tier II taxes are paid separately based on predetermined employee-employer tax rates up to a maximum amount of an employee's yearly earnings. The employee pays **4.9** percent and the employer pays **16.10** percent on the employee's first **$46,500** of railroad earnings in 1996.

RAILROAD RETIREMENT BENEFITS

Like Social Security, railroad annuities are payable to a railroad worker in the event of retirement or disability after meeting certain eligibility requirements. Annuities now are also payable to spouses, children, parents, divorced spouses, remarried widows or widowers, and divorced mothers and fathers, who meet conditions similar to those established for entitlement to Social Security benefits.

However, some dependents of railroad workers are not directly covered by the Railroad Retirement System as they would be under Social Security. For example, Social Security provides dependent children's benefits when an employee is disabled, retired, or deceased; the Railroad Retirement Act only provides children's benefits if the employee is deceased. A "special minimum guaranty" provision has been provided under the Railroad Retirement System to cover situations such as this one, where one or more members of a family are eligible for a type of Social Security benefit that is not provided by the Railroad Retirement Act. The provision states that families of railroad workers will not receive less in monthly benefits than they would have received if their railroad earnings had been covered by Social Security. Consequently, when this occurs, a railroad worker's annuity will be increased to reflect what Social Security would pay the family, unless the railroad annuity already exceeds that amount.

RAILROAD RETIREMENT ANNUITIES

The following summarizes the various annuities a railroad employee, spouse or certain dependent survivors may receive and their applicable eligibility requirements.

EMPLOYEE ANNUITIES
■ *Regular Annuities Based on Age and Service*

(1) Full annuities may be received by an employee at age 62 with 30 or more years of creditable service. Reduced retirement annuities for these employees may be received as early as age 60. **Exception:** Generally, there will be no reduction in an annuity before age 62 if the employee completed 30 years of service and attained age 60 before July 1, 1984.

2) Employees with 10 to 29 years of creditable service are eligible for full annuities at age 65. Reduced retirement annuities may be received as early as age 62.

Before receiving retirement annuities, employees must satisfy a particular requirement called the "current connection" requirement. This requirement states that an employee must have worked for a railroad for at least 12 of the months in the two and a half years (30 months) immediately preceding retirement. If an employee dies before retirement, railroad service in at least 12 of the months in the two and a half years before death will meet the "current connection" requirement needed to warrant payment of survivor benefits.

If the employee does not qualify in either of these ways, but has 12 months in some other two and a half year period, he/she may still meet the current connection requirement if he/she did not have a regular non-railroad job after the two and a half year period in which the 12 months of railroad service occurred.

It is particularly important to understand that non-railroad work in the interim before retirement can break a current connection, but self-employment in one's own unincorporated business and work for certain U.S. government agencies will not break a current connection. Once a current connection is established at the time of retirement, an employee never loses it.

Important Exception: A current connection can also be maintained, for purposes of supplemental and survivor annuities, if the employee completed 25 years of railroad service, was involuntarily terminated without fault from the railroad industry, and did not thereafter decline an offer of suitable employment in the railroad industry. Generally, where an employee has no option to remain in the service of his or her employer, the termination of the employment is considered involuntary, regardless of whether the employee does or does not receive a separation allowance.

■ Disability Annuities
(1) A **total disability** annuity may be paid to an employee at any age if the employee is permanently disabled for all **regular work** and has at last 10 years of creditable railroad service.

(2) An **occupational disability** annuity may be paid to an employee at age 60 if the employee has at least 10 years of railroad service or at any age if the employee has at least 20 years of service, when the employee is permanently disabled for his or her **regular railroad occupation**. A "current connection" provision with the railroad industry is also required for an annuity based on occupational, rather than total, disability.

Before any disability annuity can begin, a five-month waiting period after the onset of disability is required.

- *Supplemental Annuities* — A supplemental annuity may be payable to certain railroad employees who are awarded regular retirement annuities. In order to qualify for this supplement, employees must be at least age 60 with 30 or more years of creditable railroad service or at least age 65 with 25-29 years of railroad service and have a "current connection" with the railroad industry. To receive the supplemental annuity, employees must stop working (for either a railroad or for the last non-railroad employer they had before retirement), as they must to receive payment of a regular retirement annuity.

- *Vested Dual Benefit Payments* — Railroad employees, disabled or retired, who qualified for both Railroad Retirement and Social Security benefits before 1975 and who meet certain vesting requirements can receive an annuity amount called the "vested dual benefit payment," in addition to their Tier I and Tier II benefits. Although there are exceptions, individuals who were fully qualified for both Social Security and Railroad Retirement pensions as of December 31, 1974 and had a "current connection" with the railroad industry will receive this dual benefit payment.

Since vested dual benefit payments are funded by annual appropriations from U.S. Treasury general revenues (rather than from Railroad Retirement payroll taxes and other revenues that finance over 90 percent of the retirement system's benefits), payment of these dual benefits depends on the time and amount of these annual appropriations. If appropriations are not sufficient to meet estimated benefit payments, individual payments are reduced by proration. When appropriations are delayed by Congress, payments are withheld until the funds are actually made available to the Railroad Retirement program.

SPOUSE ANNUITIES

Before any annuity can be paid, a spouse must take the same steps that an employee would take to receive an annuity. The spouse must file an application for benefits, stop working, and give up any right to return to work for a railroad or for the most recent non-railroad employer, if applicable.

- *Annuity at Age 62* — If a retired employee is age 62 with 10-29 years of service, the employee's spouse is also eligible for an annuity at age 62. Early retirement reductions of up to 25 percent are applied to the spouse annuity if the spouse retires before age 65.

- *Annuity at Age 60* — If a retired employee is age 60 with 30 years of service, the employee's spouse is also eligible for an annuity at age 60. Certain early retirement reductions are applied to this kind of spouse's annuity if the employee retires before age 62, unless the employee attained age 60 and completed 30 years of service prior to July 1, 1984. If a 30-year employee retires at age 62, an age reduction is not applied to the spouse annuity even if the spouse retires at age 60 rather than age 62.

- *Annuity When Caring for an Employee's Child* — A spouse of an employee qualified for an age and service annuity is eligible for a spouse annuity at any age when caring for the employee's child, if the child is under age 16 or became disabled before age 22. In some cases, benefits may continue on a partial basis until the child attains age 18.

- *Special Annuity Provision for a Divorced Spouse* — An annuity may also be payable to the divorced wife or husband of a retired employee, if their marriage lasted for at least 10 years, both have attained age 62, and the divorced spouse has not remarried at the time she or he applies for benefits.

DUAL RAILROAD RETIREMENT ANNUITIES

If **both** a husband and wife are 10-year railroad employees and either of them had any railroad service **before** 1975, both can receive employee and spouse Railroad Retirement annuities. If **both** started railroad employment **after** 1974, they may each receive only their own annuity or spousal annuity, whichever is greater.

SURVIVOR ANNUITIES

The following annuities are payable only to those survivors who meet the various eligibility requirements established by the Railroad Retirement Act.

- *Annuity for a Widow (or Widower) Caring for an Employee's Child* — An annuity can be paid to an employee's widow(er) at age 60, or at any age if the widow(er) is caring for a child of the employee and the child is under age 16 (18 in some cases) or a child who became totally disabled before age 22.

- *Annuity for a Permanently Disabled Widow/Widower* — A widow(er) who is permanently disabled and unable to work at any regular employment can receive an annuity as early as age 50.

- *Annuity for an Unmarried Child* — An unmarried child can receive an annuity if underage 18; while age 18 and in full-time attendance at an elementary or secondary school; or at any age if permanently disabled before age 22.

- *Annuity for a Dependent Grandchild* — A dependent grandchild can qualify for benefits on the same basis as a child if both the child's parents are deceased or disabled.

- *Annuity for a Dependent Parent* — An employee's dependent parents can receive annuities at age 60 if they were dependent on the employee for at least half of their support.

SPECIAL PROVISIONS

Under certain conditions, survivors' benefits may also be payable to a divorced spouse or remarried widow(er). Benefits are limited to the amounts Social Security would pay, and are less than the amount of the survivor annuity otherwise payable.

AMOUNT OF ANNUITIES

Due to the complexities of the Railroad Retirement laws, the need for lifetime earnings records, and the various annuities that a railroad worker may be entitled to, it is quite difficult — and generally not practical — for individuals to try to estimate their own annuities or the benefits due their spouse and dependents. Any of the Railroad Retirement Board district offices will furnish annuity estimates upon request for an employee with at least 10 years of railroad service.

Those planning to retire in the near future should note: the total amount of retirement benefits (not including any vested dual benefits) payable to an employee and spouse at the time the employee's annuity begins is limited to an individual maximum determined by the Railroad Retirement Board. Although this maximum may limit the amount of benefits payable at the time the employee retires, benefits increase after retirement for any cost-of-living adjustments. It is advisable that all near-term prospective railroad retirees contact the nearest Railroad Retirement Board district office **several months** before they retire in order to obtain annuity estimates and to verify their eligibility dates.

MEDICARE COVERAGE

As indicated in the introduction to this chapter, anyone who is eligible for an annuity under the Railroad Retirement Act, whether as an employee or as a dependent, is eligible for Medicare. Railroad retirees are covered by the same provisions and requirements as are individuals covered under Social Security; consequently, the information contained in Chapter 4 on Medicare is applicable to all railroad employees and their dependents. However, the Railroad Retirement Board does have certain responsibilities in this regard since railroad employees and their dependents are covered by Medicare's health insurance plan. In particular, the board is responsible for designating specific *carriers* which handle only the Medicare claims of individuals under the Railroad Retirement System. A listing of these carriers and the processing centers is contained in Chapter 4.

FEDERAL TAXATION OF BENEFITS

Since 1984, a certain portion of Tier I retirement and survivors' benefits is subject to federal income tax in exactly the same manner as Social Security benefits. In addition, any special minimum guarantee payments received, which insure that an employee's benefit will at least equal the amount that would be payable to a family under Social Security, are treated the same as Social Security benefits for federal taxation purposes.

Consequently, retirees must consider a part of these benefits as taxable income if their adjusted gross income plus non-taxable interest income and half of their Social Security equivalent benefits exceed a certain base amount. The base amount is: $25,000 for an individual; $32,000 for a married couple filing jointly; and $0 (zero) for a married individual filing separately who lived with his or her spouse during any part of the year. However, the Tier I portion treated in this manner is limited to an amount equivalent to a Social Security benefit.

Higher income retirees should be aware that beginning with taxable year 1994, a larger amount of Social Security benefits, and those Railroad Retirement Tier I benefits equivalent to Social Security benefits, may be subject to Federal income tax. For individuals whose income exceeds $34,000 and for couples whose income exceeds $44,000, up to 85 percent of Social Security and Railroad Retirement Tier I benefits will be taxable in 1996 and subsequent years.

For Railroad Retirement annuities **beginning before July 2, 1986**, Tier I benefits exceeding Social Security equivalent benefits are subject to federal taxation and are taxable under the three-year recovery rule, which allows retirees to first recover their lifetime pension contributions from cumulative benefit payments before benefits become subject to income tax. Employee contributions are considered to be the amount of Railroad Retirement payroll taxes paid by the employee over and above comparable Social Security payroll taxes. However, vested dual benefit payments and Railroad Retirement supplemental annuities are considered non-contributory and taxable immediately.

The Tax Reform Act of 1986 eliminated, for annuities **beginning after July 1, 1986**, the three-year recovery rule for contributory private pensions which had been applicable to Railroad Retirement benefits. Under the new tax law, Railroad Retirement benefits exceeding Social Security—equivalent levels will be taxable immediately upon retirement, but on a prorated basis to allow for previously-taxed contributions and estimated life expectancies.

The Railroad Retirement Board issues two benefit information statements each year in January to help annuitants comply with the federal tax laws concerning their railroad benefits. The first statement, white form RRB-1099, shows the amount of any Social Security equivalent benefits or special minimum guarantee payments. The second statement, green form RRB-W-2P, shows the amounts of Railroad Retirement benefits over and above Social Security-equivalent benefits, plus any vested dual benefits and supplemental annuities; it also shows the amount of benefits taxable under the three-year rule after subtraction of the employee's contribution.

Unless the employee requests that taxes not be withheld, they are withheld for all U.S. citizens or residents whose Railroad Retirement benefits in excess of the Social Security-equivalent level total more than certain annual threshold amounts. Any amounts withheld during the taxable year will be reflected on the annual statement issued by the Railroad Retirement Board.

ITEMS OF PARTICULAR IMPORTANCE TO RAILROAD RETIREMENT BENEFICIARIES

There are several provisions, rules and requirements of the Railroad Retirement Act which are important because they affect the annuities and benefits of Railroad Retirement beneficiaries. The following briefly summarizes some of these items of particular importance to most beneficiaries.

- **Limitations on Earnings** — Tier I and vested dual benefit components of employee and spouse retirement annuities are subject to limitations on earnings outside the railroad industry and will be reduced if the earnings limits are exceeded. As in the case of Social Security beneficiaries — under age 65 — who exceed earnings limits, $1 in Railroad Retirement benefits is deducted for each $2 earned in a calendar year that exceeds the exempt amount. For those individuals age 65-69, the deduction will be $1 in benefits for every $3 earned over the exempt amounts.

  'There is no limitation in earnings after an annuitant reaches age 70. For individuals age 65-69, the annual earnings limit is $12,500 in 1996; for those under age 65, the limit is $8,280.

  Also, if an annuity is based on disability, there are certain work restrictions that can affect payment, depending on the amount of earnings of the disabled annuitant.

- **COLAs (Cost-of-Living Adjustments)** — The Tier I portion of both employee and spouse annuities is increased annually, and payable on January 1, by the same percentage as are Social Security benefits. The Tier II portion is normally increased annually, whenever Tier I benefits are increased, by 32.5 percent of the Tier I cost of-living increase rate. In January 1996, an increase of 0.8 percent of Tier II benefits was granted. Tier I benefits were increased by 2.6 percent.

■ *Lump-Sum Death Benefit* — When an employee dies, a lump-sum benefit payment is payable to the estate of the employee only when there are no immediate survivors eligible for monthly annuity benefits. Unlike Social Security, if there are no immediate survivors, this benefit may be paid to a funeral home or to the person who paid the burial expenses of the deceased employee. The lump-sum payment is almost always $255 if the deceased worker had completed 10 years of railroad service **after** 1974. In those cases where the deceased worker was credited with 10 years of service before January 1, 1975, the average benefit payable is approximately $850.

■ *Residual Lump-Sum Death Benefit* — In addition to the lump-sum death benefit, Railroad Retirement provides an additional lump-sum death benefit called the "residual payment," for which an insured status is not required. It is, in effect, a refund of a deceased employee's pre-1975 Railroad Retirement taxes plus an allowance in lieu of interest.

Survivors should understand, before receiving a residual payment, that the payment is reduced for any retirement benefits that have been paid on the basis of the employee's railroad service, and for any survivor benefits previously paid by either the Railroad Retirement Board or the Social Security Administration. A residual cannot be paid if there are immediate or potential monthly survivor benefits payable. However, a widow, widower or parent who would be eligible in the future **before attaining age 60**, may elect to waive future rights to monthly benefits in order to receive the residual payment.

It is of critical importance to know that this action also waives rights to Medicare based on the deceased employee's railroad service. Once a residual is paid, no further benefits are payable on the basis of the employee's railroad earnings. The residual payment is made to the employee's widow or widower, children, grandchildren, parents, brothers and sisters, or estate, in that order of precedence.

■ *Survivors' Benefits Transfer to Social Security* — If a deceased employee does not have at least 10 years of railroad service and a "current connection" with the railroad industry, survivors' benefits are payable under Social Security. The Railroad Retirement Board will automatically transfer jurisdiction to the Social Security Administration.

■ *Social Security Benefit Payments* — In those cases where a retired or disabled Railroad Retirement annuitant is also eligible for Social Security benefits, the Social Security Administration will determine the amount due and inform the Railroad Retirement Board. The Board will then issue a combined monthly benefit check to the annuitant.

   The Board reduces the annuitant's Tier I amount by the amount of the Social Security benefit. This is because the Tier I portion is based on combined Railroad Retirement and Social Security credits, figured under Social Security formulas, and approximates what Social Security would pay if railroad work were covered by that system. This benefit reduction follows principles of Social Security law, under which a beneficiary may receive only the higher of any two benefits payable.

■ *Possible Reductions in Annuities:*

— Like Social Security, the Tier I portion of a workers annuity may be reduced, under certain circumstances, when the annuitant receives worker's compensation or public disability benefits. It may also be reduced when the annuitant receives, after 1985, a federal, state or local government pension based partially or wholly on employment not covered by Social Security.

— The Tier I portion of a spousal annuity may be reduced also for receipt of any federal, state or local pension separately payable to the spouse based on the spouse's own earnings. If the employment on which the public pension is based was covered under the Social Security Act on the spouse's last working day, the reduction does not apply.

OF INTEREST TO MANY RAILROAD EMPLOYEES
AND RETIREES

The following rules and provisions affect a vast number of active and retired railroad workers and their families. Please help spread the word to others who may not be aware of them.

- **Retiree Earnings Limits:** *Tier II* and *Supplemental Annuity* payments are not normally subject to earnings deduction. However, the rules differ for retired railroad employees and spouses who have again begun work for their most recent employer — if that employer is not a railroad. Such working railroad retirees are subject to an additional earnings deduction of **$1** for each **$2** of compensation received, up to a maximum reduction of 50%. This deduction must be paid even if the retiree's earnings do not exceed the Tier I exempt earnings limits. In addition, these deductions *continue* to apply after the retiree reaches age 70 — unlike Tier I and Vested Dual Benefits earnings deductions, which stop at age 70.

- **Divorced Spouse Annuity:** A spouse annuity may be payable to the divorced wife or husband of a retired employee if their marriage lasted for at least 10 years, both have attained age 62 for a full month, and the divorced spouse is not remarried. In general, the amount of a divorced spouse's annuity is equal to what Social Security would pay in the same situation and therefore, less than the amount of the spouse annuity otherwise payable. The award of a divorced spouse's benefit does not affect the amount of the employee's annuity, nor does it affect the amount of the Railroad Retirement annuity that may be payable to a current spouse.

- **Railroad Retirement Payroll Taxes:** Currently, all contributions to 401(k) deferred compensation plans are subject to Railroad Retirement payroll taxes. Any 401(k) plans under Railroad Retirement law are now treated the same way as 401(k) plans under Social Security law. The value of employer-paid group-term life insurance premiums that exceed $50,000 are also subject to Railroad Retirement payroll taxes.

- **Special Restrictions for Disability Annuitants:** The amount disabled railroad retirement employee annuitants can earn without reducing their benefits is $400 per month, exclusive of disability-related work expenses. While a disabled employee's annuity is not payable for any month in which he or she earns more than $400 in any employment or self-employment, withheld payments will be restored if earnings for the year are less than $5,000. Otherwise, the annuity is subject to a deduction of one month's benefit for each multiple of $400 earned over $4,800.

■ *Retiring Employees Required to Relinquish Rights to Railroad Jobs:* An employee annuity based on age cannot be paid until the employee terminates railroad employment and gives up any rights to return to work for a railroad employer. Regardless of age and/or earnings, no Railroad Retirement annuity is payable for any month in which a retired employee, spouse or survivor works for a railroad. A disabled annuitant's employment rights are not relinquished until the employee becomes eligible for a supplemental annuity, attains age 65, or the employee's spouse files for an annuity — whichever comes first.

OBTAINING ADDITIONAL INFORMATION

This discussion was intended to give only a brief overview of the many benefits and provisions contained in the Railroad Retirement System. Further information or clarification of the specifics involved in the program, as well as assistance that you may need in determining your benefits, may be obtained from any of the Railroad Retirement Board district offices.

Any of the offices that you may contact will also provide, upon request, several pamphlets that detail the provisions of the Railroad Retirement Act, Medicare's hospital and medical insurance programs, and the provisions of the Railroad Unemployment Insurance Act. This important Act, not discussed in this section, provides benefits to a qualified rail worker who has been without income because of unemployment or illness. Payments may be made only after all other payments, such as salary or vacation pay, have been exhausted. The Railroad Retirement Board also administers the benefits provided by the Railroad Unemployment Insurance Act.

SUMMARY OF RAILROAD RETIREMENT TAXES AND BENEFITS — 1996

Wage Base on Which Railroad Retirement Taxes and Benefits are Calculated: (This is the maximum amount of an employee's compensation on which taxes are paid.) (1) **Tier I**	**$62,700** [**All earnings above $60,600** for Medicare Hospital Insurance (HI) tax]
(2) **Tier II**	**$46,500**
Railroad Retirement Tax Rate: (Percentage of the Wage Base) (1) **Tier I** **Employees and Employers**	**7.65%** on earnings up to $62,700; **1.45%** Medicare (HI) tax on all earnings over $62,700.
(2) **Tier II** **Employees** **Employers**	**4.90%** **16.10%**
Maximum Amount of Annual Regular Retirement Taxes: (total of Tier I and Tier II taxes): (1) **Employees**	**$ 7,075.05**
(2) **Employers**	**$12,283.05**
(Because the Medicare HI tax of 1.45% — included in RR Tier I taxes — applies to all earnings over $62,700, employees earnings over $62,700, and their employers, will pay more in retirement taxes than indicated.)	
Monthly Benefits: Average amount of benefits for: (1) Regular RR employees (per person)	**$ 1,135**
(2) Employee and spouse (combined benefit)	**$ 1,590**
(3) Aged widow (or widower)	**$ 820**

SUMMARY OF RAILROAD RETIREMENT TAXES AND BENEFITS — 1996
(continued)

Cost-of-Living Increase (percent)(*):	
(1) **Tier 1** (Based on the rise in the Consumer Price Index from the 3rd quarter of one year through the 3rd quarter of the next year.)	**2.6%**
(2) **Tier 11** (Represents 32.5 percent of the CPI increase.)	**0.8%**
Lump Sum Death Benefit:	
(1) Average (approximate) benefit payable if deceased worker was credited with 10 years of service **before** Jan. 1, 1975	$ 850
(2) Amount payable when the deceased worker had completed 10 years of railroad service **after** Dec. 31, 1974	$ 255
Retiree Earnings Limit: (This is the maximum amount an individual can earn without having any benefits withheld.)	
(1) Tier I and Vested Dual Benefits	
■ *Under Age 65* (Benefits are reduced by $1 for every $2 of earnings in excess of this amount.)	$ 8,280
■ *Age 65-69* (Benefits are reduced by $1 for every $3 of earnings in excess of this amount.)	$12,500
Important: If 1996 is the first year a Railroad Retirement annuity is payable, deductions in 1996 payments apply *only* to those months in which earnings are more than **$690** for beneficiaries *under age 65*, or over **$960** for those *age 65-69*	
■ *After age 70* (An individual can earn any amount and *not* lose benefits.)	No limit
(2) Tier II and Supplemental Annuity Payments (Generally not subject to earnings deduction.)	No limit

(*) Vested Dual Benefit payments and Supplemental Annuities also paid by the Board are **not** adjusted for the CPI increase.

LISTING

Railroad Retirement Board Offices

The following offices of the Railroad Retirement Board provide either full or part-time service to employees covered under the Railroad Retirement Act, their spouses or survivors. They will assist you by answering questions regarding your annuities, explaining your benefits, providing insurance claim forms and other informational pamphlets as well as assisting you with any retirement problems you may have. You can visit or call any of these district offices for assistance between the hours of 9:00 A.M. and 3:30 P.M.

ALABAMA
950 - 22nd St., Rm. 426
Birmingham, AL 36203
Tel: (205) 731-0019

ARIZONA
522 N. Central
Phoenix. AZ 85002
Tel: (602) 379-4841

ARKANSAS
900 S. Shackleford Rd.,
Suite 512
Little Rock, AR 72211
Tel: (501) 324-5241

CALIFORNIA
1515 W. Cameron Ave., Suite 360
West Covina, CA 91790
Tel: (818) 814-8844

1301 Clay St., Suite 392N
Oakland, CA 94612
Tel: (510) 637-2973

2985 Fulton Ave.
Sacramento, CA 95821
Tel: (916) 979-2055

COLORADO
177 Custom House
20th and Stout Sts.
Denver, CO 80201
Tel: (303) 844-4311

CONNECTICUT
414 Chapel St., Rm. 203
New Haven, CT 06511
Tel: (203) 773-2044

DISTRICT OF COLUMBIA
1310 - G Street, NW
Suite 520
Washington, DC 20005
Tel: (202) 272-7707

FLORIDA
299 E. Broward Bldg., Suite 405
Fort Lauderdale, FL 33301
Tel: (305) 356-7372

400 West Bay St., Rm. 315
Jacksonville, FL 32202
Tel: (904) 232-2546

501 Polk St., Rm. 100
Tampa, FL 33602
Tel: (813) 228-2695

GEORGIA
101 Marietta St., Suite 2306
Atlanta, GA 30323
Tel: (404) 331-2841

124 Barnard St., Rm. B-105
Savannah, GA 31412
Tel: (912) 652-4267

ILLINOIS
844 N. Rush St., Rm. 112
Chicago, IL 60611
Tel: (312) 751-4500

132 S. Water St., Suite 517
Decatur, IL 62525
Tel: (217) 423-9747

101 N. Joliet Street
Joliet, IL 60434
Tel: (815) 740-2101

1615 - 5th Ave., Suite 517
Moline, IL 61265
Tel: (309) 764-0028

INDIANA
1300 S. Harrison St., Rm. 3161
Fort Wayne, IN 46802
Tel: (219) 423-1361

50 S. Meridian, Suite 303
Indianapolis, IN 46204
Tel: (317) 226-6111

IOWA
210 Walnut St., Rm. 921
Des Moines, IA 50309
Tel: (515) 284-4344

KANSAS
444 S.E. Quincy, Rm. 180
Topeka, KS 66683
Tel: (913) 295-2655

155 N. Market St., Rm. 125
Wichita, KS 67202
Tel: (316) 269-7161

KENTUCKY
629 South 4th Ave.
Rm. 301
Louisville, KY 40201
Tel: (502) 582-5208

LOUISIANA
501 Magazine St., Rm 925
New Orleans, LA 70130
Tel: (504) 589-2597

1724 E. 70th St., Rm. C
Shreveport, LA 71105
Tel:(318) 676-3022

MAINE
66 Pearl St.
Portland, ME 04104
Tel: (207) 780-3542

MARYLAND
300 W. Pratt St., Rm. 260
Baltimore, MD 21201
Tel: (410) 962-2550

MASSACHUSETTS
U.S.P.O. & Courthouse Bldg.,
121 High St., Rm 301
Boston. MA 02208
Tel: (617) 424-5790

MICHIGAN
477 W. Mich. Ave., Suite 1990
Detroit, MI 48226
Tel: (313) 226-6221

MINNESOTA
515 W. First St., Rm. 125
Duluth, MN 55802
Tel: (218) 720-5301

180 E. 5th St., Suite 195
St. Paul, MN 55101
Tel: (612) 290-3491

MISSISSIPPI
100 W. Capitol St., Rm. 1003
Jackson, MS 39269
Tel: (601) 965-4229

MISSOURI
601 E. 12th St., Rm., 258
Kansas City, MO 64106
Tel: (816) 426-5884

1222 Spruce St., Rm. 1213
St. Louis, MO 63103
Tel: (314) 539-6220

MONTANA
2900 Fourth Ave., N. - Rm. 101
Billings, MT 59101
Tel: (406) 247-7375

NEBRASKA
106 S. 15th St., Rm. 1011
Omaha, NE 68102
Tel: (402) 221-4641

NEW JERSEY
970 Broad St., Rm. 1435B
Newark. NJ 07102
Tel: (201) 645-3990

NEW MEXICO
300 San Mateo, N.E. - Rm. 401
Albuquerque, NM 87108
Tel: (505) 262-6405

NEW YORK
Clinton Ave. & Pearl Sts., Rm.
264
Albany, NY 12201
Tel: (518) 431-4004

111 W. Huron St., Rm. 1106
Buffalo, NY 14202
Tel: (716) 551-4141

1400 Old Country Road,
Suite 204
Westbury, NY 11590
Tel: (516) 334-5940

26 Federal Plaza, Rm. 3404
New York, NY 10278
Tel: (212) 264-9820

NORTH CAROLINA
800 Briar Creek Rd.,
Rm. AA-405
Charlotte, NC 28218
Tel: (704) 344-6118

NORTH DAKOTA
657 Second Ave., N., Rm. 219
Fargo, ND 58107
Tel: (701) 239-5117

OHIO
36 E. 7th Street, Rm. 201
Cincinnati, OH 45202
Tel: (513) 684-3188

1240 E. 9th St., Rm. 907
Cleveland, OH 44199
Tel: (216) 522-4053

131 N. High St., Rm. 630
Columbus, OH 43215
Tel: (614) 469-5562

234 Summit St., Rm.321
Toledo, OH 43604
Tel: (419) 259-7442

20 Federal Plaza West, Rm. M-11-B
Youngstown, OH 44503
Tel: (216) 746-6338

OKLAHOMA
215 McGee Ave., Rm. 130
Oklahoma City, OK 73102
Tel: (405) 231-4771

OREGON
1220 S.W. 3rd Ave., Rm. 377
Portland, OR 97204
Tel: (503) 326-2143

PENNSYLVANIA
615 Howard Ave., Rm. 209
Altoona, PA 16603
Tel: (814) 946-3601

228 Walnut St., Rm. 504
Harrisburg, PA 17108
Tel: (717) 782-4490

1421 Cherry St., Suite 660
Philadelphia, PA 19102
Tel: (215) 656-6993

100 Forbes Ave., Rm. 775
Pittsburgh, PA 15222.
Tel: (412) 644-2696

Route No. 6 ,Carbondale Hwy.
Scranton, PA 18508
Tel: (717) 346-5774

TENNESSEE
710 Locust St., Rm. 126
Knoxville, TN 37902
Tel: (615) 545-4500

167 N. Main St., Rm. 109
Memphis, TN 38103
Tel: (901) 544-3274

223 Cumberland Bend Dr.,
Nashville, TN 37228
Tel: (615) 736-5131

TEXAS
819 Taylor St., Rm. 10G02
P.O. Box 17420
Ft. Worth, TX 76102
Tel: (817) 334-2638

1919 Smith, Suite 845
Houston, TX 77002
Tel: (713) 653-3045

727 E. Durango, Rm. A-423
San Antonio, TX 78206
Tel: (210) 229-6155

UTAH
125 S. State St., Rm. 1205
Salt Lake City, UT 84147
Tel: (801) 524-5725

VIRGINIA
200 Granby Mall, Rm. 616
Norfolk, VA 23510
Tel: (804) 441-3335

704 E. Franklin St., Suite 232
Richmond, VA 23219
Tel: (804) 771-2997

210 First St., S.W., Suite 460
Roanoke, VA 24002
Tel: (540) 857-2335

WASHINGTON
155 - 108th Ave., N.E., Suite 201
Bellevue, WA 98004
Tel: (206) 553-5483

920 Riverside Ave., Rm. 492
Spokane, WA 99201
Tel: (509) 353-2795

WEST VIRGINIA
640 - 4th Ave., Rm. 112
Huntington, WV 25721
Tel: (304) 529-5561

WISCONSIN
310 W. Wisconsin Ave., Suite 1300
Milwaukee, WI 53203
Tel: (414) 297-3961

Chapter 4

Medicare

What You Should Know About Its Coverage

Chapter Highlights

As in the discussion on Social Security, a special Topic Index immediately follows the introduction to this chapter to facilitate locating items of particular interest to the reader.

Medicare

What You Should Know About Its Coverage

When in 1965, President Johnson signed the Social Security Amendments establishing Medicare, it was the beginning of one of the most important programs available to you today. In 1995, this federal health insurance program provided over $181.5 billion dollars in health care benefits to the elderly and other beneficiaries. It has become the second most costly Federal domestic program — exceeded only by Social Security. Today, with almost one out of every nine Americans insured through Medicare, it has been expanded to provide health insurance coverage not only to individuals 65 years of age and older, but also to people of any age with permanent kidney failure and to many disabled persons. In 1996, there are over 37 million Medicare beneficiaries.

Medicare is administered by the Health Care Financing Administration. However, it is your local Social Security office that takes your application for Medicare, assists you in filing claims and provides information you may need concerning the program. Medicare consists of two separate parts — a **hospital insurance portion**, referred to as **Part A**, and a **medical insurance portion**, called **Part B**. The hospital insurance will help pay for your hospital care and certain follow-up care, such as care received in a skilled nursing home. The medical insurance portion will assist in the payment of your doctor's services and many of the medical services that the hospital insurance does not cover.

Medicare does not cover all of your medical care costs nor was it intended to do so. In fact, older Americans spend as large a percentage of their income on health care needs (15 percent) as they did prior to the existence of Medicare. There will be several costs, called deductibles and copayments, that you will be required to pay. These costs and other factors affecting the care you receive under Medicare will be explained in the following discussions of each portion of your Medicare insurance. The important role of supplemental insurance policies, frequently called "Medigap" policies, which assist you with some of the costs not covered by Medicare is discussed separately in the next chapter.

While reading the information contained in this chapter, keep in mind that you have certain very important rights as a Medicare patient. These rights are yours regardless of your financial circumstances or the severity of your illness or injury. They should not be denied to anyone! They are listed here for you to know and remember well.

Your Rights!

- **The right to receive proper and quality care in the diagnosis and treatment of your illness or injury.**

- **The right to be fully informed about your care, Medicare coverage and the length of your hospital stay.**

- **The right to appeal decisions concerning your care or hospital discharge.**

New State Counseling Services for Medicare and Medicaid Beneficiaries

In late 1993, $10 million in federal grants were given to nearly all 50 states to set up Medicare/Medicaid counseling programs that would help beneficiaries with many of the problems they frequently encounter in dealing with these programs— such as doctors over charging, appeals on Medicare/Medicaid decisions, and rectifying errors in their claims for health care reimbursement. Based on a highly effective volunteer program—the *Medicare/Medicaid Assistance Program (MMAP)*—begun over 16 years ago by the American Association of Retired Persons (AARP), the state programs also offer counseling on obtaining long-term care and Medigap insurance policies plus eligibility requirements for Medicaid. To locate the counseling services in your state, contact your local Area Agency on Aging or your local AARP Chapter for assistance.

Topic Index

MEDICARE AND THE PROSPECTIVE PAYMENT SYSTEM

Before reading this discussion of Medicare, it would be helpful for you to have an understanding of the system under which hospitals are paid by Medicare for the care and services you receive from them.

KEEPING HOSPITAL COSTS UNDER CONTROL

At the time Medicare and Medicaid (a federal-state medical assistance program for the needy) were established, Congress could not have predicted that by 1982 these essential programs for the elderly and disabled would cost the nation over $67 billion in that year alone. Even more shocking was that hospital costs in 1982 accounted for almost two-thirds of the $50.9 billion spent for the Medicare program.

With the rate of hospital costs in 1982 exceeding 300% the rate of inflation, Congress realized that it had to do something to contain them. It passed a bill, which was signed into law by President Reagan in April 1983, establishing what is now known as the Prospective Payment System. This new system completely changed the method by which hospitals are paid for Medicare patients. The Prospective Payment System is in use today, affecting over 5,600 hospitals throughout our country.

Under this method of payment, hospitals are reimbursed for the care they provide to Medicare patients on the basis of a pre-set (fixed) rate for each category of illness or diagnosis. These categories are known as Diagnosis Related Group classifications or simply "DRGs". There are 467 of them which cover the majority of illnesses and injuries. Each DRG classification was determined on the basis of certain physical characteristics, such as age and sex, and on treatment procedures used in the care of a patient. The rates set for each category are updated annually and vary in different areas based on urban or rural settings and the prevailing wage scales. Also, hospitals may receive special additional reimbursements for extraordinarily long hospitalization or expensive patient care.

YOUR HOSPITAL INSURANCE PROTECTION IS NOT AFFECTED!

Of utmost importance to you as a Medicare beneficiary is that this system of payment to hospitals does not change your Medicare hospital insurance protection. Neither is it used to determine the length of your stay in a hospital nor the extent of care you receive.

To ensure that hospitals do not cut back on needed services, on the care of patients or discharge them prematurely to minimize costs, Congress set up safeguards so that patients would not suffer from lack of quality care. The Health Care Financing Administration was instructed to establish *Peer Review Organizations (PRO)* in each state, composed of physicians and other medical professionals, to monitor the performance of hospitals and to ensure that needed medical care is properly provided. In addition, each Peer Review Organization investigates individual patient complaints alleging (a) inadequate care, (b) improper refusal of admission to a hospital, or (c) premature discharge from the hospital. The appeal process will be discussed later in this chapter.

Even though the Prospective Payment System is not a perfect system and has some very important issues of concern associated with it, such as the premature discharge of patients, it is a better system than the one it replaced, which was completely ineffective in controlling hospital costs — thus threatening the solvency of the Medicare program.

LIMITATION ON DOCTOR'S CHARGES

In 1996, federal law prohibits doctors from charging Medicare beneficiaries more than 115 percent of the "Medicare Approved Amounts" for their services. However, there are currently nine states that have laws which could further reduce your medical costs as a beneficiary. If you live in one of the following states, call either your state Office on Aging or the telephone number listed below about the laws in your state.

The nine states with "Charge-Limit" laws are: Connecticut (Toll Free: 800-443-9946); Massachusetts (Toll Free: 800-882-2003); Minnesota (Toll Free: 800-657-3591); New York (Toll Free: 800-342-9871); Ohio (Toll Free: 800-899-7127); Pennsylvania (Tel: (717)783-8975; Rhode Island (Toll Free: 800-322-2880); and Vermont (Toll Free: 800-642-5119).

MEDICARE HOSPITAL INSURANCE (PART A)

Eligibility Requirements for Premium-Free Insurance — Since this portion of your insurance is financed through part of the Social Security taxes you paid while you were working, you are automatically eligible at age 65 at no cost (premium-free) to you if (1) you are entitled to Social Security or Railroad Retirement benefits; or (2) you have worked long enough to be insured under Social Security or the Railroad Retirement system; or (3) you are eligible for Medicare through your federal employment.

Even if you have not reached the age of 65, you are also eligible if (1) you have been entitled to Social Security disability benefits for 24 months or (2) have worked long enough in federal employment and meet the requirements of the disability program. Those who are entitled to a Railroad disability annuity or retirement benefits based on disability, may also be eligible for the hospital insurance. They should contact their Railroad Retirement office.

In addition, certain other individuals may be eligible for hospital insurance. They include a spouse, divorced spouse, widow or widower, or dependent parents age 65 or older; disabled widows or widowers, disabled divorced spouses under the age of 65 and disabled children 18 years or older.

Those in need of maintenance dialysis or a kidney transplant due to kidney failure are eligible for premium-free hospital insurance at any age. They should inquire of their Social Security or Railroad Retirement office as to how they may qualify.

Coverage for Those Not Eligible for Premium-Free Insurance — Any individual who does not meet the basic eligibility requirements described but attains the age of 65, can purchase Medicare hospital insurance (Part A). The **monthly premium** for 1996 is $289 which, though expensive, may be the only hospital insurance that some individuals can obtain because of their age or health. There is also a requirement that these individuals must enroll and pay the monthly premium in 1996 of $42.50 for the Part B medical insurance portion.

Your Enrollment — If you are already receiving Social Security or Railroad Retirement checks, your hospital insurance protection should start automatically at the age of 65. All others will have to apply for enrollment. They should contact their local Social Security or Railroad Retirement office well in advance of their 65th birthday, so there is no delay in coverage from their time of eligibility.

WHAT MEDICARE HOSPITAL INSURANCE COVERS

Your hospital insurance will help pay for inpatient hospital care, as well as care provided in a skilled nursing facility, your home or a hospice. It does not include your doctor's services, since they are covered under Medicare's medical insurance (Part B).

A skilled nursing facility is one that is certified by its state as a qualified facility, or nursing home with the capability to provide skilled nursing care, rehabilitative services, and other specialized related health services. For Medicare certification, it must also meet requirements of the Health Care Financing Administration and be approved for Medicare payment. In this regard, most nursing homes are not considered skilled nursing facilities. Also, there are hospitals and hospices, referred to as "non-participating," that are not approved for payment by Medicare. **Always** ensure that the hospital, skilled nursing home or hospice you choose is approved for participation in the Medicare program before using any of its services.

The amount that Medicare hospital insurance pays is limited by a specific period of time which is known as a "benefit period." This is simply a way of measuring the use of services and determining your share of the costs (copayments) for your medical care. A benefit period starts when you enter a hospital or skilled nursing facility and ends when you are discharged and have been out for 60 days in a row. Your hospital insurance protection is **renewed** every time you begin a new benefit period. There is no limit on the number of benefit periods you can have for hospital or skilled nursing facility care.

When You Are Hospitalized (Inpatient Hospital Care) — When you are hospitalized, Medicare will help pay for up to 90 days of your hospitalization costs in each benefit period. During the first 60 days it pays for all covered services except the first $736. This is the hospital insurance deductible that you are responsible for paying. You pay this deductible only once in each benefit period even if you are discharged and readmitted before the benefit period ends. For the 61st through 90th day, you must pay $184 a day; Medicare pays the rest.

Unusually Long Hospital Stays — When you are hospitalized for more than 90 days in any benefit period, you have available for use what are called reserve days. For each **reserve** day you use, you are required to pay $368 per day and Medicare pays the rest. Medicare hospital insurance provides you with 60 reserve days throughout your lifetime to help pay for an unusually long hospital stay. Once a reserve day is used, you never get it back. They are not renewable. You may use these reserve days at your own discretion. However, when you decide not to use any of your reserve days, you must notify the hospital in writing ahead of time. If you do not let the hospital know in advance, the extra days of hospitalization will automatically be taken from your reserve days. Patients who have private insurance that covers payment for extended hospitalization may elect to save their reserve days for future use when they might not have this private coverage.

What Medicare Pays for Those Who are Hospitalized — Medicare will help pay for the following services and supplies when you are hospitalized:

- A semiprivate room (extra charges for a private room may also be covered if the room is determined to be medically necessary for the care of the patient);
- All regular nursing services except those of private duty nurses;
- All meals, including special diets;
- Costs of an intensive care unit, coronary care unit or other special care unit;
- Drugs furnished by the hospital during your stay;
- Blood transfusions furnished by the hospital except for the first three pints of blood in **each** benefit period;
- Laboratory tests, X-rays and other radiology services, including radiation therapy billed by the hospital;
- Medical supplies such as casts and surgical dressings;
- Use of medical equipment or appliances, such as a wheelchair;
- Rehabilitation services, such as physical therapy, occupational therapy, and speech pathology services;
- Operating and recovery room costs, including hospital costs for anesthesia services. However, charges for the doctor (anesthe-

siologist) or the nurse (anesthetist) who administers the anesthesia are covered under the medical insurance portion (Part B) of Medicare and consequently, are generally billed separately from hospital costs. Anesthetists are registered nurses who have taken postgraduate study in anesthesia and have passed the required exam for certification. Nurse anesthetists perform about half of all anesthesias in the U.S.

Limited Coverage in a Psychiatric Hospital — Your hospital insurance portion of Medicare will pay for up to 190 days of care in a participating psychiatric hospital throughout your lifetime. Coverage by Medicare and any copayments you are required to pay are the same as with any other hospitalization throughout the 190 days of care you may receive in a psychiatric hospital. However, your 60 reserve days **cannot** be used for any stay in a psychiatric hospital.

Skilled Nursing Facility Care **(Nursing Home)** — After a hospital stay, Medicare hospital insurance will help pay for up to 100 days of care in a participating skilled nursing facility, if your doctor determines you need special skilled nursing or rehabilitation services. Your hospital insurance will pay for all covered services for the first 20 days. From the 21st through 100th day, it will pay all covered charges except for $92 per day which you must pay. Covered services in these facilities include:

- semiprivate rooms
- all meals
- regular nursing services
- rehabilitation services
- blood transfusions, except the first three pints of blood
- drugs
- medical supplies and appliances, such as wheelchairs.

IMPORTANT: If you are not certain whether a nursing home is a skilled-nursing facility or if it is approved by Medicare, ask someone in the facilities business/administration office. If you have additional questions, call Social Security and they will contact the Health Care Financing Administration to obtain the answers.

Home Health Care — Even though home health care coverage is limited, either your Medicare hospital insurance or medical insurance will pay for the approved cost of unlimited home visits from a participating home health agency when you are confined to your home.

For you to be eligible, your doctor must certify that you need home health care. Also, the doctor must prescribe a home health care plan which includes part-time skilled nursing care, physical therapy, or speech therapy.

Currently, Medicare will cover up to 21 days of daily care with a maximum of 35 hours per week. If needed, intermittent care will be covered after this initial period if all of the requirements for home health care continue to be met.

The 35 hours per week can include not only skilled nursing care but also help in bathing, dressing, grooming, toileting, eating, exercising, walking, and changing bed linens. Anyone who needs more than the 35 hours will have to obtain privately paid care since Medicare will not cover above this amount.

Covered home services include part-time skilled nursing care, physical therapy, speech therapy, home health aides, occupational therapy, part-time services of home health aides, medical social services, medical supplies and durable medical equipment. In addition, Medicare will pay 80 percent of the approved costs for durable medical equipment.

Hospice Care to Help the Terminally Ill — Medicare hospital insurance will help pay for hospice care for terminally ill people if the care is provided by a Medicare-certified hospice. Additionally, the patient must elect to receive hospice care instead of other medical care. This type of care may be either at a hospice facility or at the home of the patient. Be certain that the hospice organization you select is approved for Medicare payment before agreeing to receive their care.

Hospice care basically includes pain relief, symptom management and most support services. Medicare will pay for this care *for as long as a doctor certifies the need.* There is full Medicare coverage for the following hospice services:

- nursing services
- doctors' service provided under the hospice program
- drugs, including outpatient drugs for pain relief and symptom management
- physical therapy, occupational therapy and speech pathology services

- home health aide and homemaker services

- medical social services

- medical supplies and appliances

- short-term inpatient care, including respite care

- counseling.

In addition, your insurance will pay part of the cost of outpatient drugs and inpatient respite care. The patient is responsible for 5 percent of the cost of outpatient drugs or $5 toward each prescription, whichever is less. Respite care is a short-term inpatient stay in order to give time off to the individual who regularly assists in the home care of the patient. For inpatient respite care, the patient pays five percent of the Medicare allowed rate. Although it varies slightly depending on the area of the country, in 1996, the *approximate* cost is $5 per day. Although it is limited to stays of no more than five days in a row, respite care helps provide a much needed rest to those who have the continual responsibility of caring for the patient.

MEDICARE MEDICAL INSURANCE (PART B)

The medical portion of your Medicare insurance will help pay for doctors' services, outpatient hospital care, outpatient physical therapy and speech pathology services, home health care and other health services and supplies which are not covered by the hospital insurance portion. The majority of services generally needed by individuals with permanent kidney failure are covered only by the medical portion (Part B) of Medicare insurance.

Payment for your approved medical care under this portion of your Medicare insurance follows the same basic guidelines. After you meet the annual medical insurance deductible of $100, Medicare will pay 80 percent of the approved charges for the care and services you receive throughout the year. You pay the remaining 20 percent of the approved charges, which is called a copayment.

Eligibility and Enrollment — Since there are no requirements other than age to obtain this portion of your Medicare, anyone 65 or older can enroll in Medicare **medical** insurance. Enrollees must pay a monthly premium, which may vary upward depending upon the time they enroll. In 1996, the basic monthly insurance premium is $42.50.

Be aware that there is a special provision, called the *Variable Insurance Premium*, which ensures that individuals — in particular, low-income individuals — will not have their net Social Security benefit checks reduced because of an increase in the Medicare medical premium from one year to the next.

Individuals who receive Social Security or Railroad Retirement benefits are automatically enrolled in Medicare medical insurance at the same time they become entitled to Medicare hospital insurance — unless they contact their Social Security or Railroad Retirement office and request otherwise. All other persons should apply for medical insurance as soon as they are eligible by contacting their local Social Security or Railroad Retirement office. By applying as soon as you are eligible, you avoid paying costs higher then the basic premium.

Specific Enrollment Periods — Medicare medical insurance differs from Medicare hospital insurance because medical insurance has specified enrollment periods. Three months before you first become eligible for medical insurance, a seven-month enrollment period begins, lasting through the third month after your eligibility begins. If you enroll during the three months before you are eligible, your insurance protection begins immediately on the day you are eligible. If you enroll during the months after you become eligible, coverage will start one-to-three months from the date of enrollment.

There is also a general enrollment period from January 1 through March 31 each year. You can enroll during this period if: (1) you have never had Medicare medical insurance, or (2) if you had the medical insurance but cancelled it. However, if you wait to enroll during the general enrollment period (unless your eligibility period coincides with the January 1-March 31 period), your premium will be 10 percent higher than the basic premium for each 12 month period you were eligible but not enrolled. If you enroll during the general period, medical insurance coverage starts during the following July.

The late enrollment penalty does not apply to workers aged 65 or older (and their spouses aged 65 or older) who are covered by an employer's group health insurance plan. In 1986, this late enrollment penalty waiver was extended to include workers aged 70 and older; previously, workers had to fall in the 65-70 year range. Under the waiver rule, the seven-month enrollment period begins when the employer's health insurance coverage ends or when the employee retires, whichever comes first. Thus, even if the employee became eligible for medical insurance according to Medicare's age requirements, no penalty will apply for the months the employee is covered by the employer's group health insurance.

The 1986 ruling also amended the prior requirement that the enrollee be covered by both the employer's group insurance and Medicare hospital insurance for the penalty to be waived. Now, the enrollee need only be covered by the employer's group health insurance to avoid the late enrollment penalty. Under the new rule, anyone currently paying a premium penalty under the old law can have the penalty reduced or removed if such an action is allowed by the 1986 ruling. Contact your Social Security office to apply for a premium change if the new ruling is applicable to you.

ONCE YOU ARE ENROLLED

After you have been enrolled in Medicare Part A, Part B, or both, you will receive a health insurance card which you should guard as carefully as one of your credit cards. Your insurance card shows the Medicare insurance protection you have, the date your protection began and your health insurance claim number. All enrollees, including spouses or dependents, receive separate insurance cards and different claim numbers. In most cases, your claim number will be your Social Security number with a capital letter added at the end of it. **Always carry your card!** Its information is needed for you to receive services covered by Medicare.

SERVICES COVERED BY MEDICAL INSURANCE (PART B)

With certain conditions or limitations, the following medical services and supplies are covered by your medical insurance:

Physician Services
- Your doctors' services received in their offices, in a hospital, in a skilled nursing facility, in your home or any other location in the U.S. These services include: medical and surgical care including anesthesia, diagnostic tests and procedures that are part of your treatment, radiology and pathology services provided by doctors to hospital inpatients;

- Cosmetic surgical care and services which are required due to an accidental injury or to improve the functioning of a malformed part of the body;

- A second doctor's opinion concerning a recommended surgery;

- Covered inpatient care by a physician in a Canadian or Mexican hospital under specified circumstances.

Outpatient Services
- Outpatient **hospital** services which include:
  — services in an emergency room or outpatient clinic
  — laboratory tests billed by the hospital
  — X-rays and other radiology services billed by the hospital
  — radiation therapy given under the supervision of a doctor
  — medical supplies such as splints and casts
  — drugs and biologicals which cannot be self-administered
  — blood transfusions furnished to you as an outpatient;

- Certain outpatient surgical procedures performed in a Medicare certified **outpatient surgical center**;

- Medically necessary outpatient physical therapy or speech pathology services;

- Outpatient services from a comprehensive outpatient rehabilitation facility (CORF). These are facilities which provide skilled rehabilitation services and are approved for Medicare payment. Covered services include physicians' services, physical, speech, occupational and respiratory services and therapies, counseling and other related services;

- Covered diagnostic tests and services provided by an independent laboratory that accepts Medicare assignment;

- Outpatient treatment of a mental illness;

- Rural health clinic services;

- Emergency outpatient care from a **non-participating** hospital if it is the nearest hospital equipped to handle the emergency.

Services from Other Medical Professionals
- Dental care when it involves (1) surgery of the jaw or related structures or (2) setting fractures of the jaw or facial bones or (3) services that would be covered when provided by a doctor;

- Optometrists' services for examinations related to the condition of aphakia, the absence of the natural lens of the eye;

- Chiropractor's manual manipulation of the spine to correct a subluxation that can be demonstrated by X-ray (this is the only chiropractor treatment that is covered);

- Covered services for foot care by a licensed podiatrist.

Special Items of Coverage

- Pap smears (cervical cancer screening) every three years;

- Mammograms every other year for Medicare beneficiaries 65 and older. Disabled Medicare beneficiaries ages 35 through 39 can get one baseline mammogram while those 40 to 49 can obtain one screening every two years. If a person is at high risk for breast cancer, they can receive *yearly* exams;

- Pneumococcal vaccination and any immunizations required because of an injury or immediate risk of infection, such as the Hepatitis B vaccine (cost of these immunizations is covered whether or not the Part B annual deductible has been met);

- Artificial limbs and eyes;

- Prosthetic devices needed to substitute for an internal body organ, including heart pacemakers, corrected lenses needed after a cataract operation, colostomy or ileostomy bags and other related supplies, breast prostheses as well as surgical brassieres after a mastectomy;

- Doctor-ordered portable diagnostic X-ray services in the home;

- Ambulance transportation when the ambulance, equipment and personnel meet Medicare requirements and when transportation in any other vehicle could endanger the patient's health (Medicare does not pay for ambulance use from your home to a doctor's office);

- Unlimited number of pints of blood or units of red blood cells — except for the first three pints or units in each calendar year;

- Can pay for insertion of a cochlear implant within the ear. This implant is frequently referred to as an "artificial ear" which can simulate hearing in deaf people with intact auditory nerves.

Medical Supplies and Equipment

- Drugs and biologicals that **cannot** be self-administered;

- Orthopedic shoes when they are part of a leg brace;

- Arm, leg, back and neck braces;

- Certain surgical dressings, splints, casts and similar medical supplies;

- Durable medical equipment, either rented or purchased, whichever is less costly to you and Medicare, as determined by the Medicare Insurance Carrier. Durable medical equipment consists of items that can be used repeatedly but which are not generally useful to an individual when there is no longer an injury, or illness. Examples include home dialysis systems, wheelchairs, oxygen equipment, patient lifts, overbed trapezes, walkers, suction machines, positive pressure breathing machines, safety side rails, bedside commodes, crutches, canes, aerosol therapy units and hospital beds.

OBTAINING A SECOND OPINION

Since Medicare will pay in the majority of cases for the opinion of a second doctor regarding surgery your doctor has recommended, it is advisable to obtain a second opinion before agreeing to the surgery unless it is an emergency situation and time is of the essence.

Obtaining a second opinion does not mean you do not have confidence in your doctor, but rather that you want to make certain you have examined all possible alternatives in relation to the risks, costs, discomfort or possible side effects of the surgery.

Most doctors understand your concerns and will suggest that you obtain another doctor's opinion before making a final decision. In fact, they will probably suggest the name of another doctor to contact for a second opinion. Other sources for recommendations may include your friends and relatives, family physician or internist, a local physician referral service of your hospital or the surgical department of a nearby medical school or center.

A SPECIAL PROVISION FOR OLDER PEOPLE WHO ARE STILL EMPLOYED

If you are 65 or older and either you or your spouse is working, a special rule administered by the Equal Employment Opportunity Commission may be applicable to you. The rule states an employer with 20 or more employees must offer his employees and their spouses who are 65 and older the same health insurance plan that it provides for its younger employees.

You may either accept or reject the plan offered by your employer. If you accept the employer's plan, it becomes your primary insurer which means that it pays first for any covered health care service you may receive. If you are eligible for Medicare hospital insurance (Part A), you should also enroll in it, since it does not cost you anything and may pay secondary benefits for some services that your employer's plan did not completely pay. Your decision on whether to enroll in or keep Medicare's medical insurance (Part B), which requires payment of a monthly premium, should be based on how fully your employer's plan covers your medical care costs. As previously discussed in this chapter, there is a "no penalty" rule for delayed enrollment in Medicare's medical insurance (Part B) for those employed individuals, 65 or over, who have an employer's health insurance plan.

If you elect Medicare as your primary insurer, your employer's plan cannot pay supplemental benefits for Medicare covered services. The employer's plan can provide coverage only for those services that are not covered by Medicare, such as prescription drugs and routine dental care.

Your employer should furnish you the information you need concerning your coverage under the private group plan; however, you should contact either your local Social Security or Railroad Retirement office, as appropriate, for further information on how your Medicare insurance benefits are affected by an employer's group plan.

WHAT MEDICARE DOES NOT COVER

Many services and supplies that you need for your care or rehabilitation may not be covered by either portion of your Medicare insurance. Foremost among these is what Medicare considers: (1) custodial care, (2) care that is not considered reasonable and necessary, (3) health care organizations and professionals that are not approved for Medicare payments (referred to as "non-participating"), and (4) care provided in a foreign hospital, except in a Canadian or Mexican hospital under specified situations. Puerto Rico, the Virgin Islands, Guam, American Samoa, and the Northern Mariana Islands are considered part of the United States.

"Custodial care" is care given by individuals without professional skills or training who are, however, able to fulfill the patient's personal needs, such as bathing, dressing, walking, feeding and giving medicines. At present, most of the care provided to individuals suffering from Alzheimer's disease is considered custodial and is **not** covered by Medicare.

In many cases, the phrase "care that is not reasonable and necessary" is subjective and requires a determination of eligibility by Medicare intermediaries, carriers, or the Peer Review Organizations in each state. This determination will take several factors into account, the most important of which is the patient's total physical condition and whether medical personnel are needed to assist in the care of the patient.

In some cases where Medicare disclaims all liability, it will not pay for **any** of your medical costs. The following are the most significant situations in which Medicare does not provide coverage:

- When you are awarded workers' compensation for a job-related illness or injury (your workers' compensation is responsible for paying for all related health care services);
- When you are eligible for a Federal Black Lung payment, which includes payment of medical services needed to treat the ailment;
- When you are covered by the Veterans Administration for treatment of a service-connected illness or injury;
- When any other government or military health program pays for the medical care and supplies.

Medicare may assume a **secondary** payer responsibility in the following circumstances:

- When your eligibility for Medicare insurance is based on a kidney disease that requires dialysis or a kidney transplant; in this case your employer's health insurance plan is generally the primary payer during a specified 12 month period.

- When you are in an accident, your automobile insurance medical coverage, or the other driver's insurance, no fault insurance or other liability insurance may be the first to pay your medical care costs.

- If you or your spouse are over 65 and working, either employer's health plan may be the primary payer.

When any of these circumstances occur, you should contact your Social Security or Railroad Retirement office concerning your coverage under Medicare in order to avoid any misunderstanding or delay in payment of your medical costs.

SERVICES AND SUPPLIES NOT COVERED BY MEDICARE

Some frequently used services and supplies for which Medicare does not usually pay are:

- **prescription drugs** and other medications,

- **routine physical examinations** and any **tests** related to them (except for the coverage provided for pap smears and mammograms),

- **dentures** and **routine dental care**,

- **eyeglasses** and **hearing aids**, and examinations to prescribe or fit them,

- **private duty nurses**, **cosmetic surgery**,

- **the first three pints of blood** used under either medical or hospital insurance. Non-coverage is a very important aspect of your insurance protection and is explained further in the next section.

TRANSPLANT COVERAGE

Heart transplants, though performed with increasing frequency in recent years, are not covered by Medicare **except** for those patients who can meet the provisions and stringent requirements established by the Department of Health and Human Services (DHHS). In addition, recently the DHHS announced that adult liver transplants for **certain conditions** will be covered by Medicare in a hospital approved for such transplants.

REPLACING BLOOD

As previously indicated, either your hospital or medical insurance will help pay for the whole blood, units of packed red blood cells, or blood components that you may need. This payment also includes any costs for administration, blood processing and storage. When you receive blood in a hospital or from a facility approved under your hospital insurance, Medicare will pay, in each benefit period, for all of the blood costs except for the first three pints of blood. You are responsible for either replacing these three pints or for paying a nonreplacement fee.

Replacement blood can be from yourself, from another person, or obtained via coverage from any blood assurance plan you have that replaces the blood for you.

The cost of any blood that you receive as an outpatient or as part of the other covered services under Medicare's medical insurance is paid by Medicare in the same way as all other services covered under Part B, except for nonreplacement fees for the first three pints of blood received in each calendar year. Starting with the fourth pint of blood, Medicare's medical insurance will pay 80 percent of the approved charges for all blood used after you have met Part B's $100 annual deductible.

MEDICARE COVERAGE OF FEDERAL EMPLOYEES

Since January 1983 all federal and postal employees and members of Congress have been covered under Medicare and pay the hospital insurance tax portion of Social Security. They are eligible for Medicare hospital insurance at age 65 once they have enough quarters of work coverage. Their federal employment in and after 1983 will count towards their eligibility for the hospital insurance protection in the same way that other work covered by Social Security counts. Also, those federal employees on an agency's rolls in January 1983 may credit **any** prior federal service toward Medicare eligibility **if** it is needed to qualify for hospital insurance.

The following table shows the number of quarters a federal employee must work to be eligible at age 65:

If you reach 65 in:	Number of quarters of coverage needed:
1986-1989	32
1990-1993	36
1994 or later	40

Federal employees can qualify for hospital insurance before age 65 if they become disabled and meet the specific eligibility requirements of the Social Security disability insurance programs. Those who need kidney dialysis or a kidney transplant due to permanent kidney failure, and have enough quarters of coverage, are eligible at any age for hospital insurance. Also, under certain conditions, spouses or other family members of federal employees may be entitled to Medicare's hospital insurance protection.

At the same time they become entitled to hospital insurance, federal employees can also enroll in the medical insurance portion of Medicare (Part B) and pay the required monthly premium. They do not need any quarters of coverage to be eligible for voluntary medical insurance.

For those individuals age 65 or older who are still employed by the federal government, their Government Employee's Health Plan is the primary insurer and payer of medical care and services within the limits of the plan. Medicare is the secondary payer of these costs.

It is not possible to cover here all matters concerning federal employees and their Medicare coverage. Therefore, you should address any questions that arise to either your local Social Security office or your agency's personnel office.

ELIGIBILITY FOR BOTH MEDICARE AND VETERANS BENEFITS

If you are eligible for both Medicare and veterans' health benefits, you may choose to get treatment under either program. However, you must be aware of the following concerning the payment for care and services provided to you:

■ Medicare cannot pay for services you receive from Veterans Affairs (VA) hospitals or other VA facilities, except for certain emergency hospital services; and

■ Medicare generally cannot pay if the VA pays for VA-authorized services that you get in a non-VA hospital or from a non-VA physician.

Since July 1986, the VA has been charging some veterans who have non-service connected conditions coinsurance for treatment in a VA hospital or medical facility, or for VA-authorized treatment by non-VA sources. The VA charges coinsurance when the veteran's income exceeds a particular level. If the VA charges you coinsurance for VA-authorized care by a non-VA physician or hospital, Medicare may be able to reimburse you, in whole or in part, for your VA coinsurance obligation.

Important: Medicare cannot reimburse you for VA coinsurance for services furnished by VA hospitals and facilities, unless the services are emergency inpatient or outpatient hospital services. Then, the Medicare payment is subject to Medicare deductible and coinsurance amounts.

Any questions about whether the VA or Medicare should pay for your doctor and other Medicare medical services should be directed to your Medicare carrier.

BE AWARE, YOU COULD LOSE YOUR MEDICARE COVERAGE!

In certain circumstances, your Medicare coverage can abruptly end. You could lose your Medicare hospital insurance (Part A) protection under any one of the following conditions:

- If you are entitled to Social Security benefits on your spouse's work record, your protection will end if your entitlement to those benefits ends.

- When you have hospital insurance as the spouse of a federal employee, your protection will end if you divorce before your marriage has lasted 10 years. If you have insurance based on your own Social Security work record or your own federal employment, this rule does not apply to you since your benefits are not affected by a divorce.

- If you are buying the hospital insurance portion of Medicare, your protection will end if you cancel your medical insurance portion. However, you **can cancel** your hospital insurance (Part A) and still continue your medical insurance (Part B).

- Your Medicare medical insurance (Part B) protection will end if:
  — your premiums are not paid;
  — you voluntarily cancel the insurance.

HOSPITAL AND MEDICAL INSURANCE CLAIMS

The Health Care Financing Administration contracts with private insurance organizations in each state to handle Medicare payments for the medical services and supplies you receive as a Medicare beneficiary. The organizations which handle hospital insurance claims (Part A) from hospitals, skilled nursing facilities, home health agencies and hospices are called **intermediaries**. Those organizations under contract with the government for handling medical insurance claims (Part B) for a specific geographical area are called **carriers**.

In general, insurance claims for care you received under your hospital insurance are submitted to the intermediary by the hospital or facility where you received your care. After the intermediary has reviewed the claim, you will be mailed a "Medicare Benefits" notice explaining the decision made on the claim, the services Medicare paid, and the amount of your copayments. Be sure to keep all notices you receive to ensure that you have a complete record showing paid deductibles, services received during each benefit period, and reserve days that you may have used.

As of September 1, 1990, all doctors, supplies and other providers of services must submit Medicare claims for you for all covered services under Medicare medical insurance (Part B). Also, they must submit the claims within one year of providing the care, service or item to you.

Important: You should notify your Medicare carrier if your doctor or supplier refuses to submit a Part B Medicare claim for services furnished on or after September 1, 1990 if you believe those services may be covered by Medicare.

For Medicare *medical insurance* claims, there are two methods of payment. The first method is called *assignment*. This is when a doctor or supplier agrees that the total charge for any covered service will be no more than the charge approved by Medicare. Under assignment, you cannot be billed for more than 20% of Medicare's approved charge, regardless of the actual amount of the bill; Medicare pays the other 80% after you satisfy the annual deductible. In order to avoid any possible discrepancies concerning the fulfillment of your $100 deductible, you should save every receipt you receive for paid medical expenses that are covered by your Medicare medical insurance portion.

The second method of payment is called *non-participating*. This occurs when the doctor or supplier does not accept assignment and bills you for his or her actual charge. This amount is almost always more than the charge normally approved by Medicare. When this occurs, Medicare still pays 80% of the approved charge after you meet the yearly deductible, but you can be billed for more than the charge approved by Medicare. The law limits the amount doctors can bill patients in excess of the Medicare approved fee to **115%** in 1996. Although the doctor or supplier does not accept assignment, he/she must still submit your claim to Medicare in accordance with the new law.

For example, if your doctor does not accept assignment and charges you $230 for a procedure that Medicare has limited to an approved amount of $200, you would have to pay $30 above your regular copayment charge of $40 (20 percent of the approved $200 Medicare charge). This example assumes you have already met your annual deductible of $100. The total that you would have to pay is $70 which is $30 more than if your doctor accepted assignment of Medicare charges. You can readily see why it is to your financial advantage to find a doctor or supplier who will accept assignment on all Medicare claims.

"Medicare-Participating" doctors or suppliers are those who accept assignment. Always ask your physicians or suppliers if they accept assignment, or check with your local Social Security office or your State and Area Offices on Aging for the names of those who do. These offices maintain a "Medicare-Participating Physician/Supplier" directory of the doctors and suppliers in your area accepting assignment. This directory can also be ordered, *free,* from the carrier servicing your Medicare Part B claims.

FILING BY BENEFICIARIES OF UNASSIGNED PART B CLAIMS

There will be times when you may need to file your own Medicare Part B claims, called "unassigned claims." These claims would include the following:

- Services provided before September 1, 1990;

- Services not covered by Medicare for which you want a formal Part B coverage determination;

- Services provided on or after September 1, 1990 that your doctor or supplier refuses to submit for you, even though submission is required by law;

- Services provided outside the United States (Medicare coverage of services outside the United States is very limited and must meet special rules);

- Used durable medical equipment purchased from a private source.

The form used to submit your claim is called "A Patient's Request for Medicare Payment" (Form 1490S). You can obtain this form directly from your Medicare carrier.

When completing the claim form, you should fill in each section as indicated on the back of the form in order to avoid delays in processing your claim. The most common mistakes made by individuals submitting claims that result in delays are:

- failure to sign the claim form;

- failure to include the Medicare claim number, including the letter at the end of the number;

- failure to send the claim to the correct carrier's address;

- failure to send an itemized bill.

Keep a copy of all claims and itemized bills for your records in case there is a need to inquire about your claim. The listing at the end of this chapter contains the various state carriers, their addresses and telephone numbers. Be sure to send your claim to the carrier in the area where you received the services. If you need further assistance, contact your carrier or Social Security office.

All individuals who are entitled to Medicare under the Railroad Retirement system must send their claims to the Travelers Insurance Company offices for their area. A list of these offices follows the listing of the state Medicare carriers.

BE SURE YOU ARE BILLED ONLY FOR CARE YOU RECEIVED

As health care costs rise, so do your costs for Medicare coverage. One way to help keep these costs down is to carefully review every medical bill you receive from any health care provider or supplier and every explanation of benefits form you receive for a submitted claim. This procedure can help uncover possible fraud or inaccurate billing which significantly increase the costs of the Medicare program.

In your review, look for the discrepancies that might appear and be sure that they are corrected or, if necessary, report them to the Medicare intermediary (Part A claims) or carrier (Part B claims) that handles your claims. If either do not respond adequately to your report of fraud or abuse, you should call the DHHS Office of Inspector General toll-free Hotline — **800-368-5779**.

Here are some common discrepancies to be aware of in the review of your billing:

- You are billed for certain services or supplies you never received.

- The number of billed services or supplies is greater than those you actually received, including the period of time you may have rented any durable medical equipment.

- The charges are greater than you generally paid for the same service or supplies in the past.

- A duplication of a billing has been submitted for payment.

TIMELY SUBMISSION OF MEDICARE CLAIMS

All claims must be submitted within specific time limits. You always have at least 15 months in which to submit claim. In some cases you have up to 27 months to send in claims. However, it is advisable to submit claims as the bills are received. The time limits shown here are currently approved time limits. Be sure your doctor or supplier submits any claims for you within these limits:

Services Received Between:	Claims Must Be Submitted By:
Oct. 1, 1993 and Sept. 30, 1994	Dec. 31, 1995
Oct. 1, 1994 and Sept. 30, 1995	Dec. 31, 1996
Oct. 1, 1995 and Sept. 30, 1996	Dec. 31, 1997

MEDICARE CLAIMS FOR SOMEONE WHO DIES

Generally, you do not have to be concerned about filing hospital insurance claims for someone who dies since these claims are submitted by the hospital, facility, agency or hospice that was providing the covered services at the time of the death. Payment will be made directly to the facility, as with all other hospital insurance claims.

However, for claims under Medicare's medical insurance, there are special provisions and rules for submitting claims for a patient who dies. Basically, these provisions cover the following two categories:

- ***When a bill has already been paid***. If a bill was paid by the patient or with funds from the patient's estate, payment will be made either to the estate's representative or to a surviving member of the immediate family. When you or someone else has paid the bill for the patient, payment can be made, upon submission of a claim, directly to you or to the person who paid the bill.

- ***When a bill has not been paid***. If the doctor or supplier has not submitted a claim for the deceased person, the individual who has the legal obligation to pay the bill for the deceased person may submit the medical insurance claim either before or after paying the bill. Medical insurance payment will be made directly to that person.

Keep a Record and Seek Assistance — The payment of any amount that was not paid by Medicare, or copayments that are due, must be paid either from the deceased's estate or by the individual who has the legal obligation to pay these charges. Consequently, if you are responsible for these additional payments, you should maintain a record of all bills that have been paid and any bills not paid for which a claim must be submitted.

It is advisable to contact your Social Security or Railroad Retirement office for assistance whenever you are responsible for handling the claims of a deceased beneficiary.

APPEALING AN UNFAVORABLE DECISION — IT'S YOUR RIGHT

Whenever you disagree with a decision regarding your medical or hospital care under Medicare coverage, you have the right to appeal the decision. Understanding the various courses of appeal that are available to you is essential to properly exercising this right.

Hospital Insurance Appeals (**Medicare Part A**) — Of particular concern to many Medicare beneficiaries is that they may be discharged from a hospital while still needing the hospital's care. Currently the Health Care Financing Administration requires that all Medicare patients, upon admission to a hospital, receive notice of their rights while a hospital patient. This includes hospital care, discharge rights and appeal procedures. In addition, Medicare requires that hospitals inform patients at least 48 hours (two full days) in advance of a scheduled discharge.

If you receive a discharge notice and feel you are being discharged too soon, you or someone authorized to represent you should **immediately** notify your state's Peer Review Organization that you want to appeal the discharge. See the PRO listing found at the end of this chapter. These organizations are under contract with Medicare to review hospital treatment of Medicare patients. They are required to review your case and arrive at a decision within three working days after having received your appeal. If their decision supports your request for continued hospitalization, you can remain in the hospital under Medicare payments until the next discharge decision is reached. However, if the Peer Review Organization denies your request, you become liable for all hospital costs starting the third day after receiving the original written notice of your pending discharge. Thus, it is **critical that you appeal immediately** upon receipt of your notice.

Your Peer Review Organization should also be contacted whenever you have been denied Medicare coverage for admission to a hospital or if you feel you are receiving inadequate hospital care or services.

Whenever you disagree with any decision of the Peer Review Organization, you can request a hearing by an Administrative Law Judge of the Social Security Administration, if the amount in question is $200 or more. Your appeal request must be submitted in writing within 60 days of the decision. If the decision is still unsatisfactory to you, and the amount involved is $2,000 or more, you can appeal to a Federal Court; otherwise the decision by the Administrative Law Judge is final.

Appeals of decisions regarding hospital insurance coverage involving (1) a skilled nursing facility, (2) home health care, or (3) hospice care, should be submitted through the responsible Medicare Intermediary. Your local Social Security or Railroad Retirement office can be contacted for assistance in filing this type of appeal.

Medical Insurance Appeals (**Medicare Part B**) — Appeals of claims made under your Medicare medical insurance coverage must be submitted to the Medicare carrier that handled the claim. If you disagree with the decision on appeal, and the amount Medicare would pay if the appeal was fully approved is $100 or more, you can request a hearing by the carrier. You can include any other claims you have had reviewed within the last six months to reach the $100 amount needed to request a hearing. The hearing officer's decision is considered final for claims in the amount of $100 to $500. If you are dissatisfied with the hearing officer's decision, and the amount of the claim is over $500, you can have your claim reviewed by an Administrative Law Judge. If the claim in question is still not resolved in your favor and involves more than $1,000, you can appeal to a Federal Court.

SPECIAL RULING FOR SOME SERVICES NOT COVERED BY MEDICARE

In some cases, it is quite possible that you had no way of knowing or you could not *reasonably* be expected to know (i.e., you had not received a written notice) that certain services or care would not be covered by your Medicare insurance protection. If this happens, and the claim you submit is denied because the services were not considered medically necessary, but rather custodial care, payment may still be approved through the appeal process.

The denial notice that you will receive will include the instructions necessary for reconsideration of your claim. A provision in Medicare coverage permitting payment under these conditions is called a "waiver of benefit liability." If you need additional help in submitting an appeal based on this special ruling, contact your local Social Security or Railroad Retirement office.

GETTING DOCTOR COSTS UNDER CONTROL

Despite the controls established to reduce hospital expenditures, Medicare's costs have still tripled in the last ten years. Medicare now costs over $100 billion per year, largely due to rising payments to physicians. In fact, the total costs paid by Medicare to physicians have risen at a rate of more than 15 percent per year. Consequently, to control rising doctor's costs, Congress — under the Omnibus Budget Reconciliation Act of 1989 — enacted a new system for paying doctor's bills. This system will be phased in over the next five years.

The law affects how much you spend out-of-pocket for doctors' fees and how much Medicare will reimburse doctors for their services as follows:

- The law required the implementation of a national fee schedule under which the Medicare-approved payment (adjusted for local costs) for a given treatment or service would be the same for all doctors in the same region of the country. Currently, doctors charge Medicare for their services on the basis of what they consider is "customary, prevailing and reasonable" for a service in their area. The new payment schedule emphasizes primary and preventive care by allowing higher fees for services related to this type of care. Payments are reduced for certain high technology care and surgery.

- The law limits the amount doctors can bill patients in excess of the Medicare-approved fee. Since 1993, doctors can only charge **115%** of the approved fees. In 1991, doctors could charge only 125% of the new fees; in 1992, the maximum amount allowed was 120%. If you paid more in the past than the charge limit, you should ask for a refund. If you cannot get a refund or reduction, call your Medicare Carrier and ask for assistance.

Important: Any physician who knowingly charges more than these amounts is subject to severe sanctions by the government.

- The law requires doctors to fill out and submit claims on behalf of patients after September 1, 1990. This includes doctors who do not accept the Medicare-allowed amount as full payment for their services.

- The law prohibits doctors from referring patients to clinical laboratories in which the doctors have financial interests.

MEDICARE COVERAGE HEADLINES

Several changes over recent times will affect millions of Medicare beneficiaries. Unfortunately, a vast number of beneficiaries are still unaware of them. They are listed below to ensure that you are aware of their effect on your Medicare coverage of health care and services.

- ***"QMB" Program:*** An important program to help low-income Medicare beneficiaries, begun over two years ago, has been found to be underscribed. Fewer than half of all eligible beneficiaries have enrolled in the program, or begun receiving any of its benefits. Called the *Qualified Medicare Beneficiary* (QMB) program, it provides financial assistance from state Medicaid funding to eligible low-income beneficiaries.

Individuals who qualify will have their monthly Medicare premiums and certain out-of-pocket expenses paid by their state Medicaid program. Although each state sets its own guidelines, in general, to be eligible for this financial assistance, a Medicare beneficiary must have (1) an annual income level at or below the national poverty level (in 1996, this is $7,980 for a single person, $10,608 for a couple) and limited assets (in 1996, up to $4,000 value for a single person, excluding home, car and burial plot; $6,000 for a couple) and (2) cannot have access to other significant financial resources. See Chapter 6 for a further explanation of the *QMB* program.

If you believe you qualify for this program, contact your state or local welfare office or social service agency immediately to apply.

■ *Medicare Coverage Changes:* Effective in mid-1993, Medicare began paying for flu shots and the costs of therapeutic shoes for those suffering from severe diabetic foot disease.

■ *Immunosuppressive Drugs:* Currently, Medicare medical insurance will help pay for drugs used in immunosuppressive therapy for one year, beginning with the date of discharge from an inpatient hospital stay during which a Medicare-covered organ transplant was performed.

■ *Pap Smears:* Although routine physical examinations and tests directly related to such examinations are not covered by Medicare, it will pay for pap smears of beneficiaries at three-year intervals.

■ *Respite Care:* Covered only under the hospice program, respite care covers a short-term inpatient stay in a facility to give temporary relief to the person who regularly assists the patient with home care. Each inpatient respite care stay cannot exceed five consecutive days. The patient pays 5% of the Medicare-allowed rate which varies depending on the area of the country.

■ *Outpatient Treatment of Mental Illness Coverage:* Services for outpatient treatment of a mental illness is subject to a special payment rule. Medicare pays 50% of approved charges for all services: the beneficiary pays the remaining 50%. The rule only affects payment for outpatient services from doctors, comprehensive outpatient rehabilitation facilities (CORFs), physician assistants, and psychologists.

- *Independent Clinical Laboratory Services:* Medicare approves certain independent laboratories which accept assignment to perform specific diagnostic tests. **Not** *all* laboratories are approved by Medicare and some laboratories are approved only for certain kinds of tests. Before any tests are performed, ask whether or not they will be covered by Medicare.

- *Coverage of Optometrists' Services:* Medicare now pays for certain health care portions of an eye examination performed by an optometrist. Previously, only ophthalmologists' (medical doctors specializing in the functions and diseases of the eye) services were covered, unless the Medicare patient had cataract surgery. Under the new law, the following optometrist (an individual who is not a medical doctor but is trained to test eyes for vision defects and prescribe glasses or contact lenses) services are covered: the eye health part of an eye examination performed because of a patient's symptoms or complaint, treatment for eye disease, and glasses or contact lenses, for individuals who have had cataract surgery. As in the past, coverage is **not** provided for other prescription glasses, contact lenses or the part of an eye examination that determines a lens prescription.

- *Mammogram Coverage:* Medicare now pays up to $55 for a mammogram every other year for Medicare beneficiaries 65 and older. Disabled beneficiaries can get them more frequently depending on their age and risk of developing breast cancer.

- *Medicare Claim Problems:* After you have contacted your Medicare carrier several times concerning a problem with either the submission of a claim or its payment and a satisfactory response is not forthcoming, contact either SSA via its toll-free telephone service, your local Social Security office or by writing or calling directly to: HCFA Bureau of Program Operations/Inquiries, 6325 Security Blvd., Baltimore, MD 21207, Tel: (301) 966-5994.

MEDIGAP INSURANCE LAW

If you are a Medicare beneficiary planning to buy additional health insurance to supplement Medicare, commonly called "Medigap" insurance, a 1990 law will help you obtain this coverage that was frequently denied in the past.

For Medicare beneficiaries age 65 or older, the law provides a one-time, six-month period during which you can select a Medigap policy and be assured that you will not be turned down for health reasons. The six month period always begins the first month in which a beneficiary, age 65 or older, enrolls in Medicare Part B (Medical Insurance).

During the open enrollment period, a Medigap insurer may not deny you a policy or place conditions on the issuance or effectiveness of a policy based on your health status, past claims experience, or medical condition. If you are in poor health, an insurer may not discriminate against you by charging you a higher premium than it charges anyone else enrolling during this period.

Whenever you enroll in Medicare, it is important to remember that if you are 65 years or older and a new enrollee in Medicare Part B, the first six months your coverage is in effect is your Medigap open enrollment period.

If you are age 65 or older and your Part B benefits have already begun, you still may be entitled to some part of the six month Medigap open enrollment period. To determine whether you qualify, add six months to the Part B effective date on your Medicare card. If the resulting date is in the future, you have time to take advantage of this new provision.

If you do not qualify for Medigap open enrollment, you still may be able to purchase a Medigap policy. However, if you are in poor health, you may have to shop around to find a policy.

MEDICARE *SELECT* . . .
A NEW MEDIGAP INSURANCE OPTION

In 1992, a new Medigap insurance option was made available to Medicare beneficiaries in 15 states. The new option — called Medicare *SELECT*— differs from standard Medigap insurance. Under the Medicare *SELECT* provisions, Medicare beneficiaries may be charged a lower premium in return for agreeing to use the services of particular health care professionals, referred to as "preferred providers"

The Medicare *SELECT* option was initially available only in Alabama, Arizona, California, Florida, Indiana, Kentucky, Michigan, Minnesota, Missouri, North Dakota, Ohio, Oregon, Texas, Washington, and Wisconsin. In 1995, Congress expanded the program to include all 50 states and extended it for three years. It will be up for reauthorization in 1998.

Private insurance companies offer Medicare *SELECT* insurance as they do standard Medigap policies. Each company that offers Medicare *SELECT* has its own network of preferred providers.

When a person with a Medicare *SELECT* policy receives services from a preferred provider, Medicare will pay its share of the approved charges. Then, as is true under other Medigap policies, the Medicare *SELECT* insurer will pay some or all of the balance of the bill, depending on the limits of the particular Medicare *SELECT* policy.

Medicare *SELECT* policies may pay reduced or no benefits if the policy holder receives care outside of the preferred provider network, unless the care is required for a medical emergency. If you need further information on this new Medigap insurance option, contact your state insurance counseling office as indicated in the listing beginning on page 234.

SUMMARY OF 1996 MEDICARE COVERAGE
Hospital Insurance (Part A)

(This part of Medicare is **free** to all Social Security beneficiaries. Others who want this coverage pay a monthly premium of **$289***.)

Covered Services	Benefit Period (1) (days of coverage)	What Medicare Pays
Hospitalization	First 60 days	**All** costs except the **$736** deductible, which you pay. (2)
	61st to 90th day	**All** costs above **$184** per day, which you pay.
	91st to 150th day *Reserve Days (3)*	**All** costs above **$368** per day, which you pay.
	Beyond 150 days	Medicare provides no coverage; *you must pay all costs.*
Post-Hospital Skilled Nursing Facility Care	First 20 days	**All** costs.
	21st to 100th day	You pay **$92** per day and Medicare pays **all** remaining costs.
	Beyond 100 days	You pay **all** costs. Medicare pays nothing after 100 days.
Home Health Care	Up to 21 days of daily care, at a maximum of 35 hours per week. (Intermittent/ part-time care provided afterwards if all requirements are met.)	**All** costs for home health care visits and services that are medically needed.
Hospice	Two 90-day periods and one 30-day (May be extended under certain conditions	**All** costs except certain limited costs which you pay for out-patient drugs and inpatient respite care.
Blood	When needed	**All** blood except the first 3 pints which you pay for or replace.
Psychiatric Hospital Care	190 days (lifetime)	Helps pay up to a lifetime maximum of **190 days**. You must pay for all additional days.

* See footnote on following page.

SUMMARY OF 1996 MEDICARE COVERAGE
Medical Insurance (Part B)
(Basic Monthly Insurance Premium = $42.50)

Covered Services	What Medicare Pays
Medical Expenses — Doctors' services and.other medical services, therapy and supplies in or out of the hospital	80% of the approved amount for services rendered after the annual deductible has been met. You pay the **$100** annual deductible **plus** the remaining **20%** balance of the amount approved by Medicare.
Outpatient Hospital Treatment — Unlimited treatments as medically needed	80% of the approved amount. You pay the remaining 20% of the approved amount **plus** the **$100** deductible if it has not already been paid for the year.
Blood — Unlimited number of pints	80% of the approved amount after the **first three pints.** You pay for the **first three pints** plus the remaining 20% of the approved amount.
Outpatient Treatment for Mental Illness	There is no longer any actual dollar limitation. Instead, a beneficiary pays 50% of approved charges. Medi care will pay the remaining 50% on all approved care after the annual deductible is met.

FOOTNOTES FOR HOSPITAL INSURANCE (PART A):

* In 1996, the monthly premium for Part A coverage is $289. However, if you or your spouse have at least 30 quarters of employment in jobs covered by Social Security but not enough quarters to qualify for premium-free Part A coverage, the monthly fee for Part A in 1996 is $188. You must also apply for Part B. As is true for Part B coverage, you can only apply for Part A during specified enrollment periods.

(1) A benefit Period begins on the first day you receive services as an inpatient in a hospital and ends after you have been out of the hospital or skilled nursing facility for 60 days in a row.

(2) You must pay a $736 deductible during each Benefit Period.

(3) These are called Reserve days. You receive 60 of them to use in your lifetime. They are not renewable and may be used *only* once.

LISTING

Medicare Claim Offices for Railroad Retirement Beneficiaries

There are only two Travelers Insurance Company processing centers that handle the Medicare insurance claims of **all** Railroad Retirement beneficiaries, including those entitled to both Railroad Retirement and Social Security benefits.

If you receive Railroad Retirement benefits, your claim should be sent to the processing center serving your state to avoid any delay in payment. Additionally, any doctor or supplier of medical items who submits an insurance claim for you should be given the correct Traveler's Insurance office for the processing of your claim.

You may write or call the following centers if you have any questions concerning your claims or your Medicare coverage. To reach either center, call the nationwide toll-free telephone number: 800-833-4455. Contact your area Railroad Retirement Board office if you need any additional information. (See the listing of these offices in Chapter 3.)

PROCESSING CENTER I

Use the mailing address and telephone numbers listed below if you live in the following states: **Alabama, Connecticut, Delaware, District of Columbia, Florida, Georgia, Illinois, Indiana, Kentucky, Maine, Maryland, Massachusetts, Michigan, Mississippi, New Hampshire, New Jersey, New York, North Carolina, Ohio, Pennsylvania, Puerto Rico, Rhode Island, South Carolina, Tennessee, Vermont, Virginia, West Virginia.**

> The Travelers Insurance Company
> Railroad Medicare Claim Office
> P.O. Box 10066
> Augusta, GA 30999
> Toll Free: 800-833-4455

PROCESSING CENTER II

Use the mailing address and telephone numbers listed below if you live in the following states: **Alaska, Arizona, Arkansas, California, Colorado, Hawaii, Idaho, Iowa, Kansas, Louisiana, Minnesota, Missouri, Montana, Nebraska, Nevada, New Mexico, North Dakota, Oklahoma, Oregon, South Dakota, Texas, Utah, Washington, Wisconsin, Wyoming.**

> The Travelers Insurance Company
> Railroad Medicare Claim Office
> P.O. Box 30050
> Salt Lake City, UT 84130
> Toll Free: 800-833-4455

Railroad Retirement Fraud and Abuse Hotline

Any Railroad Retirement beneficiary who has reason to believe that a doctor, hospital, or other provider of health care services is performing unnecessary or inappropriate services or is billing Medicare for services not received, may call the Railroad Retirement toll-free *Hot Line*. The Hot Line has been installed by the Railroad Retirement Board's Inspector General to receive any evidence of such fraud or abuse of the Medicare Program. (The Hot Line should not be used for questions about Medicare policy, delayed claims or payments.)

In Illinois, you may call **1-312-751-4336**; outside Illinois, call (toll-free) **1-800-772-4258**. Or you may send your complaints in writing to: RRB, OIG, Hot Line Officer, 844 N. Rush Street, Chicago, Illinois 60611.

LISTING

Medicare State Claim Offices

The following listing contains the Medicare carrier offices that handle Medicare insurance claims for each state. Your claim form should be sent — by the doctor or other provider of medical services and items (except in those cases described earlier in this chapter) — to the state where you **received** the medical-care, items, or services. If you need to file your own claim, you can get the proper form, HCFA-1490S, by calling or writing your Medicare carrier.

In several cases, you will note that a particular carrier may handle various areas within a state or in a nearby state. In this case, the areas they serve are listed separately above the named insurance carrier. Your claim should be sent to the carrier that handles the area in which you received the care or services. This will avoid any possible delay or confusion in the handling of it.

Since many of the states have toll-free telephone numbers for use **within** their states, it is advisable for you to utilize this service whenever you need help in answering questions concerning your claims. (Some of the toll-free numbers can be used by neighboring states.)

Medicare insurance claims for those under the Railroad Retirement system **must be submitted** to the Travelers Insurance Company offices that serve their region. See the listing that precedes this one for the address of these offices.

ALABAMA
  Medicare Blue Cross-Blue Shield of Alabama
  P.O. Box 830-140, Birmingham, AL 35283
  Tel: (205) 988-2244
  Toll Free: 800-292-8855

ALASKA
Medicare, Aetna Life and Casualty
P.O. Box 1998, 200 S.W. Market Street
Portland, OR 97207
Tel: (503) 222-6831
Toll Free: 800-452-0125

AMERICAN SAMOA
Medicare/Hawaii Medical Services Association
P.O. Box 860, Honolulu, HI 96808
Tel: (808) 944-2247

ARIZONA
Medicare, Aetna Life and Casualty,
10000 N. 31st Avenue, P.O. Box 37200, Phoenix, AZ 85069
Tel: (602) 861-1968
Toll Free: 800-352-0411

ARKANSAS
Medicare, Arkansas Blue Cross and Blue Shield,
A Mutual Insurance Company
P.O. Box 1418, Little Rock, AR 72203
Tel: (501) 378-2320
Toll Free: 800-482-5525

CALIFORNIA
Counties of: Los Angeles, Orange, San Diego, Ventura, Imperial, San Luis Obispo, Santa Barbara
Medicare, Transamerica Occidental Life Insurance Co.,
Box 30540, Los Angeles, CA 90030
Tel: (213) 748-2311
Toll Free: 800-675-2266

All Other Areas in the State
Medicare Claims Department
Blue Shield of California, Chico, CA 95976

In Northern California area codes 209, 408, 415, 510, 707, 916:
Tel: (916) 743-1583
Toll Free: 800-952-8627

In Southern California area codes 213, 310, 619, 714, 805, 818, 909:
Tel: (714) 796-9393
Toll Free: 800-848-7713

COLORADO
Medicare/Blue Shield of North Dakota
Governor's Center II
600 Grant St., Suite 600
Denver, CO 80203
Tel: (701) 282-0691
Toll Free: 800-247-2267

CONNECTICUT
Medicare, The Travelers Insurance Company
538 Preston Ave., P.O. Box 9000, Meriden, CT 06454
Tel: (203) 728-6783 (in Hartford)
        (203) 237-8592 (in the Meriden area)
Toll Free: 800-982-6819

DELAWARE
Xact Medicare Services
P.O. Box 890065, Camp Hill, PA 17089
Toll Free: 800-851-3535

DISTRICT OF COLUMBIA
Xact Medicare Services
P.O. Box 890065, Camp Hill, PA 17089
Toll Free: 800-233-1124

FLORIDA
Medicare, Blue Shield and Blue Cross of Florida, Inc.
P.O. Box 2360, Jacksonville, FL 32231
Tel: (904) 355-3680
Toll Free: 800-333-7586

GEORGIA
Medicare/Aetna Life & Casualty
P.O. Box 3018, Savannah, GA 31402
Tel: (912) 920-2412
Toll Free: 800-727-0827

GUAM
Medicare, Aetna Life and Casualty
P.O. Box 3947, Honolulu, HI 96812
Tel: (808) 524-1240

HAWAII
Medicare, Aetna Life and Casualty
P.O. Box 3947, Honolulu, Hi 96812
Tel: (808) 524-1240
Toll Free: 800-272-5242

IDAHO
CIGNA Medicare
3150 N. Lakeharbor Lane, Suite 254
P.O. Box 8048, Boise, ID 83707
Tel: (208) 342-7763
Toll Free: 800-627-2782

ILLINOIS
Blue Cross and Blue Shield of Illinois
Medicare Claims, P.O. Box 4422, Marion, IL 62959
Tel: (312) 938-8000
Toll Free: 800-642-6930

INDIANA
Medicare Claims, Part B, Associated Insurance Companies, Inc.
P.O. Box 7073, Indianapolis, IN 46207
Tel: (317) 842-4151
Toll Free: 800-622-4792

IOWA
Medicare Claims, IASD Health Services, Inc.
Blue Cross and Blue Shield of Iowa
636 Grand Avenue, Des Moines, IA 50309
Tel: (515) 245-4785
Toll Free: 800-532-1285

KANSAS
Counties of: Johnson, Wyandotte
Medicare, Blue Shield of Kansas City
P.O. Box 419840, Kansas City, MO 64141
Tel: (816) 561-0900
Toll Free: 800-892-5900

All other areas in state:
Medicare, Blue Cross/Blue Shield of Kansas
1133 S.W. Topeka Blvd., Topeka, KS 66629
Tel: (913) 232-3773
Toll Free: 800-432-3531

KENTUCKY
AdminaStar of Kentucky
P.O. Box 37630
Louisville, KY 40233-7630
Tel: (502) 425-6759
Toll Free: 800-999-7608

LOUISIANA
Medicare, Arkansas Blue Cross & Blue Shield
P.O. Box 83830, Baton Rouge, LA 70884
Tel: (504) 529-1494 (in New Orleans)
       (504) 927-3490 (in Baton Rouge)
Toll Free: 800-462-9666

MAINE
Medicare/C and S Administrative Services
P.O. Box 1000, Hingham, MA 02044-9191
For Non-assigned Claims
P.O. Box 2222, Hingham, MA 02044-9193
Tel: (207) 828-4300
Toll Free: 800-492-0919

MARYLAND
Counties of: Montgomery, Prince Georges
  Xact Medicare Services
  P.O. Box 890065
  Camp Hill, PA 17089
  Toll Free: 800-233-1124

All other areas in state:
  Trail Blazer Enterprises
  P.O. Box 5678
  Timonium, MD 21094
  Toll Free: 800-492-4795

MASSACHUSETTS
  Medicare/C and S Administrative Services
  P.O. Box 1000
  Hingham, MA 02044
  Tel.: (617) 741-3300
  Toll Free: 800-882-1228

MICHIGAN
  HCSC
  Michigan Medicare Claims
  P.O. Box 5544
  Marion, IL 62959
  Tel: (313) 225-8200
  Toll Free: 800-482-4045

MINNESOTA
Counties of: Anoka, Dakota, Fillmore, Goodhue, Hennepin, Houston, Olmstead, Ramsey, Wabasha, Washington, Winona
  Medicare, The Travelers Insurance Company
  8120 Penn Avenue, South,
  Bloomington, MN 55431
  Tel: (612) 884-7171
  Toll Free: 800-352-2762

All other areas in state:
  Medicare, Blue Shield of Minnesota
  P.O. Box 64357,
  St. Paul, MN 55164
  Tel: (612) 456-5070
  Toll Free: 800-392-0343

MISSISSIPPI
  Medicare, The Travelers Insurance Company
  P.O. Box 22545,
  Jackson, MS 39225
  Tel: (601) 956-0372
  Toll Free: 800-682-5417

MISSOURI

Since this state is divided into many geographical areas for the handling of Medicare claims, you should use the toll free telephone service provided to verify which carrier serves you. In general the following counties are serviced by Blue Shield: Andrew, Atchison, Bates, Benton, Buchanan, Caldwell, Carroll, Cass, Clay, Clinton, Daviess, DeKalb, Gentry, Grundy, Harrison, Henry, Holt, Jackson, Johnson, Lafayette, Livingston, Mercer, Nodaway, Pettis, Platte, Ray, St. Clair, Saline, Vernon, Worth

Medicare, Blue Shield of Kansas City
P.O. Box 419840, Kansas City, MO 64141
Tel: (816) 561-0900
Toll Free: 800-892-5900

All other areas in state:
Medicare, General American Life Insurance Company
P.O. Box 505, St. Louis, MO 63166
Tel: (314) 843-8880
Toll Free: 800-392-3070

MONTANA

Medicare, Blue Shield of Montana
2501 Beltview, P.O. Box 4310, Helena, MT 59604
Tel: (406) 444-8350
Toll Free: 800-332-6146

NEBRASKA

Medicare, Blue Cross/Blue Shield of Nebraska
P.O. Box 3106
Omaha, NE 68103
Tel: (913) 232-3773 (Service site in Kansas)
Toll Free: 800-633-1113

NEVADA

Medicare, Aetna Life Insurance Company
P.O. Box 37230, Phoenix, AZ 85069
Tel: (602) 861-1968
Toll Free: 800-528-0311

NEW HAMPSHIRE

Medicare/C and S Administrative Services
P.O. Box 1000, Hingham, MA 02044-9191
For Non-assigned Claims
P.O. Box 2222, Hingham, MA 02044-9193
Tel: (207) 828-4300
Toll Free: 800-447-1142

NEW JERSEY

Xact Medicare Services
P.O. Box 890065
Camp Hill, PA 17089
Toll Free: 800-462-9306

NEW MEXICO
Medicare Claims/Administration, Aetna Life and Casualty of Oklahoma
P.O. Box 25500, Oklahoma City, OK 73125
Toll Free: 800-423-2925
In Albuquerque, call: (505) 821-3350

NEW YORK
Counties of Bronx, Columbia, Delaware, Dutchess, Greene, Kings,
Nassau, New York, Orange, Putnam, Richmond, Rockland, Suffolk,
Sullivan, Ulster, Westchester:
Medicare, Empire Blue Cross/Blue Shield of New York
P.O. Box 2280, Peekskill, NY 10566
Tel: (516) 244-5100
Toll Free: 800-442-8430

County of Queens:
Medicare, Group Health, Inc.
P.O. Box 1608, Ansonia Station, New York, NY 10023
Tel: (212) 721-1770

All other areas in state:
Medicare, Blue Shield of Western New York
33 Lewis St., Binghamton, NY 13905
Tel: (607) 772-6906
Toll Free: 800-252-6550

NORTH CAROLINA
Connecticut General Life Insurance Company
P.O. Box 671, Nashville, TN 37202
Tel: (919) 665-0348
Toll Free: 800-672-3071

NORTH DAKOTA
Medicare, Blue Shield of North Dakota
711 - 2nd Ave., N., Fargo, ND 58102
Tel: (701) 277-2363
Toll Free: 800-247-2267

NORTHERN MARIANA ISLANDS
Medicare/Aetna Life & Casualty
P.O. Box 3947, Honolulu, HI 96812
Tel: (808) 524-1240

OHIO
Medicare, Nationwide Mutual Insurance Co.
P.O. Box 57, Columbus, OH 43216
Tel: (614) 249-7157
Toll Free: 800-282-0530

OKLAHOMA
Medicare Administration, Aetna Life and Casualty
701 N.W. 63rd Street, Suite 100, Oklahoma City, OK 73116
Tel: (405) 848-7711
Toll Free: 800-522-9079

OREGON
Medicare Administration, Aetna Life Insurance Company
200 S.W. Market Street, P.O. Box 1997, Portland, OR 97207
Tel: (503) 222-6831
Toll Free: 800-452-0125

PENNSYLVANIA
Xact Medicare Services
Box 890065, Camp Hill, PA 17089
Toll Free: 800-382-1274

PUERTO RICO
Medicare/Triple-S, Inc.
Call Box 71391, San Juan, PR 00936
Toll Free: 800-749-4900 (In Puerto Rico metro area)
             800-981-7015 (Outside metro area)

RHODE ISLAND
Medicare, Blue Shield of Rhode Island
444 Westminster Street, Providence, RI 02903
Tel: (401) 861-2273
Toll Free: 800-662-5170

SOUTH CAROLINA
Palmetto Govt. Benefits Administrators
Medicare Part B Operations
P.O. Box 100190
Columbia, SC 29202
Tel: (803) 788-3882
Toll Free: 800-868-2522

SOUTH DAKOTA
Medicare, Blue Shield of North Dakota
711 - 2nd Ave., N., Fargo, ND 58102
Toll Free: 800-437-4762

TENNESSEE
CIGNA Medicare
P.O. Box 1465, Nashville, TN 37202
Tel: (615) 244-5650
Toll Free: 800-342-8900

TEXAS
Medicare, Blue Cross/Blue Shield of Texas, Inc.
P.O. Box 660031, Dallas, TX 75266
Tel: (214) 235-3433
Toll Free: 800-442-2620

UTAH
Medicare, Blue Shield of Utah
P.O. Box 30269, Salt Lake City, UT 84130
Tel: (801) 481-6196
Toll Free: 800-426-3477

VERMONT
Medicare/C and S Administrative Services
P.O. Box 1000, Hingham, MA 02044-9191
For Non-assigned Claims
P.O. Box 2222, Hingham, MA 02044-9193
Tel: (207) 828-4300
Toll Free: 800-447-1142

VIRGIN ISLANDS
Medicare/Triple-S, Inc.
Call Box 71391, San Juan, PR 00936
Tel: (809) 773-9548 (in St. Croix)
     (809) 774-7915 (in St. Thomas)
Toll Free: 800-474-7448 (In U.S. Virgin Islands)

VIRGINIA
Counties of: Arlington, Fairfax. Cities of Alexandria, Falls Church, Fairfax
Xact Medicare Services
P.O. Box 890065, Camp Hill, PA 17089
Toll Free: 800-233-1124

All other areas in state:
Metro Health Care
P.O. Box 26463, Richmond, VA 23261
Tel: (804) 330-4786
Toll Free: 800-552-3423

WASHINGTON
Aetna Life Insurance Company
Medicare Part B
P.O. Box 91099
Seattle, WA 98111-9199
Tel: (206) 621-0359
Toll Free: 800-372-6604

WEST VIRGINIA
Medicare, Nationwide Mutual Insurance Co.
P.O. Box 57, Columbus, OH 43216
Tel: (614) 249-7157
Toll Free: 800-848-0106

WISCONSIN
Medicare, Wisconsin Physicians' Service
Box 1787, Madison, WI 53701
Tel: (608) 221-3330 (in Madison)
Toll Free: 800-944-0051

WYOMING
Medicare, Blue Cross/Blue Shield of Wyoming
P.O. Box 628, Cheyenne, WY 82003
Tel: (307) 632-9381
Toll Free: 800-442-2371

LISTING

Durable Medical Equipment Regional Carriers

REGION A
States of Connecticut, Delaware, Maine, Massachusetts, New Hampshire, New Jersey, New York, Pennsylvania, Rhode Island, Vermont

Travelers Insurance Company
P.O. Box 6800
Wilkes-Barre, PA 18773-6800
Toll Free: 800-842-2052

REGION B
District of Columbia and states of Illinois, Indiana, Maryland, Michigan, Minnesota, Ohio, Virginia, West Virginia, Wisconsin

AdminaStar Federal, Inc.
P.O. Box 7031
Indianapolis, IN 46207-7031
Toll Free: 800-270-2313

REGION C
States of Alabama, Arkansas, Colorado, Florida, Georgia, Kentucky, Louisiana, Mississippi, New Mexico, North Carolina, Oklahoma, South Carolina, Tennessee, Texas, Puerto Rico, and the U.S. Virgin Islands

Palmetto Government Benefits Administrators
Medicare DMERC Operations
P.O. Box 100141
Columbia, SC 29202-0141
Toll Free: 800-213-5452

REGION D
States of Alaska, Arizona, California, Hawaii, Idaho, Iowa, Kansas, Missouri, Montana, Nebraska, Nevada, North Dakota, Oregon, South Dalota, Utah, Washington, Wyoming, American Samoa, Marianna Islands, and Guam

CIGNA Medicare
P.O. Box 690
Nashville, TN 37202
Toll Free: 800-899-7095

LISTING

State Peer Review Organizations (PROs)

As you now are aware, every state is required to have a Peer Review Organization to oversee Medicare utilization within its hospitals. These Peer Review Organizations are listed here by state.

Since you must act expeditiously to appeal your disagreement with a hospital's notice of discharge, it is advisable for you, or whoever is assisting you, to call your state Peer Review Organization **immediately** for assistance to ensure that your appeal is handled without delay. Many states have toll-free (except when noted otherwise) *Hotline* telephone numbers specifically set-up in order to respond to your needs as quickly as possible. Be certain to use the Hotline telephone number *before* using any local number that may be indicated in this listing.

ALABAMA
Alabama Quality Assurance
Foundation
One Perimeter Park South
Suite 200 North
Birmingham, AL 35243
Tel: (205) 942-0785
Hotline: 800-760-3540

ALASKA
Professional Review
Organization for Washington
10700 Meridan Avenue, North
Suite 100
Seattle, WA 98133
Tel: (206) 364-9700
Hotline: 800-445-6941
          (907) 562-2252
          (local-Anchorage)

AMERICAN SAMOA/GUAM
Hawaii Medical Services Association
818 Keeaumoku Street
P.O. Box 860
Honolulu, HI 96808
Tel: (808) 944-3581
Hotline: 808-944-3586
          (Collect-Out-State)

ARIZONA
Health Services Advisory
Group, Inc.
301 E. Bethany Home Rd., B-157
Phoenix, AZ 85012
Tel: (602) 264-6382
Hotlines:800-626-1577
          800-359-9909
          (In-State)

ARKANSAS
Arkansas Foundation for
Medical Care, Inc.
809 Garrison Avenue
P.O. Box 2424
Fort Smith, AR 72902
Tel: (501) 785 2471
Hotlines:800-824-7586
          800-272-5528
          (In-State)

CALIFORNIA
California Medical Review, Inc.
60 Spear Street, Suite 500
San Francisco, CA 94105
Tel: (415) 882-5800
Hotlines: 800-841-1602 (In-State)
            415-882-5800
            (Collect-Out/State)

COLORADO
Colorado Foundation for
Medical Care
2821 South Parker Road
P.O. Box 17300
Denver, CO 80217
Tel: (303) 695-3300
Hotlines: 800-727-7086 (In-State)
            303-695-3333
            (Collect-Out/State)

CONNECTICUT
Connecticut Peer Review
Organization, Inc.
100 Roscommon Drive
Suite 200 North
Middletown, CT 06457
Tel: (203) 632-2008
Hotlines: 800-553-7590 (In-State)
            203-632-2008
            (Collect-Out/State)

DELAWARE
West Virginia Medical Institute, Inc.
3001 Chesterfield Pl.
Charleston, WV 25304
Tel: (304) 346-9864
Tel: (708) 357-8770
Hotlines: 800-642-8686 ext. 266
      (Region-DE,DC,MD,PA,VA)
            655-3077
            (Local-Wilmington)

DISTRICT OF COLUMBIA
Delmarva Foundation for
Medical Care, Inc.
9240 Centreville Road
Easton, MD 21601
Tel: (410) 822-0697
Hotlines: 800-645-0011
            800-492-5811 (In-State)

FLORIDA
Florida Medical Quality
Assurance, Inc.
Suite 700
Tampa, FL 33607
Tel.:(813) 281-0795
Hotline: 800-844-0795 (In-State)

GEORGIA
Georgia Medical Care Foundation
57 Executive Park South,Suite 200
Atlanta, GA 30329
Tel: (404) 982-0411
Hotline: 800-282-2614 (In-State)

HAWAII
Hawaii Medical Services
Association
818 Keeaumoku Street
P.O. Box 860
Honolulu, HI 96808
Tel: (808) 944-3581
Hotline: 808-944-3586
            (Local-Oahu/Collect)

IDAHO
Professional Review
Organization for Washington
Suite 100
10700 Meridian Avenue, North
Seattle, WA 98133
Tel: (206) 364-9700
Hotlines: 800-445-6941
            208-343-4617
            (Local-Boise/Collect)

ILLINOIS
Crescent Counties
Foundation for Medical Care
1001 Warrenville Road
Lisle, IL 60532
Tel: (708) 769-9600
Hotline: 800-647-8089

INDIANA
Sentinal Medical Review
Organization
2901 Ohio Boulevard
P.O. Box 3713
Terre Haute, IN 47803
Tel: (812) 234-1499
Hotline: 800-288-1499

IOWA
Iowa Foundation for Medical Care
6000 Westown Parkway
West Des Moines, IA 50266
Tel: (515) 223-2900
Hotline: 800-752-7014 (In-State)

KANSAS
Kansas Foundation for
Medical Care, Inc.
2947 S.W. Wanamaker Drive
Topeka, KS 66614
Tel: (913) 273-2552
Hotline: 800-432-0407 (In-State)

KENTUCKY
Sentinal Medical Review
Organization
10503 Timberwood Circle
Suite 200
P.O. Box 23540
Louisville, KY 40223
Tel: (502) 339-7442
Hotline: 800-288-1499

LOUISIANA
Louisiana Health Care Review Inc.
8591 United Plaza Blvd., Suite 270
Baton Rouge, LA 70809
Tel: (504) 926-6353
Hotline: 800-433-4958 (In-State)

MAINE
Health Care Review, Inc.
Henry C. Hall Building
345 Blackstone Blvd.
Providence, RI 02906
Tel: (401) 331-6661
Hotlines: 800-541-9888/
          528-0700 (In-State)
          207-945-0244
          (Collect-Out/State)

MARYLAND
Delmarva Foundation for
Medical Care, Inc.
9240 Centreville Rd.
Easton, MD 21601
Tel: (410) 822-0697
Hotlines: 800-645-0011
          800-492-5811 (In-State)

MASSACHUSETTS
Massachusetts Peer Review
Organization, Inc.
235 Wyman Street
Waltham, MA 02154
Tel: (617) 890-0011
Hotlines: 800-252-5533 (In-State)
          617-890-0011
          (Collect-Out/State)

MICHIGAN
Michigan Peer Review
Organization/Suite 200
40600 Ann Arbor Road
Plymouth, MI 48170
Tel: (313) 459-0900
Hotline: 800-365-5899

MINNESOTA
Foundation for Health
Care Evaluation
2901 Metro Drive, Suite 400
Bloomington, MN 55425
Tel: (612) 854-3306
Hotline: 800-444-3423

MISSISSIPPI
Mississippi Foundation for
Medical Care, Inc.
735 Riverside Drive
P.O. Box 4665
Jackson, MS 39296
Tel: (601) 948-8894
Hotline: 800-844-0600 (In-State)

MISSOURI
Missouri Patient Care Foundation
505 Hobbs Road, Suite 100
Jefferson City, MO 65109
Tel: (314) 893-7900
Hotline: 800-347-1016

MONTANA
Montana-Wyoming Foundation
for Medical Care
400 North Park
Helena, MT 59601
Tel: (406) 443-4020
Hotlines: 800-479-8232 (In-State)
          406-443-4020
          (Collect-Out/State)

NEBRASKA
Iowa Foundation for Medical
Care/Sunderbruch Corp.
6000 Westown Parkway, Suite 350E
West Des Moines, IA 50266
Hotlines: 800-247-3004 (In-State)
          800-422-4812
          (Collect-Out/State)

NEVADA
Peer Review
675 East 2100 South, Suite 270
Salt Lake City, UT 84106
Tel: (702) 385-9933
Hotlines: 800-558-0829 (In-State)
          702-385-9933
          (Collect-Out/State)
          702-826-1996 (Reno)

NEW HAMPSHIRE
New Hampshire Foundation
Medical Care
15 Old Rollinsford Road, Suite 302
Dover, NH 03820
Tel: (603) 749-1641
Hotlines: 800-582-7174 (In-State)
          603-749-1641
          (Collect-Out/State)

NEW JERSEY
Peer Review Organization of
New Jersey, Inc.
Central Division
Brier Hill Court, Bldg. J East
Brunswick, NJ 08816
Tel: (908) 238-5570
Hotlines: 800-624-4557 (In-State)
          201-238-5570
          (Collect-Out/State)

NEW MEXICO
New Mexico Medical Review
Association
707 Broadway N.E., Suite 200
P.O. Box 27449
Albuquerque, NM 87125
Tel: (505) 842-6236
Hotlines: 800-279-6824 (In-State)
          842-6236
          (Local-Albuquerque)

NEW YORK
Island Peer Review
Organization, Inc.
1979 Marcus Avenue, 1st floor
Lake Success, NY 11042
Tel: (516) 326-7767
Hotlines: 800-331-7767 (In-State)
          516-326-7767
          (Collect-Out/State)
          326-7767
          (Local-Metro/N.Y.C.)

NORTH CAROLINA
Medical Review of North
Carolina, Inc.
5625 Dillard Drive, Suite 203
P.O. Box 37309
Cary, NC 27511-9227
Tel: (919) 851-2955
Hotline: 800-682-2650 (In-State)
         (Local/Collect)

NORTH DAKOTA

North Dakota Health Care
Review, Inc.
900 N. Broadway Avenue, Suite 301
Minot, ND 58701
Tel: (701) 852-4231
Hotlines: 800-472-2902 (In-State)
       701-852-4231
       (Collect-Out/State)

OHIO

Peer Review Systems, Inc.
P.O. Box 6174
757 Brooksedge Plaza Dr.
Westerville, OH 43081
Tel: (614) 895-9900
Hotlines: 800-589-7337 (In-State)
      800-837-0664
      (Out-of-State)

OKLAHOMA

Oklahoma Foundation for
Peer Review, Inc.
5801 Broadway Extension
Suite 400
Oklahoma City, OK 73118
Tel: (405) 840-2891
Hotline: 800-522-3414 (In-State)

OREGON

Oregon Medical Professional
Review Organization
1220 S.W. Morrison, Suite 200
Portland, OR 97205
Tel: (503) 279-0100
Hotlines: 800-344-4354 (In-State)
      503-279-0100
      (Local-Portland/Collect)

PENNSYLVANIA

Keystone Peer Review
Organization, Inc.
777 East Park Drive, P.O. Box 8310
Harrisburg, PA 17105
Tel: (717) 564-8288
Hotline: 800-322-1914 (In-State)

PUERTO RICO

Puerto Rico Foundation for
Medical Care
Mercantile Plaza, Suite 605
Hato Ray, PR 00918
Tel: (809) 753-6705
Hotlines: 809-753-6705/
      753-6708

RHODE ISLAND

Health Care Review, Inc.
345 Blackstone Blvd.
Providence, RI 02906
Tel: (401) 331-6661
Hotlines: 800-662-5028 (In-State)
      (401) 331 661
      (Collect-Out/State)
      800-221-1691
      (Region/N.England Wide)

SOUTH CAROLINA

Medical Review of North Carolina
Suite 203
P.O. Box 37309
5625 Dillard Drive
Cary, NC 27511
Tel: (919) 851-2955
Hotline: 800-682-2650 (In-State)

SOUTH DAKOTA

South Dakota Foundation for
Medical Care
1323 South Minnesota Avenue
Sioux Falls, SD 57105
Tel: (605) 336-3505
Hotline: 800-658-2285

TENNESSEE

Mid-South Foundation for
Medical Care
6401 Poplar Avenue , Suite 400
Memphis, TN 38119
Tel: (901) 682-0381
Hotline: 800-489-4633

TEXAS

Texas Medical Foundation
Barton Oaks Plaza Two, Suite 200
901 Mopac Expressway South
Austin, TX 78746
Tel: (512) 329-6610
Hotline: 800-725-8315 (In-State)

UTAH

Utah Peer Review Organization
675 East 2100 South
Suite 270
Salt Lake City, UT 84106
Tel: (801) 487-2290
Hotline: 800-274-2290

VERMONT

New Hampshire Foundation for
Medical Care
15 Rollinsford Road, Suite 302
Dover, NH 03820
Tel: (603) 749-1641
Hotlines: 800-772-0151 (In-State)
          802-655-6302
          (Collect Out/State)

VIRGINIA

Medical Society of Virginia
Review Organization
1606 Santa Rosa Rd., Suite 200
P.O. Box K-70
Richmond, VA 23288
Tel: (804) 289-5320
Hotlines: 800-545-3814
          (Region-DC,MD,VA)
          289-5397
          (Local-Richmond)

VIRGIN ISLANDS

Virgin Islands Medical Institute
P.O. Box 1566,Christiansted
St. Croix, VI 00821
Tel: (809) 778-6470
Hotline: 809-778-6470
         (Local/Collect)

WASHINGTON

Professional Review
Organization for Washington
10700 Meridian Avenue, North
Suite 100
Seattle, WA 98133
Tel: (206) 364-9700
Hotlines: 800-445-6941
          368-8272
          (Local-Seattle)

WEST VIRGINIA

West Virginia Medical
Institute, Inc.
3001 Chesterfield Pl.
Charleston, WV 25304
Tel: (304) 346-9864
Hotlines: 800-642-8686 Ext. 266
          346-9864
          (Local-Charleston)

WISCONSIN

Wisconsin Peer Review
Organization
2909 Landmark Place
Madison, WI 53713
Tel: (608) 274-1940
Hotline: 800-362-2320 (In-State)

WYOMING

Montana-Wyoming Foundation
for Medical Care
400 North Park, 2nd Floor
P.O. Box 5117
Helena, MT 59601
Tel: (406) 443-4020
Hotlines: 800-497-8232 (In-State)
          (406) 443-4020
          (Collect-Out/State)

Chapter 5

Health Insurance

It's Critical to You

Chapter Highlights

Health Insurance

It's Critical to You

With the rising cost of hospitalization, medical care, medication, and long-term care at home or in a nursing facility, adequate health insurance coverage is more critical than ever. But, for the estimated 41 million Americans — of which over 26 million are workers — with no coverage at all, the 60-plus million with too little coverage, and the countless others with the wrong kind of insurance, just one serious illness could become the most disastrous financial event of a lifetime. Be aware that the average cost per day of a hospital stay is more than $1,300!

The Department of Health and Human Services estimates that over 6 million of the under-65 population are financially devastated by a catastrophic health incident each year. More astonishing in a wealthy nation like ours: over one and a half million families each year have at least one member who was refused medical care because of inadequate funds or lack of insurance. Currently, nearly one-half of all widows and two-thirds of all divorcees have no private health insurance to help them pay for medical care.

Almost everyone could benefit from improved health insurance protection. Even the elderly and disabled covered by Medicare benefits need supplemental health insurance to help pay for many out-of-pocket costs not covered by Medicare, such as long-term nursing home care, in-home care, outpatient prescription drugs and doctors' charges that exceed the Medicare-approved rates. Nor does Medicare cover expenses for hearing, dental and optical care, or products for which the elderly spend millions of dollars out-of-pocket each year. And, for the one out of five Americans affected by mental disorders or illnesses, most health policies — including Medicare — provide very minimal coverage for treatment or hospitalization.

Because America's health system is private (not socialized), commercial health insurance policies are Americans' only sources of aid in meeting the costs of health care. You must be well-informed to be able to select a health insurance policy that will give you adequate health-care protection. However, with the huge number of companies offering varying policies at a wide range of prices, selecting the right policy is not an easy task. Currently, there are over 1,500 companies in the U.S. who provide policies with varying benefits, costs, limitations and exclusions. Even the nationally-recognized *Blue Cross-Blue Shield* has over 60 different policies, with a daunting maze of complex plans to sort through.

This discussion of health insurance does not address the intricacies and costs of the numerous policies available throughout the nation. However, it does provide important information to clarify health insurance issues and to help you select the right policy for you. The chapter is divided into two parts: Section I, "Health Insurance Information Everyone Should Know," and Section II, "Health Insurance for Those on Medicare."

Medicare Beneficiaries Take Note . . .

While this chapter explains the ten standard Medigap plans mandated by the new Medigap insurance law, be sure to read Chapter 4 on Medicare (p. 179) for other important provisions of the new law. In particular, be aware of the **one-time, six-month open enrollment period**, during which no insurer can refuse to sell you Medigap insurance for health reasons, or charge you a higher premium because of poor health!

Chapter 4 also explains the new Medicare option, Medicare *SELECT*. Medicare *SELECT* gives beneficiaries the option of lower insurance premiums if they agree to choose their medical practitioners from the list of "preferred providers" designated by the insurance companies.

Always remember! The more benefits an insurance policy provides, the more it will cost. Carefully assess both your anticipated health care needs and your ability to pay a policy's monthly premiums. Obtain all the information and assistance you can before making a final choice. Your State Insurance Regulator's office and many of the organizations listed in Chapter 11 can provide useful, up-to-date information on the new standard Medigap policies and Medicare *SELECT* option.

SECTION I

Health Insurance Information Everyone Should Know

This section contains information that can help everyone — including Medicare beneficiaries — understand the various commercial health insurance policies available throughout the nation.

BASIC TYPES OF PRIVATE HEALTH INSURANCE

Health insurance can be divided into two general types: *Group Health Insurance* and *Individual Health Insurance*. Both are structured on a "fee-for-service" approach, where insurance companies provide reimbursement for the health care services specified by the insurance policy.

Consumers can also purchase alternative plans which provide health care directly to their members rather than reimbursing them for services provided by others. These alternative plans include pre-paid plans, like *Health Maintenance Organizations* (HMOs) and *Independent Practice Associations* (IPAs). A third option, the *Preferred Provider Organization* (PPO), contracts with independent doctors and one or more hospitals to furnish health care services to its members more cheaply than the standard costs for such services.

Group and individual health insurance plans, HMOs, IPAs and PPOs are each discussed more fully below to promote understanding of the choices available to you in obtaining adequate, reasonable coverage for yourself and your family.

Group Health Insurance

Group health insurance is designed to cover several people under a single policy, with a designated group policyholder responsible for paying the premiums. These policies are available to workers through their employers, and to members of labor unions, credit unions, associations and other organizations that have group insurance as one of their benefits. These policies also cover the insured person's immediate family (with some exceptions).

Group plan premiums are usually less costly than individual plans. Although coverage varies according to the particular plan, it is usually broader than the coverage available in an individually-purchased plan. Coverage by most group plans begins after a waiting period specified by the group policyholder (for example, employees must work full-time for a specified period before their coverage will begin).

An important **advantage** of group health insurance is that a person's physical condition will not usually adversely affect eligibility. A major **disadvantage** is that coverage will end when the person leaves the group. Thus, one could lose coverage quite abruptly, even on the day membership or employment ends, or within 30 days thereafter.

Most group policies have an option which allows the insured person to convert from the group policy to an individual policy with the same insurance company. However, the option must be exercised within a given period and the individual policy will cost more and probably have fewer benefits than the group policy.

Group Health Insurance Continuation Law— Consolidated Omnibus Budget Reconciliation Act (COBRA)

Until 1986, many individuals, their spouses and dependents lost their group health insurance because of a loss or reduction in employment, divorce, or the death or retirement of a spouse who was insured by the group plan. Dependents of the insured became ineligible for coverage under the group plan because they became too old for "dependents' coverage."

As part of the 1986 Consolidated Omnibus Budget Reconciliation Act, a law was passed to help many individuals retain health insurance that they would have lost due to changes in work or family status. The law, which is not retroactive, requires state and local governments (except the District of Columbia) and private employers with 20 or more workers to offer terminated employees the right to continue coverage within two weeks after the employees' eligibility for group insurance ends. The individual must respond within 60 days of the notice or lose the right to continue the insurance coverage. However, continued coverage requires that the insured individual pay **both** the employer and employee portions of the premium plus a two percent fee for administrative costs. Although this may sound rather expensive, the group insurance plan is usually much more afford-able than any individual plan **and** it generally provides much better coverage. Plus, group insurance does not require you to pass a physical examination — it will provide coverage even if you have poor health or are normally considered high-risk.

The law states that the following individuals are eligible to continue their employer's group health insurance plan:

- workers who become unemployed or whose hours are cut — as well as their spouses and dependents — as long as the worker was not terminated for gross misconduct;
- widows and dependent children of former employees; divorced or separated;
- divorced spouses and dependent children;
- spouses not eligible for Medicare and dependent children of retiring workers;
- a former employee's dependent children who become ineligible for whatever reason — including children who pass the maximum age allowed under the group plan;
- workers, spouses and their dependents if the employer files for bankruptcy (enacted in 1987, this group was not previously covered by the Continuation Law).

In most cases, coverage can continue for up to three years for all except unemployed workers (and their dependents), who are covered for up to 18 months. However, coverage will end earlier if: (1) the insured person fails to pay the premiums; (2) he/she becomes eligible for another group's coverage through employment or remarriage; (3) he/she becomes eligible for Medicare; or (4) the employer stops providing the group health plan as a benefit for **all** employees.

Individual Health Insurance

Individual health insurance policies vary considerably in cost and coverage. Individual insurance can be purchased to cover only an individual or to include all family members under the one policy. This insurance is generally purchased because: (1) the individual does not have group insurance; (2) because he/she wants to supplement group insurance with benefits not provided under the group policy; or (3) to obtain additional coverage for a costly long-term illness or accident not covered by the existing policy. Most Medicare beneficiaries purchase individual supplemental policies to pay for health care costs not covered by Medicare. These policies, explained in the second section of this chapter, are called *Medicare supplement insurance* policies — commonly referred to as *Medigap* policies.

PRE-PAID HEALTH PLANS

Pre-paid health plans are offered by *Health Maintenance Organizations* (HMOs) and *Independent Practice Associations* (IPAs) — a form of HMO. Currently, over 60 million individuals are enrolled in Health Maintenance Organizations (HMOs), which provide enrollees with required health care services they need **plus** preventive care, all for a fixed annual premium. The enrollee usually pays no deductibles or large copayment towards these services. Consequently, HMO members usually save a lot on out-of-pocket expenses. However, members must receive their health care at an HMO facility or from HMO physicians. The available services vary considerably, but generally include:

- **Standard Medical Services** — routine office visits, X-rays and diagnostic tests, hospital and surgical care, emergency care, etc.

- **Preventive Services** — check ups, mammograms, and other preventive examinations. In addition, HMOs frequently provide eyeglasses, hearing aids, dental care and prescription drugs as standard benefits, unlike most insurance policies, which normally only cover these at additional cost to the insured.

HMOs operate in different ways. Many have their own salaried physicians and facilities, while others contract with other group medical practices (who maintain their own health centers) to provide health care services to the HMO members.

Another form of HMO is called an *Independent Practice Association* (IPA). Under this arrangement, the HMO contracts with several independent (private practice) physicians who provide health care services directly to HMO members. The HMO reimburses the physicians either based on a schedule of annual fixed fees for a defined package of services, or on a fee-for-service basis. Many individuals prefer IPAs because they offer a wider choice of doctors and convenient medical facilities.

Since 1985, Medicare coverage was extended to certain federally approved Health Maintenance Organizations (including IPAs) thus allowing Medicare beneficiaries to choose either a pre-paid HMO plan or a more traditional supplement insurance plan to pay for health care and services as they are provided. Because they offer an important alternative to private Medicare supplement policies, the costs and coverage these HMOs/IPAs provide to Medicare beneficiaries are discussed in Section 2 of this chapter.

Evaluate Carefully before Joining

At first glance, an HMO may appear to be the best way to meet your health care needs at a reasonable, fixed price without any deductibles or copayments. However, you should carefully evaluate the particular HMO that interests you (remember all HMOs are not the same) and determine whether you would be satisfied with its coverage and services. Consider the following when evaluating an HMO:

- **Services:** Determine what services the HMO provides and compare them to those provided by your present health insurance policy or one that you would consider buying.

- **Financial Status:** Be sure the HMO is well established and secure. If it has a parent organization, also check that organization's financial status.

- **Costs:** Determine how much you will pay per month and what copayments may be required. Compare these costs with those of a traditional policy offering similar benefits and care.

- **Emergencies:** Determine whether the HMO will pay for emergency care and, if so, how much it will cover when you are away or unable to use their doctors or facilities.

- **Doctors' Qualifications:** Check the qualifications of the doctors affiliated with the HMO. How many are "Board Certified" or "Board Eligible?" Find out the rate of turnover in the past two years, and the type of specialists available. "Board Certified" means the doctor has passed certain tests in his/her specialty, while "Board Eligible" means the doctor has completed his/her residence training but has not passed the final certifying tests. Both indicate medical competence in the specialty.

- **Other Specialists:** Find out what provisions the HMO has for members who need a specialist in an area not covered by any HMO-affiliated physicians.

- **Complaints:** Contact HMO members, if possible, to find out what complaints they may have about the HMO's services or care. Ask your State Insurance Regulator or State Consumer Protection office if they have complaints filed about the HMO. Also, find out how the HMO handles complaints about care or the doctor who provided it.

- **Appointments:** Find out how the HMO handles appointments (first-come/ first-served, restricted to a particular time, etc.) and determine the length of an average wait for an appointment.

- **Personal Considerations:**
  — Is the location of the HMO facility or physicians' offices convenient to you?
  — Are you willing to accept doctors assigned by the HMO rather than those of your own choosing?
  — Many HMOs also use nurse-practitioners and physicians' assistants to help with doctors' workloads; would you be willing to see one of these instead of a doctor?
  — Would you be satisfied with the hospitals the HMO uses?

PREFERRED PROVIDER ORGANIZATIONS (PPOs)

Preferred Provider Organizations provide enrollees with health care services and treatments at substantially discounted fees. PPOs draw from the network of independent physicians and hospitals that have negotiated contracts with them (this network is usually formed by an employer or insurance company to treat the plan's members). Usually, PPO members may use any doctor or hospital of their choice, but receive greater reimbursement for charges from a doctor or hospital (called "preferred provider") allied with the PPO. The PPO usually reimburses the member 80 percent or more for bills issued by a physician or hospital allied with the PPO, while limiting reimbursement for non-affiliated doctors to 50 percent or less.

There are several advantages to PPO coverage: medical out-of-pocket expenses are more predictable and less costly; insurance premiums are considerably lower; enrollees have a greater choice of physicians or hospitals than with some HMOs.

PPOs are **not approved** to participate in Medicare, although a limited number of demonstration projects are underway to determine whether or not approval would be justified. Consequently, Medicare beneficiaries must be aware that PPOs are not currently available to provide approved health care to them.

SPECIFIC TYPES OF GROUP AND INDIVIDUAL HEALTH INSURANCE

Basic Medical Insurance Policies

Basic medical insurance policies generally cover the basic costs of hospital, medical and surgical care. Most policies have specific time and dollar limits on benefits. Generally, they cover hospital room and board, operating and recovery rooms, surgeons fees (limited by a surgical fee schedule, which states specific amounts for all operations), intensive care units, laboratory and other diagnostic tests, X-rays, anesthesia services and doctors' fees for in-hospital medical visits. Most other medical care costs, such as for visits to a doctor's office, are not often covered.

Major Medical Insurance Policies

Major medical insurance policies provide broader coverage than basic medical insurance and usually provide greater protection against the costs of serious illnesses, accidents, and continuing chronic illnesses. When an insurance company offers policies that combine basic and major medical plans into one policy, the result is called a *comprehensive* policy.

Medicare Supplement Insurance *(Medigap)* Policies

Medicare supplement insurance policies provide benefits to help pay for what Medicare does not cover. They cover deductibles, copayment-payments and other out-of-pocket costs that Medicare beneficiaries have to pay. Generally, most private Medigap insurance policies follow the Medicare guidelines and will not pay for non-Medicare approved services. See the next section on insurance for Medicare beneficiaries for more details.

Hospital Confinement Indemnity Insurance Policies

Confinement indemnity policies pay a fixed fee — per day, per week, or per month (depending on the policy) — when a person is hospitalized. Benefits are usually paid directly to the insured and are not based on actual hospitalization costs. Most policies have a waiting period before they pay benefits. In other words, you usually have to be in a hospital for a certain number of days before you receive an indemnity.

Long-Term Care Policies

Although still in their infancy, commercial long-term care insurance policies are receiving more attention from insurance companies, the public, and the government. Currently, the average cost of nursing home care ranges between $25,000 and $30,000 per year, and the average professional in-home health care visit averages between $45 and $60 per visit. The financial ability to cover such costs is of critical concern to almost every American — whether 45, 65, or older. Most of us have a deep inner fear of having to pay the enormous costs associated with a catastrophic illness or injury that requires long-term care.

Even Medicare covers only limited expenses for the long-term care of a patient with an acute illness, and provides almost nothing for in-home or nursing home care for a patient with a chronic injury or illness, such as Alzheimer's disease. Consequently, private insurance companies are finally looking at expanding their markets to cover the last remaining gap in health insurance and Medicare coverage: long-term health care insurance.

According to the Department of Health and Human Services, about 130 companies now sell long-term care insurance. Currently, over 2 million policies have been sold, and the market is expected to grow enormously in the next few years. Since these policies are still experimental, they continue to change and vary widely in cost, coverage and benefits. Thus, it is almost impossible to present a detailed analysis of those that are currently offered. However, some characteristics are shared by most long-term care policies.

Most policies provide coverage for each day of care in a nursing home, with some coverage for in-home health visits for a limited benefit period. The majority offer very little coverage for in-home care and are basically geared to covering nursing home care only. The benefit periods, including a waiting period of approximately 90 days before payments begin, range anywhere from one to three years, with a few providing coverage up to six years. For those that offer in-home care coverage, there is generally a limit of 180 days to two years of coverage within the total maximum benefit period.

The daily amount each policy actually pays for nursing home care varies even more widely, from $10 per day to $100 per day, generally depending on the cost of the policy. Annual premiums can cost anywhere from several hundred dollars to several thousand depending on the amount and type of benefits provided.

Policies restrictions and provisions also vary, but often include:

- restricted coverage for skilled nursing or intermediate care facilities (nursing home), **excluding** custodial-type nursing homes, where most chronic long-term patients are placed.

- requirement that the covered person be hospitalized before he/she enters a nursing home. This is an important restriction, since over 60 percent of patients who enter nursing homes are not hospitalized before entry.

- some policies do not cover care for certain illnesses.

Unfortunately, the current long-term insurance policies still don't address long-term or in-home care for the majority of people because of the high cost of such care and the exorbitant costs for the few policies that do provide sufficient coverage for long-term care. However, new long-term policies are being developed continually. Perhaps more affordable policies with better benefits and coverage for the average person will appear in the near future.

If You Buy — Buy with Caution!

When considering the purchase of a long-term policy, it is absolutely essential that you contact **several** companies and do in-depth comparison shopping. The discussion at the end of this section, "Sources of Free Information and Assistance", lists some good resources on long-term insurance.

Above all, be sure you understand each policy's costs, maximum and per-day benefits, types of nursing facilities covered, in-home benefits, waiting period provisions, other restrictions that may preclude payment for illnesses such as Alzheimer's disease, and renewal provisions. Be aware that the best policies are almost always the most expensive ones. *Of utmost importance:* be sure the policy you select provides adequate protection at a realistically affordable cost. Nothing could be more disastrous than to purchase a policy whose premiums would create a financial hardship for you and your family. Remember, insurance is a contingency plan — you don't want to pay more for the insurance plan than you might pay for the actual care. Nor do you want to invest so much that you lose a disproportionate amount of money — especially because you may never require the coverage long-term insurance provides.

Limited Benefit Policies

Benefits provided by these policies are usually extremely limited, and vary widely from policy to policy. Due to their restrictive nature, these policies **should never be used** as a substitute for basic medical insurance; rather, they should be purchased when appropriate, to supplement basic coverage. They are categorized as follows:

■ **Dental Insurance** — Although now often offered with group insurance policies, special insurance to cover dental care can also be purchased separately. Dental insurance coverage is usually limited to routine dental care and dental injuries, with some reimbursement for restorative services, such as crowns, caps and dentures.

■ **Specified Illness or Injury Insurance** — Generally only covers expenses which accrue from the particular illness, injury or circumstances specified in the policy. The most common policies cover one of the following:
  — Cancer care in a hospital
  — Intensive care unit
  — Heart Attacks
  — Accidents
  — Disability which prohibits an individual from working. .

RENEWALS, RESTRICTIONS AND EXCLUSIONS

The particular wording and terms found in a health insurance policy define exactly:

- what services and care are actually covered by a policy;
- what coverage may be excluded;
- how much the insurance company or health care plan will pay;
- how much the insured person will have to pay out-of-pocket;
- whether the policy can be renewed on its expiration date.

Unless you understand the language of the policy, you may purchase insurance that will not provide the coverage you need. The following is a brief explanation of certain terms and provisions contained in most policies. It should help you to understand and evaluate an insurance policy.

- **Pre-existing conditions** — medical problems that a person has been treated for before purchasing insurance coverage. The pre-existing condition may prevent coverage of the particular disorder for a period of six months, one to two years, or even longer.

- **Exclusions** — ailments not covered by the policy (like Alzheimer's disease) and/or injuries resulting from war or military service, aviation, attempted suicide or intentionally self-inflicted injuries.

- **Waiting period** — period of time (established in the policy) after the policy is in effect but before the insured can receive benefits.

- **Coordination of benefits provisions** — to prevent multiple or excessive payments for a particular medical expense, the policy allows a person to receive a set maximum benefit amount or to collect on only one policy. Although this provision generally applies to different policies with the same insurance company, some policies have an "Insurance with Other Insurers" provision. Under this provision, an insurance company will usually only pay a portion of the benefits where the insured has other valid policies providing the same coverage and the insurer is aware of these other policies.

- **Renewal provisions** — one of the most important provisions to consider before you buy a particular policy. A health insurance policy is written for a limited time, usually a year, and must be renewed, at the end of each term. The following summarizes the basic renewal provisions:

— *Renewable for life/guaranteed renewable / noncancelable:* The insured is guaranteed the ability to renew for life or until he/she reaches an age specified in the policy.

— *Conditionally renewable:* The insured can renew this policy, usually until he/she reaches a specified age. However, the company can drop a particular type of policy for a given area, precluding renewal for everyone covered under the policy. This does not happen often, but it can.

— *Optional renewable:* The Insurance company may decide not to renew the policy at the end of the term.

— *Term or nonrenewable:* This policy cannot be renewed at the end of the term.

GLOSSARY OF HEALTH INSURANCE TERMS

The following glossary contains a few terms used frequently in most health insurance policies. However, the terms "assignment" and "participating physician or supplier" apply only to Medicare and Medicare supplement insurance policies.

- **actual charge** — the amount a physician or supplier bills a patient for a particular medical service, supply or equipment.

- **assignment** — a process through which a doctor or supplier agrees to accept the Medicare program's payment as payment in full except for specific copayment-insurance and deductible amounts required from the patient.

- **copayment** — a type of cost-sharing in which the insured person pays a specific amount, usually in dollars rather than a percentage, for covered services. The insurer pays the rest of the cost. Similar to copayment-insurance, except the amount paid does not usually vary with the cost of the service.

- **cost-sharing** — a way of paying for care and services in which the insured person has to pay some out-of-pocket costs to receive care. The total costs are shared with the insurance company or Medicare.

- **deductible** — a fixed amount that an insured person pays each year for covered medical services. Any amount above the deductible is covered by insurance.

- **intermediate care facility (nursing home)** — a facility that provides institutional services, board and lodging to patients who need consistent specialized care but do not need the more intensive level of care provided in a skilled nursing facility. Medicare and many private insurance policies limit their coverage to *skilled* nursing facilities.

- **participating physician or supplier** — a physician or supplier who agrees to accept assignment on all Medicare claims.

- **reasonable charge** — the amount allowed by an insurance company or Medicare for a given service or health care item. The amount is usually based on the common charge for the item or service in the local area.

- **Skilled nursing facility (nursing home)** — a facility which provides care for patients who have just completed a stay in a hospital and need intensive care or rehabilitation.

ADVICE ABOUT BUYING HEALTH INSURANCE

Although most insurance agents and companies are honest and try to sell health insurance policies that customers need and can afford, some are dishonest and unscrupulous, particularly when dealing with the elderly. These agents and companies will often employ deception to sell insurance policies to the unsuspecting consumer.

In a joint hearing several years back on health insurance fraud, the House Subcommittee on Health and Long-Term Care and the Subcommittee on Housing and Consumer Interests disclosed some shocking deceptions and fraud perpetrated on the elderly by certain insurance agents.

In some cases, the agents sold policies that duplicated the customer's Medicare coverage but which did not pay for any additional benefits. Some individuals were "conned" into replacing a policy with a new one that offered "better" coverage; however, the agent failed to mention that the switch would leave the individual without coverage for six months or more because the new policy had an unexplained waiting period during which benefits were not paid.

Unbelievable as they sound, these deceptions continue to occur! Consequently, you must be alert to the possibility of dealing with a dishonest agent or company, even though they are in the minority. Again, *most insurance agents and companies are trustworthy.*

With the extremely high cost of procuring health insurance, it is absolutely essential that you carefully evaluate all policies you are considering and the insurance companies selling them.

The following suggestions may prove helpful when you shop for health insurance:

- Learn about the insurance company and agent with whom you are dealing. A company must meet certain qualifications to sell insurance in your state, so contact your State Insurance Regulator's office (listed at the end of this chapter) to make sure the company and agent are approved. Also, insurance agents must be licensed by your state and are required to carry state-issued proof (certificate or card) that shows their name and the company they represent. Always ask to see this state-issued certificate or card — **do not accept** a commercial business card as proof of licensing.

- Always try to find a local agent who is readily available to help you with questions or claims.

- Never be rushed by an insurance agent's or company's high-pressure tactics. Take as much time as you need to review the policy thoroughly and compare it with other policies from different companies. The comparison shopping you do can save you money and ensure that you get the best coverage.

- Whenever possible, discuss the policy you are considering with a family member or friend before you sign the application and agree to buy.

- Whenever possible, buy only one policy that adequately covers your health care needs rather than several policies that may overlap or duplicate coverage.

- Watch out for exclusions for pre-existing conditions, etc. Be sure to know exactly when the policy begins paying benefits and whether any medical conditions are permanently excluded from coverage.

- Be wary about changing or replacing policies you already have. However, *don't keep a policy that doesn't meet your current health care needs or which duplicates coverage.* **Always** keep an old policy in force until the new policy begins to actually pay benefits. This precaution will protect you in case the new policy has a waiting period or certain exclusions for pre-existing conditions that your current policy covers.

- Know the policy's renewal provisions and in particular whether the company can refuse to renew your individual policy.

- Since most policies have some type of limit on benefits (expressed generally in dollars payable or number of days for which payment will be made), be sure to determine the maximum benefits stated in the policy. Do not rely on the agent's comments without seeing the amounts in writing. Read the policy **yourself!**

- Always ask whether the policy has a "free look" provision which gives you time (usually 10 to 30 days) in which to look over the policy after you receive it and to return it for refund of the initial premium if you don't want it.

- Obtain as much information as you can to thoroughly evaluate any special offers for reduced-price group benefit insurance — aimed at the elderly — advertised on television, radio, or by mail. Although many of these plans appear to be good bargains at first glance, they may provide very little coverage for the cost.

- **Always** fill out an insurance policy application completely and accurately before signing it to prevent future claims from being denied or the policy from being cancelled because of errors or omissions. Do not leave any blank spaces to filled in later by the agent or anyone else. It is very important that you read the **entire** policy and application before signing it or agreeing to purchase. If you have poor eyesight and cannot read it properly, make sure you have a friend or family member — not the agent — read it to you.

- **Never** pay cash for the insurance premium. Always pay by check, money order or bank draft made out to the insurance company (never to the agent).

KEEPING A RECORD OF YOUR POLICIES

You should maintain a current record of all your health insurance policies so that the information is readily available in an emergency. Also, keep all original policies in a safe place and let a family member, friend or your authorized representative know where you keep them.

Be sure to include the correct name, telephone number and permanent address of the insurance agent and company which issued the policy. In addition, obtain the company's toll-free telephone number if available, to help save money on long distance calls.

SOURCES OF FREE INFORMATION AND ASSISTANCE

Several sources of health insurance information and assistance are readily available — **without charge.** Two that may prove extremely helpful are the offices of your **State Insurance Regulator** and **State Consumer Protection Department**. Both offices provide up-to-date consumer guides on insurance, and information about state and federal insurance laws, your rights as a policy holder, and insurance companies that do business in your state. The offices' consumer complaint departments can help you solve insurance problems you have been unable to resolve with an insurance agency or company. A listing of the State Insurance Regulators appears at the end of this chapter; a listing of State Consumer Protection Offices is found at the end of Chapter 10, following the discussion of "Legal Assistance for the Elderly."

Other sources of health insurance information which can help you select an insurance company or policy are:

- **The Health Insurance Association of America** — offers several publications on health insurance policies, Medigap policies and long-term care policies. The Association offers a listing, by state, of the insurance companies that sell long-term insurance policies. Other Association pamphlets include: *Consumers' Guide to Long-Term Care* and *What You Should Know About Health Services.*

To order copies of the listing, the two publications mentioned, or any other publications on health insurance policies, write to:

Health Insurance Association of America
1025 Connecticut Ave., NW Suite 1200
Washington, DC 20036

- **The American Council of Life Insurance** — offers several booklets on health insurance, life insurance, and annuities. The Council also has a listing of companies that offer long-term health care policies throughout the nation. Request the listing or policy information by writing to:

American Council of Life Insurance
1001 Pennsylvania Ave., NW
Washington, DC 20004

Be sure to specify the type of policy information you wish to receive.

- Your public library is probably one of the best sources of information available. Call or visit to review their collection of pamphlets, books, magazines and reference materials on health insurance. Tell your librarian the type of policy you need or the information you seek. He/she will help you obtain the latest information on the ever-changing world of insurance.

One of the library's most useful reference books is *Best Ratings*. The book — published by A.M. Best and Co. — rates most large insurance companies in the U.S. based on their financial strength. An insurance company's rating indicates the security of any policy purchased from the company. Naturally, it's always best to seek a company with the highest possible rating (A+ is the highest rating).

- Many associations and organizations concerned with older individuals (several are listed in Chapter 11) offer publications on health insurance, including Medigap and long-term care policies. These publications are almost always free to members. However, you may sometimes have to wait a few weeks for a publication, depending on its availability.

- Retired federal employees enrolled in the Federal Employees Health Benefits Program (FEHBP) and Medicare Parts A and B, should direct questions about the FEHBP plan's coverage to their FEHBP plan's carrier or they should call or write for general information on retirement and health benefits to:

U.S. Office of Personnel Management
Retirement and Insurance Group
P.O. Box 14172
Washington, DC 20044
Tel: (202) 606-0500

OF IMPORTANCE TO FEDERAL AND POSTAL WORKERS AND RETIREES . . .

Under the Federal Employees Health Benefits Program (FEHBP), federal and postal workers and retirees have over 300 health maintenance organizations plus 19 fee-for-service *(traditional) insurance* plans to choose from during each year's "open season." If you are such a worker or retiree and also eligible for Medicare, it is crucial that you learn about the coverage provided by both Medicare and the various FEHBP plans high and standard options. Towards this end, before selecting an FEHBP plan, be sure to read as many brochures on the various plans as you can. These brochures are available directly from the insurance providers' offices or from the Office of Personnel Management.

If you are a federal retiree with Medicare, the standard option will generally cover you sufficiently. However, if your spouse is not yet eligible for Medicare and is covered only under your FEHBP plan, you should weigh the cost benefits of a lower premium for a standard option plan and the coverage it provides against the higher premium of the high option plan — especially if your spouse is in poor health. If you elect to take the higher option, you can shift to the standard option when your spouse becomes eligible for Medicare.

SECTION II

Health Insurance For Those On Medicare

Medicare never covers all of the health care costs that a beneficiary may incur. Thus, most beneficiaries find it necessary to obtain additional health insurance to help pay the deductibles, copayment-payments and out-of-pocket costs not covered by Medicare. Although Medicare's coverage has been somewhat expanded in recent years, Medicare still only covers care in a "*skilled* nursing home" — while the majority of nursing homes are not skilled. Also, Medicare only provides limited coverage for nursing home care for a patient with a long-term **acute** illness or injury; it provides no coverage at all for patients with long-term **chronic** conditions.

In addition, Medicare only pays up to the maximum amounts it has set for medical services, and it does **not pay at all** for services it does not consider medically necessary. Before you select additional health insurance to supplement Medicare's coverage, you should become familiar with what Medicare does cover so you can determine which private commercial policy will cover most or all of your out-of-pocket costs. Innumerable insurance companies and agents are eager to sell you policies to supplement your Medicare coverage. But, no matter how much you spend for this additional coverage, it's likely you still won't be covered completely. Therefore, you should carefully evaluate candidate policies to see which will provide the most coverage for the best value.

The majority of insurance companies offer various types of health insurance policies to Senior Citizens in addition to the standard Medicare supplement insurance that most Medicare beneficiaries purchase. Many of these alternate policies were covered in Section I of this chapter. Be aware that just because you have Medicare doesn't always mean you need additional insurance. Sometimes such insurance only duplicates the benefits you already have. Workers and their spouses 65 and older, and disabled beneficiaries under 65 who are covered by an employer group health care plan, should note that their company plan is primarily responsible for covering their health care costs; Medicare only helps supplement this insurance by paying for some services and costs not covered by the group health policy.

This section limits its discussion to Medicare supplement insurance policies and alternative pre-paid health plans which Medicare beneficiaries may now choose to provide for their health care. While only 9 percent of Medicare beneficiaries are currently enrolled in pre-paid health plans, these plans are becoming more popular and are expected to increase another 20 percent within the next year because they offer beneficiaries a health care option that can save them money and provide better preventive care than most typical health insurance plans.

MEDICARE SUPPLEMENT INSURANCE (*MEDIGAP* POLICIES)

Since Medicare's enactment in 1965, many private insurance companies have sold supplement insurance policies — *Medigap* policies — to help fill in the "gaps" in health care service and costs that are not covered by Medicare. Consequently, when choosing Medicare supplement insurance, you should look for a policy which covers as many major gaps in Medicare coverage as possible. Three major gaps (discussed later in this section) are:

- Medicare deductibles and copayments

- items and services not covered by Medicare

- costs exceeding Medicare's "approved charges."

Understanding these deficient areas (gaps) in your Medicare coverage will enable you to effectively evaluate and select a Medigap policy. Be sure to compare several Medigap policies because, while they all follow Medicare guidelines for covered services and benefits, they can vary considerably in price and the additional (non-gap) services they may provide. This additional coverage can include partial payment for outpatient drugs and medications, routine physical examinations, certain immunizations, and several other items not normally covered by Medicare. However, just as Medicare sets "approved amounts" for services, most Medigap policies also set predetermined approved amounts for services, and generally exclude those services and care that Medicare does not cover.

"First Things First"

Before you examine or evaluate any Medigap policies, you should be aware of three provisions of federal law:

- Medicare supplement policies are not connected with the federal government or the Medicare program. The government does not sell or service these policies, or endorse any particular one. They are sold only by private insurance companies, Blue Cross, and Blue Shield. It is against the law for any insurance company or agent to state or suggest that they represent the Medicare program or any government agency.

- Federal law prohibits any insurance company or agent from knowingly selling you a policy that duplicates Medicare coverage or any private health insurance policy that you already own *without* notifying you in writing of this duplication.

- By law, insurance companies are prohibited from discriminating unfairly against the consumer by raising rates or limiting coverage.

SUMMARY OF MEDICARE'S "GAPS" IN COVERAGE

The following summary of Medicare coverage highlights the gaps this coverage leaves in your total health care. Information about what Medicare does cover appears in Chapter 4.

- **Gap 1 — Medicare deductibles and copayment-payments:** In 1996, you are responsible for paying the following Medicare deductibles and copayments:

  — *Hospitalization (Part A)* after you pay the 1996 deductible of **$736**, Medicare pays all other allowable charges for the first 60 days of in-patient hospital care during a benefit period. For days 61 through 90, you pay a copayment-insurance charge of **$184** per day. If you need more than 90 days of hospitalization in any benefit period, you may draw on your 60 lifetime reserve days. You must also pay a copayment-insurance charge of **$368** per day for each reserve day used. In each case, you must pay a **$736** deductible during each benefit period.

— *Skilled Nursing Facility Care (Part A)* Medicare will help cover up to 100 days per benefit period of in-patient care in a skilled nursing facility. Medicare pays all approved charges *except* for a daily copayment-insurance charge of **$92**, which you must pay for days 21 through 100.

— *Medical Insurance Coverage (Part B)* beneficiary pays the first **$100** of allowable charges (annual one-time deductible). For the rest of the calendar year, Medicare pays 80 percent of all allowable charges for most services. The remaining 20 percent, plus all charges in excess of Medicare's allowable amounts, must be paid by the beneficiary.

The first thing a Medigap policy should provide is coverage of the deductibles and copayments that Medicare expects its beneficiaries to pay out-of-pocket.

■ **Gap 2 — Items and services not covered by Medicare:** Medicare only covers services it considers reasonable and medically necessary, and provides limited coverage for treatment of mental illness (including hospitalization). Currently, Medicare's coverage for hospitalization in a psychiatric hospital cannot exceed 190 days in an entire lifetime.

The following summarizes the major services and supplies **not** usually **covered** under Medicare hospital (Part A) or Medical (Part B) insurance. Many supplemental insurance policies will provide coverage for some of these services. Find a policy that offers the most coverage at the best cost.

— Chiropractic services;   — Routine foot care;
— Cosmetic surgery;   — Health care outside the
— Custodial care;   United States;
— Dental care;   — Homemaker services;

— Prescription and non-prescription drugs purchased outside a hospital;

— Eyeglasses and eye examinations for prescribing, fitting, or changing eyeglasses;

— Personal convenience items in your room at a hospital or skilled nursing facility such as a phone or television;

— Routine physical examinations and tests directly related to such examinations;

— Private duty nurses;

— Private room in a hospital or nursing home;

— Custodial services performed by immediate relatives or members of your household.

— Hearing aids and hearing examinations for prescribing, fitting, or changing hearing aids;

— Immunizations except pneumococcal and Hepatitis B vaccinations or immunizations required because of an injury or immediate risk of infection;

— Self-administered injections, such as insulin;

— Long-term care (nursing homes);

— Meals delivered to your home;

— Full-time nursing care in your home;

— Orthopedic shoes, unless they are part of a leg brace and are included in the orthopedist's charge;

■ **Gap 3 — Costs that exceed Medicare's "approved charges":** Medicare will pay up to a maximum amount it has determined to be "reasonable" for each covered service or supply. Always ask your doctors and medical suppliers whether they accept "assignment" of Medicare benefits. Although doctors and suppliers do not have to accept assignment, many do — which can save you a lot in out-of-pocket expenses. However, when the doctor/supplier won't accept assignment, the beneficiary pays any cost charged by a physician or supplier that exceeds the approved maximum.

Since many doctors and medical suppliers charge more than the "approved" Medicare amounts for services and supplies, it is advantageous to have a supplement policy that sets higher limits than Medicare's for the same services or supplies, or which pays a portion of the difference. Because these additional out-of-pocket costs are common and can be quite expensive, you should consider the extent to which a Medigap policy will help cover them.

MEDIGAP INSURANCE REFORM

To protect Medicare beneficiaries against Medigap marketing abuses, Congress enacted a Medigap reform law in 1990. In effect in all states except Minnesota, Massachusetts and Wisconsin, the law standardizes and simplifies the Medigap policies offered by all insurance providers. (These three states were exempted from the law because they already had alternative Medigap standarization programs in effect before the federal legislation standarizing Medigap policies was enacted. If you live in these states, contact your state insurance department to find out what Medigap coverage is available.)

The new law defines ten standard benefit packages developed by the National Association of Insurance Commissioners which must be designated "A" through "J"—with A always being the lowest-cost "core" plan, and J providing the most extensive (and probably most expensive) coverage for those who want to purchase maximum available coverage. Insurers cannot change or eliminate the letter designations but can add words to clarify them. Annual average costs for the standard policies range from approximately $400 to $600 for Plan A to a high of $1,200 to $1,800 for Plan J.

Before any firm which sells Medigap insurance can offer Plans B through J, it must provide the government-mandated Plan A. Every insurer's Plan A must include the same minimum—or core—set of benefits. Insurers can also provide any or all of the nine other plans, each of which must include: (1) the core benefits and (2) the additional benefits for each plan mandated by law. Any other benefits the insurer may wish to offer in one of the plans are not covered by the law. The prices of Plans B through J may vary, but within state (maximum) guidelines.

To help Seniors compare Medigap policies from different providers, the law also requires insurers to use the same wording and formats to describe all government-mandated benefits. To be competitive, insurers may add benefits to those required by law, or lower their prices below government-set maximums. The Medigap law is not intended to restrict insurers from offering more than the government mandates, but to make sure that when Seniors compare different insurers' Medigap plans, they know the minimum coverage they should expect from each insurance policy. Thus, shopping for Medigap becomes a question of comparing prices and non-legislated "extras" before making a final selection.

Mandatory Core Benefits

The core coverages that must be provided in all insurers' Plan A packages as well as all other policies are:

- Medicare Part A co-payment for days 61-90 of a hospital stay;

- Medicare Part A co-payment for each lifetime reserve day (91-150), plus an additional 365 days of inpatient hospital care once Medicare coverage has been exhausted;

- 20% co-payment for Medicare Part B services once the Part B deductible is met;

- the first 3 pints of blood used in a calendar year, under Medicare Parts A and B.

Additional Benefits of Plans B through J

Insurers need not provide any or all of Plans B through J, but if they do provide one or more of the plans, each plan must include in addition to the core benefits of Plan A the benefits listed below:

- **Medicare Part A deductible**—Plans B through J must cover the yearly deductible for Part A hospitalization.

- **Medicare Part B deductible**—Plans C, F, and J must include the $100 deductible for Part B that beneficiaries must pay.

- **Skilled nursing home care**—Plans C through J must include the co-payment for days 21-100 of skilled nursing home care. This does not cover custodial nursing home care; it only covers short stays in a nursing home for those who need skilled care or rehabilitation.

- **Excess Part B charges** (Only for Medicare-approved services)—Plans F, I, and J must cover 100% of the balance of charges that exceed Medicare's approved fees; Plan G must cover 80% of the balance.

- **Foreign travel emergencies**—Plans C through J must cover 80% of medically necessary emergency care needed during a trip outside the U.S. after a $250 deductible is met.

- **At-home recovery**—If you are eligible for Medicare-paid home health care after an injury or illness, Plans D, G, I, and J pay for visits by a personal care aide to help with eating, bathing, dressing, personal hygiene, etc.

- **Prescription drugs**—Plans H and I offer a "basic" benefit for prescription drugs. After a $250 deductible is met, the basic benefit pays for 50% of all prescription drug costs up to $1,250. Plan J extends the same coverage up to $3,000.

- **Preventive medical care**—Plans E and J cover up to $120 per year of preventive care (physical examinations, serum cholesterol screenings, hearing tests, etc.) ordered by a doctor.

AN ALTERNATIVE APPROACH:
FEDERALLY-QUALIFIED HMOs

For the past several years, the federal government has contracted with private health pre-payment plans to provide services to Medicare beneficiaries, giving beneficiaries a health care alternative to the standard Medicare program. These pre-paid plans essentially comprise Health Maintenance Organizations (HMOs), a few similar pre-paid "Competitive Medical Plans" (CMPs) and the new Medicare SELECT health insurance product as explained in Chapter 4 on Medicare.

Each HMO/CMP must be federally approved to participate in Medicare and must at least duplicate the services covered by Medicare. Once an HMO/CMP is approved, Medicare will pay it a fixed monthly amount based on the average expense normally paid by Medicare beneficiaries for Medicare medical insurance (Part B) premiums less deductibles and copayment-insurance. The beneficiary also pays the HMO/CMP a premium to cover Medicare's required deductibles and copayment-insurance amounts plus the costs of any additional HMO/CMP services not covered by Medicare. Beneficiaries continue to have the Medicare Part B medical insurance premium deducted from their Social Security checks. The premium paid to the HMO/CMP is **not** the premium for Medicare medical (Part B) insurance.

There are several reasons that Medicare beneficiaries enroll in approved HMOs/CMPs. Some of the most frequently cited included:

- HMOs/CMPs save them money.
- The plans charge a fixed monthly amount which makes it easier to budget for total health care expenses.

- HMOs/CMPs don't require a payment each time a service is provided.
- Many provide several services not covered by Medicare at no cost or for a nominal fee.
- Almost all care is provided at one location.
- Emergency care is available continuously around the clock.
- There are usually no claim forms to complete.

Some of the most frequently cited disadvantages include:

- The choice of a doctor is limited.
- There are often long waiting periods to see a doctor.
- Beneficiaries must use the HMO's/CMP's hospital(s).
- The patient is often treated by a physician's assistant rather than a doctor.
- The setting is a clinic rather than an intimate private practice office.

If you are interested in belonging to a federally-approved HMO/CMP, there are a few requirements in addition to paying the monthly premium. They are as follows:

- You must live in the area served by the HMO/CMP.
- You must have Medicare Part B medical insurance.
- You must not be entitled to Medicare coverage because of kidney failure requiring dialysis or kidney transplant.
- You must agree to follow the HMO's/CMP's rules.

Once you have joined an HMO/CMP, if you become dissatisfied for any reason, you can terminate your membership at any time. Individuals who need help locating an HMO/CMP in their area or in an area to which they are moving can contact their local Social Security office or use the new nationwide toll-free telephone service: 800-772-1213. Social Security has a national directory of Medicare participating pre-payment plans (HMOs/CMPs) listed by state and plan number. If Social Security cannot provide a current telephone number, obtain the full name and address of the HMO/CMP so you can obtain a telephone number from directory assistance.

LISTING

State Insurance Regulators

Each of our states has a commissioner or other official who is responsible for overseeing the laws and regulations governing all types of insurance and insurance businesses within the state. A primary function of these regulators is to protect your interests as an insurance policyholder. Even though many people look to the insurance commission to help resolve complaints against insurance companies, few people realize that the commissions provide many other helpful services to the public. Foremost among these services are counseling services regarding insurance needs for the elderly. Also the commissions often offer publications which will assist you in determining which insurance policies may satisfy your needs.

Many of the state insurance offices have recently established special telephone numbers solely to provide insurance counseling services. These numbers are designated in this listing by the letters "**IC**" preceding the telephone number. Contact your state insurance regulator for assistance by either calling or writing to the offices listed below.

ALABAMA
Insurance Department
135 South Union Street, #181
Montgomery, AL 36130
Tel: (334) 269-3550
IC Tel: 800-243-5463

ALASKA
Department of Insurance
800 E. Diamond, Suite 560
Anchorage, AK 99515
Tel: (907) 349-1230
IC Tel: 800-478-6065

AMERICAN SAMOA
Insurance Department
Office of the Governor
Pago Pago, AS 96797
Tel: 011-(684)633-4116

ARIZONA
Insurance Department
2910 N. 44th St.
Phoenix, AZ 85018
Tel: (602) 912-8444
IC Tel: 800-432-4040

ARKANSAS
Insurance Department
400 University Tower Bldg.
1123 S. University Ave.
Little Rock, AR 72204
Tel: (501) 686-2900
IC Tel: 800-852-5494

CALIFORNIA
Insurance Department
300 S. Spring Street
Los Angeles, CA 90013
Toll Free: 800-927-4357
Tel: (213) 897-8921

COLORADO
Insurance Division
1560 Broadway, Suite 850
Denver, CO 80202
Tel: (303) 894-7499 ext. 356
IC Tel: 800-544-9181

CONNECTICUT
Insurance Department
P.O. Box 816
Hartford, CT 06142
Tel: (203) 297-3800
IC Tel: 800-443-9946

DELAWARE
Insurance Department
841 Silver Lake Blvd.
Dover, DE 19904
Tel: (302) 739-4251
Toll-Free: 800-282-8611
IC Tel: 800-336-9500

DISTRICT OF COLUMBIA
Insurance Department
441 - 4th Street N.W.
Suite 850 North
Washington, DC 20001
Tel: (202) 727-8000
IC Tel: (202) 994-7463

FLORIDA
Department of Insurance
State Capitol Plaza, Level 11
200 E. Gaines St.
Tallahassee, FL 32399
Tel: (904) 922-3100
IC Tel: (904) 922-2073

GEORGIA
Insurance Department
2 Martin L. King, Jr. Drive
Room 716 West Tower
Atlanta, GA 30334
Tel: (404) 656-2056
IC Tel: 800-669-8387

GUAM
Insurance Department
378 Chalan San Antonio
P. O. Box 2796
Tamuning, GU 96911
Tel: 011 (671) 477-5144

HAWAII
Insurance Division
P.O. Box 3614
Honolulu, HI 96811
Tel: (808) 586-2790
IC Tel: (808) 586-0100

IDAHO
Insurance Department
700 W. State St., 3rd Fl.
Boise, ID 83720
Tel: (208) 334-4350
IC Tel: 800-247-4422 (S.W.)
        800-488-5725 (N.)
        800-488-5764 (S.E.)
        800-488-5731 (C.)

ILLINOIS
Insurance Department
320 W. Washington St., 4th Fl.
Springfield, IL 62767
Tel: (217) 782-4515
IC Tel: 800-548-9034

INDIANA
Insurance Department
311 W. Washington St.,Suite 300
Indianapolis, IN 46204
Tel: (317) 232-2395
Toll Free: 800-622-4461
IC Tel: 800-452-4800

IOWA
Insurance Division
Lucas State Office Bldg., 6th Fl.
E. 12th and Grand Sts.
Des Moines, IA 50319
Tel: (515) 281-5705
IC Tel: (515) 281-5705

KANSAS
Insurance Department
420 S.W. 9th Street
Topeka, KS 66612
Tel: (913) 296-3071
Toll Free: 800-432-2484
IC Tel: 800-432-3535

KENTUCKY
Insurance Department
215 W. Main St., P.O. Box 517
Frankfort, KY 40602
Tel: (502) 564-3630
IC Tel: 800-372-2973

LOUISIANA
Insurance Department
P.O. Box 94214
Baton Rouge, LA 70804
Tel: (504) 342-5301
IC Tel: 800-259-5301

MAINE
Bureau of Insurance
State Office Building
State House, Station 34
Augusta, ME 04333
Tel: (207) 582-8707
IC Tel: 800-750-5353

MARYLAND
Insurance Administration
501 St. Paul Place
Baltimore MD 21202
Tel: (410) 333-2793
IC Tel: 800-243-3425

MASSACHUSETTS
Insurance Division
470 Atlantic Ave.
Boston, MA 02210
Tel: (617) 521-7777
IC Tel: (617) 727-7750

MICHIGAN
Insurance Bureau
P.O. Box 30220
Lansing, MI 48909
Tel: (517) 373-0240
IC Tel: (517) 373-8230

MINNESOTA
Insurance Department
Department of Commerce
133 E. 7th St.
St. Paul, MN 55101
Tel: (612) 296-4026
IC Tel: 800-882-6262

MISSISSIPPI
Insurance Department
P.O. Box 79
Jackson, MS 39205
Tel: (601) 359-3569
Toll Free: 800-948-3090

MISSOURI
Department of Insurance
P.O. Box 690
Jefferson City, MO 65102
Tel: (314) 751-2640
Toll Free: 800-726-7390
           (within state)
IC Tel: 800-390-3330

MONTANA
Insurance Department
126 N. Sanders
Mitchell Bldg., Rm. 270
P.O. Box 4009
Helena, MT 59601
Tel: (406) 444-2040
IC Tel: 800-332-2272

NEBRASKA
Insurance Department
941 "0" St., Suite 400
Lincoln, NE 68508
Tel: (402) 471-2201
IC Tel: (402) 471-4506

NEVADA
Dept. of Business & Industry
Division of Insurance
1665 Hot Springs Rd.
Carson City, NV 89710
Tel: (702) 687-4270
Toll Free: 800-992-0900
IC Tel: (702) 367-1218

NEW HAMPSHIRE
Insurance Department
169 Manchester St.
Concord, NH 03301
Tel: (603) 271-2261
Toll Free: 800-852-3416
IC Tel: (603) 271-4642

NEW JERSEY
Insurance Department
20 W. State Street
Roebling Bldg.
Trenton, NJ 08625
Tel: (609) 292-5363
IC Tel: 800-792-8820

NEW MEXICO
Insurance Department
PERA Building, P.O. Drawer 1269
Santa Fe, NM 87504
Tel: (505) 827-4500
IC Tel: 800-432-2080

NEW YORK
Insurance Department
160 West Broadway
New York, NY 10013
Tel: (212) 602-0203 (NYC)
Outside NYC:
Toll Free: 800-342-3736
Outside of state:
IC Tel: 800-333-4114

NORTH CAROLINA
Insurance Department
Dobbs Bldg., P.O. Box 26387
Raleigh, NC 27611
Tel: (919) 733-0111
Toll Free: 800-662-7777
IC Tel: 800-443-9354

NORTH DAKOTA
Insurance Department
600 E. Boulevard
Bismarck, ND 58505
Tel: (701) 328-2440
Toll Free: 800-247-0560
IC Tel: 800-247-0560

OHIO
Insurance Department
2100 Stella Court
Columbus, OH 43215
Tel: (614) 644-2673
Toll Free: 800-686-1526
IC Tel: 800-686-1578

OKLAHOMA
Insurance Department
P.O. Box 53408
Oklahoma City, OK 73152
Tel: (405) 521-6628
IC Tel: (405) 521-6628

OREGON
Department of Consumer &
      Business Services
Senior Health Insurance
470 Labor & Industries Bldg.
Salem, OR 97310
Tel: (503) 378-4484
IC Tel: 800-722-4134

PENNSYLVANIA
Insurance Department
Strawberry Square, 13th Fl.
Harrisburg, PA 17120
Tel: (717) 787-2317
IC Tel: 800-783-7067

PUERTO RICO
Commissioner of Insurance
Fernandez Juncos Station
P.O. Box 8330
San Juan, PR 00910
Tel: (809) 722-8686
IC Tel: (809) 721-5710

RHODE ISLAND
Insurance Division
233 Richmond Street, Suite 233
Providence, RI 02903
Tel: (401) 277-2223
IC Tel: 800-322-2880

SOUTH CAROLINA
Department of Insurance
P.O. Box 100105
Columbia, SC 29202
Tel: (803) 737-6180
Toll Free: 800-768-3467
IC Tel: 800-868-9095

SOUTH DAKOTA
Insurance Department
500 E. Capitol Ave.
Pierre, SD 57501
Tel: (605) 773-3563
IC Tel: (605) 773-3656

TENNESSEE
Department of Commerce
    & Insurance
500 James Robertson Parkway
Nashville, TN 37243
Tel: (615) 741-4955
Toll Free: 800-525-2816
IC Tel: 800-525-2816

TEXAS
Department of Insurance
333 Guadalupe Street
P.O. Box 149091
Austin, TX 78714
Tel: (512) 463-6500
IC Tel: 800-252-3439

UTAH
Insurance Department
3110 State Office Bldg.
Salt Lake City, UT 84114
Tel: (801) 538-3805
Toll Free: 800-429-3805
IC Tel: 800-606-0608

VERMONT
Dept. of Banking & Insurance
State Office Building
89 Main St., Drawer 20
Montpelier, VT 05620
Tel: (802) 828-3302
IC Tel: 800-828-3302

VIRGINIA
Bureau of Insurance
1300 E. Main Street
P.O. Box 1157
Richmond, VA 23209
Tel: (804) 371-9741
IC Tel: 800-552-4464

VIRGIN ISLANDS
Commissioner of Insurance
Kongens Gade 18
St. Thomas, VI 00802
Tel: (809) 774-2991
IC Tel: (809) 774-2991

WASHINGTON
Insurance Department
4224 - 6th Ave. SE, Bldg. 4
Lacey, WA 98504
Tel: (360) 753-7300
Toll Free: 800-562-6900
IC Tel: 800-397-4422

WEST VIRGINIA
Insurance Department
2019 Washington Street, E.
Charleston, WV 25305
Tel: (304) 558-3386
Toll Free: 800-642-9004
IC Tel: (304) 558-3317

WISCONSIN
Insurance Department
P.O. Box 7873
Madison, WI 53707
Tel: (608) 266-0103
Toll Free: 800-236-8517
IC Tel: 800-242-1060

WYOMING
Insurance Department
Herschler Building
122 West 25th Street
Cheyenne, WY 82002
Tel: (307) 777-7401
Toll Free: 800-438-5768
IC Tel: 800-438-5768

Chapter 6

Low Income Programs

For Those In Need

Chapter Highlights

The information on the programs described in this chapter is current as of early 1996. Most of the eligibility requirements will not change, except for the amount of income and resources that an individual may have and still qualify for the various programs. Do not be overly concerned that minor increases in your income may disqualify you from these programs: eligible persons' income levels are generally raised each year to conform with the established federal poverty guidelines and cost-of-living increases. In 1996, the national poverty income levels are $7,740 for one person and $10,360 for a married couple. Congress reviews all means-tested programs each year to ensure that changes in eligibility standards do not exclude the nation's neediest individuals.

Low-Income Programs

For Those in Need

Five major low-income government programs provide direct cash support or in-kind benefits, like medical care, to the nation's needy. These programs are: **Supplemental Security Income, Medicaid, Food Stamps, Hill-Burton Program of Free Hospital Care,** and the **Qualified Medicare Beneficiary (QMB)/Specified Low-Income Medicare Beneficiary (SLMB) programs**. If you are typical of most people in the U.S., you are probably either unaware of these programs, confuse them with other government programs like Social Security and Medicare, or — even worse — don't know that you are eligible. Consequently, many of you who need the help these programs provide will never receive their benefits and assistance. For example, studies of the Food Stamp program indicate that a vast majority of older people eligible for food stamps — almost half of all eligible households — never even apply for them.

It is essential that you learn about these five programs and your own eligibility so that, if the need arises, you know where to turn for assistance. These programs are referred to as "means-tested" because eligibility is based on income that falls below a certain level. Except for the Hill-Burton program, which is based strictly on gross income and size of family, the applicant's assets must also be below certain levels, and he/she must meet other eligibility criteria before any benefits can be granted.

Fortunately, despite the large numbers of people in need, most of you will probably never require the assistance of any of these programs. However, for those who do not receive Social Security and Medicare benefits and have relatively few resources and low incomes, or for those who care for family members or friends who need such assistance, the information in this chapter may be extremely helpful — now or in the future.

SUPPLEMENTAL SECURITY INCOME

Supplemental Security Income, or SSI, is a federal program which provides a guaranteed minimum monthly income (by check) to low-income individuals who are aged, blind, or disabled. SSI was enacted by Congress in 1972 as the first federal program to establish a uniform, national income floor and to ensure the economic security of America's neediest individuals by providing them with a guaranteed annual income. Since its inception in January 1974 with about 3.2 million individuals receiving benefits, SSI has expanded its eligibility standards so that currently, over 7 million people receive SSI benefits.

SSI was designed to consolidate three state-level programs — Old Age Assistance, Aid to the Blind, and Aid to the Permanently and Totally Disabled — and administer them at the federal level. With this consolidation, Congress sought to eliminate the discrepancies in eligibility requirements and benefit amounts from state to state. To ensure that recipients of benefits from the more generous state programs were not adversely affected by SSI, Congress mandated that any state whose benefit levels had been higher than SSI's would have to supplement the SSI payments to make up the difference. Consequently, current SSI benefits still vary from state to state because, while the federal government pays a uniform base amount to recipients, many states add to that amount from their own funds.

Because of the two programs' similar initials, many people confuse SSI with Social Security (SS). While SSI is administered by the Social Security Administration, the Administration does not provide any of its financing: SSI is entirely funded by federal general revenues.

SSI's assistance can be extremely important — even crucial — to many low-income, blind, and handicapped individuals. However, too many of these people are not even aware of the program's existence. It is estimated that half (over 2 million people) of the elderly eligible for SSI don't receive benefits from the program. This discussion of SSI is designed to familiarize you with the program's provisions and your own possible eligibility for its benefits.

BASIC ELIGIBILITY REQUIREMENTS

To be eligible for SSI benefits in 1996, you must:
1. *reside* in the *U.S.* or the *Northern Mariana Islands,* and
2. *be a U.S. citizen; or be a foreign national lawfully admitted to the U.S.; or*
be a foreign national residing in the U.S. who is in the process of receiving Immigration and Naturalization Service permission to stay.

If you meet these requirements, you must:
1. *have limited income and resources,* ***and***
2. *be 65 or older;* ***or***
be blind with vision of no better than 20/200 or a limited visual field of 20 degrees or less with the best corrective lenses. However, if you are visually impaired but not blind, you may still qualify for SSI as a disabled person; or be disabled by a physical or mental impairment which prevents you from performing any substantial gainful work. This impairment must be expected to last for at least 12 months or to result in death.

If you care for a child under 18, he/she may also be considered blind or disabled and receive SSI benefits (check with Social Security to ascertain his/her eligibility).

If you meet the basic criteria for SSI eligibility, your approval and benefit amount will depend on the amount of income and resources you already have. If you are married, Social Security considers the total resources of you and your spouse. If you are a sponsored alien, the sponsor's resources may be considered in addition to yours. For children under 18, Social Security considers the income and resources of the parents or guardians.

RESOURCES

Resources are items that you own, such as real estate, personal property, a car, savings and checking account balances, cash, and stocks and bonds. However, Social Security does not consider the following resources:

- The house you live in and the land it occupies;

- Personal and household goods and insurance policies, depending on their value;

- $4,500 of the value of a car (if your car is worth more than $4,500, Social Security only considers the amount by which the car's value exceeds $4,500);

- Burial plots for you and members of your immediate family;

- Up to $1,500 of burial funds for you plus up to $1,500 in burial funds for your spouse;

- Any real estate which cannot be sold because (1) it is jointly owned and selling it would deprive the other owner(s) of a place to live; or (2) its sale is barred by law; or (3) the owner's reasonable efforts to sell it have been unsuccessful.

NOTE: *Until 1988, if you transferred any assets (rather than sold them) in the 24 months before you applied for SSI, Social Security would consider the transfer made solely for the purpose of becoming eligible; therefore, the uncompensated value of the assets were considered part of your resources. However, a recent change in the SSI law allows Social Security to waive this rule in cases where considering these assets resources would cause the SSI applicant undue hardship.*

After deducting these allowances, a single adult or child can qualify in 1996 for SSI if his/her resources do not exceed **$2,000**. A married couple can have joint resources of up to **$3,000** in 1996.

INCOME

Under the SSI program, "income" means anything received that can be used to meet a person's needs for food, clothing or shelter. This includes not only cash and checks, but also "in kind" items, such as food and housing, as well as some items that would not be considered income for federal or other tax purposes. Income is divided by SSI into two categories as follows:

- *Earned income* includes wages, net-earnings from self-employment, earned income tax credit payments, and income received from sheltered workshops.

- *Unearned income* includes Social Security benefits, workers' or veterans' compensation, pensions, "in-kind" support and maintenance, annuities, rent and interest received.

However, Social Security does not consider all income when deciding whether a person qualifies for SSI. It allows certain items to be excluded when determining whether an individual meets the income limits. Anyone whose countable income falls below the annual established income limits is considered "income eligible" for SSI benefits. These limits depend on whether you do not work or if you work as follows:

- *If you do not work:* no matter where you live, you may be able to get SSI if your monthly income is less than *$490* for one person or *$725* for a couple.

- *If you work:* you may be able to get SSI if all of your income from working is less than *$1,025* a month for one person or *$1,495* a month for a couple.

The following income is **not** counted when determining whether an individual meets the income limit:

$20 of any income (earned or unearned) in a month; **plus**

$65 of earnings in a month, plus half of any earnings in excess of the $65.

In addition, the following items are excluded when an applicant's income is calculated:

- home energy assistance from approved home energy suppliers
- food, clothing, shelter, or home energy assistance from nonprofit organizations
- food stamps
- need-based assistance from a state or local government or Indian tribe
- home-grown produce consumed by the household
- housing assistance from a federal housing program run by state or local governments
- incentive allowances and certain types of reimbursement for individuals in certain training programs.

Also, disabled or blind workers can deduct from their considered incomes certain impairment-related items that are critical to their ability to work:

- **Medical Devices** — wheelchairs, hemodialysis equipment, braces, and prostheses, such as artificial hips, arms, and legs;

- **Attendant Care** — help getting ready for work and/or going to and from work, assistance required immediately upon arrival home from work, readers for the blind; interpreters for the deaf;

- **Transportation** — extraordinary costs, like modification to a vehicle;

- **Drugs and Medical Services** — regularly-prescribed medical treatment or therapy required to control a condition, such as anticonvulsant drugs, chemotherapy, anti-depressant medication, etc.;

- **Home Modifications** — changes to the outside of the home which make it easier for the person to get to and from work, such as ramps and/or railings.

SSI BENEFIT AMOUNTS

In 1996, the basic federal SSI payment for a single adult or child is $470 per month; the basic payment for an eligible married couple is $705 per month. However, as explained earlier, the amount you actually receive may exceed the basic payment because your state may add to that amount from its own funds.

OTHER IMPORTANT SSI RULES

Several provisions of SSI may affect your eligibility and receipt of benefits:

- If you qualify for Social Security or another kind of benefit, you must apply for it. You may still receive SSI in addition to other benefits if the amount of income you receive from Social Security or another source falls below SSI's allowable maximum.

- You cannot receive both SSI and Aid to Families with Dependent Children. If you qualify and apply for both, you can select the program that is best for you.

- Disabled SSI recipients must accept any vocational rehabilitation services offered to them.

- If you live in a city or county rest home, halfway house, or other public institution, you will probably not be eligible for SSI. However, there are some exceptions; you may still qualify for SSI if:

  — you live in a publicly-operated community residence which serves no more than 16 people;

  — you live in a public institution primarily so you can attend approved educational or job training classes that will help you get a job;

  — you live in a public emergency shelter for the homeless, in which case you can receive SSI payments for up to six months in any nine-month period;

  — you live in a public or private institution for which Medicaid is paying more than half the cost of your care, in which case SSI will pay you a monthly "needs allowance" of up to $30 plus any additional state allowance.

- Because having a permanent residence is not a requirement for SSI eligibility, homeless people who meet the basic eligibility criteria may also qualify for SSI benefits. Social Security has special arrangements with community organizations (shelters, churches, soup kitchens, etc.) that help the homeless. They make sure these organizations help the homeless apply for SSI and provide a "mail drop" where the homeless persons can receive their monthly checks.

- If you receive SSI benefits, you are probably also eligible for Food Stamps, Medicaid, and state and/or county social services. If you are disabled or blind, these state/county services may include job skills training, job placement, and training for independent living.

- If you are blind or disabled and recover while participating in an approved vocational rehabilitation program, you can continue to receive SSI benefits while continuing the program, if continued participation would increase the chance that the cure (and your eventual removal from SSI's rolls) would be permanent.

- Disabled employed SSI recipients may receive cash benefits until their income exceeds SSI limits for allowable income. However, in 1996, the disabled recipient's SSI payments are reduced by $1 for every $2 earned in excess of $65.00 per month. For example, someone who earned $67.00 per month (that is, $65.00 + $2.00) would have his/her monthly SSI payment reduced by $1.00.

APPLYING FOR SSI

As with other federal assistance programs, SSI requires you to present certain documents and information when you apply. The inability to present these documents and data will delay approval of your application until they are submitted and verified. If you cannot locate any of the required items listed below, contact Social Security.

It is important that you do not delay in applying for SSI. The program does not pay benefits retroactively. When you apply for SSI, make sure you bring the following information to the Social Security office:

- Social Security card or other record of your Social Security number;

- Birth certificate (original or certified copy) or oldest available proof of age;

- *If you are disabled or blind:* medical records or names and addresses of all doctors, hospitals, and clinics that have treated you; names and addresses of any social workers familiar with your disability;

- Information about your income and assets, such as payroll slips, copies of tax returns, bank books, insurance policies, car registration, and burial fund records.

CHANGES IN STATUS THAT MUST BE REPORTED TO SOCIAL SECURITY

Your approval for SSI benefits is based on your financial status, physical condition, and living situation at the time you apply. Therefore, you must inform Social Security of any changes that could affect your eligibility for SSI or the amount of your SSI benefits. This change must be reported by the 10th day of the month after the month in which the change took place (for example, if your income increases in September, you must report this increase to Social Security by October 10th). Your failure to report such changes can result in penalties or even loss of entitlement to any future SSI benefits.

While an improvement in your circumstances may affect your SSI benefits, this is not always the case. **Do not** fail to report such a change out of fear that your benefits will be cut. The penalty for not reporting such a change is far worse than any effects the change might have on your benefit check. The following changes must be reported by SSI beneficiaries:

- **Change in Resources** — increase or decrease in cash, checking, savings, or Christmas club account balance; certificate of deposit; stocks and bonds; real estate other than your home;

- **Change in Income** — increase or decrease in cash, checks, or non-cash income, such as food, clothing, or shelter;

- **Change in Living Arrangements** — increase or decrease in the number of people living in your home; your move into or out of someone else's home;

- **Change of Address.**

APPEALS

You always have the right to appeal if Social Security rejects your application for SSI, stops your checks, or reduces the amount of your benefits. To appeal any Social Security decision about your SSI eligibility or benefit amount, you must appeal within 60 days of receiving the notice of Social Security's decision.

An appeal can include four steps: (1) reconsideration, (2) hearing by an Administrative Law Judge, (3) review by an Appeals Council, and (4) filing a suit in federal district court. These steps are similar to those taken by Social Security recipients when appealing a decision about their Social Security benefits. In the same way, an appeal may be settled during any one of these steps; it needn't progress through all four.

For more information about the SSI appeals process, contact your local Social Security office for assistance and to request the pamphlet entitled *Your Right to Question the Decision on Your SSI Claim.* This pamphlet explains each of the four steps in detail.

SSI CAN HELP YOU . . . BUT ONLY IF YOU APPLY!

The Supplemental Security Income program can give you much needed financial assistance when you have nowhere else to turn. Because the minimum Social Security benefit was eliminated in 1981, many of America's neediest people do not receive enough Social Security to survive. These people rely on the assistance provided by SSI.

While the procedures for determining your eligibility — your age, physical condition, resources, and income — can be complicated, Social Security is there to help. When you apply, they will accurately determine whether your circumstances qualify you for SSI, and how much your benefits will be. If you are over 65, blind, or disabled and have a low income, contact your local Social Security office **immediately** to apply for SSI.

SUMMARY OF BASIC SSI ELIGIBILITY REQUIREMENTS
(Effective January 1, 1996)

I. Eligible Individuals Must Be:

■ **Aged**	65 or over
	or
■ **Blind**	with vision no better than 20/200 or with a limited visual field of 20 degrees or less with the best corrective lenses.
	or
■ **Disabled**	With a physical or mental impairment which prevents substantial gainful work and which is expected to last at least 12 months or to result in death.

and

II. Eligible Individuals Must Have Income And Resources No Greater Than:

■ **Income**	(1) *If you don't work:* $490 in a month for a single person; $725 a month for a couple. (2) *If you work:* $1,025 in a month for a single person; $1,495 a month for a couple.
■ **Resources**	$2,000 for an individual, $3,000 for a couple not counting home, car, personal effects and household goods of reasonable value.

---

(1) Not all income is "countable." In particular, income that is not counted includes: (1) $20 of any income (earned or unearned) in a month; plus (2) $65, of earnings in a month; and (3) only half of earnings over $65 per month.

MEDICAID

Medicaid is a medical assistance program which is financed by both federal and state tax dollars. It was created by the Social Security Act Amendments of 1965 to help pay medical costs for needy persons of all ages, in particular those receiving welfare benefits and those with low income. Currently, Medicaid is providing assistance for more than 36 million individuals at an estimated total federal/state annual projected cost of over $156 billion. An ever increasing portion of Medicaid's expenditures have been for nursing home care. Approximately 89 percent of all public expenditures for nursing home care are paid by Medicaid, and over 50 percent of all nursing home residents are Medicaid beneficiaries.

Many people confuse Medicaid with Medicare. Medicare, as explained earlier in Chapter 4, is a federal **insurance** program under the Social Security Act that helps pay the health care costs for people 65 years of age or older, regardless of their income, and for certain disabled persons under 65 receiving Social Security benefits. It is financed by monthly premiums paid by the insured persons and the federal government. Medicaid is not an insurance program that individuals help finance. It is a joint federal-state **assistance** program that can help pay the monthly Medicare premium, its deductible and coinsurance costs and many other medical costs that Medicare does not pay, of which the most important to our elderly is extended custodial care in a nursing home. Medicare is the same in all states and is administered by the Social Security Administration,whereas Medicaid programs vary and are administered by the states.

The eligibility provisions for the Medicaid program are complex due to its interrelationship with other programs, such as Aid to Families with Dependent Children (AFDC) and Supplemental Security Income (SSI), as well as to the flexibility given to the various states under its regulations. States design their own programs within federal guidelines; consequently, definitions and limitations on eligibility and services vary from state to state. However, all participating states **must** cover at least the following services for recipients:

- inpatient hospital services
- outpatient hospital services
- other laboratory and x-ray services

- rural health clinic services
- family planning services
- skilled nursing facility services and home health services for individuals 21 and older
- early and periodic screening, diagnosis and treatment for individuals under 21
- physicians' services
- family planning services and supplies
- nurse-midwife services.

Most of the states' Medicaid programs also pay for several other services, such as nursing homes or long-term facility services, inpatient psychiatric care for those under 21 or over 65, dental care, prescribed drugs, eyeglasses, clinic services, and other diagnostic, screening, preventive and rehabilitative services.

CATEGORICALLY NEEDY AND MEDICALLY NEEDY

All states establishing Medicaid programs must provide medical assistance to those referred to as the "Categorically Needy." These are individuals receiving federal financial assistance under Aid to Families with Dependent Children or Supplemental Security Income. Generally, eligibility under this category includes a person who (1) is aged 65 or older, blind or disabled, or is a member of a family with children deprived of the support of at least one parent, and (2) is determined to be financially eligible on the basis of limited income and resources.

In many of our states, individuals who do not receive federal financial assistance and who are not determined to be "Categorically Needy" because of their incomes may still be eligible for their state's Medicaid program. They are referred to as the "Medically Needy." In general, these are individuals whose medical costs are quite high in relation to their income and who meet certain specific requirements established by their states. Some nominal fees may be imposed for services that are offered to the "Medically Needy."

States and territories that provide for **both** of these categories — "Categorically Needy" and "Medically Needy" — include:

Arkansas
California
* Connecticut
District of Columbia
Florida
Georgia (limited program)
* Hawaii
* Illinois
Iowa
Kansas
Kentucky
Louisiana
Maine
Maryland
Massachusetts
Michigan
* Minnesota
Montana
Nebraska

* New Hampshire
New Jersey
New York
* North Carolina
* North Dakota
Northern Mariana Islands
* Oklahoma
Pennsylvania
Puerto Rico
Rhode Island
Texas
Utah
Vermont
Virgin Islands
* Virginia
Washington
West Virginia
Wisconsin

Currently the remaining states cover only those individuals — "Categorically Needy" — who are eligible for Aid to Families with Dependent Children and Supplemental Security Income. They are:

Alabama
Alaska
Colorado
Delaware
Guam

Idaho
* Indiana
Mississippi
* Missouri
Nevada

New Mexico
* Ohio
South Carolina
South Dakota
Wyoming

* The foregoing states in both lists marked with an asterisk use their own standards, which are generally more strict, to determine Medicaid eligibility rather than use the national SSI standards used by most states.

Arizona, Tennessee and Oregon do not participate in the Medicaid program. They have a separate federal assistance program which is approved to operate as a Section 1115 Demonstration Program.

DETERMINING YOUR ELIGIBILITY

When applying for Medicaid services, you will be asked about your income and what assets you own. Income is any money a family receives as wages, pensions, retirement benefits or support payments. Assets include such items as cash, money in the bank, property, automobile, medical insurance and the cash or loan value of your insurance policies or the policies of any other household members. If your income and resources fall within the eligibility levels, you will be eligible for Medicaid assistance. However, even if your income is too high, you may still be eligible if your medical bills, when subtracted from your income, bring you below the eligibility levels needed to qualify. The process of subtracting your medical bills from your income to become eligible for Medicaid is called "spend-down."

If you are denied Medicaid because of the value of your total resources or assets, you may become eligible for Medicaid when your assets fall to or below the eligibility levels. This could result from loss of resources or by a change that reduces the value of your assets. Individuals will generally not be considered eligible for a period of time when they transfer, give away or sell property for less than fair market value within two years prior to applying for Medicaid, if the transfer was performed solely for the purpose of establishing eligibility. Remember that this is a program intended to assist those who have very limited incomes and assets.

Since each state determines its own Medicaid eligibility requirements within federal guidelines, it is not feasible to discuss each state's complex eligibility requirements. However, if you believe you maybe eligible because of your low income or medical expenses, contact your state's Medicaid agency immediately to apply for this program.

RECENT LEGISLATIVE CHANGES

Several recent changes in federal law will affect older Americans' eligibility to receive Medicaid. The following briefly describes the most important legislative changes:

- As part of the 1993 Omnibus Budget Reconciliation Act, major changes in Medicaid's treatment of trusts and transfers of assets for those seeking Medicaid eligibility became effective on August

10, 1993. Of utmost importance is that these changes included extending the ineligibility period when certain assets are given away from 30 months to 36 months—sometimes even longer— and disallowing certain trusts previously approved under Medi- caid's eligibility rules. In addition, the law requires every state to initiate estate recovery programs for nursing home and long-term care Medicaid expenses of deceased recipients. Since these changes are quite complex, be certain to seek the advice of an attorney who is knowledgeable of the new rules *before* applying for medi- caid assistance.

■ The law now allows states to provide Medicaid coverage for home and community-based services for those elderly who would otherwise require nursing home care.

■ The law allows widows/widowers who lose their eligibility for Supplemental Security Income benefits due to receipt of widow(er)'s benefits to receive Medicaid if they are under 65 and, thus, cannot receive Medicare.

■ States must pay all Medicare premiums, deductibles, and copay- ments for beneficiaries who do not qualify for Medicaid but whose incomes fall below 100% of the federal poverty line. States must also pay the Medicare Part B premiums for those individuals whose incomes exceed the national poverty by up to 20% in 1996. For further information on this requirement, see page 266 of this chapter.

■ States must increase the amount of income and assets that may be kept by a beneficiary whose spouse's long-term nursing care is covered by Medicaid. This provision protects elderly spouses from being impoverished by having to spend-down all of their resources and income simply to qualify for Medicaid. The law states that, in 1996, the spouse of a nursing home resident could keep at least $1,254 per month income up to a maximum of $1,918 per month **plus** $15,348 to $76,740 of jointly-held assets (this is in addi- tion to the family home) — with increases scheduled for future years — and still qualify for Medicaid.

ONCE YOU ARE APPROVED FOR MEDICAID

If you qualify for Medicaid, you will receive a medical card or other form of identification, which varies among the states, showing that

you are authorized to receive Medicaid benefits. You should closely
guard your Medicaid authorization because you will need it each time
you require Medicaid services. Do not let anyone else use it, and
promptly report its loss to the administering offices, as well as any
change in circumstances that might affect eligibility, such as an
increase in income, assets or a change in family members.

You do not usually pay for any medical services; however, those
"Medically Needy" recipients of Medicaid **may**, in some states, be
charged an enrollment fee or a limited portion of their medical costs.

If you are also eligible for Medicare, present both the Medicaid
authorization and the Medicare card when requesting medical services.
Charges rendered for services to Medicaid/Medicare recipients are
first billed to Medicare. If any "third party" insurance is available to
pay all or part of the medical expenses of a recipient, that party should
be identified. Any medical insurance you have including veteran's
coverage, Medicare or other medical coverage — such as court or
insurance settlements — must pay for the care before payment is
made by Medicaid. If there is a delay and Medicaid pays before the
"third party" pays, a refund must be made to the state when you receive
payment from the "third party."

WHERE TO GO FOR ASSISTANCE

Despite the stringent requirements for obtaining assistance, Medicaid
is an invaluable program to help those whose resources are limited
and who cannot afford medical assistance or long-term care. If your
application for Medicaid is denied, you may request a hearing by an
administrative officer of your state's Department of Social Services. **Do
not hesitate** to request a hearing if you are denied this assistance.

For further information regarding your state's Medicaid program,
contact your state's Medicaid agency or the office in your locality that
administers the program. Local Medicaid offices come under the aegis
of various offices within each state — Department of Social Services,
Public Health or State Welfare offices. Call your Area Agency on
Aging or Human Services Information number if you have difficulty
locating the nearest Medicaid office.

FOOD STAMP PROGRAM

The Food Stamp program helps low-income Americans increase their food purchasing power by issuing them food stamps. By combining food stamps with their available income, the recipients can afford a more nutritious diet. Enacted by Congress in 1964, the Food Stamp program was revamped by the Food Stamp Act of 1977 which expanded the categories of persons eligible, and strengthened the program's integrity. It is now the third largest government assistance program — after Medicaid and subsidized housing — with an annual anticipated expenditure in 1996 of over $24 billion and an average of 27 million participants each month.

The federal government pays for all food stamp benefits plus 50 percent of most state and local administrative costs. The Department of Agriculture's Food and Nutrition Service is responsible for federal administration and supervision of state participation. The Service also develops national policies and regulations. At state and local levels, the state Social Services department (or Welfare department) administers the aspects of the program that deal directly with recipients, such as eligibility for and issuance of stamps. Apply directly for food stamps through these state/local departments; however, if you live in a household in which all members receive Supplemental Security Income (SSI), you should apply for food stamps at your local Social Security office.

Although the food stamp program is not generally considered an elderly nutrition program, its benefits could be an important deterrent against the malnutrition which afflicts an estimated 50 percent of low income elderly individuals. Unfortunately, nearly half of needy older Americans never even apply for food stamps. Consequently, they never receive the program's aid in purchasing food. To increase elderly participation in the program, special provisions have been made for them, including more liberal treatment of shelter costs, medical expenses, and assets (discussed later under "Eligibility Requirements").

All eligible applicants receive food stamps in amounts determined by their household sizes and incomes. The stamps enable them to buy food items in authorized grocery stores. Food Stamps are treated just like cash by the stores, who simply forward them to commercial banks for cash or credit. The stamps cannot be used to buy non-food items, such as alcoholic beverages, tobacco products, household supplies like soap or paper products, medicines or vitamins, or for hot ready-to-eat foods or food that will be eaten in the store. The Food Stamp program is strictly designed to help fund purchases of *nutritious* food items by and for the food stamp recipient and his/her immediate family.

1996 ELIGIBILITY REQUIREMENTS

All U.S. citizens, legally permanent aliens, and certain other legal aliens are eligible to apply for food stamps. Even if some members of a household do not meet these requirements, those who do may qualify for food stamps. The program is non-discriminatory by law and is available to all eligible persons. Eligibility for food stamps is determined strictly on the basis of financial need — which is assessed by considering size of household, income and resources, and assets available to the household.

To receive food stamps, households must meet certain tests called *resource (or asset) and income tests.*

■ **Resource/Asset Test**
   To be eligible for food stamps, household assets must not exceed:
   — $2,000 worth of resources for households with no Senior members;
                                        or
   — $3,000 worth of resources for households with at least one member aged 60 or older.

   Certain resources are not considered; these include:
   — individual's home and surrounding lot
   — household goods
   — personal belongings
   — life insurance policies.

   Resources that are considered include:
   — cash and money in checking and saving accounts
   — stocks and bonds
   — land and buildings (other than the individual's home and lot) that do not produce income.

■ **Income Test**

All households with no elderly member or member who receives certain disability payments must meet **both** the national gross and net monthly income limits shown in the table below; households with an elderly (60 years or older) or disabled member only have to meet the **net** income limit. Households which exceed these limits are not eligible for food stamps.

Although it does not apply to many individuals, an additional income eligibility requirement applies **only** to elderly or disabled individuals who maintain a separate household *but* share living arrangements with other individuals. (This does not include those individuals who rent rooms or quarters within the confines of another household.) The local food stamp office will explain this requirement if it applies to your particular situation.

Income Limits throughout the Nation
(October 1995 — September 1996)

Household Size	Net Monthly Income Limits (1)	Gross Monthly Income Limits (1)
1 person	$ 623	$ 810
2 persons	836	1,087
3 persons	1,050	1,364
4 persons	1,263	1,642
5 persons	1,476	1,919
6 persons	1,690	2,196
7 persons	1,903	2,474
8 persons	2,116	2,751
Each additional member	+214	+278

(1) The limits in Alaska and Hawaii are higher by 25 and 15 percent, respectively.

Gross income is a household's total, nonexcluded income, before any deductions have been made (e.g., for tax). Income includes any money that a household earns, plus any money received on a regular basis, such as self-employment income, Social Security benefits, unemployment insurance, pensions, public assistance, child support and veteran's benefits. Net income is gross income minus any deductions allowed by the program.

From October 1995 — September 1996, these allowable deductions are:

- 20 percent of earned income:

- A standard deduction per month:
  — $134 per household in the 48 contiguous states and District of Columbia (higher deductions apply in Alaska and Hawaii)

- A dependent-care deduction — when applicable — for care which is work related (not to exceed $200 per month per household for all areas). Dependent care includes day care for children and disabled adults that is required to enable a household member to work, look for a job, or get training or education leading to a job;

- Households may receive an extra shelter cost deduction (also called a higher shelter cost deduction). Extra shelter costs include the costs of fuel, utilities and rent or mortgage payments that exceed 50 percent of the household's income. This deduction cannot exceed the following amounts *except* for households with an elderly or disabled person:

  — $247 per household in the 48 contiguous states and District of Columbia (higher deductions allowed in Alaska and Hawaii)

  (There is *no* limit on the amount of the extra shelter deduction for households with elderly or disabled individuals.)

- Medical costs for an elderly or disabled household member which exceed $35 per month in all areas if these costs are not covered by insurance, Medicare, or Medicaid.

WHAT TO BRING WITH YOU WHEN YOU APPLY FOR FOOD STAMPS

To apply for food stamps, you must have a person-to-person interview at the food stamp office. You must bring documentation to support your eligibility claim. Housebound individuals who are unable to get to the office in person may appoint an authorized representative.

In addition to forms of identification, such as a driver's license or birth certificate, you must bring the following items with you when you apply for food stamps:

- Social Security numbers for all household members;

- Proof of legal alien status for non-U.S. citizens;

- Proof of your monthly earnings, such as recent pay stubs; proof of other income received by anyone else for whom the application is being made;

- Copy of check or benefit statement from Social Security, pensions and SSI, and any other **unearned** income;

- Unreimbursed medical bills for expenses over $35 incurred by household members who are 60 years or older or disabled;

- Bank books or current bank statements and savings bonds owned by anyone in the household;

- Receipts of childcare costs (babysitting in the home is included) and for disabled adult care;

- Utility and rent bills. Homeowners must also bring proof of mortgage and property tax payments.

APPLY NOW!

If you have difficulty buying enough food to have three nutritious meals every day, but are unsure whether your income or resources are too great or that you are just not poor enough to qualify, **go at once** to your local food stamp office. Let them determine your eligibility. Even if you only get the minimum food stamp allotment each month, it will still help you buy the food you need. This program was designed to help you, but you must apply for its assistance. You may be surprised to learn that, after the allowed deductions, you **are** eligible!

APPEALS

If you are denied food stamp benefits and disagree with the disapproval, or if you feel that you have not received the correct amount of food stamps, you have the right to appeal. To do this, immediately contact the supervisor of your local food stamp office. If you are still dissatisfied after the supervisor reviews your application, you may request to have your case reviewed by a "fair hearing official." If your problem is still not satisfactorily resolved after the hearing, contact your local legal aid or legal services office for assistance.

AFTER YOU APPLY

After you complete your application and interview, you will receive a notice stating that you were either approved or rejected for food stamps. If you are approved, the notice will tell you the number of food stamps you will receive — called your "coupon allotment" — and when you must reapply. The amount of your food stamp benefit is based on your net income and the number of people in your household.

Not everyone who is eligible for food stamps receives the maximum amount nor does he/she necessarily receive the minimum amount. The following table shows the maximum amount of monthly food stamp benefits (allotments) a household can receive:

Maximum Monthly Food Stamp Allotments
(October 1995 — September 1996)

Household Size	48 States and District of Columbia
1 person	$119
2 persons	218
3 persons	313
4 persons	397
5 persons	472
6 persons	566
7 persons	626
8 persons	716
Each additional person	+90

(The allotments in Alaska and Hawaii are higher by 25 and 15 percent, respectively.)

By federal law, approved individuals should receive their first food stamps within 30 days of applying. In emergencies where an individual needs food stamps immediately, he or she will receive expedited service and should receive stamps within five calendar days.

HILL-BURTON PROGRAM OF FREE HOSPITAL CARE

A special program providing free hospital or other health care to those individuals without insurance and unable to pay for needed health care because of their limited incomes, was established by Congress in 1946. This program is called the Hill-Burton Uncompensated Services Program, but has become known as "the program of free hospital care" because hospitals provide most of the services and care each year under this program. It is administered by the Department of Health and Human Services through ten regional offices.

Under this program, funds were given to hospitals and other health facilities for construction and modernization in exchange for the facilities' agreement to provide a reasonable volume of services each year to persons unable to pay. In addition, these services were to be made available to all persons residing in the hospital's area. In the 1960s, this program was quite well known. However, since the enactment of Medicare and Medicaid (whose patients are generally not included in this program), and because of the lack of additional funds in the federal budget for this particular program, the Hill-Burton Free Hospital Care program frequently goes unnoticed within communities that have hospitals that are currently obligated to provide free care. There are innumerable hospitals throughout the country that must still provide free care over the next several years. You should be aware of this program if you have a low income, insufficient hospital insurance, and are not eligible for Medicare or Medicaid coverage.

HOW THE PROGRAM WORKS

Under the Hill-Burton program, a hospital or health care facility can choose the type of services it will provide free to patients. Each providing facility only pays hospital costs; it does not cover any private doctor's bills. Each hospital is required to give a certain amount of free care each year, but it can stop once it has fulfilled the required amount.

To obtain this free care, you must request it from the hospital's admission office. The hospital will provide you with an "Individual Notice" that explains the services provided and the income levels qualifying for free care. Income refers to your total annual cash receipts, before taxes, from all sources. The qualifying amounts are based upon the Community Services Administration (CSA) Income Poverty Guidelines established by the federal government. Hospitals use these guidelines to set their own qualifying income levels; however, they cannot set eligibility levels greater than twice the established federal guidelines. Hospitals frequently raise their eligibility levels to the maximum allowed (called category C levels) which is double the poverty levels shown below.

The following income guidelines are currently applicable in all states and the District of Columbia except Alaska and Hawaii. The levels for Alaska and Hawaii are considerably higher and can be obtained from your hospital.

FEDERAL QUALIFYING INCOME LEVELS
1996

Size of Family Unit	Poverty Guideline
1 member	$7,740
2 members	10,360
3 members	12,980
4 members	15,600
5 members	18,220
6 members	20,840
7 members	23,460
8 members	26,080

(For family units with more than 8 members, add $2,620 for each additional member)

APPLYING FOR ASSISTANCE

If your income qualifies you for the hospital's free care, you should request an application form from the admissions office. You may apply either before or after you receive care in the hospital. The hospital will ask you to include proof of your income, such as a pay slip or recent income tax form, with your application. *Of utmost importance:* In many cases, if your income is greater than the basic federal income guidelines, but not more than double, the hospital may still decide to give you free services or reduce the charges for your care. Consequently, it is advisable for you to apply under any circumstances when your income is not sufficient to pay for your hospital care.

After completing the application, you should ask for a "Determination of Eligibility." The hospital has two full days to determine your eligibility and respond. If your application is denied, you may file a complaint with the Department of Health and Human Services' regional office serving your area.

Important! Hill-Burton facilities must provide services without discrimination on the basis of race, color, national origin, religion, or creed. Also, they may not discriminate against Medicare or Medicaid patients.

You may obtain assistance with filing your complaint, or any information concerning this program, by calling the toll-free "Hill Burton Hot Line" — **800-638-0742**. Maryland residents should call **800-492-0359**, or write to:

> Division of Facilities Compliance
> Hill-Burton Project Office
> Department of Health and Human Services
> Room 11-25, Parklawn Building, 5600 Fishers Lane
> Rockville, Maryland 20857

MEDICARE BENEFICIARY ASSISTANCE PROGRAMS

In 1988, the *Qualified Medicare Beneficiary(QMB)* program was enacted as a mandatory program by Congress as part of the Medicare Catastrophic Coverage Act of 1988. Although the Act was later repealed, the QMB program was retained to ensure that as many low-income Medicare beneficiaries as possible would receive assistance in paying the cost-sharing expenses of Medicare. Under the QMB program, state Medicaid programs are required to pay Medicare's Part A Hospital and Part B Medical Insurance premiums, deductibles, and co-insurance amounts for certain elderly and disabled persons with low-incomes and very limited assets .

To qualify for the QMB program, an individual must:

- be entitled to Medicare Hospital Insurance Part A;

- have an annual income at or below the national poverty guidelines;

■ must have limited resources such as bank accounts, stocks, bonds and etc. Generally, when resources or assets are considered in qualifying as a QMB, a personal home, one automobile, burial plots, home furnishings, personal jewelry and life insurance are not counted.

In January 1993, the government expanded the *Qualified Medicare Beneficiary Program* to cover more low-income beneficiaries. The *Specified Low-income Medicare Beneficiary (SLMB)* program covered those people whose incomes exceeded the national poverty level by up to 10% in 1993 and 1994. In 1995 and 1996, the amount by which SLMB income can exceed the poverty level increased to 20%. Although the SLMB program augments the existing QMB program, state Medicaid programs are only required to pay the Medicare Part B premiums for those eligible as an SLMB.

To qualify as a QMB in 1996, an individual's annual income cannot exceed $7,980 (about $665 per month) and resources cannot exceed $4,000; a couple's income cannot exceed $10,608 (or $884 per month) and resources cannot exceed $6,000. To qualify as a SLMB, a person must meet the same criteria as a QMB except for income, which can be $794 per month for an individual, $1,057 per month for a couple. As with a QMB, SLMB resources cannot exceed $4,000 for an individual, $6,000 for a couple.

The programs differ in two features other than income:

1) States only pay the SLMB's Medicare Part B monthly premiums, whereas for QMBs, the states pay both Medicare Part A and Part B premiums, deductibles, co-payments, and other out-of-pocket medical expenses.

2) SLMB eligibility may be retroactive for three calendar months, whereas QMB eligibility is not retroactive.

Both the QMB and SLMB programs are supervised by the federal Health Care Financing Administration but are administered by state Medicaid offices which make the determination as to who is eligible for assistance. If your income is low, immediately contact your state Medicaid office or local social services agency to apply. For more information about these programs, you may call the Health Care Financing Administration's toll-free telephone number: **800-638-6833.**

OTHER LOW-INCOME ASSISTANCE PROGRAMS

In addition to the five programs described in this chapter, several other federal and state programs provide assistance to low-income individuals. Since the features and requirements of these programs vary greatly from state to state, and sometimes even within a state, it is not feasible to discuss each of them here. However, some of these programs are covered in Chapter 1 in the section on "Federal Programs that Provide Benefits and Assistance to Older Americans." The following federal, state and local government programs should not be overlooked in your search for assistance.

■ **Subsidized Housing Assistance Programs** — These programs vary considerably throughout the nation and, unfortunately, are often very limited in the amount of affordable, decent housing they provide for the many who need it. However, two federal programs administered at the state or local level are of particular significance:

— **Section 8 Housing** program which provides rental subsidies to low- or moderately low-income households to help finance housing in the private sector;

— **Section 202 Elderly Housing** program which provides subsidized rental housing to elderly and handicapped individuals.

In addition, the **Farmers Home Administration** provides loans and grants to individuals in rural areas to help meet their housing needs. Since available housing and funds for all of these programs is limited, eligible individuals should not delay in applying with their local public housing agency or the local office that administers the various housing programs.

■ **Low-Income Home Energy and Weatherization Assistance Programs** — Both of these programs provide eligible households with financial assistance — directly or through vendors — to help meet home heating and cooling costs, and to provide energy related crisis intervention aid and low-cost house weatherization, such as insulation and storm windows and doors. Since the states administer these programs under broad federal guidelines, they may establish their own benefit structures and eligibility rules and requirements. Consequently, the type and amount of benefits vary considerably from state to state.

- **Aid to Families with Dependent Children** — This program provides cash welfare payments for needy children and their parent or other relative who takes care of them. To be considered "needy," a child must have been deprived of parental support or care because his/her father or mother is continuously absent from home, incapacitated, deceased or unemployed. States administer this program within federal limitations and guidelines but set their own benefit levels, establish income and resource limits and decide who is in need.

- **General Assistance Programs** — This assistance is provided by state or local governments to needy individuals who do not qualify for major welfare programs or whose assistance payments do not meet their basic living needs. It is often provided to unemployed people who are ineligible for Aid to Families with Dependent Children or unemployment insurance benefits, or to those who have exhausted their unemployment benefits. Because they are funded by state or local jurisdictions, these assistance programs are not available in all states. Where the programs are available, their eligibility requirements and benefits vary considerably, even within the same state.

Although it may take considerable effort to obtain information about these programs, it is very important to find out which ones are available in your community and to **apply at once**, since there is often a considerable waiting period between when you apply and when you receive benefits. If you have any difficulty in locating in your community the offices administering these programs, contact your local Area Agency on Aging for assistance.

Chapter 7

Health and Shelter

What They Can Mean to You

Chapter Highlights

Health and Shelter

Important Considerations in Life

This chapter discusses three issues of immense concern to older individuals: (1) health and welfare, (2) care of a loved one in a nursing home or at home and (3) finding a new place to live. This discussion couldn't possibly answer every question you may have about these important topics. However, it should guide you towards the answers and help you need.

PART I

Health and Well Being . . . A Priority

Despite their belief that good health is very important, a vast majority of Seniors have not taken the actions required to ensure a long and healthy life. To do this, you must first learn about what can affect your health and what preventive measures will help ensure your well-being.

This discussion is not intended to be a complete medical resource; however, it does contain a listing of clearinghouses and centers that **can** answer almost any medical question you may have *and*, best of all, most of the information they provide is **free!** This discussion also touches on illnesses or health topics of interest to many older individuals, such as high cholesterol, Alzheimer's disease and tinnitus. Be aware that this discussion only provides an overview of these topics — it is not meant to be exhaustive. Additional information can be readily obtained from *your doctor* or from the sources in the listing at the end of this section.

CRITICAL HEALTH CONCERNS OF
OLDER AMERICANS

With preventive medicine becoming a major medical focus of society, older Americans are naturally concerned about the illnesses and major causes of death in their age group. According to the National Center for Health Statistics, the current leading causes of death for people 65 and over, in order of prevalence, are:

1. Heart diseases
2. Cancer
3. Cerebrovascular diseases (strokes)
4. Chronic obstructive pulmonary diseases (such as asthma, emphysema and bronchitis)
5. Pneumonia and influenza (flu)
6. Diabetes mellitus
7. Accidents
8. Arteriosclerosis (hardening of the arteries)
9. Kidney dysfunctions (including nephritis, nephrotic syndrome and nephrosis)
10. Septicemia (blood poisoning)
11. Chronic liver diseases
12. Hypertension
13. Suicide
14. Ulcers of the stomach and duodenum.

A disturbing element in these statistics is the inclusion of accidents, which could largely be prevented, and suicide, which is a frequently-ignored problem among the elderly. Some important suggestions for accident prevention are discussed later in this chapter.

Alzheimer's disease, which accounts for more than three-fourths of mental illness in older individuals, is considered by some medical experts to be one of the leading secondary causes of death in the United States. It is not included in official statistics because of the difficulty diagnosing and reporting it as a primary cause of death. This baffling degenerative brain disorder will be discussed further in this chapter.

Osteoporosis, a severe degenerative thinning of the bones, is an ailment that most often affects the elderly, in particular elderly women. It is estimated that nine out of ten women over the age of 75 are affected by it. Although responsible for many bone fractures, leading to hospitalization and degeneration of an individual's health and physical capabilities, the ailment is not considered a primary cause of death, but rather a significant **secondary** cause of death.

I hope that by discussing these causes of death, you will be encouraged to take every action necessary to prevent them, or at least detect them in their early stages when treatment is still effective. Great strides have been made in treating many of these illnesses, especially when detected early. Heart disease, for instance, the leading cause of death among all ages, declined by over 28 percent since 1970. Death from strokes declined even more dramatically during this period — by 49 percent. Of individuals who suffer major strokes each year, over two-thirds will survive; a third of these will recover fully, and a large number of the remaining recoverees will regain much of their prior capability. Most strokes could be prevented by reducing certain high risk factors, such as hypertension, sedentary behavior, stress, high cholesterol diets, overweight and smoking.

Cancer is the most feared **and** most treatable of the chronic diseases. With the great advances in prevention, detection and treatment, almost **half of all cancer cases can be put into complete — and permanent — remission** by modern treatment methods. Even breast cancer, the second leading cancer causing death in all women, and the number one cancer killer in elderly women, can be, with early detection, completely reversed in almost 100 percent of all cases. Treatment of prostate cancer in men, by radiation therapy or surgical removal of the cancerous tissue, has nearly the same rate of success — without necessarily causing impotency, **if** the disease is detected early enough for treatment to be effective. Despite the effective treatment rate that can result from early detection, the American Cancer Society estimates that there are over 120,000 cases yearly of prostate cancer in men (1 in every 11), with a projected death rate of more than 30,000 individuals. (The Society recommends that all men over 40 get a yearly prostate exam.)

It is important to heed **all warning signs,** such as fatigue, sleepless-ness, nausea, or bleeding, that could signal the onset of an ailment. Your program of early detection and prevention should include regular visits to your physician, and increased awareness of your own health. If you notice the onset of any of these symptoms, contact your doctor **immediately.** Early treatment can significantly reduce the severity of these illnesses, and allow you to lead a long, produc-tive life.

The National Institutes of Health has compiled a list of warning signs for the following diseases:

- **Heart Attack**
    - Chest pain or pressure, most often in the center of the chest. Frequently, the pain radiates to the neck or left shoulder or goes down the left arm. The pain is often described as constricting or vise-like, as if a rope were being pulled tightly around the chest, or it resembles a heavy weight pressing down on the chest.
    - General weakness
    - Pale, ashen appearance; feeling cold while possibly sweating profusely
    - Shortness of breath
    - Nausea.

- **Stroke**
    These are the symptoms of transient ischemic attack (TIA) which, left untreated, can lead to a major stroke.

    - Intermittent numbness, tingling or weakness in the arm or leg, or on one side of the face
    - Temporary blindness in one or both eyes
    - Temporary difficulty with speech
    - Loss of strength in a limb.
    Other danger signals are unusual or unexplainable headache, dizziness, drowsiness, nausea and vomiting, abrupt person-ality changes or impaired judgment.

- **Cancer**
    - Change in bowel or bladder habits, such as increased urina-tion, diarrhea or constipation
    - A sore that does not heal
    - Unusual bleeding or discharge

— Thickening or lump in breast or elsewhere
— Indigestion or difficulty swallowing
— Obvious change in wart or mole
— Nagging cough or hoarseness.

More specifically, the National Foundation for Cancer Research emphasizes the need to watch for the following cancer symptoms which occur commonly in older individuals:

Lung Cancer
Persistent cough
Coughing up blood
Shortness of breath

Breast Cancer
Lump in the breast
Changes in breast shape
Nipple discharge

Colon and Rectum Cancer
Change in bowel habits
Bleeding from the rectum
Blood in the stool

Prostate Cancer
Frequent or difficult urination
Blood in the urine
Frequent lower back pain with
the above symptoms

Uterus, Ovary and Cervix Cancer
Bleeding after menopause
Unusual vaginal discharge
Enlargement of the abdomen
Pain during intercourse

Skin Cancer
A sore that does not heal
Change in shape, size or color
of a wart or mole
Sudden appearance of a mole

■ **Diabetes**
— Excessive thirst, and often, hunger
— Frequent urination
— Unexplained weight loss
— Fatigue, a "run down" feeling
— Blurred vision
— Itchy skin
— Slow-healing cuts and bruises
— Nausea and vomiting
— Tingling or numbness in the hands or feet, possibly resulting from reduced circulation.

VITAMINS AND MINERALS

While most people know their basic dietary requirements — carbohydrates, proteins, fats, along with vitamins and minerals — most of them don't know how these nutrients act in their bodies. Armed with the understanding that vitamins and minerals are good for them, they assume that more is always better. As a result, they frequently take megadoses, unaware of the damage they may be doing.

While carbohydrates, fats, and proteins are the body's "crude oil," vitamins are the refining chemicals that convert that oil to "high octane gas" — providing the body with the pure energy it needs to function. There are 13 essential vitamins. If you omit any one of them from your diet, a deficiency will develop, with all the short- and long-term side effects.

The body does not manufacture its own vitamins except for Vitamin D, which you probably get enough of through exposure to sunlight, or ultraviolet rays (although too much exposure poses its own hazards). They must be obtained from your food or — in those cases when you cannot possibly eat a balanced diet — from supplements. Most people understand the role of minerals even less than that of vitamins. Minerals have two functions: (1) they are the building blocks for bones and soft tissues, and (2) they regulate body functions like heartbeat, blood clotting, the internal pressure of body fluids, nerve responses, and transportation of oxygen from the lungs to the tissues. The body requires certain minerals in fairly large quantities: calcium, phosphorous, potassium, chloride, sodium, magnesium, and sulfur. Other minerals — the "trace minerals" — are required in very small amounts. These include iron, manganese, copper, iodine, zinc, cobalt, fluorine, and selenium.

Every day, the medical community is learning more about how vitamins and minerals function in the body. We do know that Vitamins A, D, E, and K — even more than the other vitamins — should be taken in **limited** doses, because they are fat-soluble: whatever the body doesn't use immediately it stores in the fat and the liver. When too much is stored this way, the excess vitamins act as toxins. Megadoses of Vitamin A can cause headaches, nausea, diarrhea, and even liver and bone damage. Megadoses of Vitamin D can cause kidney damage. The other vitamins are water-soluble, meaning the body can't store them. Instead, the body uses what it needs and excretes the rest, along with its other waste products.

Taking too much of any mineral — even if the amount only exceeds your recommended daily allowance by a little — can upset the body's functions, reduce your ability to perform physical tasks, and contribute to health problems such as anemia, bone demineralization and fracture, cramping, constipation, diarrhea, and neurological disease. Taken in too-high doses, some minerals can actually prevent the body's absorption of other minerals (for example, taking too much zinc will cause a copper deficiency).

Each year, Americans spend over $3 billion for vitamin and mineral supplements. Over 75 percent of Americans over 60 take some kind of nutritional supplement regularly. Yet the use of vitamin and mineral supplements poses a serious problem for the elderly, because of their susceptibility to illness, and the changes in their digestive and absorptive functions. Also, because older people are more likely to take other medications along with these supplements, they run a greater risk of problematic drug interactions.

Yet, because older people are usually aware of the importance of proper nutrition — although they often have nutritionally-inadequate diets due to food intolerances, inability to digest certain foods, ingestion of medications which reduce the body's absorption of certain nutrients, or simply out of bad habit — they tend to take more dietary supplements than any other age group. However, except for those whose illnesses require vitamin supplements or whose medicines prevent them from getting enough vitamins and minerals from their food, most people **do not need** dietary supplements. It is possible to get all the nutrients your body needs by simply eating a *well-balanced diet.*

Even those who cannot eat certain foods — like people with lactose (milk sugar) intolerance (which can be overcome by adding *lactase,* the enzyme that breaks down lactose, to liquid dairy products before ingesting them) — will find that, with a little ingenuity, they can get everything they need from the food they eat.

To understand just how much of each nutrient your body requires, you should become familiar with the U.S. Recommended Daily Allowance (U.S. RDA) for each one (see the table below of vitamins, minerals, and their U.S. RDAs for adults). A U.S. RDA — as defined by the Food and Drug Administration — is the recommended total

U.S. RDAs FOR VITAMINS AND MINERALS

VITAMINS

Fat-Soluble Vitamins:

Vitamin A (Retinol)	5000 I.U.
Vitamin D (Calciferol)	400 I.U.
Vitamin E (Tocopherol)	30 I.U.
Vitamin K	(No established RDA)

Water-Soluble Vitamins:

Vitamin C (Ascorbic Acid)	60.0 mg
Folic Acid (Folacin)	0.4 mg
Vitamin B1 (Thiamine)	1.5 mg
Vitamin B2 (Riboflavin)	1.7 mg
Niacin (Niacinamide)	20.0 mg
Vitamin B6 (Pyridoxine)	2.0 mg
Biotin	0.3 mg
Pantothenic acid	10.0 mg
Vitamin B12 (Cyanocobalamin)	6.0 mcg

MINERALS

Calcium	*1000.00 mg
Iron	18.00 mg
Phosphorus	1000.00 mg
Magnesium	400.00 mg
Zinc	15.00 mg
Copper	2.00 mg
Iodine	150.00 mcg

*In 1984 the National Institutes of Health recommended an increase to 1,500 mg of calcium for older *women.*

Note: *Selenium and chromium* are considered essential to the body's daily needs but do not have an established U.S. RDA. Recommended for these minerals are: 50-200 mcg.

amount of any nutrient to be ingested in a day. Nutrient amounts are measured in milligrams (1/1000 of a gram), micrograms (1/1000 of a milligram), or international units (I.U.). If you do buy a dietary supplement, be sure to compare the supplement amount with the U.S. RDA for that nutrient. Most supplements' labels list the percentage of the U.S. RDA they provide.

Of utmost importance: before taking any dietary supplement, it is advisable to consult with your doctor or a licensed nutritionist. Again, the best — and safest — source of all nutrients is food.

WHO IS YOUR DOCTOR?

"Who is your doctor?" — this is a question older people often ask their family, friends and acquaintances. For as we get older and chronic health conditions are likely to increase, our doctor of many years has either retired, moved away or died. Even when we don't lose our regular doctor, we may develop illnesses which require treatment by another doctor — a specialist in a field of medicine with which we are not familiar. In the hopes of getting a good recommendation, thousands of older individuals begin their search for a new doctor or specialist by asking the same question: "Who is your doctor?"

The task of finding a new doctor at this time in your life is not always easy, especially since advances in medicine lead to a continuous array of new specialties. This section tries to clarify the selection process and the different specialists frequently required by older individuals.

PRIMARY CARE DOCTORS

If your initial concern is finding a doctor to provide general care — usually referred to as a **primary care doctor** — you should look for an internist or family physician who is experienced in geriatric medicine. Since very few doctors have actually been trained to specialize in illnesses associated with old age, most of these specialists — known as geriatricians — have obtained their special training through actual care of the elderly. With the ever-increasing number of elderly individuals, and the accompanying demand for geriatric medical care, many medical schools now require their students to have some specialized geriatric training. However, it will be years before the supply of geriatricians will meet the demand.

Internists are either medical doctors (M.D.s) who diagnose and treat disease in adults but do not perform surgery or **osteopaths** — Doctors of Osteopathy (D.O.s). Osteopaths are fully-trained and qualified as licensed physicians, and practice all branches of medicine and surgery. Although osteopaths focus on the musculoskeletal system and may use palpation and applied manipulative procedures to treat certain disorders, they are not chiropractors, bone specialists or physical therapists. Over 85 percent of the nation's approximately 23,000 osteopaths provide primary health care to individuals and families. The remaining 15 percent are specialists in surgery, internal medicine, radiology or psychiatry.

A family physician is certified as a Specialist in Family Practice and must be recertified every six years. Family physician training includes six broad areas of medicine: surgery, internal medicine, psychiatry, obstetrics and gynecology, pediatrics and community medicine. The scope and variety of their medical knowledge enables family physicians to treat almost all types of human illness.

You can feel confident choosing any one of these three doctors as your primary care physician.

MEDICAL SPECIALISTS

To give you the best possible care, your primary care doctor may find it necessary to confer with or refer you to one of the following medical specialists:

- *Anesthesiologist* — specializes in anesthesiology and administering anesthetics during surgery and other medical procedures.
- *Cardiologist* — treats heart diseases and malfunctions.
- *Dermatologist* — treats skin disorders.
- *Endocrinologist* — treats glandular disorders, such as thyroid, adrenal and pituitary.
- *Gastroenterologist* — specializes in diseases of the digestive system.
- *Gynecologist* — specializes in the female reproductive system.

- *Hematologist* — treats blood disorders.

- *Neurologist* — treats disorders of the nervous system.

- *Neurotologist* — surgeon who specializes in nerve disorders of the ear.

- *Oncologist* — treats tumors and cancer.

- *Ophthalmologist* — diagnoses and treats optical disorders, performs surgery, and prescribes drugs, eyeglasses and contact lenses.

- *Orthopedist* — specializes in diseases of the bones and joints and correction of deformities.

- *Otologist* — specializes in the ear and its disorders.

- *Otorhinolaryngologist* — (commonly referred to as an ENT — ear, nose and throat — specialist) treats diseases of the ear, nose and throat.

- *Pathologist* — specializes in determining the causes of diseases and resulting changes (pathology) in the body's tissues, organs and blood.

- *Proctologist* — treats disorders of the colon, rectum and anal canal.

- *Psychiatrist* — treats mental and emotional disorders and illnesses; prescribes medications and counsels patients; performs diagnostic tests to determine whether patients have related physical problems.

- *Rheumatologist* — specializes in arthritis and rheumatism.

- *Urologist* — specializes in the urinary system of both sexes, including the bladder and kidneys; treats disorders of the male reproductive system.

CHOOSING A DOCTOR

There are several ways to obtain a recommendation for a doctor:

- Ask people you know for the names of their doctors.

- Ask your county medical society or local Area Agency on Aging for a recommendation of local doctors.

- Contact your local medical referral service.

- For those who live in certain areas of the U.S., a new service provided by the Consumer Health Services offers assistance in locating almost any type of doctor, chiropractor, podiatrist or dentist in the local area of the caller. Call toll-free **800-362-8677** (800-DOCTORS). The program, which is expanding, is now available in the Chicago, Fort Worth/Dallas, Denver, Washington D.C. (and the metro areas of Virginia and Maryland), Kansas City, Milwaukee, Houston, Pittsburgh, and Philadelphia metropolitan areas. New York is already scheduled for service in the near future.

Once you have obtained several recommendations, be very careful to select the one that is right for you. Begin by calling or visiting the doctor's office. Be sure to ask the following questions:

- What are the doctor's credentials? Is he/she affiliated with any medical societies or associations?

- What is the doctor's experience with older individuals?

- Does the doctor accept assignment for Medicare or whatever other medical insurance you carry?

- What arrangements does the doctor have for seeing patients after hours, at home, or in an emergency?

- With which hospitals in the community is the doctor associated?

- What are his/her hours, office fees and billing procedures?

Once these questions have been answered to your satisfaction, arrange for an appointment to meet the doctor(s) you are considering and discuss your medical concerns. Then make your selection. You should like the doctor you choose and feel confident in him/her. If you don't like a particular doctor, continue your search until you find a doctor with whom you are completely comfortable.

UNDERSTANDING BLOOD CHOLESTEROL

Although you often hear otherwise, blood cholesterol — in limited quantities — is good. The body uses cholesterol to produce essential substances, like cell walls and hormones, and to perform other vital functions. Since the amount of cholesterol the body uses is very limited, blood cholesterol levels that are too high pose very dangerous risks.

High blood cholesterol is one of the three major **controllable** risk factors contributing to heart disease, the other two being high blood pressure and cigarette smoking. Most heart attacks are caused by arteriosclerosis. Arteriosclerosis occurs when cholesterol, fats, and other substances build up in the walls of the arteries, thus clogging the flow of blood to the heart.

Like other lipids (fats) and lipid-like substances, cholesterol is not water-soluble. Therefore, to make cholesterol and lipids transportable in the body, the liver wraps them in protein packages called *lipoproteins.*

Blood cholesterol is found in both the low-density lipoproteins (LDL) — which is of most concern when considering blood cholesterol levels — and in the high-density lipoproteins (HDL). Low-density lipoproteins contain the highest concentrations of cholesterol, and may be responsible for depositing cholesterol in the artery walls. For this reason, LDLs are often referred to as the "bad" cholesterol. By contrast, high-density lipoproteins contain higher concentrations of protein and low concentrations of cholesterol. HDLs are believed to remove cholesterol from the cells in the artery walls, transporting it back to the liver for removal from the body. Research has demonstrated that people with higher levels of HDL than LDL have lower incidences of heart disease, which is why HDL has come to be called the "good" cholesterol.

To help prevent heart disease, it is essential that you determine your blood cholesterol levels through simple blood tests. Blood cholesterol is measured in terms of milligrams per deciliter (mg/dl): which means the number of milligrams of cholesterol found in 1/10 of a liter of blood. NIH's National Heart, Lung and Blood Institute (NHLBI) has just published the following guidelines for blood cholesterol:

If your total cholesterol level is:	and your LDL is:	your cholesterol level is:
less than 200 mg/dl	less then 130 mg/dl	desirable
200 to 239 mg/dl	130 to 159 mg/dl	borderline high-risk
240 mg/dl and higher	160 mg/dl and higher	high-risk

Currently, the average total blood cholesterol level for middle-aged men and women is about 215 mg/dl.

It is not so much the total blood cholesterol that is of concern as the **ratio** of LDL to HDL. Sometimes, even if your LDL is slightly higher than desirable, it might be offset by a high HDL. Thus, just because your total blood cholesterol is high, a low LDL coupled with a high HDL may reduce your cause for concern. Conversely, even if your LDL is "desirable," an HDL that is extremely low (less than 35 mg/dl) may still put you at risk. Because there are so many factors involved in determining safe blood cholesterol levels, **you should always check with your doctor:** only he/she is qualified to determine whether your cholesterol levels are healthy.

If your cholesterol levels **are** higher than desirable, you can reduce them by (1) increasing your HDL level **and** (2) lowering your LDL level. You will probably be able to accomplish this by exercising regularly, not smoking, and most important, reducing your intake of fats (ideally no more than 20 grams per day), especially if you're over-weight. If you do need to lose weight, you'll be amazed how much you can lose while still eating all the calories you want **if you just limit your fat intake.** In addition, your diet should be modified to include lots of complex carbohydrates such as fruits and vegetables, especially starchy vegetables like potatoes, sweet potatoes and legumes *and* few or no refined foods containing bleached flour and white sugar.

The National Cholesterol Education Program of NHLBI has recent-ly published a free 51-page booklet entitled *Eating to Lower Your High Blood Cholesterol.* The booklet gives the latest nutritional informa-tion on the foods to eat and those to avoid to reduce blood choles-terol levels. To obtain this free booklet or other current information about blood cholesterol, write to:

> National Institutes of Health
> National Heart, Lung and Blood Institute
> National Cholesterol Education Program/C-200
> Bethesda, MD 20892

ALZHEIMER'S DISEASE

Alzheimer's disease is a disorder that affects the cells of the brain and eventually produces serious intellectual impairment. The resulting mental impairment affects not only the victims, but also their families and loved ones. As the illness progresses, it brings about adverse changes in the individual's mental and neurological functions. Most notable are changes such as frequent forgetfulness leading to almost complete memory loss, confusion, agitation, irritability, lack of concentration, judgment and orientation. Even though this disease is progressive in nature, it does vary among those afflicted in degree and rate of progression. Unfortunately, there is still no cure nor do we know how to prevent this illness, but progress is being made in the research of it.

Despite the estimated 4 million older individuals — with projections of over 14 million by year 2040 — affected by Alzheimer's, **do not become concerned** over occasional forgetfulness. The majority of us, young and old, forget at times what we were about to say or pull out a drawer and forget for a moment what we were looking for.

Despite our limited knowledge about Alzheimer's, many of its symptoms can be controlled or reduced with proper medical care. It is absolutely essential that the Alzheimer's victim seek the care of a physician — preferably one who has a thorough understanding of this illness and its treatment in relationship to the other physical ailments that may exist in an elderly patient. Due to the emotional impact this illness has on family members, they should also receive help from the physician, who can guide them in the caring of their loved one, and help them understand this disease and how to cope with the patient's erratic behavior.

An outstanding organization which can assist you or someone in your family who has this disease is the Alzheimer's Disease and Related Disorders Association (ADRDA). This nonprofit voluntary health organization continually works to make the public more aware of this disorder, to provide support for those affected by it, and to aid in research efforts and the advocation of legislation that responds to the needs of Alzheimer's patients and their families. Contact them either by calling their 24-hour toll-free information and referral number, 800-272-3900 or by writing to them at 919 North Michigan Avenue, Suite 1000, Chicago, Illinois 60611.

ARTHRITIS AND PARKINSON'S . . . DEBILITATING ILLNESSES AFFECTING MILLIONS OF SENIORS

ARTHRITIS

An estimated 37 million Americans are afflicted with America's number one crippling disease — arthritis. One in every seven people and one in every three families will suffer from arthritis sometime during their lifetime. Over 7 million Americans are currently disabled by arthritis. Often thought of as only affecting older people, arthritis attacks people of all ages, including 50,000 children. A chronic disease; arthritis persists throughout life.

Arthritis, which means inflammation of the joint, actually refers to more than 100 different rheumatic diseases. The five most common types of arthritis and the estimated number of people affected by them are: *osteoarthritis* (16 million Americans), *rheumatoid arthritis* (7 million), *ankylosing spondylitis* ("spinal arthritis" — nearly 2.5 million), *gout* (1.8 million) and *systemic lupus erythematosus* (nearly 500,000, over 400,000 of whom are women).

Although cures are not yet available, treatment has advanced considerably. However, there are more fraudulent treatments for arthritis than for any other disease in America, so be extremely cautious about buying any product that claims to cure arthritis or its symptoms. Anyone afflicted with arthritis should only take treatments prescribed by a doctor.

The Arthritis Foundation, founded in 1948, is the only national volunteer health association committed to finding the causes, cures and prevention for arthritis in its many forms. It consists of 71 chapters and divisions throughout the nation which help millions of Americans learn more about this illness and how to cope with it. Write or call toll-free for free information on arthritis or membership in the Arthritis Foundation: Arthritis Foundation, P.O. Box 1900, Atlanta, GA 30326 (Toll Free: 800-283-7800).

PARKINSON'S DISEASE

Over 2.5 million Americans are thought to suffer from Parkinson's disease, generally referred to simply as "Parkinson's". According to NIH statistics, this number increases by 20-30,000 new cases each year.

Parkinson's is a degenerative, debilitating, progressive disease of the central nervous system which originates in the brain's thalamus. Its symptoms, devastating to its victim, include slowly spreading tremors, muscular weakness, rigidity or paralysis (often in the face), and a peculiar, shuffling gait. Although there is no known cure, several medications combat the symptoms of Parkinson's, arresting the tremors for a period of time.

Recently, a ray of hope for Parkinson's victims occurred with the first significant advance in its treatment in many years. A new drug — Deprenyl — was proven to slow the progression of the disease in some cases. Deprenyl has been approved by the FDA and is now available by prescription.

The National Parkinson's Foundation is the world's leading center for research, treatment, therapy and rehabilitation of those with Parkinson's and related neurological disorders. The Foundation disseminates extremely helpful publications to the general public, including where to get help and current reports from the medical profession. Contact the Foundation by writing or calling: National Parkinson Foundation, 1501 N.W. 9th Avenue, Miami, FL, 33136, Tel. (in Miami) (305) 547-6668, Toll Free (Florida) 800-433-7022, Toll Free (other 49 states) 800-327-4545.

ACCIDENTAL HYPOTHERMIA AND HYPERTHERMIA — DANGEROUS EXTREMES IN BODY TEMPERATURE!

One of the physical changes that occurs as we age is that our bodies do not adjust as efficiently to temperature changes. Unresponsiveness to temperature can be caused by conditions such as circulatory problems, diabetes, strokes, damaged hearts, or the body's reaction to many medications. Consequently, older individuals are much more susceptible to accidental **hypothermia** (called "cold stress") — a sudden drop in body temperature to 95°F (35°C) or below — and to **hyperthermia** (called "heat stress") — an extreme jump in body temperature to 104°F (40°C) or higher. Keep in mind that normal body temperature is approximately 98.6°F (37°C).

Both of these conditions are very dangerous to the elderly, in particular those with heart and circulatory disorders or diabetes. If not treated promptly, hypothermia and hyperthermia can result in death. Each condition is discussed below to make you aware of its symptoms and of the precautionary measures you can take to avoid them.

HYPOTHERMIA (COLD STRESS)

Hypothermia is caused by an excessive loss of heat from the body. Although it usually occurs when an individual is exposed to severe cold without sufficient protection, it can occur in older individuals in temperatures above freezing.

Only special low-reading thermometers, like those used by medical professionals can register hypothermic temperatures. However, if you shake your home thermometer down extremely well, it may record low body temperatures. If your thermometer **does** register a temperature below 95°F (35°C) — or if it doesn't register any temperature — call for emergency help **immediately!** While waiting for help to come, insulate the victim with blankets, towels or anything dry — **do not** use hot baths, electric blankets or hot water bottles. Do not raise the victim's feet, as this could further depress the body temperature, or give him/her any food or drink.

Because most home thermometers will not record lower body temperatures, you must rely on the following symptoms to determine whether or not a person is experiencing cold stress:

- slurred speech
- slow or irregular breathing and heart rate
- muscle stiffness, particularly in the neck, arms, and legs
- confusion and drowsiness
- cool or cold, extremely pale skin. (The skin may also have large, irregular blue or pink spots.)
- puffy or swollen face
- loss of consciousness

- shivering (note that shivering is not always present in older individuals with hypothermia).

Here are some precautionary measures you can take to safeguard your well-being in cold weather:

- Stay where it is the warmest — avoid exposure to even moderately cold temperatures whenever possible. Set heating thermostats to at least 65°F (18.3°C); higher if you are ill.
- Dress warmly:
  — Wear several loose layers of lighter-weight clothing.
  — When going outside, wear a windproof outer garment: winds and breezes lower body temperature faster than body heat can be replaced.
  — Wear a hat and scarf (between 30 to 40 percent of body heat is lost through the head).
  — Stay dry — if your clothes and/or shoes get wet, change **immediately!**
  — Eat a nutritious, well-balanced diet every day.
  — Exercise moderately on a regular basis.
  — Use extra blankets in bed since cold stress can develop during sleep.

HYPERTHERMIA (HEAT STRESS)

Heat stress can occur either during a prolonged heat wave or when an unexpected rise in external temperature is so sudden that the body does not have enough time to adjust. Do not become alarmed if you simply feel hot, uncomfortable or listless, since these feelings usually pose no threat unless they persist for a long time. However, if you have the following symptoms, seek emergency assistance **immediately!**

- body temperature — measured rectally — rises to 104°F (40°C) or higher
- rapid heartbeat
- diarrhea
- dizziness
- nausea
- cramps

- dry skin (with no sweating)
- overall weakness or fatigue
- chest pain
- breathing problems
- mental changes such as mood swings or disorientation.

The following precautionary measures should be taken during periods of intense heat:

- Stay indoors in an air-conditioned room. If you do not have air conditioning, spend as much time as possible in cool malls, museums, stores, libraries, Senior Centers, or other air conditioned buildings.

- If you do not have air conditioning, use a fan to help circulate air. Lower window shades or blinds.

- Avoid using your stove during the hottest time of day to cut down on any additional heat.

- Take several cool baths or showers.

- Stay out of the sun; if you must go outdoors, wear a hat to protect your head and/or use an umbrella. Also, wear light-colored, light-weight, loose-fitting clothes that permit evaporation of sweat (preferably natural fabrics like cotton).

- Eat light meals and avoid hot foods.

- Avoid any strenuous activity and curtail your normal activities.

- Drink plenty of water and/or fruit juices.

- Do not drink any alcoholic beverages — these act as diuretics and cause rapid water loss from the body.

A word of advice to those living alone: During a severe cold spell or heat wave, ask friends, relatives or neighbors to check on you at least once or twice a day to see how you are doing. If you have no one to check on you regularly, call your local Area Agency on Aging to see if they have a volunteer visiting program that could look in on you or, if not, see whether they have a telephone check-in service available for housebound individuals in periods of extreme heat or cold.

IMMUNIZATIONS

After reaching a certain point in our adulthood, most of us frequently ignore or overlook particularly important immunizations. Since the ability to counter an illness tends to decrease with advancing age, we should take every precaution available to avoid contracting a vaccine preventable illness at a vulnerable time in life.

The following immunizations are recommended by the U.S. Public Health Service and most physicians for older individuals. If you have not already received them, contact your physician or local public health service about obtaining these important immunizations.

- **_Tetanus_** — This immunization protects individuals against lock-jaw, which is caused by bacteria (tetanus spores) entering the body through a wound or cut made by a tainted object. While many people assume that tetanus occurs **only** when someone receives a deep puncture wound from a dirty or rusty object such as a nail or knife, the truth is **over half** the wounds infected with tetanus bacteria each year are caused by minor household injuries that frequently go untreated until the onset of infection. The first tetanus immunization is usually given to an infant as part of the DPT vaccination which also includes diphtheria and pertussis (whooping cough) vaccines. You should receive a DPT booster shot at least once every 10 years to retain your level of immunity. However, many physicians recommend that individuals who are cut by dirty or rusty objects, or who get cuts that leave dirt beneath the skin, obtain booster shots if they have not had one in the last five years. According to the U.S. Public Health Service, adults who have never received the initial primary inoculation should not obtain the DPT combination vaccination but rather the DT vaccine for adults, which excludes the pertussis vaccine.

- **_Diphtheria_** — Although the incidence of diphtheria has declined considerably with the use of the diphtheria toxoid vaccination, it is estimated that less than half of our over-60 population is adequately protected against this disease. As stated above, the DPT vaccine, or DT inoculation for adults immunizes for both diphtheria and tetanus. A follow-up booster shot should be received every 10 years.

■ *Influenza* — Even though over 50 million people are afflicted each year by the flu, less than 25 percent of our elderly obtain the influenza vaccine which provides significant protection against flu infections. This vaccine has been effective in drastically reducing the number and severity of cases each year. The immunization should be obtained every fall. In many communities, it is administered free or at a minimal cost by the local public health service office. Coverage by Medicare has been provided since 1993.

■ *Pneumococcal Pneumonia* — The vaccination least known to most people is the one that protects against pneumonia, one of the leading causes of death in the nation. This vaccination can protect an individual against 23 different strains of the pneumococci bacteria which causes over 87 percent of all pneumococcal disease. Individuals over 65 and those with chronic illnesses are the most susceptible and constitute the largest portion of the more than 50,000 Americans who die each year from pneumonia. The vaccination (which can provide protection for three to five years) may be taken at any time during the year. For those who are eligible, the cost of this vaccination is completely covered by the medical portion of Medicare (Part B) explained in Chapter 4.

■ *Measles* — Though most of us consider measles a childhood illness, it also affects a great many elders. When an adult contracts measles, the illness can be extremely severe, and may result in brain damage or even death. A one-time inoculation with the live virus vaccine can provide protection throughout a lifetime. Most physicians recommend that any adult over 50 who has never received a primary vaccination or did not have measles as a child obtain this vaccination to ensure immunity from this disease.

It is advisable to keep a record of the dates of any immunizations you have received. These dates should be kept in your medical records.

ACCIDENTS

According to the National Safety Council, the elderly are the victims of **23 percent** of all accidental deaths. Each year over 24,000 elderly die from accidental injuries. With attention to your own safety and by taking a few precautionary measures, you can do much to lower these statistics. In particular, pay attention to what you can do to prevent (1) **falls** — which are the most common causes of accidental deaths — (2) **motor vehicle accidents** — which are the second greatest cause of accidental deaths among the elderly — and (3) **burns** that become increasingly difficult to recover from as you age, regardless of their degree of severity.

The following precautions are strongly recommended to help prevent many of these types of accidents:

- Illuminate all walking and bedroom/sleeping areas sufficiently to allow clear vision, especially at night. Use night lights — which are very economical — wherever possible to avoid tripping over any objects or furniture.

- Make sure your bathtubs have non-skid mats or strips in them. Bars attached to the walls, or to the sides of the bathtub, will help greatly when getting in and out of your bathtub.

- Set your water heater thermostats to no more than 120 degrees to avoid scalding accidents.

- Make sure your carpeting and rugs are not frayed or loose and do not slide easily. Tack down any loose carpeting on stairs. Put some double-stick tape on the back of throw rugs to prevent them from sliding.

- Install sturdy handrails on both sides of your stairways so that they are strong enough to support your entire weight if you should stumble or fall. Make sure you always grasp a handrail when ascending or descending steps. Keep stairways well lighted at all times.

- While on **any** medication, don't drink alcohol unless the doctor approves.

- **Never** smoke in bed!

■ Don't put any cigarette butts in a trash can or receptacle without first pouring water over them.

■ Be sure you have smoke detectors on all levels of your home and check them frequently to ensure they are operable. If your smoke detector is battery-operated, the battery should be replaced once a year or sooner if the low warning alarm or warning light comes on.

■ Know in advance how you can exit safely and quickly — especially from your bedroom — in case of a fire.

■ Always turn a heating pad off before going to sleep.

■ Don't cook when wearing loose clothing or clothing made of materials that can easily catch fire, like sleeping apparel.

■ Do not overload an extension cord with appliances.

■ Keep all electrical appliances and extension cords away from sinks or water. Always remember ... when appliances are plugged into a socket, the wires can still conduct electricity if they come in contact with water **even** when the appliance switch is turned off.

■ Take your time getting up from bed or a chair so that you don't become faint or dizzy.

■ Don't lock yourself in your own home so securely that you can't get out in an emergency. Have locks installed that are easily and quickly opened from the inside.

■ When walking outside after it has rained or snowed, look at the pavement frequently to avoid any potential trouble spots and take extra precaution when crossing the street. At night, wear bright clothing, carry a flashlight and, whenever possible, have someone accompany you.

■ When you travel by car, try to drive less often at night, during busy times, on wintry and slick roads, and for long periods of time. **Always use your seat belt!** Since it is normal with advancement in age to lose some reaction time, you should drive more **cautiously.** This is for your well-being and that of others.

HEALTH HEADLINES

While many of you may have read or heard about the following health news items, I am including them here for those who may not be aware of them. The health benefits described here could help millions, so it's important that you be aware of them. This section will only take a few minutes to read, but these are minutes that could make a tremendous difference in your life or in the lives of those for whom you are caring.

- In early 1993, two new drugs, *tacrine* and *beta interferon*, for the treatment of Alzheimer's disease and Multiple Sclerosis were recommended by advisory expert panels for approval by the Food and Drug Administration(FDA). Although neither drug is a cure-all for either illness, both represent milestones in the treatment against these devastating diseases. *Tacrine*, commercially known as Cognex, has shown to provide significant benefits to about 12% of Alzheimer patients in delaying their memory loss and impaired physical capabilities. *Beta interferon*, used in the treatment of Multiple Sclerosis (MS) patients, appears to reduce MS attacks and decrease the number of brain lesions that develop.

- In March 1990, the National Institutes of Health (NIH) announced that massive injections of a readily available drug — Methylprednisolone — within 8 hours of spinal injury could significantly reduce the risk of paralysis. The drug reduces the swelling and spinal deterioration that cause paralysis. The drug also diminishes the severity of disability that usually follows such injuries. Researchers have found Methlyprednisolone given intravenously within the first hours of the injury will help even the most severe spinal cord injury patients.

- A new prescription drug, misoprostol (marketed by G.D. Searle under the brand name *Cytotec*) was approved by the FDA to prevent stomach ulcers in millions of arthritis patients who take NSAIDS (nonsteroidal anti-inflammatory drugs, such as aspirin, ibuprofen, naproxen, and piroxicam). The new drug — the first to treat NSAID-induced ulcers, according to the FDA — allow our elderly and ulcer-prone patients to continue taking their current arthritis medications without fear of gastrointestinal bleeding. Cytotec could help over 37 million Americans who have arthritis.

■ In April 1990, it was reported that an experimental cancer drug, *2-CDA* (2-Chlorodeoxyadenosine) had produced remission in 11 of 12 patients suffering from a rare form of leukemia, called hairy cell leukemia. Two other drugs (Interferon and Deoxycoformycin) have already been approved by FDA for treatment of hairy cell leukemia. Both drugs are less effective than 2-CDA and produce serious side effects. The only unwanted side effect of 2-CDA is a fever that lasts a few days. The drug also shows promise in fighting the more chronic lymphocytic leukemia. The new drug awaits final approval by the FDA, but is expected to receive it in the very near future.

■ One of the largest pharmaceutical companies in the U.S., G.D. Searle, sponsors a special program called the *Searle Patients in Need Program*. Through this program, Searle gives away several of their cardiovascular and hypertensive drugs (including Calan, Nitrodisc, Norpace and Aldactone) to low-income individuals who cannot afford to buy them. Recently, Searle added its new drug Cytotec to the program. Upon a doctor's request, Searle will issue certificates to be used by the patient when purchasing these prescribed medications. The pharmacist accepts the certificate as payment at the time the drugs are dispensed. In turn, the pharmacist submits the certificate to Searle for payment. This is truly one of the finest programs available to the millions of uninsured and low-income individuals who desperately need these medications. Many other pharmaceutical companies have in the past year begun to follow suit.

■ Throughout the country a new form of health therapy has been emerging: **pet therapy!** In nursing homes and even some hospitals — despite some resistance to changing rules which prevent visits from pets — healthy pets (dogs and cats) can be brought for regular visits with confined patients. The result has been phenomenal, with improvement in the patients' psychological conditions (and often, as a result, their physical conditions). Studies have shown that pets in almost any type of environment can have a remarkably positive influence on an individual's well-being.

Consequently, many organizations — perhaps within your own community — are gathering "pet volunteers," lovable, clean and healthy animals, to visit patients on a regular basis in nursing homes and hospitals that participate in pet therapy programs. Most Area Agencies on Aging are familiar with programs available in your area. Contact them for further information.

- For those who suffer from continual chronic pain from arthritis, back problems, migraine headaches, neuralgia or any other physical condition which creates ongoing, often unbearable pain, there is now a home therapy to reduce or even eliminate chronic pain. This therapy **does not use any medication.** Instead, it is provided by a biomedical device called **TENS** (transcutaneous electrical nerve stimulation) which has been used in hospitals and pain clinics for several years. The small unit can be worn on a belt or held in the hand. It works by lightly attaching electrodes to the painful area, then stimulating the nerve cells in that area at the press of a button. The electrodes' current enables the body to block the pain messages. It is also believed that TENS helps stimulate production of the body's own pain-relieving chemicals (endorphins).

   At a doctor's recommendation, Medicare will pay for a 30-day trial period when the TENS supplier does not provide a free trial period. Medicare will also cover 80% of the Medicare-approved cost of the unit if it is determined that TENS is effective in reducing the patient's pain **and** a doctor recommends purchase of the unit. Contact your physician if you would like more information on this form of therapy and the TENS home unit.

- *Aspirin Shown to Cut Heart Attacks and Strokes:* A study published in 1991 in the *New England Journal of Medicine* concluded that daily doses of aspirin could cut the risk of strokes by as much as 50 percent among patients suffering from Atrial Fibrillation — a common heart condition that causes over 70,000 strokes each year. The report also supported the findings of several other studies, which concluded that aspirin, because of its anticlotting properties, can dramatically reduce the risk of heart attacks.

LISTING

Clearinghouses and Centers for Health Information and Assistance

The following clearinghouses, centers and toll-free health information telephone numbers are sponsored either by private organizations or the federal government. They have been selected for presentation here because they can provide an abundance of health information and assistance on various health topics of interest to older individuals. Included are two new programs of particular importance to people concerned with their vision and hearing. These programs are made available by the Foundation of the American Academy of Ophthalmology and the Occupational Hearing Services; they are described in the sections on *Eye Care* and *Hearing and Speech*. All of the groups listed offer most of their services at no cost. Groups that primarily serve professional health-care providers are not included in this listing.

The services offered vary but they include publications, recorded messages or personalized counseling services that respond to your questions with either direct answers or referrals to others who may be of help. You can either write or call those sources where both an address and telephone number are indicated. All others provide assistance **only** through their telephone service. Since there is **no charge** for the majority of services and information provided, **you are encouraged to use them as often as needed.**

If you are not satisfied with the information received and need further assistance on a particular subject, call the **Health Information Center** of the Office of Disease Prevention and Health Promotion (which is listed here under "Health"). Its staff will be eager to help you obtain additional information on almost any health topic.

Acquired Immune Deficiency Syndrome (AIDS)

National AIDS Information Clearinghouse
P.O. Box 6003, Rockville, MD 20849
Toll Free: 800-458-5231

Offers information to callers on AIDS, including symptoms, possible causes, and recommended preventive measures.

National Institute of Allergy & Infectious Disease
Office of Communications, Building 31, Room 7A-32, 9000 Rockville Pike, Bethesda, MD 20892
Telephone: (301) 496-5717

The Institute conducts and supports research on infectious and allergic diseases and on immunology. It currently has a major responsibility for research of AIDS. In addition to providing consumer materials on AIDS, the Institute dispenses information on allergies, bacterial meningitis, sinusitis, poison ivy allergy, mold allergy, pollen allergy, dust allergy, insect allergy, asthma, rabies, viruses, sexually transmitted diseases, viral hepatitis, genital herpes, Reyes syndrome, toxoplasmosis, tuberculosis, and the immune system.

Public Health Service AIDS Information Hotline
Toll Free: 800-342-2437

Provides information to the public on the prevention and spread of AIDS.

Aging

National Institute on Aging Information Center
P.O. Box 8057, Gaithersburg, MD 20857
Telephone: (301) 495-3455

The Institute conducts and supports biomedical, social, and behavioral research and training related to the aging process, diseases and other special problems and needs of the aged. Consumer materials are available on menopause, nutrition, arthritis, cancer, aging, Alzheimer's disease, constipation, diabetes, exercise, hearing, high blood pressure, osteoporosis, medicines, senility, flu, urinary incontinence, skin care, and dental care.

Two special informational packets on Aging and Alzheimer's disease are also available.

Alcoholism

National Clearinghouse for Alcohol and Drug Information
P.O. Box 2345, Rockville, MD 20852
Telephone: (301) 468-2600

The clearinghouse provides current information on alcohol related subjects, alcohol use and abuse, and on programs focusing on the prevention of and treatment for drug abuse. Also provides referrals to organizations for treatment and counseling.

Alcoholism and Drug Addiction Treatment Center
Toll Free: 800-382-4357

Provides referrals to local facilities where individuals can seek help.

Alzheimer's Disease

Alzheimer's Disease & Related Disorders Association
70 East Lake Street, Suite 600, Chicago, IL 60601
Toll Free: 800-272-3900
       800-572-6037 in Illinois

Offers information on publications about Alzheimer's disease and related disorders available from the Association. Gives referrals to local chapters and support groups.

National Institute of Neurological and Communicative Disorders and Stroke
Building 31, Room 8A-06
9000 Rockville Pike, Bethesda, MD 20892
Telephone: (301) 496-5924

The Institute conducts and supports research on the causes, prevention, diagnosis, and treatment of neurological and communicative disorders and stroke. It currently plays a major role in the research of Alzheimer's disease. Consumer materials are available on this disease, as well as on acoustic neuroma, amyotrophic lateral sclerosis, aphasia, autism, cerebral palsy, dementias, epilepsy, Friedreich's ataxia, Huntington's disease, multiple sclerosis, muscular dystrophy, myastenia gravis, neurofibromatosis, Parkinson's disease, shingles, spina bifida, spinal cord injury, stuttering, torsion dystonia, stroke, head injury, Gaucher's disease, Niemann-Pick disease, Fabry's disease, TaySachs disease, Farber's disease, metachromatic leukodystrophy, and lipid storage diseases.

Arthritis

Arthritis Foundation
1314 Spring Street, NW, Atlanta, GA 30309
Telephone: (404) 872-7100

A national voluntary health organization which provides information and services to people with arthritis, including referrals to
doctors and clinics.

National Institute of Arthritis and
Musculoskeletal and Skin Diseases
Information Office, Building 31, Room 4C-05
9000 Rockville Pike, Bethesda, MD 20892
Telephone: (301) 496-8188

Established in 1986 as an Institute within the National Institutes of
Health, it conducts and supports research and related programs in
the field of arthritis, musculoskeletal and skin diseases. Consumer
materials are available on arthritis, osteoporosis, lupus erythematosus,
back ailments, psoriasis, acne, ichthyosis, epidermolysis bullosa,
vitiligo and Paget's disease.

Cancer

Cancer Information Service
Toll Free: 800-422-6237

The Cancer Information Service is a telephone inquiry system which
supplies information about cancer and cancer-related resources to
the general public and to cancer patients and their families. Callers
are automatically put in touch with the office serving their area. Inquiries
are handled by health educators and trained volunteers.

AMC Cancer Information
Toll Free: 800-525-3777

Provides current information on causes of cancer, prevention, methods
of detection and diagnosis, treatment and treatment facilities, rehabilitation, and counseling services.

Dental Health

National Institute of Dental Research
Public Reports and Inquiries Section
Building 31, Room 2C-35, 9000 Rockville Pike, Bethesda, MD 20892
Telephone: (301) 496-4261

The National Institute of Dental Research was established to improve dental health through education and research. Consumer publications are available on dental health, fluoride treatment, temporomandibular joint disease, canker sores, periodontal disease, dental sealants, dental implants and other mouth problems.

Diabetes

National Diabetes Information Clearinghouse
Box NDIC, 9000 Rockville Pike, Bethesda, MD 20892
Telephone: (301) 468-2162

The Clearinghouse, a service of the National Institute of Diabetes and Digestive and Kidney Diseases, distributes its own publications on diabetes, as well as other related materials either at no cost or minimal cost to the public. Consumer materials are available on diabetes, foot care, nutrition, insulin, blood glucose monitoring, eye care and various other related subjects.

American Diabetes Association
Telephone: (703) 549-1500 in Virginia and DC metro area
Toll Free: 800-232-3472

Provides free printed materials, newsletter, and health education information on diabetes. Also gives physician referrals and support group assistance information.

Digestion

National Digestive Diseases Information Clearinghouse
Box NDDIC, 9000 Rockville Pike, Bethesda, MD 20892
Telephone: (301) 468-6344

This is a service of the National Institute of Diabetes and Digestive and Kidney Diseases. Various publications are available on diabetes, endocrinology, metabolic diseases, digestive diseases and nutrition, and kidney, urologic and blood diseases.

Drug Abuse

National Clearinghouse for Alcohol And
Drug Abuse Information
P.O. Box 2345, Rockville, MD 20852
Telephone: (301) 468-2600

See the discussion on this clearinghouse in the preceding section under ALCOHOLISM.

National Cocaine Hotline
Toll Free: 800-262-2463

Answers questions on the health risks of cocaine and provides counseling to individuals who use cocaine, their friends and families. Also provides referrals.

NIDA Helpline
Toll Free: 800-662-4357

This is a service of the National Institute on Drug Abuse. It provides referrals and general information on drug abuse and on AIDS as it relates to intravenous drug users.

Eye Care

Eye Care Helpline (National Eye Care Project)
The Foundation of the American Academy of Ophthalmology
P.O. Box 6988. San Francisco, CA 94101
Toll Free: 800-222-3937

The National Eye Care Project is a public service program sponsored by the Foundation of American Academy of Ophthalmology and state ophthalmological societies throughout the country. Its purpose is to provide medical and surgical eye care to the nation's elderly, particularly those who are disadvantaged.

Medical eye care from participating ophthalmologists is available at no out-of-pocket cost by calling the toll free Helpline which is operated nationwide. All U.S. citizens and legal residents, age 65 or over who have medical eye problems are eligible for this assistance if they don't have a personal eye physician and have difficulty in paying for medical eye care.

Eligible callers will be mailed the name of an eye physician in their area who has volunteered to see Helpline patients. If the patient does not have Medicare or other insurance, there is no charge for the ophthalmologist's service. If a patient does have insurance, this pays the cost of care in full.

Helpline patients will not receive a bill for eye care services from the physician. Eyeglasses, medication and hospital care are not included in the program. Ophthalmologists and other volunteers within local communities will work to make these available, where possible.

National Eye Institute
Information Office, Building 31, Room 6A-32
9000 Rockville Pike, Bethesda, MD 20892
Telephone: (301) 496-5248

The National Eye Institute has primary responsibility within the National Institutes of Health for supporting and conducting research aimed at improving the prevention, diagnosis, and treatment of eye disorders. Consumer materials are available on eyes, diabetic retinopathy, low vision, ocular histoplasmosis, retinitis pigmentosa, macular degeneration, glaucoma, cataracts and various other eye disorders.

Food Safety

USDA's Meat and Poultry Hotline
Telephone: (202) 447-3333 in District of Columbia
Toll Free: 800-535-4555

A service of the Food Safety and Inspection Service of the U.S. Department of Agriculture. Answers consumers questions on meat or poultry products regarding food safety and consumption. Will assist in determining whether items should be eaten or discarded.

The telephone numbers shown above may also be used by individuals who use telecommunications devices. However, there may be some delay when a TDD caller is put on hold. If this occurs, the caller should not hang up since the call will be answered as soon as a counselor is available.

Hansen's Disease

American Leprosy Missions
Telephone: (201) 794-8650 in New Jersey
Toll Free: 800-543-3131

Answers questions and distributes materials on Hansen's disease which is the clinical name for leprosy.

Headache

National Headache Foundation
Toll Free: 800-843-2256
        800-523-8858 in Illinois

Provides information and literature on headaches and treatment.

Health

Health Information Center
Office of Disease Prevention and Health Promotion
P.O. Box 1133, Washington, DC 20013
Telephone: (301) 565-4167
Toll Free: 800-336-4797

Formerly known as the National Health Information Clearinghouse, its name was changed in 1986 to the Health Information Center. This important center assists the public in locating needed health information through the identification of information resources. Health questions are referred to the appropriate resources that in turn respond directly to inquirers. It also prepares and distributes publications and directories on health and health promotion topics.

Hearing and Speech

(See Chapter Ten for additional organizations that help the deaf and hearing impaired.)

Dial A Hearing Screening Test
Occupational Hearing Services
P.O. Box 1880, Media, PA 19063
Toll Free: 800-345-3277 in Pennsylvania
        800-222-3277

This is a new service available in the majority of states which provides for a free hearing screening test and referral to ear doctors if the caller fails testing. The service allows callers to check their own hearing by dialing a local phone number and listening to four test signals for each ear. The recordings provide pertinent medical information associated with hearing problems and referral to local hospitals and clinics.

To find out the phone number and sponsor in your area, call the toll-free telephone number shown above. When you call these toll-free numbers, an operator will give you the phone number and instructions for your calling area.

Hearing Helpline
Telephone: (703) 642-0580 in Virginia
Toll Free: 800-327-9355

Provides information on better hearing and the prevention of deafness. A service of the Better Hearing Institute.

National Association for Hearing and Speech Action Line
Telephone: (301) 897-5700 in Maryland
Toll Free: 800-638-8255

Offers information on hearing and speech problems and distributes materials on speech-language pathologists and audiologists (certified by the American Speech-Language Hearing Association), hearing aids, and other topics related to hearing and speech.

National Hearing Aid Helpline
Toll Free: 800-521-5247

Provides information on hearing aids and distributes a directory of hearing aid specialists certified by the National Hearing Aid Society.

Heart Disease

National Heart, Lung and Blood Institute
Information Office, Building 31, Room 4A-21
9000 Rockville Pike, Bethesda, MD 20892
Telephone: (301) 496-4236

The Institute's primary responsibility is the scientific investigation of the heart, blood vessels, lung, and blood diseases and disorders. Consumer materials are available on Cooley's anemia, heart disease, arteriosclerosis, congestive heart failure, extrasystoles, cholesterol, hyperlipoproteinemia, pulmonary embolism, varicose veins, emphysema, chronic obstructive pulmonary disease, heat stroke, angina, stroke and blood transfusions.

High Blood Pressure

High Blood Pressure Information Center
P.O. Box 30105, Bethesda, MD 20814
Telephone: (301) 951-3260

The Information Center is a service of the National Heart, Lung and Blood Institute. Consumer information is provided through the Center on high blood pressure, sodium, blood pressure measurement devices and other related subjects.

Kidney Diseases

American Kidney Fund
Toll Free: 800-638-8299
          800-492-8361 in Maryland

Grants financial assistance to kidney patients who are unable to pay treatment costs. Also provides information on organ donations and kidney-related diseases.

Liver Diseases

American Liver Foundation
Telephone: (201) 256-2550 in New Jersey
Toll Free: 800-223-0179

Provides information on liver diseases, including fact sheets. Also makes physician referrals.

Lung Diseases

LUNGLINE
National Asthma Center
Te!ephone: (303) 355-5864
Toll Free: 800-222-5864

Answers questions about asthma, emphysema, allergies, smoking, and other respiratory and immune system disorders. Questions are answered by registered nurses or other health professionals.

National Heart, Lung and Blood Institute
Information Office, Building 31, Room 4A-21
9000 Rockville Pike, Bethesda, MD 20892
Telephone: (301) 496-4236

See the discussion on this Institute in the preceding section under HEART DISEASE.

Lupus Erythematosus

Lupus Foundation of America
Telephone: (301) 670-9292
Toll Free: 800-558-0121

Provides information packets on systemic lupus erythematosus. Makes referrals to local chapters, which serve as support groups.

Mental Health

National Institute of Mental Health
Public Inquiries Branch, Parklawn Building, Room 15C-05
5600 Fishers Lane, Rockville, MD 20857
Telephone: (301) 443-4513

Answers general inquiries from the public on mental health and provides information on schizophrenia, depressive illness, psychological stress and other mental disorders.

Multiple Sclerosis

National Multiple Sclerosis Society
Toll Free: 800-624-8236 (to obtain general information by mail)
             800-227-3166 (for specific questions)

Answers questions on multiple sclerosis and provides written information on request.

Organ Donations

The Living Bank
Toll Free: 800-528-2971

Operates a registry and referral service for people wanting to commit their tissues, bones, vital organs, or bodies to transplantation or research.

Organ Donor Hotline
Toll Free: 800-243-6667
         800-666-1884 in Virginia

Offers information and referrals for organ donation and transplantation. Answers requests for organ donor cards.

Orphan Drugs and Rare Diseases

National Information Center for
Orphan Drugs and Rare Diseases
P.O. Box 1133, Washington, DC 20013
Toll Free: 800-456-3505

The Center responds to inquiries on rare diseases (those with a prevalence in the United States of 200,000 or fewer cases), and orphan drugs (medicines not widely researched or available). This is a service of the Office of Disease Prevention and Health Promotion.

Osteoporosis

National Institute of Arthritis and
Musculoskeletal and Skin Diseases
Information Office, Building 31, Room 4C-05
9000 Rockville Pike, Bethesda, MD 20892
Telephone: (301) 496-8188

See the discussion on this institute in the preceding section under ARTHRITIS.

Paralysis/Spinal Cord Injuries

The following organizations and services offer information on spinal cord injuries and other forms of paralysis, including printed materials and referrals to organizations and support groups.

American Paralysis Association
Telephone: (201) 379-2690 in New Jersey
Toll Free: 800-225-0292

National Organization on Disability
Toll Free: 800-248-2253

National Rehabilitation Information Center
Toll Free: 800-346-2742

National Spinal Cord Injury Association
Toll Free: 800-962-9629

Paralyzed Veterans of America
Telephone: (202) 872-1300

Spinal Network
Toll Free: 800-338-5412

Parkinson's Disease

National Parkinson Foundation
1501 N.W. 9th Ave. - Bob Hope Road, Miami, FL 33136
Telephone: (305) 547-6666 in Miami area
Toll Free: 800-433-7022 in Florida
        800-327-4545

Answers questions about Parkinson's disease and provides written information on request. Gives referrals to physicians.

Parkinson's Education Program
Telephone: (714) 250-2975 in California
Toll Free: 800-344-7872

This service provides written materials including newsletters, glossary of definitions, and a publications catalog. It offers patients support group information and doctor referrals.

Plastic Surgery

American Society of Plastic and Reconstructive Surgeons
Toll Free: 800-635-0635 (includes Canada)

Provides referrals to board-certified plastic surgeons. Offers pamphlets describing procedures and results of some operations.

Smoking

Office on Smoking and Health
Rhodes Building Mail Stop K-12
1600 Clifton Road, NE, Atlanta, GA 30333
Telephone: (301) 443-1690

The Office on Smoking and Health has primary responsibility within the federal government for programs of information and education as a means of reducing premature death and disability associated with tobacco use, particularly of cigarettes. A major function is to respond to written and telephone inquiries related to the scientific and technical aspects of smoking and health. Various publications are available free to the public.

Tinnitus

American Tinnitus Association
P.O. Box 5, Portland, OR 97207
Telephone: (503) 248-9985

Over 36 million Americans suffer from a disorder called "tinnitus" which is characterized by a continual ringing or noise (buzzing/hissing) in the ears. It can be so persistent and unbearable to eventually cause serious illness. The American Tinnitus Association provides information to tinnitus sufferers about available treatments and referrals to professionals. The Association also sponsors self-help groups throughout the country so that individuals can communicate their experiences with others and share their particular ways of coping with tinnitus.

Urological Disorders/Urinary Incontinence

National Association for Continence
P.O. Box 8310
Spartanburg, SC 29305
Toll Free: 800-252-3337

Provides education and assistance to incontinence sufferers, their families, and professionals responsible for their care.

Simon Foundation for Continence
P.O. Box 815, Wilmette, IL 60091
Toll Free: 800-237-4666

Provides information on incontinence and ordering information for a quarterly newsletter and other publications.

Venereal Diseases

VD Hotline (Operation Venus)
Toll Free: 800-227-8922

Provides free and confidential information on sexually transmitted diseases and gives referrals for diagnosis and treatment.

Vision Impairment

(See Chapter Ten for additional organizations that help the blind and visually-impaired.)

American Council of the Blind
Telephone: (202) 467-5081 in the District of Columbia
Toll Free: 800-424-8666

Offers information on blindness. Also provides referrals to clinics, rehabilitation organizations, research centers, and local chapters.

American Foundation for the Blind (AFB)
Telephone: (212) 620-2147
Toll Free: 800-232-5463

Provides information on visual impairments, blindness, and on AFB services, products, and publications.

Don't Forget to Get Your Annual Flu Shot!

Every year 50-60,000 older people die from influenza or pneumonia — a severe and often fatal complication of the flu. The winter flu outbreaks of 1990 and 1991 will be remembered as two of the worst in history, reaching epidemic proportions throughout the nation.

Flu vaccinations are crucial for the elderly and for individuals who have heart or lung disorders. Most communities offer free or reduced-cost flu immunizations for Seniors and disabled people. *Remember:* The flu vaccination has been covered by Medicare since 1993.

PART II

After the Hospital Stay ...
Nursing Homes/Hospices/
Home Care

NURSING HOMES

One of the hardest decisions to make is whether to institutionalize a loved one when they are seriously ill. Often, sadness, guilt, and fear of not doing the right thing make an already difficult decision nearly impossible. It is essential, however, that you distance yourself from these feelings so you can make a rational decision ... a decision that considers the needs of the patient first and foremost. Remember, the nursing facility you select may become the patient's home for life.

Before you begin to consider a particular nursing home, you should know that there are three types of facilities designed to provide varying levels of long-term care:

- **Skilled Nursing Facilities** (SNF) — provide 24-hour nursing services for people with serious health care needs that do not require the intense level of care provided in a hospital. In addition, rehabilitation services may also be provided. Many SNFs are federally certified to participate in Medicare or Medicaid.

- **Intermediate Care Facilities** (ICF) — nursing homes which are usually federally certified to participate in Medicaid but not Medicare. They provide less extensive health care than SNFs. Nursing and rehabilitation services are provided in some facilities, but not 24 hours. These homes are designed for persons who can no longer live alone but need minimal medical supervision or assistance and help with personal and/or social care.

- **Board and Care Facilities** — provide shelter, supervision and care, but do not offer medical and skilled nursing services. Unlike the SNF and ICF facilities, board and care facilities are not licensed to receive reimbursement under Medicare and Medicaid. In some·

states, residents of board and care facilities may receive financial assistance through a state supplement to Supplemental Security Income (SSI).

Before you settle on a nursing home, be sure you have the resources to pay for it. It's not a good idea to rely on Medicare, because it only covers acute care in a skilled nursing home for a very limited time. Most private insurance policies, if they cover nursing homes at all, have very limited coverage for skilled or intermediate care facilities. In other words, the patient and/or his/her family will probably have to pay for the nursing home themselves. And nursing home costs can add up to thousands of dollars a year. However, for older people with limited resources, few remaining assets, and who are unable to pay for a nursing home, Medicaid will pay for the care. However, the choice of nursing homes for Medicaid recipients is limited to those which accept Medicaid and which have an opening.

Fortunately, new legislation protects the spouses of nursing home patients from impoverishment by preventing their need to "spend down" all their resources simply to qualify for Medicaid.

When you finally do select a nursing facility, you should be absolutely satisfied with your selection before making any commitment. Learn as much as you can about the medical services the facility provides: are there nurses on duty 24 hours a day? Is the facility clean? Is its atmosphere relatively pleasant? Is it designed with accident-prevention features? How are its dining room and food? What is its fire safety record? Does it provide an adequate recreation area(s)? Are the patient's room and toilet facilities clean and comfortable? It is essential that you ask every question you think of; if you are choosing a nursing home for someone else, put yourself in that person's place when thinking of what to ask.

Your local library and Area Agency on Aging can direct you to books and brochures on how to choose a nursing home. In addition, the American Health Care Association has an outstanding free pamphlet entitled *Thinking About a Nursing Home?* To request it, contact:

American Health Care Association
1201 L Street, NW
Washington, DC 20005
Tel: (202) 842-4444

Of utmost importance: Every state has an *Ombudsman Program* which consists of volunteers who visit assigned nursing homes to act as friendly advocates, monitoring conditions and actively representing residents' needs and interests. If you find that your loved one is being mistreated or is not receiving proper care, contact your local ombudsman **immediately** through your local Area Agency on Aging.

HOSPICES

Although it has been covered by Medicare since 1983, hospice care is still a vague concept to many people. A hospice is not so much a specific place but rather, an approach to caring for the terminally ill that allows them to live their final days as free as possible from pain and mental anguish.

Hospice care is usually provided in the patient's own home, with arrangements for eventual inpatient care, if necessary, in a facility or part of a facility designated for hospice care. Hospice services may include:

- physician services
- nursing care
- medical appliances and supplies
- drugs to manage symptoms and relieve pain
- home health aide and homemaker services
- therapy
- medical social services
- counseling
- respite care to temporarily relieve the primary caregiver.

Almost all hospice services are covered by Medicare, Medicaid, Blue Cross, and most other major insurance companies. If the patient receives hospice care from a Medicare-certified hospice, Medicare hospital insurance pays almost the entire cost (see Chapter 4, "Medicare," for details); there are no deductibles or copayments, except for limited cost-sharing for outpatient drugs and respite care.

However, to be eligible for Medicare hospice coverage, the patient must meet four conditions:

1. Eligibility for Medicare (Part A) Hospital Insurance;

2. Certification of terminal illness by the patient's doctor and the hospice facility;

3. Signature of a statement by the patient indicating a choice of hospice care rather than Medicare's standard benefit for terminal illness;

4. Receipt of care from a Medicare-certified hospice program only (the patient's doctor or the hospice agency or organization will tell you whether the hospice program is Medicare-certified).

Throughout the nation, hospice organizations provide compassion, comfort, and understanding to the terminally ill and their families. If you or someone in your family is terminally ill, contact any local hospice to learn more.

HOME CARE

For most of us, a time will come when we or someone we love will need health care at home. While such care cannot duplicate the medical efficacy of nursing home or hospital services, most people would much rather be cared for at home, in familiar surroundings, by those they love. And, home care — while occasionally trying — also provides tremendous satisfaction to the caregiver, who can be confident that he or she has done everything possible for the loved one.

Admittedly, there is a downside to home care: the demands on the time, energy, and resources of caregivers, if uninterrupted, can lead them to resent their loved ones and even forget why they didn't just "put them in a nursing home." Fortunately, almost every community has recognized the realities of home care. As a result — in addition to local private home health agencies — these communities offer various types of free or very low-cost home services to help provide for the personal needs of the sick or housebound. These include homemaker services, home-delivered meals, daily communication by phone or visit, adult day care, loans of medical equipment, counseling, and social activities.

Plus, support groups for patients — especially victims of diseases like Alzheimer's and cancer — and their families provide information and emotional support. Chapter 10 discusses the many home services provided by local Area Agencies on Aging especially for those who provide home care for a sick loved one.

Medicare's coverage of in-home care is extremely limited and, even then only applies to part-time, intermittent skilled nursing care or physical, occupational, or speech therapy at home. Also, before Medicare will consider covering the care, the patient's doctor must set up a home treatment plan. However, once the home services are approved, Medicare will usually pay for them in full. On the other hand, prescription drugs, full-time nursing care, and custodial services are not covered. Chapter 4, "Medicare," enumerates and explains Medicare's coverage of home care.

Before you commit yourself to a home care agency, ask the following questions:

- How long has the agency been in business? (This is a good indicator of its reliability.)
- Is the agency licensed by the state? (Most states require such a license.)
- Is it Medicare-certified?
- Will the agency continue care if Medicare or other reimbursement sources are exhausted?
- What are the eligibility requirements for the agency's services?
- Will a nurse or therapist visit your home to evaluate your needs?
- Does the agency have a written care plan?
- What are the agency's fees for the services it provides? What financial arrangements does it require to pay for these services?
- How do they arrange for emergencies?

To find a home care agency in your community, ask your doctor or hospital discharge planner for a referral, or check your yellow pages under the health-related headings. Most states have home care associations that can help you locate a good agency. To locate your state's home care association, contact:

National Association for Home Care
519 C Street, NE, Stanton Park
Washington, DC 20002
Tel: (202) 547-7424

The National Association will also provide — upon request — brochures on in-home care and selecting a home care agency.

If you are taking care of a loved one at home, you probably know how difficult it can be to find the necessary medical supplies. And you are surely aware how frightening the patient finds the prospect of an emergency — and summoning the necessary help — when you aren't home. The following discussions are designed to help you address both issues.

MEDICAL EMERGENCY HOME ALERT SYSTEMS

For millions of frail elderly and handicapped individuals, the thought of being alone at home when a medical emergency strikes, and perhaps unable to summon help, is terrifying. For those who have already experienced such a situation, the memory of waiting and praying for someone to find them is an episode that continues to haunt them — robbing them of their peace of mind. Fortunately, most communities now have emergency alert systems that can help individuals lead independent lives, secure that when an emergency occurs they can readily summon help.

The available home alert systems go by a variety of names such as *Lifeline, Lifecall, Lifewatch* and other similarly descriptive terms. Lifeline, the first such system available to the public, currently has more than 100,000 subscribers in the U.S. and Canada monitored by over 2,000 centers located in various hospitals. Costs for the subscriber's initial equipment for the many systems available throughout the U.S. vary anywhere from $300 to $900, with monthly service costs generally ranging from $10 to $20. In some communities, those who have limited resources can get help from local governments, churches and service organizations to defray the system's cost.

Although the systems vary somewhat in how they operate and type of equipment and services provided, the basic principle is the same. A small device, which is worn comfortably around the neck or carried in a pocket, can be activated by a hand-squeeze to transmit a signal to a monitoring center through a transmitter unit attached to the telephone. Most transmitters used in the various systems work even when a telephone is off the hook and also have a battery powered backup which takes over whenever there is a power failure in the home. Consequently, the system operates continually.

When the monitoring center, usually located in a nearby hospital, receives a signal for help, it immediately calls the subscriber to determine whether it was a false alarm. If there is no answer, the center calls a pre-arranged contact individual (generally a family member or friend who lives close by) to go to the subscriber's home, check on the individual, and relay his or her condition back to the center so it can send appropriate assistance. If the center cannot reach a contact person, a rescue squad is dispatched to the subscriber's home. Since the subscriber may be unable to admit the rescuers, they are instructed to break in if necessary.

Over the last 10 years, the availability of the emergency alert systems has increased dramatically, even extending into some remote rural areas. The sophistication of the available systems has also improved — allowing more rapid response to subscriber medical emergencies, as well as handling other types of emergencies, like fire or robbery attempts.

To find out what systems are available in your area, contact one of several sources in your community: a local hospital or medical center, the Better Business Bureau, Senior Centers, the Area Agency on Aging or Human Services Information office. It is essential that you thoroughly investigate any system you may consider buying for its effectiveness, its past performance in the community, and its total cost, which includes monthly service charges plus the rental/purchase price for the home-based equipment.

OBTAINING MEDICAL SUPPLIES AND EQUIPMENT

For many individuals, especially those in rural areas or less populated cities, it can often be frustrating and difficult to obtain medical supplies, equipment and personal care items for a patient at home. While items used widely on a regular basis (bandages and dressings, diabetic aids, incontinent supplies, bed pans, urinals, wheelchairs, canes, etc.), can generally be purchased at a local drugstore, others (like mastectomy needs, laryngectomy/tracheostomy supplies, catheters, ostomy pouches, support garments, hospital-type beds, portable commodes or bath tub chairs), are often unavailable or very expensive in many areas of the country.

The first place to look for these items is your local drugstore. Because of demand, many drug stores stock some items that would not normally be maintained in their inventories. However, if your drugstore's inventory is very limited, the pharmacist may direct you to a local medical supplier or one further away who will fill phone orders. If your pharmacist cannot give you the name of a supplier, look in the yellow pages of your local telephone directory under "Medical Equipment and Supplies" or "Surgical Supplies," then visit or call to obtain the catalogs of those you find to determine whether they sell equipment, personal care items, or both.

Another good source of local supplier recommendations is your doctor. Call your doctor's office and ask for the name of a medical supplier that retails the items you need.

Once you have located a local supplier, you may also want to investigate a mail-order medical specialty house to do some comparison shopping for the best price and inventory. There are several mail-order suppliers throughout the country. Some organizations like the American Association of Retired Persons (mentioned in Chapter 11) sell their members reasonably priced medical supplies and small equipment in addition to their pharmacy items and medications. Also, Sears has a special Home Health Care catalog which contains a wide selection of medical supplies and equipment. Call and ask them to send you the catalog.

Lastly, if you still can not find a reliable mail-order company with a wide selection of items, contact one of the national suppliers listed below. Ask them to send you a catalog and information on their billing, payment, ordering and shipping procedures, guarantees and return policies. Although Medicare beneficiaries generally must prepay for items purchased, these companies will submit directly the required Medicare claim forms for your reimbursement.

- **Medical Market Place** (located in Minnesota)
  Toll Free: 800-328-0141

■ **Bruce Medical Supply** (located in Massachusetts)
      Toll Free: 800-225-8446

Referral to the aforementioned companies in no way constitutes advertising for them or their product, or a recommendation that you buy from them rather than from another company. They are included only as a resource for people who cannot find another reliable medical supplier.

SOURCES OF INFORMATION

The following national organizations have a variety of consumer publications on nursing homes, hospices and home care available upon request to members and non-members. Most publications are either free or cost very little.

**American Association of
Retired Persons**
Health Advocacy Services
601 E Street, NW
Washington, DC 20049
Tel: (202) 434-2277

Hospice Association of America
519 C Street, NE
Washington, DC 20002
Tel: (202) 547-5263

**American Health Care
Association**
1201 L Street, NW
Washington, DC 20005
Tel: (202) 842-4444

**National Council of Catholic
Women**
1275 K Street, NW, Suite 975
Washington, DC 20005
Tel: (202) 682-0334

National Consumers League
Suite 928-N
815 15th Street, NW
Washington, DC 20005
Tel: (202) 639-8140

**The National Council on the
Aging, Inc.**
409 Third Street, SW
Washington, DC 20024
Tel: (202) 479-1200

National Hospice Organization
Suite 901
1901 N. Moore Street
Arlington, VA 22209
Tel: (703) 243-5900

PART III

Housing . . . Consider Your Options Carefully

At some time in our lives almost all of us feel that our living situations no longer suit our way of life. Some of us find our houses too big — particularly once the children move away. For those left alone when their spouses die, the family house is not only too big, but maintaining it becomes a problem, and affording it can become an unbearable financial burden.

Others simply decide that their old homes and neighborhoods no longer offer what they want. The cost-of-living may be too high, family members may have moved far away, the climate may become increasingly less tolerable, or the community focus may no longer reflect their own interests and concerns (a neighborhood you moved into because it had lots of families with small children may not have much to offer now that your children have grown up and moved away).

While there is still a nationwide need for affordable housing for the elderly, most communities have some type of retirement home or complex that is both reasonably priced and designed to meet the needs of Senior Citizens. Much of this retirement housing is designed for the many, many older people who want to live independently. Other residences are geared towards those who want their meals furnished, housekeeping services supplied, social activities on the premises, and easily-accessible medical services in case they get sick.

Because the range of living options for the elderly — and the cost for same — is so broad, it is important that you obtain as much information as you can, and consider each one carefully, comparing its features with your needs — present and anticipated — and desires. You may want to discuss your options with family and friends. Your local library, housing authority, and Area Agency on Aging are all good resources for information on the latest housing options targeted at retirees. The Agency, in particular, is usually up-to-date on the housing available, or soon to become available, in your area. It can also direct you to programs like shared housing in your community.

Visiting and reviewing all the housing you consider will take some time and effort, but remember — you are selecting your home . . . a home you will want to live in for many years to come.

The following housing programs and types of retirement housing are available in most communities.

- **Congregate Housing and Senior Apartments:** Designed for elderly individuals who are mostly independent, but who require some assistance from staff and social support from other residents, these facilities are usually for rent. Some are privately funded while others are publicly assisted. In communities with congregate housing and/or Senior apartments for low-income Seniors, potential residents must apply for a rent subsidy with the local housing authority.

- **Accessory Apartments:** These units are usually converted from space in larger houses and have their own outside entrances, kitchens, and baths. Accessory apartments are often created by families who wish to have their elderly relatives live with them, but who also want the relative to live independently.

- **Retirement Communities:** These communities vary widely — especially in cost — throughout the country. Many contain single-family homes, rental apartments, condominiums, and cooperatives which are sold or rented. Like any other community, most retirement communities provide only basic services like police and fire protection. Others offer transportation, meals, and some in-home services, such as housekeeping.

- **Life Care Communities:** The newest housing option for the elderly, life care communities (also referred to as continuing care communities) provide "graduated care" which enables residents to move from private apartments into the community's nursing home or skilled nursing home if and when the need arises. When they apply, residents make a one-time payment for their living space, then pay a monthly fee for the services provided by the community (sometimes including basic medical care). The operation and financing of these communities vary widely from state to state.

   Because their costs vary — initial payments can range from $15,000 to $175,000, with monthly fees ranging from $150 to $2,000 — you should always learn everything you can about any life care community you consider; focus especially on the financial solvency of the community, and **always** seek the advice of an attorney before signing a contract.

- **Shared Housing:** Shared houses or apartments bring together two or more unrelated individuals, enabling them to share living expenses while maintaining their own personal living space (e.g., a bedroom). Housemates share expenses like rent, utilities, and — if desired — groceries, and can share responsibility for the housekeeping and chores. Most importantly, shared housing brings people together. Arrangements for shared housing can be made by an individual, through local organizations or through the Area Agency on Aging.

- **Adult Homes:** Adult homes are also known as Adult Care, Sheltered Care or Residential Care. They provide room, board, and help with daily living activities for four or more adults under the same roof. In some cases, residents share rooms. Generally, the facility or person in charge is licensed by state and local authorities.

- **Elderly Cottage Housing Opportunity (ECHO):** ECHO housing — or "granny flats" — originated in Australia. They are not apartments as "flats" may suggest, but rather, self-contained units designed for temporary installation on the side or in the backyard of a house. ECHO units let elderly relatives live near their families while maintaining their freedom and independence. However, local zoning ordinances often do not permit ECHO units. Check with your local housing authority for further information.

- **Mobile Homes:** Offering many of the features and advantages of an ECHO unit, a mobile home is usually located in a mobile home community which provides connections to electricity and water. Because they can be moved, the elderly residents can relocate along with their families, if desired.

REVERSE MORTGAGES
(HOME EQUITY CONVERSION MORTGAGES)

Three out of every four Seniors over 65 own their homes. Eighty percent of these Seniors no longer pay a mortgage. The amount of equity tied up in these houses is estimated at $700 billion to $1 trillion. But, since six out of every ten elderly, single homeowners have incomes as low as $5,000 or less, the vast number of them are "house rich, cash poor," and lack adequate funds to pay for support services, home maintenance, and other daily needs.

Many Seniors who own their homes and who want to continue to live in them now have a way to obtain the money they need to meet their daily living expenses: a Reverse Mortgage, or Home Equity Conversion Mortgage. A Reverse Mortgage uses the equity in the Senior's home as security on a loan. The Reverse Mortgage differs from a conventional home equity loan in that the homeowner does not pay the lender monthly — rather, the lender pays the home-owner.

The Mortgage amount is based on the amount of equity in the home and, in most cases, can be paid either as a lump sum or in monthly installments.

Although reverse mortgages have helped thousands of people, in the past, older individuals have had difficulty obtaining them. To obtain such loans, Seniors resorted to private entrepreneurs or banks which provided very little protection to the Senior borrower and had to pay high interest rates with short terms. In many cases, when the note came due, these Seniors were forced to sell their home to payback the borrowed money. Some have lost everything they had. However, there are several reputable institutions that not only handle reverse mortgages for older people but actively seek the business of the 20 million plus individuals over 65 who live in their own homes. Unfortunately those lenders who do not have federal insurance protection for the borrower may not be able to make the payments to the homeowner. *A strong word of advice*: avoid any reverse mortgage that is not insured by the federal government.

FEDERALLY INSURED REVERSE MORTGAGES

Congress, in an effort to help Seniors secure reverse mortgages without fear, passed the Housing and Community Act of 1987. The Act authorizes the HUD Federal Housing Administration to implement a five-year *Home Equity Conversion Mortgage Insurance Demonstration* (HECMID) program which would insure 2,500 loans for homeowners age 62 or older. Eligible homeowners must live in homes which they own nearly 100%. All 2,500 loans were granted in such a short period that Congress passed 1990 legislation to increase the number of authorized HECMID loans to cover 25,000 reverse mortgages over the next five years. This increased authorization will enable many more Seniors to take advantage of the program.

Under this program, homeowners can choose from three payment options:

- tenure — monthly payments as long as the borrower occupies the home as his or her principal residence;
- term — monthly payments for a fixed period;
- line-of-credit — enables the borrower to draw money as needed up to a maximum amount.

The HUD home equity conversion program guarantees that borrowers may continue to live in their houses until they move, sell, or die. Homeowners may sell their property at any time, and retain any proceeds that exceed the amount needed to pay off the mortgage. In addition, they cannot be forced to sell their home to pay off the mortgage.

Anyone interested in the HECMID program or would like more information on these reverse mortgages, can call or write: American Association of Retired Persons, Home Equity Conversion Center, 601 E Street, NW, Washington, DC 20049, Tel: (202) 434-2277. In addition, any FHA-insured lender in your community who is HUD-approved will be able to provide you with information concerning federally-insured reverse mortgages.

PATIENT SELF-DETERMINATION BILL ENACTED!

Overwhelmingly approved by Congress as part of 1990's Omnibus Budget Reconciliation Act, the Patient Self-Determination Act (PSDA) took effect on December 1, 1991. It governs all health care facilities that receive Medicare or Medicaid funding — nearly every health care facility in the U.S.

The Act requires medical facilities to advise patients of their legal options under state law regarding acceptance or refusal of life-sustaining medical treatments, as well as their right to formulate advance directives, such as Living Wills and Durable Powers of Attorney for Health Care.

PSDA strengthens the patient's rights and holds health care facilities accountable to those they serve. Failure to comply with the PSDA can result in the loss of federal funding. In addition, the law requires the Department of Health and Human Services to educate the public about legal right-to-die options.

Chapter 8

Dying, Death and Funerals

What to Do at a Difficult Time

Chapter Highlights

Dying, Death and Funerals

What to Do at a Difficult Time

To almost everyone, death is one of the most difficult subjects to discuss. In fact, many consider it to be a "taboo" subject that just shouldn't be discussed until someone dies. However, given the many decisions people face when their spouse or someone they are close to dies, and with the high costs of funerals (currently, the average cost of a funeral — excluding the cemetery plot and grave marker — is over $4,000), it is imperative that individuals prepare themselves to deal with one of life's most difficult and stressful events: the loss of someone they love.

I have limited this chapter to brief explanations of those items that are most significant to the majority of individuals. The chapter is divided into three sections: Section I, "General Considerations," Section II, "When Death Occurs," and Section III, "After Death. " I suggest you read the last section a few times, because it discusses how to handle grief and carry on with life after the loss of a loved one. Even if it doesn't seem pertinent to you now, it may prove extremely beneficial in the future. And, if you are friendly with someone who has recently suffered such a loss, you may help your friend enormously by telling him or her about what you have read.

SECTION I

General Considerations

LIVING WILLS: DECLARING YOUR RIGHT TO DIE

With the rapid advancement in medical technology and the ability to sustain life even when death is imminent, many individuals fear the possibility of being kept alive by artificial means when there is no chance of recovery from an illness or accident.

In hopes of preventing measures that can only prolong their dying, millions of people have signed declaration documents requesting the right to die with dignity and without artificial prolongation of their lives by modern medical technology. These declarations are known in most states as *Living Wills*. Briefly stated, Living Wills are legal documents — signed, dated and witnessed — which allow individuals to declare their wishes **in advance** regarding the use of life-sustaining procedures when they are dying. Living Wills are flexible documents: they can be modified as various concerns arise to prohibit all artificial sustenance or only specific treatments (such as mechanical respirators and intubation for feeding) when death is inevitable.

A Living Will also contains a "Durable Power of Attorney" (explained in Chapter 10, in the section on "Legal Assistance") provision for the appointment of a person who has the power to make medical treatment decisions for the individual making the will in the event he/she is unable to do so. In states that have not passed Living Will legislation, the Durable Power of Attorney can legally make health care decisions for a person who has become incompetent.

All states and the District of Columbia have now passed some form of "Advanced Directive," "Living Will," "Natural Death," or "Right to Die" legislation to make documents like Living Wills legally binding under most conditions.

Each state's requirements for making a Living Will declaration vary according to the laws of that state. To obtain further information and free copies of Living Wills or the similar declaration documents valid in your state, call or write to the following helpful organization:

> Choice In Dying
> 200 Varick Street
> New York, NY 10014
> Tel: (212) 366-5540

BODY, ORGAN, AND TISSUE DONATIONS

With the number of successful transplants increasing each year because of new drugs which help prevent the body's rejection of transplanted organs, there is a critical need for more organ and tissue donors. The American Council on Transplantation estimates that over 5,000 medically-evaluated patients await corneas for transplants, 20,000 await kidneys, 2,500 await hearts, 200 await hearts *and* lungs, 2,000 await livers, and 200 await pancreases. Although it takes only one adult donor to provide three to four persons with skin grafts, the need for skin donors has also increased tremendously.

In 1968, a national organ and tissue donor registry was founded for U.S. residents — the Living Bank. Currently, this outstanding organization has over 300,000 registered donors and supplies the necessary donor registration forms and cards to anyone requesting information on organ and tissue donation. The Living Bank functions as a national referral agency. At the time of a donor's death, the Bank attempts to fulfill the donor's wishes by contacting the nearest transplant facility, organ or tissue bank, or medical school (in the case of body donation), according to the donor's wishes and physical condition at the time of death. If an individual has registered with other organ banks, medical schools, or, in many states, by signing the back of a driver's license, no conflict arises with the Living Bank registration because the Bank works with all other organizations to use donations.

If you are interested in donating your organs, tissue or body, the following information may answer your questions about such donations:

- Organ donations are legally-binding on survivors by the Uniform Anatomical Gift Act if the donor properly completed a Uniform Donor Card. However, most donations will not be accepted unless the next of kin approves. Consequently, the Living Bank advises donors to inform their families of their wishes and to have their next of kin witness the signature of their donor forms and cards.

- There is generally no charge to your family or estate for the removal of any organ or tissue.

- Once organs or tissues are removed, the body is returned to the family or power of attorney. Since there is no disfigurement or delay in funeral services, an open casket funeral can be held.

- Individuals who wish to donate their bodies to a medical school for medical research and educational endeavors should register with the nearest medical school as well as complete the Uniform Donor Card. The Living Bank will provide names and addresses of medical schools near you. However, many medical schools already have more than enough body donations. You may want to check with your target school to ascertain their needs and what procedures the school uses to dispose of the remains once the studies have been completed.

- There is almost no age limit for donation of eyes, skin and bone. While some age criteria apply for donations of vital organs, the condition of the tissue or organ at the time of death is a more significant factor in determining whether a donor organ or tissue can be used.

If you wish to receive a Uniform Donor Card and form or simply want additional information on donations, call or write to:

> The Living Bank
> P.O. Box 6725
> Houston, TX 77265
> Toll Free: 800-528-2971

MEMORIAL SOCIETIES

Although they have existed since 1939 and currently number over 150 in the U.S., with another 25 or more in Canada, memorial societies are unknown to the majority of Americans. These nonprofit organizations, staffed almost completely by volunteers, advocate (1) preplanning of funerals, (2) the freedom to plan funerals that conform with one's values and beliefs, and (3) availability of an economically manageable funeral. Societies do not sell merchandise or provide any funeral services directly. Instead, they arrange contracts and agreements with funeral providers to take care of their members when a death occurs.

Society members are encouraged to arrange for their funerals, cremations, or body donations with one of the society's cooperating morticians. Planning a funeral before death occurs eliminates many of the difficult and emotional decisions that surviving family members must make. In general, most memorial society members pay considerably less — more than 50 percent less — than non-members for funerals and cremations.

The cost of membership is low with one-time lifetime dues ranging from $10 to $25. In most cases, if a member moves out of the society's area, membership can be transferred from one participating society to another for little or no cost.

Most memorial societies belong to the Continental Association of Funeral and Memorial Societies. Founded in 1963 as a nonprofit, nonsectarian, nondiscriminatory organization, the Association ensures that high standards are maintained by its member societies. In addition, it offers reciprocity among its member societies so that members of one society who die away from home can receive the benefits of the participating society that is local at the time of death.

If you would like to join a memorial society, or if you want further information on memorial societies, call or write to:

> Continental Association of Funeral and
> Memorial Societies, Inc.
> 6900 Lost Lake Road
> Egg Harbor, WI 54209
> Toll Free: 800/458-5563

PRE-PAID FUNERALS

In planning ahead for their deaths, thousands of individuals have chosen to prepay for funeral goods and services months or even years before their deaths. Often referred to as "pre-need" plans, such prepayment arrangements can lock in the cost of the funeral, provide peace of mind to those who may not have anyone to handle their funeral arrangements, or ensure that their survivors will not be burdened with the costs and planning of a funeral at the time of death.

However, there are many disadvantages to pre-paying funeral costs. Unless death is imminent, carefully examine any pre-payment plans to ensure that the disadvantages do not outweigh the advantages. The following list of disadvantages is designed to make you aware that some pre-need plans are not as advantageous as they may seem:

- It is very difficult in today's business environment to guarantee that the plan's provider will still be in business when you die.

- If you move, it may be difficult to receive a refund or transfer the plan to another community.

- In several states, the money you pay does not have to be placed in a special trust fund. The provider can spend it to maintain the business. Consequently, when the time comes for your funeral, no money may be available to pay for your funeral costs.

- If the agreement allows for cancellation, the provider may deduct a penalty from the total amount you have already paid.

- If you decide to change (or add) to the agreed funeral services, additional costs may be added to your plan. With some plans, changes are not accepted after a certain period of time.

If you decide to buy a pre-need plan, make sure that your survivors are aware that your funeral expenses have been pre-paid, where the contract is located, and the name of the funeral home that will be responsible for handling your burial. However, it may be wiser to simply pre-arrange the funeral and set money aside in a bank account — which draws interest — to cover funeral costs.

THE FTC FUNERAL RULE

To help protect consumers against abuse and unfair trade practices when they purchase goods and services from a funeral home, in 1984 Congress enacted a very important law: the Federal Trade Commission Funeral Industry Practices Trade Regulation Rule. Commonly known simply as the "FTC Funeral Rule," it was extended early this year by the Federal Trade Commission (FTC). The law applies to all 23,000 funeral homes in the U.S. It requires the funeral provider to inform consumers **in advance** of (1) the costs of all funeral goods and services they are considering purchasing, and (2) which of these goods and services **are not** required by state and local law.

Because most funeral purchases are made immediately following the death of a loved one — at a time when the stress of grief and time constraints may cloud your judgement — it is wise to learn about the provisions of the FTC Funeral Rule now, before such purchases are imminent.

The following summary explains the provisions of the Rule:

- The funeral home must allow the consumer to purchase goods and services individually; consumers cannot be required to buy a "funeral package," although such packages may be offered as **alternatives** to individual purchases. Consumers can only be charged for those items they have selected.

- When a consumer inquires in person, the funeral home must disclose the costs of all goods and services **in writing.** If the consumer inquires by telephone, the funeral home must disclose these costs over the phone.

- Once all arrangements have been agreed to by the consumer and the funeral home, the funeral home must provide the consumer with an **itemized statement** listing all goods and services ordered. The statement must indicate the individual price of each item as well as the total cost of all goods and services. Finally, the statement must include a disclosure of the laws and/or cemetery/crematorium rules that compel the consumer to purchase any "required" goods or services.

- The funeral home may not charge the consumer for **unauthorized** embalming unless it is required by state law.

- The FTC Funeral Rule requires funeral homes from:
  — claiming that embalming or a particular type of casket, vault, or grave lining will preserve the body indefinitely;
  — making any false claims that state or local laws require vaults or grave linings in a cemetery.

- The Funeral Rule requires funeral homes to declare the following items — **in writing** — to the consumer:
  — Embalming is not required by law **except** in certain cases, such as when refrigeration is not available. Therefore, the consumer can only be required to purchase embalming when it is required by state or local law or in the case of funeral arrangements which, because they include an open casket, make embalming a practical necessity. The consumer always has the right to forego embalming when choosing a disposition like direct cremation or immediate burial. — Use of a casket for direct cremation is **not** required by law. The consumer **always** has the right to buy an unfinished wood box or alternative container for cremation.

— The funeral home will charge a fee to the consumer for **cash advance items**. Cash advance items constitute any goods and/or services purchased by the funeral home on the consumer's behalf These items may include:

- flowers
- obituary notice(s)
- pall bearers
- clergy honorarium
- music
- additional transportation
- burial clothes
- grave marker, monument, or urn
- cemetery charges for opening and closing the grave
- long distance telephone calls or telegrams
- burial vault or grave liner.

The funeral home must also inform the consumer when: (1) any service fees are added to the price of a cash advance item; (2) the funeral provider receives a refund discount, or rebate from the supplier of the cash advance item.

Always remember that the consumer has the right to choose **only** those individual funeral goods and services he/she wishes to purchase.

RESOLVING PROBLEMS OR COMPLAINTS ABOUT FUNERAL ARRANGEMENTS

Some typical consumer problems with funerals are:

- Billings by the funeral home for services or goods delivered that were not requested;

- Differences between prices charged and those originally quoted;

- Substitution of selected goods, such as the casket, without prior consent;

- Billing for services that were not performed;

- Non-completion of items or services agreed to by the funeral director.

Most problems with funerals can be resolved amicably by discussing them with the funeral director. This should **always** be the first point of contact in settling such problems or complaints. Funeral directors are well aware of their public image within the community and usually want to resolve any dissatisfaction with the funeral home's services promptly.

Unfortunately, not all problems or complaints may be resolved to your satisfaction. If they are not, you should immediately contact: (1) your local Better Business Bureau; or (2) your state or local consumer protection agency (listed in Chapter 10); or (3) the licensing board that regulates the funeral industry in your state (if necessary, ask your local librarian to help you find the address and telephone number); or (4) the National Research and Information Center (NRIC), an independent organization which arbitrates consumer complaints involving funeral directors. To contact the NRIC, call toll-free 800-662-7666 or write to:

> National Research and Information Center
> 2250 E. Devon, Suite 250
> Des Plaines, IL 60018

Although the Federal Trade Commission (FTC) cannot directly resolve individual consumer problems or disputes, the Commission may investigate consumer complaints of funeral home activities that seem to demonstrate a pattern of unacceptable conduct or practice to determine if any action is warranted. Consequently, it is advisable that you also inform the Federal Trade Commission about your particular experience. You may call or write to FTC headquarters or to one of its regional offices — preferably, the office closest to you.

FEDERAL TRADE COMMISSION OFFICE ADDRESSES

Headquarters:

> Division of Credit Practices
> Federal Trade Commission
> 6th St. and Pennsylvania Ave., NW
> Washington, DC 20680
> Tel: (202) 326-3175

Regional Offices:

10 Causeway St.	150 Williams St.	1718 Peachtree St.
Suite 11584	13th Floor	Room 1000
Boston, MA 02222	New York, NY 10038	Atlanta, GA 30367
Tel: (617) 565-7240	Tel: (212) 264-1207	Tel: (404) 347-4836

Regional Offices (continued):

668 Euclid Ave. Suite 520A Cleveland, OH 44114 Tel: (216) 522-4207	55 E. Monroe St. Suite 1437 Chicago, IL 60603 Tel: (312) 353-4423	100 N. Central Expwy. Suite 500 Dallas, TX 75201 Tel: (214) 767-5501
1405 Curtis St. Suite 2900 Denver, CO 80202 Tel: (303) 844-2271	11000 Wilshire Blvd. Suite 13209 Los Angeles, CA 90024 Tel: (213) 575-7575	915 Second Ave. Room 2806 Seattle, WA 98174 Tel: (206) 553-4656

901 Market St.
Suite 570
San Francisco, CA 94103
Tel: (415) 744-7920

FINANCIAL HELP FOR THE TERMINALLY ILL

For many terminally ill people, the cost of health care and daily living expenses is far beyond what they can afford. Consequently, many of them are doing without the help and care they need during the final stages of life.

For some of these people there is now a solution: several life insurance providers will pay reduced death benefits on life insurance policies of terminally ill customers between 50 to 80 percent (less, depending on life expectancy) of what the policy would have paid to survivors at the time of death. In exchange, the insurance company becomes the sole beneficiary of the policy. Allstate Financial Corporation and Prudential Life Insurance Company of America are just two of several insurance companies who are currently providing such arrangements.

There are many unknowns, financial risks and tax consequences associated with such payments. Therefore, it is critical that anyone considering selling their policy to an insurance company must first seek sound advice from a trusted insurance agent, lawyer, tax accountant or their State Insurance Regulator.

SECTION II

When Death Occurs

WHAT TO DO AT THE TIME OF DEATH

It is extremely difficult for most people to think clearly or make decisions immediately following the death of a loved one. Under the stress of bereavement, it requires considerable effort to take the steps required to arrange a funeral or memorial service. In some cases, the loved one may have made final preparations in anticipation of passing away. However, for most people, such arrangements have not been made.

Fortunately, family members, associates and close friends are usually more than willing to help. Their counsel may help balance consideration of the deceased's desires with the need to keep costs at a reasonable level.

Here are some tasks that should be attended to promptly following a death:

- Call your funeral home or memorial society to arrange for removal of the body.

- Sign any papers necessary for an autopsy (if required) or donation of the body or organs.

- Request as many copies as possible of the signed death certificate since several will be required for verification of death to banks, insurance companies and others who require such certification before benefits or assets can be released to the spouse or family. Generally, death certificates can be obtained from the hospital, medical facility or funeral director.

- Make arrangements to inform relatives, friends, associates and employers about the death. Ask friends and/or relatives to assist you since this is an important task with which they can be very helpful.

- Meet with the funeral director or whoever is handling the disposition of the deceased to discuss the time and place of the funeral or memorial service, the location for placement of the remains (cemetery, mausoleum crypt or above-ground tomb), casket choices, transportation of the family and any other purchases required for the funeral ceremony or other disposition of the deceased. Have someone accompany you to help make decisions.

- Keep a record of all who send flowers or charity donations so you can thank them later.

- Prepare the information necessary for a newspaper obituary notice if desired. Contact the newspaper(s) directly, or ask the funeral director to assist you.

- If you wish to extend hospitality in the form of meals or lodging to mourners who travel from outside the area, feel free to accept any help offered by others.

OTHER CRITICAL TASKS

As soon as the deceased is laid to rest, several important tasks must be performed by the surviving spouse, family lawyer, executor named in a will, or administrator if the deceased died without a will. These tasks should be completed as soon as possible so any disbursement of benefits and/or settlement of an estate can be processed without delay. The following list contains items that relate to most individuals. Naturally, this list is not all-inclusive, nor is each point applicable to everyone, because each set of circumstances can vary.

- Locate the original copy of any will prepared by the deceased.

- Make a thorough search for all documents, statements and/or papers relating to deeds of ownership (land, homes, vehicles, etc.), checking, savings, and other bank accounts, stocks, bonds, outstanding loans or monies owed to the deceased.

- If required by the state, petition the court to begin probate proceedings.

- If applicable, contact your local Social Security office to inform them of the death. Return any benefit checks that were not cashed by the deceased and apply for the Social Security "lump sum" death benefit or any Social Security survivor benefits to which you or your family may be entitled.

- If the deceased carried insurance, promptly notify all insurance companies of the death and request instructions on how to file for payments due from the policies.

- Notify all banks, credit unions, lending institutions or credit card companies of the death. Request statements, if necessary, of any balances owed or assets remaining.

- Notify the following regarding any death benefit entitlements:
  — The deceased's current employer and any former employers, such as Civil Service, that may provide death benefits based on the deceased's work record;
  — Trade unions, fraternal and other organizations to which the deceased belonged that may award death benefits to members' families;
  — Business partners and associates.

- If the deceased was a veteran, contact the regional office of the Veterans Administration to apply for any survivor and burial benefits to which your family may be entitled.

- If the deceased was an active or retired military member, contact the closest military installation for guidance and assistance from the **casualty assistance officer** to secure any survivor benefits or entitlements from the military service branch to which the deceased belonged.

- Remember, **do not make any decisions in haste.** Seek the guidance of other family members, your lawyer or other trustworthy person(s) who can properly advise you on the actions you are contemplating.

SECTION III

After Death

COPING WITH GRIEF

The death of someone you have loved and with whom you have shared part of your life engenders a grief that can be very difficult to overcome. In some cases, the stress of grief is so great that it affects both physical and mental health. For a time it may actually take away your joy in living. The grief is so real and so difficult to understand that few people know how to handle it and overcome their feelings of sadness, loneliness and remorse.

A mourning period after the loss of a loved one is a normal re-action for everyone; however, if mourning continues too long and depression sets in, it can have a very negative effect on your well-being and on everything you do. Professional help and counseling from a psychiatrist, psychologist, social worker or the clergy may be required to help overcome the pain and suffering of extreme grief. However, there are several things you can do to help alleviate grief before it reaches a crisis point. Here are some suggestions:

- Feel free to express your grief openly. Try not to continually sup-press your emotions. Family and friends will understand; they will expect and empathize with your feelings of loss.

- Try to recall the many pleasant memories of your loved one. These memories often bring joy and pleasure that can ease this difficult period.

- Start doing some form of exercise every day, even if it is simply taking a walk or doing a few warm-up exercises. You will find that the physical effort you expend will greatly enhance your mental outlook.

- Begin a hobby that you always wanted to pursue but never found the time for, or reclaim an old one you stopped doing some time back.

- Take comfort in your faith and participate in the activities and ser-vices of your church, synagogue, temple or other place of worship.

- If there ever was a time to start doing volunteer work this is it! You could help out at a hospital, school, church, Senior Center or at one of the many organizations which always need volunteers, especially the local Area Agency on Aging. Helping others can give you much satisfaction and can be one of the greatest healing agents available to you.

- Socialize as much as possible by joining organizations that interest you and attending their meetings regularly. Though this might require great effort, depending on how you feel at the time, the results will be worthwhile.

- Direct your mental activities in a new direction by taking an adult class at one of your local schools, or by participating in the Elderhostel program, a unique educational experience for the elderly involving both travel and instruction in a variety of areas. This special program is discussed in Chapter 11.

- If you are still employed, try to return to work a short time after your loss. The longer you wait, the more difficult it will be to return. Those who are not currently employed may wish to find some part-time work.

- Lastly, but critically important, **keep active** — both physically and mentally — all day long!

SELF-HELP AND SUPPORT GROUPS

Another way to help alleviate your grief and restore a meaningful perspective to your life is to join a local self-help or support group of others who, like you, have lost someone they love. It is surprising how much you can benefit from the help of the other members of these groups.

Throughout the nation, hundreds of groups or programs have been organized specifically to help widows and widowers overcome the loss of their spouses. In particular, the American Association of Retired Persons (AARP) began a program called the "Widowed Persons Service" (WPS) which is currently active in over 195 communities. This outstanding program is composed completely of volunteers who have been widowed for at least 18 months, so they have a thorough understanding of how the recently widowed feel. Since its inception in 1973, WPS has helped thousands of widowed men and women through one of the most difficult periods of their lives.

If you would like to participate in this program — or become a volunteer yourself — write to:

> American Association of Retired Persons
> Widowed Persons Service — JD
> 601 E Street, NW
> Washington, DC 20049

Other organizations can help you find a support group in your community. These include local churches, synagogues and Area Agencies on Aging. If you cannot find a support group in your own community, you can obtain information about one closest to you by writing to the National Self-Help Clearinghouse. Send your request for information with a self-addressed, stamped envelope to:

> National Self-Help Clearinghouse
> 25 W. 43rd Street, Room 620
> New York, NY 10036.

Do not hesitate to contact any of the above for assistance. This is a critical period of adjustment in your life, and you need all the help you can get.

Chapter 9

Veterans' Entitlements

You Earned Them!

Chapter Highlights

**TOLL-FREE TELEPHONE NUMBER
FOR THE VA INSURANCE CENTER
800-669-8477**
If you have any questions or need any service performed
on your VA insurance policy, call this toll-free number.

Veterans' Entitlements

You Earned Them!

The Department of Veterans Affairs (VA) was created in 1930 to make a single agency responsible for the many federal veterans' programs administered, at that time, by several government offices. Since 1930, the VA has grown dramatically as the number of veterans and their dependents has increased.

In 1930, only 4.7 million veterans were eligible for VA benefits; today there are over 26 million eligible veterans plus over 45 million of their eligible dependents. Together, these veterans and their families constitute one third of the nation's population — and their numbers are still growing and *aging*! According to VA estimates, by the year 2000, the number of veterans age 65 and older will peak at 9 million and represent 37 percent of the total veteran population.

The VA has the most comprehensive system of veterans' assistance and care in the world. It provides benefits through three VA departments: the Department of Veterans Benefits, the Department of Memorial Affairs, and the Department of Medicine and Surgery.

With an annual budget of over 35 billion dollars and more than 223,000 employees, the VA is second only to the Department of Defense. It administers the largest health care delivery system in the free world, consisting of 171 hospitals, 233 outpatient clinics, 131 nursing home care units, 39 domiciliaries and over 189 readjustment counseling centers. The VA also runs one of the federal government's major loan guarantee programs. Since World War II, this program has benefited over 12 million veterans and their dependents. The VA's program of disability compensation or pension payments pays out nearly $15 billion each year. The Administration has the eighth largest insurance program in the nation. Its national cemetery system comprises 114 national cemeteries in 38 states and Puerto Rico. More than 20 million veterans have participated in VA education and training programs since the inception of the GI Bill in 1944. The VA also sponsors numerous other programs that benefit millions of U.S. veterans and their dependents.

In considering the significance of the VA's total responsibilities, its accomplishments, and its dedication to serving so many Americans, Congress passed legislation which the President signed in October 1988, that converted the VA from an independent agency into the 14th cabinet department — the *Department of Veterans Affairs.* In January 1993, Jesse Brown, a combat-decorated Vietnam veteran, was sworn in as Secretary of Veterans Affairs by President Clinton.

UNDERSTANDING AND OBTAINING VA BENEFITS

Although millions of older Americans and their dependents receive VA benefits and services, a vast number of elderly veterans are unaware that they too are eligible. Thousands go without health care which they could receive free from the VA. Others spend their last savings to bury their spouses when a dignified burial is available from the VA at no cost.

This chapter discusses three major VA benefits available to every older American who ever served in the armed forces, his/her spouses and dependents: (1) health care for veterans; (2) disability compensation and pensions for veterans whose disabilities were caused by or aggravated during their military service; (3) veterans' burial entitlements. Questions about other benefits (educational assistance, GI loans, insurance, etc.) not covered in this chapter can be answered by any local or regional VA office (see the Listing at the end of this chapter).

If you find that you are eligible for any VA benefits or services, contact the VA office nearest you. Remember, **you earned these benefits**. Without the dedicated efforts and sacrifices you made to defend our country, America would not be the great place it is today.

ELIGIBILITY REQUIREMENTS

If your military service was completed under any conditions other than dishonorable discharge, you can qualify for VA benefits. And, based on your eligibility, your dependents and survivors may also be eligible for certain VA benefits. In some cases, individuals with undesirable or bad conduct discharges may also qualify. Their eligibility must be determined by the VA, which reviews the facts of each individual case. However, all veterans with honorable or general discharges — even if they are now in prison or on parole — are entitled to certain VA benefits.

While most veterans served in the regular armed forces, there are thousands of individuals whose military service was not recognized as "active" because it was not certified by the Secretary of Defense at the time. However, several of these groups are now recognized and certified as active. These include:

- Women's Airforces Service Pilots
- Signal Corps Women Telephone Operators, World War I
- Army Engineer Field Clerks
- Women's Army Auxiliary Corps
- Quartermaster Corps Female Clerical Employees with AEF, World War I
- Civilian Employees of Pacific Naval Air Bases who Actively Participated in Defense of Wake Island, World War II
- Reconstruction Aides and Dieticians, World War I
- Male Civilian Ferry Pilots
- Wake Island Defenders from Guam
- Civilian Personnel Assigned to Secret Intelligence Element of OSS
- Guam Combat Patrol
- Quartermaster Corps Keswick Crew on Corregidor
- U.S. Civilian Volunteers who Actively Participated in Defense of Bataan
- U.S. Merchant Seamen on Blockships in Support of Operation Mulberry
- World War II American Merchant Marine in Oceangoing Service during Period of Armed Conflict
- Civil Service Crewmembers of U.S. Army Transport Service
- Naval Transportation Service.

If you were a member of any of these groups — especially the last three, which were certified in 1988 — contact your regional VA office **immediately** to apply for a discharge certificate so you can begin receiving VA benefits.

The VA provides disability pensions and other benefits to all low-income veterans who served during wartime. The following are approved periods of wartime service:

- **Mexican Border Period** — *May 9, 1916 through April 5, 1917* for any veteran who served in Mexico, on its borders, or in adjacent waters;

- **World War I** — *April 6, 1917 through November 11, 1918; Extended to April 1, 1920* for any veteran who served in Russia; *Extended to July 1, 1921* for any veteran who served after November 11, 1918 and before July 2, 1921 as long as at least one day of service fell after April 5, 1917 and before November 12, 1918;

- **World War II** — *December 7, 1941 through December 31, 1946;*

- **Korean Conflict** — *June 27, 1950 through January 31, 1955;*

- **Vietnam Era** — *August 5, 1964 through May 7, 1975;*

- **Persian Gulf** — *August 2, 1990, and ending by Presidential proclamation or by law.*

HEALTH CARE BENEFITS

In addition to care provided at the VA hospital, the following health care benefits are available to eligible veterans:

- **Nursing Home Care** — Nursing home care is provided to convalescents or other persons whose ailments are not acute enough to require hospitalization. VA nursing home care is provided in the VA's own skilled and intermediate nursing facilities or in private nursing homes contracted by the VA to provide service to veterans.

- **Domiciliary Care** — Ambulatory self-care and home health services are provided to veterans disabled by age or disease whose ailments do not require hospitalization or nursing home treatment.

- **Outpatient Treatment** — Outpatient treatment includes: medical examination and related medical services during rehabilitation, consultation, professional counseling, and training and mental health services in connection with treatment of physical and mental disabilities. Outpatient medical treatment may be coupled with home health services as necessary or appropriate for the effective and economical treatment of disabilities. Home health care may include home improvements and structural alterations deemed necessary to assure continuation of treatment or to provide home access or essential lavatory and sanitary facilities.

- **Alcohol and Drug Dependence Treatment** — Care is provided in VA hospitals to veterans who are addicted to alcohol or drugs. After hospitalization, veterans may be eligible for outpatient care or may be authorized to continue treatment or rehabilitation in other VA-sponsored facilities, such as halfway houses and therapeutic communities.

The VA also provides outpatient medical care benefits such as dental treatment, prosthetic appliances for the disabled, readjustment counseling, and services for blind veterans. Eligible blind veterans can receive various aids and services, including:

- adjustment-to-blindness training;

- improvements and structural alterations to the home;

- low vision aids and training in how to use them;

- approved electronic and mechanical aids, and their necessary repair and replacement;

- guide dogs, including the expense of training the veteran to use the dog and the cost of the dog's medical care.

Medical, outpatient, and nursing home care and resources in VA facilities are available to all eligible veterans. However, in July 1986, the VA implemented new eligibility assessment procedures designed to give priority to veterans with service-related disabilities and illnesses and to low-income veterans.

When they apply for VA medical benefits, most veterans — regardless of age — whose medical problems are not service-connected must disclose their total income for the previous year and their current net worth. These factors are then used to determine the veterans' eligibility for VA medical care. However, the following groups of veterans are not required to make such disclosures:

- Former prisoners of war;

- Vietnam veterans with illnesses/disabilities that might be related to their exposure to certain herbicides while serving in Indochina;

Veterans exposed to ionizing radiation during atmospheric testing of nuclear weapons or during the occupation of Hiroshima and Nagasaki whose illnesses/disabilities might be related to that exposure;

- Veterans who receive VA pensions;

- Veterans of the Mexican Border period, the Spanish-American War, or World War I;

- Veterans who are eligible for Medicaid.

ELIGIBILITY OF VETERANS WITH NONSERVICE-RELATED ILLNESSES

The VA recently established two new eligibility categories for VA hospital, nursing home, and outpatient care for veterans: *"mandatory"* and *"discretionary"*.

Within these two categories, eligibility assessment procedures, based on income levels are used for determining whether nonservice-connected veterans are eligible for cost-free VA medical care. The VA must provide hospital care and *may* provide nursing home care to veterans in the "mandatory" category, and *may* provide hospital and nursing home care to veterans in the "discretionary" category if space and resources are available in VA facilities.

The law requires VA to provide hospital care to veterans in the "mandatory" category at the nearest VA facility capable of furnishing the care in a timely fashion. If no VA facility is available, care must be furnished in a Department of Defense facility or other facility with which VA has a sharing or contractual relationship. If space and resources are available after caring for "mandatory" category veterans, VA may furnish care to those in the "discretionary" category. Veterans in the "discretionary" category must agree to pay VA a copayment for their care.

Veterans in the "mandatory" category not subject to the eligibility assessment are service-connected veterans, former prisoners of war, veterans receiving VA pension, and veterans eligible for Medicaid.

The eligibility assessment which follows applies to all other nonservice-connected veterans, regardless of age:

- *MANDATORY:* Your hospital care is considered "mandatory if you are among the groups previously listed or if you are a nonservice-connected veteran and your income is $21,001 or less if single or with no dependents, or $25,204 or less if married or single with one dependent (add $1,404 for each additional dependent). Hospital care in VA facilities must be provided in VA facilities, if space and resources are available.

- *DISCRETIONARY:* Your hospital care is considered "discretionary" if you are a nonservice-connected veteran and your income is above $21,001 if single with no dependents, or $25,204 if married or single with one dependent (add $1,404 for each additional dependent). You must agree to pay an amount for your care equal to what you would have to pay under Medicare. VA may provide hospital, outpatient, and nursing home care in VA facilities to veterans in the "discretionary" category, if space and resources are available.

Copayment amounts for those considered "discretionary" in 1994 are:

— *Hospitalization and Nursing Home Care* — $736 for the first quarter (90 days) of continuous hospitalization during any 365-day period; $368 for each subsequent quarter for hospitalization. For each 90 days of nursing home care, you will be charged a copayment equal to the Medicare deductible. In addition to these changes, you will be charged $10 per day for hospital care and $5 a day for nursing home care.

Important: The Omnibus Budget Reconciliation Act of 1990 provides that veterans receiving medications on an outpatient basis from VA facilities, for the treatment of nonservice-connected disabilities or conditions, are required to make a copayment of $2 for each 30-day or less supply of medications provided. Veterans receiving medications for treatment of service-connected conditions and veterans rated 50 percent or more service-connected are exempt from the copayment requirement for medications.

CHAMPVA DEPENDENT AND SURVIVOR CARE

The VA has a program that provides medical care to eligible dependents and survivors of certain veterans, especially those with service related illnesses/disabilities or veterans who died during active duty. The program, called CHAMPVA (Civilian Health and Medical Program of the Veterans Administration), helps pay for medical services and supplies obtained by eligible veterans' dependents and survivors from civilian providers.

DISABILITY BENEFITS PROVIDING MONTHLY CASH PAYMENTS

Two benefits can provide considerable financial assistance to many older veterans: **disability compensation** and **disability pensions**.

■ Disability Compensation

Disability Compensation may be paid monthly to veterans with disabilities incurred or aggravated during military service. The amount of monthly benefits in 1996, based on the severity of the veteran's condition, ranges from $91 for a 10 percent degree of disability to $1,870 for a 100 percent disability rating. Veterans whose service-connected disability are rated at 30 percent or more are entitled to additional allowances for dependents. These allowances are determined according to the number of dependents and the degree of disability. Even higher additional benefits can be paid to veterans with 30 percent or greater disability if their spouses need the aid because they attend another person.

Most important! — There is no time limit to file a claim for service connected disability benefits. However, unless the application is filed within one year of discharge, compensation is effective only from the date of application. If the VA determines that an eligible veteran has suffered certain severe disabilities, they will pay additional compensation benefits per month to the veteran. These special benefits are determined according to each individual case.

The monthly payments for disability compensation are shown in the following table.

Compensation for
Service-Connected Disability — 1996

Percentage of Disability:	Monthly Benefit
10 percent	$ 91
20 percent	174
30 percent	266
40 percent	380
50 percent	542
60 percent	683
70 percent	862
80 percent	999
90 percent	1,124
Total disability	1,870

- **Disability Pensions**

  Disability Pensions are available to permanently, totally disabled veterans with wartime service whose income from all sources falls within prescribed limits. Unreimbursed medical expenses are taken into consideration in determining the income limitation.

  Most important! — The VA previously considered unemployed or retired veterans 65 years of age or older permanently and totally disabled for purposes of pension eligibility. The Omnibus Reconciliation Act of 1990 eliminated the presumption of disability at age 65 for pension claims after November 1, 1990. Veterans 65 or older must now establish entitlement to pension benefits based on medical evidence. Although this new rule has eliminated an automatic presumption of disability for certain older veterans, *do not refrain* — if you have a disability — from applying for a Disability Pension !

  The VA disability pension program provides the following annual benefits which are generally paid monthly. The annual payment is reduced by the amount of the annual countable income of the veteran, and of his/her spouse and dependent children. A veteran who is a patient in a nursing home, or who is determined by the VA to need an attendant, or who is permanently housebound may also be entitled to higher income limitations or additional benefits.

Pension Program Rates — 1996

	Annual Benefit
Veteran without dependent spouse or child	$ 8,246
Veteran with one dependent (spouse or child)	10,801
Veteran in need of regular aid and attendance without dependents	13,190
Veteran in need of regular aid and attendance with one dependent	15,744
Veteran permanently housebound without dependents	10,080
Veteran permanently housebound with one dependent	12,634
Two veterans married to one another	10,801
Veteran of World War I and Mexican Border Period, add to the applicable annual rate	1,867
Amount to add for each additional dependent	1,404

If you have a disability, or already receive compensation and believe your condition has worsened, which may entitle you to additional benefits, contact your nearest VA office **immediately** concerning either of these programs.

BURIAL AND DEATH BENEFITS

Burial in a national cemetery is available to all veterans whose discharges are not dishonorable, and to their spouses and dependents. Although exceptions are sometimes made, the following individuals are not eligible for burial in any national cemetery:

- A father, mother, sister, or in-law of a veteran even if the individual was dependent upon the veteran for support and belonged to the veteran's household;

- A veteran's widow who remarries. However, a veteran's widow whose remarriage is voided, terminated by death, or dissolved by annulment or divorce by a court with the authority to render such decrees, regains eligibility for burial in a national cemetery unless the Veterans Administration determines that the decree of annulment or divorce was secured through fraud or collusion;

- A spouse whose marriage to a veteran has been annulled or terminated by divorce;

- Any veteran convicted of subversive activities after September 1, 1959 has no right from the date of commission of such offense to burial in a national cemetery. Eligibility will be reinstated if a pardon is granted by the President of the United States;

- A person whose only service is active duty for training in the National Guard or Reserve Service unless he/she dies in honorable conditions during active duty, be it training or full-time service.

BURIAL IN ARLINGTON NATIONAL CEMETERY

Because Arlington National Cemetery is under the jurisdiction of the Department of the Army rather than the VA, all burials there are handled through the office of the cemetery's superintendent. Due to the limited number of available full-casket gravesites, there are specific requirements for burial in this cemetery. However, any veteran of the armed forces who is eligible for burial in a national cemetery and who is cremated may have his or her remains interred in the columbarium at the Arlington National Cemetery. Otherwise, only the following individuals, their spouses, minor children and dependent adult children (including spouses and children of individuals already buried in the cemetery) may be buried in Arlington Cemetery.

- Any person who dies on active duty in the armed forces;

- Retired military personnel included in an official service retired list who are eligible to receive compensation stemming from their military services;

- Recipients of the Medal of Honor, Distinguished Service Cross, Air Force Cross, Navy Cross, Distinguished Service Medal, Silver Star, or Purple Heart;

- Individuals who performed honorable military service and who held elective office in the U.S. Government, or served in the Supreme Court, the Cabinet, or in offices compensated at Level II under the Executive Salary Act;

- Former members of the armed forces who were separated because of a 30 percent or greater physical disability before October 1, 1949, who served on active duty (other than training), and who would have been eligible for retirement under the current provisions for retirement.

For further information about burial in Arlington Cemetery, call or write to:

Superintendent
Arlington National Cemetery
Arlington, VA 22211
Tel: (703) 695-3250

BURIAL BENEFITS

The following summary identifies the VA burial benefits that eligible veterans, their spouses and dependents may receive and the restrictions applicable to these benefits.

■ **Gravesites** — One gravesite is authorized for each eligible veteran and his/her eligible family members *except* where soil conditions require side-by-side gravesites. A gravesite cannot be reserved before it is needed for a burial. When a death occurs and interment in a national cemetery is authorized, a gravesite will be assigned in the name of the veteran.

For national cemeteries with no available gravesites there may still be space to enter cremated remains. Occasionally, full-casket gravesites become available in closed cemeteries due to disinterments or relinquishment of gravesite reservations made before 1962. Contact the cemetery's director for information on the opening of additional gravesites.

■ **Headstones or Markers** — The VA will furnish a headstone or marker to memorialize or mark the grave of a veteran buried in a national, state, or private cemetery. The VA will also provide markers to eligible dependents interred in a national or state veterans' cemetery. A memorial marker or headstone for veterans whose remains have not been recovered or identified may also be provided by the VA. Such markers are placed in the memorial section of the national cemetery. These memorial markers/headstones are furnished for those who were buried at sea, those whose bodies were donated to science, and those who were cremated and the ashes scattered.

The VA no longer reimburses part of the cost of a private headstone or marker bought after the veteran's death and placed on his/her grave. When burial occurs in a cemetery other than a national cemetery or a state veterans cemetery, the headstone or marker must be applied for separately. It is shipped at Government expense; however, the VA does not pay the cost of placing the headstone or marker on the grave.

- **Burial Allowances** — If the veteran's death is not service-connected, the VA provides a burial allowance of $300 for any veteran entitled at the time of death to VA compensation or pension payments or who died in a VA medical facility.

- **Plot or Interment Allowance** — A plot or interment allowance of $150 is available to any veteran entitled to the burial allowance, or who was discharged or retired from service because of a disability which was incurred or aggravated in the line of duty. Veterans buried in a national or other federal cemeteries are not eligible for plot allowances. The plot allowance may be paid to a state if the veteran was buried in the state's veterans' cemetery.

If the veteran's death is service-connected, VA will pay up to $1,500 in lieu of the burial and plot allowance.

- **Burial Flags** — The VA will provide an American flag to drape the casket of an eligible veteran. After the burial, the flag may be given to the next of kin, close friend or associate of the deceased. The VA may also issue a flag for a veteran who is missing in action and presumed dead.

- **Presidential Memorial Certificates** — Memorial certificates expressing the nation's recognition of the deceased veteran's service which are signed by the President are made available to the next of kin of deceased eligible veterans or of persons who were members of the armed forces at time of death. Eligible recipients include the next of kin (widow, widower, oldest child, parent, or oldest sibling), a relative or friend upon request, or an authorized representative acting on behalf of such relative or friend.

COMMON QUESTIONS ON VETERANS' BURIALS

The following answers questions often raised by veterans and their families:

- When a veteran dies during treatment in a VA medical facility, the VA will pay to transport the deceased to the place of burial.

- The VA will reimburse the estate of a deceased veteran for burial expenses that have been pre-paid to a funeral home.

- Husbands of female veterans are eligible for the same VA benefits as wives of male veterans.

- The VA will pay for and provide inscriptions of certain military awards on government-furnished headstones and markers. These awards are: Medal of Honor, Distinguished Service Cross, Navy Cross, Air Force Cross, Silver Star, and Purple Heart.

- The VA will pay for and replace a government headstone if it is cracked, broken, destroyed or otherwise made illegible. The veteran's family members or another responsible party should direct such a request, including a description of the current damaged headstone/marker, to:

    Director
    Monument Service (42)
    Veterans Administration
    Washington, DC 20420.

- When traveling overseas primarily to visit a veteran's burial site in a permanent American military cemetery or his/her memorial on a Tablet of the Missing, immediate family members (widows, parents, siblings, and guardians) may be eligible for non-fee or fee-free passports. For additional information, write to:

    American Battle Monuments Commission
    Room 5127, Pulaski Building
    20 Massachusetts Ave., NW
    Washington, DC 20314.

DEATH COMPENSATION BENEFITS

The VA provides two death benefits to help certain veterans' surviving spouse or dependents:

- **Death Pension** — Compensation payments may be authorized for spouses, unmarried children under 18 (or under 23 if the child attends a VA-approved school), and dependent parents of veterans (1) who died before January 1, 1957 from a service-connected cause or (2) whose death was nonservice-connected but who had at least 90 days of wartime service. Spouses, unmarried children and dependent parents must meet the applicable need-based standards to be considered for payment of this death pension.

- **Dependency and Indemnity Compensation (DIC)** — If a veteran dies of service related causes, DIC benefits may be paid to survivors based on the veteran's grade at the time of discharge. These benefits are greater than death pensions. Other income is not a factor in determining survivor eligibility for DIC benefits.

OF IMPORTANCE TO MANY VETERANS!

Although the following items and changes were announced several months ago, many veterans are still unaware of them and how they may effect eligibility for several VA benefits. Please help spread the word to Veterans who may not yet have heard about them.

——————————————— ★ ★ ★ ———————————————

The Defense Department has determined that Merchant Marine seamen who served in active, oceangoing service from December 7, 1941 to August 15, 1945, **are** veterans and thus eligible for discharge certificates from the armed forces. This change in status makes these individuals eligible for certain VA benefits. The decision also affects Civil Service crewmembers aboard U.S. Army Transport Service and Naval Transportation Service vessels in oceangoing service or in foreign waters during the same period.

Individuals affected by these new rulings should immediately apply for a discharge certificate by filing DD Form 2168, which is available from any VA Regional Office. The completed form should be mailed to the applicable service's office listed as follows:

Naval Military Command
(NMPC-3)
Navy Department
Washington, DC 20370-5300

Commander, US Army Reserve
PAS-EENC
9700 Page Boulevard
St. Louis, MO 63132-5000

Commandant (GMVP-1/12 MMVS)
U.S. Coast Guard
Washington, D.C. 20953.

--- ★ ★ ★ ---

WORLD WAR II "FLYING TIGERS" ELIGIBLE FOR VA BENEFITS

The Department of Veterans Affairs (VA) has announced that the famed World War II Flying Tigers have been granted veteran status. A recent Defense Department decision determined that honorably discharged members of the *American Volunteer Group* (AVG) (Flying Tigers) who served from December 7, 1941 to July 18, 1942, are potentially eligible for veterans benefits. Individuals must have an AVG discharge certificate or letter, or identification as an honorably discharged AVG member in other credible publications or documents.

In general, these newly designated veterans (or their survivors) can apply for the same benefits currently available to other veterans, including service-related disability compensation, pension, medical care, certain survivors' benefits, VA-guaranteed home loans, and burial benefits. Eligibility for specific benefits will be determined on a case-by-case basis, depending on the specifics of service and eligibility criteria for each benefit.

Before applying for veterans benefits, individuals must first apply for an Armed Forces discharge certificate by filling out DD Form 2168, which is available from any VA Regional Office or the Department of the Air Force.

--- ★ ★ ★ ---

In June 1988, the National Archives and Records Administration told the VA about its collection of computer tapes containing 10 million Army medical treatment records. These records partially fill a gap created when a 1973 fire destroyed millions of military files at a federal record center in St. Louis. The newly found records cover the years from 1942 to 1945 and from 1950 to 1954.

This discovery may enable many Army and Army Air Corps veterans of World War II and the Korean Conflict to refile for Veterans Administration disability compensation payments which had been previously denied, based on the lack of documentary evidence to support their claims.

The computerized information reflects battle injuries treated in Army hospitals and hospitalizations for other reasons. The records cover personnel who served in the Army and Army Air Corps, as well as personnel from other services who were treated in Army medical facilities. Using the new records, the VA now hopes to assist many veterans whose claims had previously been denied because no record was available to confirm medical disabilities that occurred during military service. Veterans and survivors who think their disability compensation claims may be affected should contact their nearest VA regional office for further information and assistance refiling their claims, if necessary.

APPEALS

All veterans have the right to appeal unfavorable determinations made by VA regional offices or medical centers. These determinations can only be appealed to the Board of Veterans Appeals.

Established in 1933, the Board of Veterans Appeals makes all final authoritative decisions on claimant disputes with VA determinations of benefit amounts or eligibility. The Board has a mandate to act in favor of the claimant whenever possible, with all reasonable doubt to be resolved in the individual's favor.

Personal hearings will be scheduled upon request. An appellant may be represented, without charge, by an accredited representative of a veterans' organization or any other service organization recognized by the Administrator of Veterans Affairs. An attorney may be employed for assistance but such services are limited by law to a maximum fee. The current appeals procedures are outlined below:

1. You have **one year** from the date of the notification of VA determination to file your appeal. To initiate the appeal, you

must file a "Notice of Disagreement" in which you express your dissatisfaction and request an appellate review. The Notice of Disagreement should be filed with the VA facility that made the original determination. Once this notice is filed, you may request a personal hearing on the appeal.

2. When it receives your Notice of Disagreement, the VA will send you a "Statement of the Case" justifying the determination and citing the laws and regulations applicable to your case.

3. If you still disagree with the VA's judgment, you must file a "Substantive Appeal" within 60 days after the date of the Statement of the Case or within one year from the notification of the original determination, whichever is later.

4. The Board of Veterans Appeals will review your case and render a decision.

With the passage of Public Law 100-687 in October 1988 veterans gained the right of final appeal to the U.S. Court of Veterans Appeals. The Court — which is entirely independent of the Veterans Administration — has exclusive jurisdiction to review decisions of the Board of Veterans Appeals. As an independent entity, the U.S. Court of Veterans Appeals is not bound by decisions of the VA Administrator, VA regulations, or opinions of the VA General Counsel.

Access to the Court is limited to those veterans who have submitted their claims to the Board of Veterans Appeals and have received an adverse decision from the Board. The notice of appeal must then be filed with the Court of Veterans Appeals within 120 days after the date of the letter in which the Board of Veterans Appeals rendered their decision.

The legislation of 1988 also cleared the way for veterans to further elevate VA claims appeals to higher U.S. courts, including the Supreme Court, which had historically denied having jurisdiction in most VA claims matters.

For more information on the Court's rules and procedures contact:
Court Clerk, Court of Veterans Appeals
625 Indiana Ave., NW, Suite 900
Washington, D.C. 20004
Toll Free: 800-869-8654

OBTAINING A VETERAN'S RECORD
OF MILITARY SERVICE

To obtain any veteran's health care or benefits, you must have official documentation of the veteran's discharge or separation from military service. If an individual's discharge or separation papers cannot be located, copies can be obtained from the military centers listed at the end of this section.

Submit requests in writing on Standard Form 180, *Request Pertaining to Military Records,* which can be obtained from the military centers or from your nearest VA regional office. However, **in the case of a medical emergency,** information can be obtained by phoning the appropriate section at the St. Louis, Missouri center:

- Air Force Section — (314) 538-4243

- Army Section — (314) 538-4261

- Navy/Marine Corps/Coast Guard Section — (314) 538-4141.

Any VA regional office will usually help you obtain the necessary documents in case of emergency, death, or when you have difficulty getting the information from another source.

The military departments limit their release of information from military personnel records according to protective provisions required by law. All individuals have access to most of the information contained in their own records. The next of kin — if the veteran is deceased — and federal offices (for official purposes) are authorized to receive information from a military service or medical record only as specified by law. All other requesters must have a release authorization signed by the veteran or, if deceased, by the next of kin.

Generally, there is no charge for copies of discharge or separation papers. However, a nominal fee may be charged for certain services. If your request involves a service fee, you will be notified as soon as the fee is determined. A Report of Separation (DD Form 214 or its equivalent) is required to provide the information needed to prove eligibility for most VA benefits. The discharge certificate, which only states the date and character of a discharge, is not sufficient.

WHERE TO WRITE FOR RECORDS OF DISCHARGED, DECEASED AND RETIRED MILITARY MEMBERS

Write to the center that corresponds with the branch of the military service in which the veteran served. In addition to personnel records, these centers can also supply the veteran 's past medical records when available.

Army	Air Force
National Personnel Records Center Attn: Army Military Records 9700 Page Boulevard St. Louis, MO 63132	National Personnel Records Center Attn: Air Force Military Records 9700 Page Boulevard St. Louis, MO 63132

Navy	Marine Corps
National Personnel Records Center Attn: Navy Military Records 9700 Page Boulevard St. Louis, Mo 63132	National Personnel Records Center Attn: Marine Corps Military Records 9700 Page Boulevard St. Louis, MO 63132

Coast Guard

National Personnel Records Center
Attn: Coast Guard Military Records
9700 Page Boulevard
St. Louis, MO 63132

For officers and enlisted personnel — regardless of their branch of military service — separated more than 60 years ago, records are generally maintained by the National Archives in Washington, D.C. Address your requests to:

Military Archives Division
National Archives and Records Administration
Washington, DC 20408

Contact the nearest VA regional office for the exact location of records for Reserve and National Guard members, general officers, active duty members and those individuals who are on the Temporary Disability Retirement list. Their records are not always available from the centers listed in this summary.

NATIONAL VETERANS' ORGANIZATIONS

The following national organizations provide veterans with a variety of services and extremely helpful information (newsletters, magazines, and bulletins) on changes in veterans' benefits, entitlements and assistance.

Many of these organizations have local chapters which offer veterans the chance to participate in various activities. For further information on membership — both national and local, contact the organization that interests you by calling or writing. Since membership dues are generally low, you may wish to join several of these organizations.

Air Force Association (AFA)
1501 Lee Highway
Arlington, VA 22209
Tel: (703) 247-5800

Air Force Sergeants Association (AFSA)
P.O. Box 50
Temple Hills, MD 20757
Tel: (301) 899-3500

American Veterans of WW II, Korea and Vietnam (AMVETS)
4647 Forbes Blvd.
Lanham, MD 20706
Tel: (301) 459-9600

Association of the United States Army (AUSA)
2425 Wilson Blvd.
Arlington, VA 22201
Tel: (703) 841-4300

American Legion
700 North Pennsylvania St.
Indianapolis, IN 46204
Tel: (317) 635-8411

American Legion Auxiliary
National Headquarters
777 N. Meridian Street, 3rd Floor
Indianapolis, IN 46204
Tel: (317) 635-8411

National Association for Uniformed Services (NAUS)
5535 Hempstead Way
Springfield, VA 22151
Tel: (703) 750-1342

Paralyzed Veterans of America
801 - 18th Street, NW
Washington, DC 20006
Tel: (202) 872-1300
Toll Free: 800-424-8200

Disabled American Veterans (DAV)
807 Maine Avenue, SW
Washington, DC 20024
Tel: (202) 554-3501

Jewish War Veterans of the United States
1811 R Street, NW
Washington, DC 20009
Tel: (202) 265-6280

Ladies Auxiliary V.F.W.
National Headquarters
406 W. 34th Street
Kansas City, MO 64111
Tel: (816) 561-8655

Marine Corps League
8626 Lee Highway, Suite 201
Fairfax, VA 22031
Tel: (703) 207-9588

Military Order of the Purple Heart
National Headquarters
5413-C Backlick Road
Springfield, VA 22151
Tel: (703) 354-2140

The Retired Enlisted Association (TREA)
1111 S. Abilene Ct.
Aurora, CO 80012
Tel: (303) 752-0660

The Retired Officers Association (TROA)
201 N. Washington Street
Alexandria, VA 22314
Tel: (703) 549-2311

Society of Military Widows (SMW)
5535 Hempstead Way
Springfield, VA 22151
Tel: (703) 750-1342

Veterans of Foreign Wars of the U.S. (VFW)
200 Maryland Ave., NE
Washington, DC 20002
Tel: (202) 543-2239

VA HEADLINES

The following recent news items and changes — and their possible effects on your eligibility for several VA benefits — are extremely important:

- *Critical!* The VA will help World War II veterans who were exposed to mustard gas during U.S. military experiments conducted during their military service, and who suffer from certain long-term effects of that experimentation. Veterans who were exposed will be eligible for disability compensation.

Normally, veterans applying for VA disability compensation must submit documentation with their claims that their illness or condition occurred during military service. Such documentation usually consists of a military medical record of treatment. However, because of the confidentiality of the testing and the failure by the military branches to follow up on the long-term effects to veterans, most of these experiments went undocumented. Because of this, the usual criteria will not be applied to mustard gas claims.

The recognized long-term (over one year) effects of significant exposure to mustard gas are: laryngitis, chronic bronchitis, emphysema, asthma, chronic conjunctivitis, and corneal opacities.

World War II veterans who were involved in mustard gas testing, and who suffer from one or more of these conditions, should contact the nearest VA regional office **immediately** for help filing a claim.

- *Change in Determination of Exposure to Agent Orange:* In 1991, the Secretary of Veterans Affairs ruled that Vietnam veterans with non-Hodgkin's lymphoma, a form of cancer, are entitled to disability payments based on their service in Vietnam. The Secretary acted in response to study results by the U.S. Centers for Disease Control.

  The VA will identify and reopen claims filed by veterans who served in Southeast Asia and who alleged that their development of non-Hodgkin's lymphoma resulted from Agent Orange exposure. The VA will extend as much latitude as possible to award retroactive benefits and to assist widows and children of veterans who died as a result of non-Hodgkin's lymphoma.

- *Tax-Free Fund Payments:* Veterans who served in the U.S. armed forces in Vietnam from 1961 to 1972 may receive payments from the *Agent Orange Settlement Fund,* which are not subject to federal income tax. According to the IRS, these payments — begun in 1989 — constitute damages paid for personal injury or sickness, and are excluded from taxable income. An estimated 60,000 people are eligible for payments because of sickness or disability from exposure to Agent Orange during their Vietnam tours of duty. Survivors of deceased veterans who receive payments from the Fund may also exclude the payments from federal income tax.

- *Vocational Rehabilitation:* As part of a disabled veteran's rehabilitation program, the VA will pay for tuition, books, tools or other expenses and provide a monthly living allowance. Employment assistance is also available to help the rehabilitated veteran get a job. A seriously disabled veteran may receive services and assistance to increase independence in daily living. Apply at any VA office. Veterans have 12 years after separation to apply for this benefit; however, extensions may be granted under certain conditions.

- *VA to Pay $911 Million in Insurance Dividends:* The VA announced that over $911 million in dividends will be paid in 1996 to veterans holding active policies. Dividends will be credited automatically to the 2.3 million policyholders on the anniversary dates of their policies. Policyholders may choose to receive a dividend check or to select one of nine alternate payment options. Only those policies that have been kept in force receive annual dividend distributions. No application from individual policyholders is necessary.

- *VA Urges Veterans to Refinance Home Loans:* The VA strongly encourages veterans to refinance their loans with interest rates that are *two points* or more lower than their current rate. The potential individual and collection savings to veterans are substantial. For lesser differences in rates, refinance costs eat up much of the savings. Veterans considering refinancing should contact a private lending agency in their area. If there are questions concerning eligibility for a VA-guarantee of the refinanced loan, the veteran should contact the nearest VA Regional office.

- *Compensation Payments to Certain Incompetent Veterans:* The Budget Reconciliation Act of 1990 requires that payment of compensation to a non-hospitalized incompetent veteran, with no spouse, child, or dependent parent, be suspended in any case where the value of the veteran's estate (not including the veteran's home) exceeds $25,000 until the value of the estate is reduced to less than $10,000. The Act further provides for payment of the total amount of compensation that had been withheld, should the veteran subsequently be rated competent for 90 days.

- *VA Increase Efforts to Bill Insurance Companies for Veterans Care:* In 1991, Congress authorized the VA to increase its efforts to recover from insurance companies the cost of care provided to *service-disabled veterans* for treatment of non-service-related health problems. Previously in 1986, Congress passed legislation to recover from insurance companies the cost of providing medical care to *nonservice-disabled veterans*.

The amount VA can collect from insurance companies is limited to the amount the veteran or other health-care provider would receive if the care had been furnished by a nongovernment agency. The insurance companies reimburse VA directly. Veterans are *not billed* by VA or the veteran's insurance company, and a veteran's eligibility for VA health-care services is not affected. Veterans *will not be responsible* for *uncollected claims* against their policies, nor for copayments that many policies require (portion of bills that the insured must absorb). VA's absorption of annual policy deductibles from recovered claims may satisfy the obligation of a veteran who later seeks private medical care.

VA OFFERS TOLL-FREE SERVICE FOR THE HEARING-IMPAIRED

The Department of Veterans Affairs (VA) has set up a national toll-free telephone number accessible by a telecommunications device to assist deaf and hearing-impaired veterans and their families. Veterans with this special equipment, known as a TDD, can call **1-800-829-4833** for information on VA benefits and programs.

Based at the Chicago VA Regional Office, the service is available from 8 a.m. to 4 p.m. CDT, Monday through Friday. Calls received after normal business hours and on weekends and holidays will be returned the following business day.

Nearly 230,000 veterans receive VA disability compensation for hearing loss. Throughout the United States, approximately 21 million people suffer from some degree of hearing loss. Of that number, 350,000 are totally deaf.

Veterans Administration Regional Offices

For information or help applying for veteran's benefits, write, call or visit a Veterans Benefits Counselor at any of the regional offices listed below. A new VA toll-free telephone service was recently started. With the new service, veterans and their dependents throughout the country may obtain information on their VA benefits from regional offices by calling toll-free **800-827-1000**. Callers will be automatically connected to the VA regional office closest to them.

The telephone numbers shown in this listing are subject to change. If you cannot reach one of the numbers shown, consult the listing under "U.S. Government—Veterans Administration" in the blue pages of your phone book, or contact the telephone directory assistance operator.

When you write to these offices, address your inquiry to: Veterans Administration Regional Office. If there is more than one office in your state, write to the office that serves your area.

ALABAMA
Veterans Administration Regional Office
345 Perry Hill Rd.
Montgomery, AL 36109

If you reside in the local telephone areas of:
   Montgomery 279-4866
All other areas in Alabama: 800-827-1000.

ALASKA
Veterans Administration Regional Office
2925 DeBarr Rd.
Anchorage, AK 99508

If you reside in the local telephone areas of
   Anchorage 257-4700
All other Alaska communities: 800-827-1000.

ARIZONA
Veterans Administration Regional Office
3225 N. Central Ave.
Phoenix, AZ 85012

If you reside in the local telephone areas of:
    Phoenix 263-5411
All other areas in Arizona: 800-827-1000

ARKANSAS
Veterans Administration Regional Office
Bldg. 65, Ft. Roots
North Little Rock. AR 72115

If you reside in the local telephone areas of:
    Little Rock 370-3800
All other areas in Arkansas: 800-827-1000

CALIFORNIA
Veterans Administration Regional Office
Federal Building
11000 Wilshire Boulevard
West Los Angeles, Los Angeles, CA 90024

Counties of Inyo, Kern, Los Angeles, Orange, San Bernardino, San Luis Obispo, Santa Barbara and Ventura:

Dial direct from Central LA......................................479-4011
All other areas of the above counties: 800-827-1000

If you reside in the local telephone area of:
    East LA 722-4927
Counties of Alpine, Lassen, Modoc and Mono served by:
1201 Terminal Way, Reno, NV 89520

If you reside in the above California counties: 800-827-1000

Veterans Administration Regional Office
2022 Camino Del Rio North, San Diego, CA 92108

Counties of Imperial, Riverside, and San Diego:

If you reside in the local telephone area of:
    Above counties 297-8220
All other areas of the above counties: 800-827-1000

Veterans Administration Regional Office
211 Main Street, San Francisco, CA 94105

If you reside in the local telephone area of:
    San Francisco 495-8900
All other areas of Northern California: 800-827-1000

COLORADO
Veterans Administration Regional Office
155 Van Gordon St.
Denver, CO 80225

If you reside in the local telephone area of:
Denver 980-1300
All other Colorado areas: 800-827-1000

CONNECTICUT
Veterans Administration Regional Office
450 Maine Street
Hartford, CT 06103

If you reside in the local telephone area of:
Hartford ....(203)278-3230
All other Connecticut areas: 800-827-1000

DELAWARE
Veterans Administration Regional Office
1601 Kirkwood Highway
Wilmington, DE 19805

If you reside in the local telephone area of:
Wilmington 998-0191
All other Delaware areas: 800-827-1000

DISTRICT OF COLUMBIA
Veterans Administration Regional Office
1120 Vermont Ave., NW
Washington, DC 20421
All of Washington, DC: (202) 418-4343

FLORIDA
Veterans Administration Regional Office
144 First Avenue S.
St. Petersburg, FL 33701

If you reside in the local telephone area of:
St. Petersburg..898-2121
All other Florida areas: 800-827-1000

GEORGIA
Veterans Administration Regional Office
730 Peachtree Street, NE
Atlanta, GA 30365

If you reside in the local telephone area of:
Atlanta 881-1776
All other Georgia areas: 800-827-1000

GUAM
Veterans Administration Office
U.S. Naval Regional Medical Center
P.O. Box 7613,
FPO San Francisco, CA 96630
(671) 344-9200 or 344-5260

HAWAII
Veterans Administration Regional Office
PJKK Federal Bldg.
300 Ala Moana Blvd.
Honolulu, HI 96850

Mailing: P.O. Box 50188, Honolulu, HI 96850

If you reside in the local telephone area of:
    Island of Oahu 566-1000
All other Hawaii areas: 800-827-1000

IDAHO
Veterans Administration Regional Office
805 W. Franklin St.
Boise, ID 83702

If you reside in the local telephone area of:
    Boise 334-1010
All other Idaho areas: 800-827-1000

ILLINOIS
Veterans Administration Regional Office
536 S. Clark Street, P.O. Box 8136
Chicago, IL 60680

If you reside in the local telephone area of:
    Chicago 663-5510
All other Illinois areas: 800-827-1000

INDIANA
Veterans Administration Regional Office
575 N. Pennsylvania Street.
Indianapolis, IN 46204

If you reside in the local telephone area of:
    Indianapolis 226-5566
All other Indiana areas: 800-827-1000

IOWA
Veterans Administration Regional Office
210 Walnut Street
Des Moines, IA 50309

If you reside in the local telephone area of:
    Des Moines 284-0219
All other Iowa areas: 800-827-1000

KANSAS
Veterans Administration Regional Office
5500 E. Kellogg
Wichita, KS 67218

If you reside in the local telephone area of:
    Wichita 682-2301
All other Kansas areas: 800-827-1000

KENTUCKY
Veterans Administration Regional Office
545 S. Third St.
Louisville, KY 40202

If you reside in the local telephone area of:
    Louisville 584-2231
All other Kentucky areas: 800-827-1000

LOUISIANA
Veterans Administration Regional Office
701 Loyola Ave.
New Orleans, LA 70113

If you reside in the local telephone area of:
    New Orleans 589-7191
All other Louisiana areas: 800-827-1000

MAINE
Veterans Administration Regional Office
Route 17 East
Togus, ME 04330

If you reside in the local telephone area of:
    Togus 623-8000
All other Maine areas: 800-827-1000

MARYLAND
Veterans Administration Regional Office
31 Hopkins Plaza
Baltimore, MD 21201
Counties of Montgomery and Prince Georges

If you reside in the above Maryland counties: (202) 418-4343

If you reside in the local telephone area of:
    Baltimore 685-5454
All other Maryland areas: 800-827-1000

MASSACHUSETTS

Towns of Fall River and New Bedford and counties of Barnstable, Dukes, Nantucket, part of Plymouth, and Bristol are served by:
Veterans Administration Regional Office
380 Westminster Mall
Providence, RI 02903
If you reside in the above counties: 800-827-1000

Remaining Massachusetts counties served by:
Veterans Administration Regional Office
Government Center
John F. Kennedy Federal Building
Boston, MA 02203
If you reside in the local telephone area of:
Boston 227-4600
All other Massachusetts areas: 800-827-1000

MICHIGAN

Veterans Administration Regional Office
Patrick V. McNamara Federal Building
477 Michigan Avenue
Detroit, MI 48226

If you reside in the local telephone area of:
Detroit 964-5110
All other Michigan areas: 800-827-1000

MINNESOTA

Veterans Administration Regional Office
Federal Building
Fort Snelling
St. Paul, MN 55111

If you reside in the local telephone area of:
Minneapolis 726-1454

Counties of Becker, Beltrami, Clay, Clearwater, Kittson, Lake of the Woods, Mahnomen, Marshall, Norman, Otter Tail, Pennington, Polk, Red Lake, Roseau, and Wilkin are served by Fargo, ND
If you reside in the above counties: 800-827-1000
All other Minnesota areas: 800-827-1000

MISSISSIPPI

Veterans Administration Regional Office
100 West Capitol Street
Jackson, MS 39269

If you reside in the local telephone area of:
Jackson 965-4873
All other Mississippi areas: 800-827-1000

MISSOURI
Veterans Administration Regional Office
Federal Building
400 S. 18th St.
St. Louis, MO 63103

If you reside in the local telephone area of:
    St. Louis 342-1171
All other Missouri areas: 800-827-1000

MONTANA
Veterans Administration Regional Office
Fort Harrison, MT 59636

If you reside in the local telephone area of:
    Fort Harrison/Helena 447-7975
All other Montana areas: 800-827-1000

NEBRASKA
Veterans Administration Regional Office
Federal Building
5631 S. 48th St.
Lincoln, NE 68516

If you reside in the local telephone area of:
    Lincoln 484-4001
All other Nebraska areas: 800-827-1000

NEVADA
Veterans Administration Regional Office
1201 Terminal Way
Reno, NV 89520

If you reside in the local telephone area of:
    Reno 329-9244
All other Nevada areas: 800-827-1000

NEW HAMPSHIRE
Veterans Administration Regional Office
Norris Cotton Federal Building
275 Chestnut Street
Manchester, NH 03101

If you reside in the local telephone area of:
    Manchester 666-7785
All other New Hampshire areas: 800-827-1000

NEW JERSEY
Veterans Administration Regional Office
20 Washington Place
Newark, NJ 07102

If you reside in the local telephone area of:
    Newark 645-2150
All other New Jersey areas: 800-827-1000

NEW MEXICO
Veterans Administration Regional Office
Dennis Chavez Federal Building
U.S. Courthouse
500 Gold Avenue, SW
Albuquerque, NM 87102

If you reside in the local telephone area of:
    Albuquerque 766-3361
All other New Mexico areas: 800-827-1000

NEW YORK
Veterans Administration Regional Office
Federal Building
111 W. Huron Street
Buffalo, NY 14202

If you reside in the local telephone area of:
    Buffalo 551-5191
All other areas of Western New York State: 800-827-1000

Veterans Administration Regional Office
111 W. Huron St., New York City, NY 10014

Counties of Albany, Bronx, Clinton, Columbia, Delaware, Dutchess, Essex, Franklin, Fulton, Greene, Hamilton, Kings, Montgomery, Nassau, New York, Orange, Otsego, Putnam, Queens, Rensselaer, Richmond, Rockland, Saratoga, Schenectady, Schoharie, Suffolk, Sullivan, Ulster, Warren, Washington, Westchester.

If you reside in the local telephone area of:
    New York 620-6330
All other areas in the above counties: 800-827-1000

NORTH CAROLINA
Veterans Administration Regional Office Federal Building
251 N. Main
Winston-Salem, NC 27155

If you reside in the local telephone area of:
    Winston-Salem 748-1800
All other North Carolina areas: 800-827-1000

NORTH DAKOTA
Veterans Administration Regional Office
2101 Elm St.
Fargo, ND 58102

If you reside in the local telephone area of:
    Fargo 293-3656
All other North Dakota areas: 800-827-1000

OHIO
Veterans Administration Regional Office
Anthony J. Celebrezze Federal Building
1240 East 9th Street
Cleveland, OH 44199

If you reside in the local telephone area of:
    Cleveland 621-5050
All other Ohio areas: 800-827-1000

OKLAHOMA
Veterans Administration Regional Office
Federal Building
125 S. Main Street
Muskogee, OK 74401

If you reside in the local telephone area of:
    Muskogee 687-2500
All other Oklahoma areas: 800-827-1000

OREGON
Veterans Administration Regional Office
Federal Building
1220 SW 3rd Avenue.
Portland, OR 97204

If you reside in the local telephone area of:
    Portland 221-2431
All other Oregon areas: 800-827-1000

PENNSYLVANIA
Veterans Administration Regional Office
P.O. Box 8079
5000 Wissahickon Ave.
Philadelphia, PA 19101

Counties of Adams, Berks, Bradford, Bucks, Cameron, Clinton, Columbia, Cumberland, Dauphin, Delaware, Franklin, Juniata, Lackawanna, Lancaster, Lebanon, Lehigh, Luzerne, Lycoming, Miffin, Monroe, Montgomery, Montour, Northhampton, Northumberland, Perry, Philadelphia, Pike, Potter, Schuylkill, Snyder, Sullivan, Susquehanna, Tioga, Union, Wayne, Wyoming, and York.

If you reside in the local telephone area of:
    Philadelphia 438-5225
All other areas in the above counties: 800-827-1000

    Veterans Administration Regional Office
    1000 Liberty Avenue, Pittsburgh, PA 15222

If you reside in the local telephone area of:
    Pittsburgh 281-4233
All other areas in Western Pennsylvania: 800-827-1000

PHILIPPINES
Veterans Administration Regional Office
1131 Roxas Boulevard (Manila)
APO San Francisco, CA 96440
011 (632) 521-7521, Ext. 2577 or 2220

PUERTO RICO
Veterans Administration Regional Office
U.S. Courthouse & Federal Bldg.
Carlos E. Chardon Street
San Juan, PR 00936

If you reside in the local telephone area of:
    Hato Rey ....(809)766-5141
All other Puerto Rico areas: 800-827-1000
Dial from U.S. Virgin Islands: 800-827-1000

RHODE ISLAND
Veterans Administration Regional Office
380 Westminister Mall
Providence, RI 02903

If you reside in the local telephone area of:
    Providence 273-7100
All other Rhode Island areas: 800-827-1000

SOUTH CAROLINA
Veterans Administration Regional Office
1801 Assembly Street
Columbia SC 29201

If you reside in the local telephone area of:
    Columbia 765-5861
All other South Carolina areas: 800-827-1000

SOUTH DAKOTA
Veterans Administration Regional Office
P.O. Box 5046
2501 W. 22nd Street
Sioux Falls SD 57117

If you reside in the local telephone area of:
    Sioux Falls 336-3496
All other South Dakota areas: 800-827-1000

TENNESSEE
Veterans Administration Regional Office
110-9th Avenue S
Nashville, TN 37203

If you reside in the local telephone area of:
    Nashville 736-5251
All other Tennessee areas: 800-827-1000

TEXAS
Veterans Administration Regional Office
6900 Almeda Rd.
Houston, TX 77030

Counties of Angelina, Aransas, Atascosa, Austin, Bandera, Bee, Bexar, Bianco, Brazoria, Brewster, Brooks, Caldwell, Calhoun, Cameron, Chambers, Colorado, Cormal, Crockett, DeWitt, Duval, Edwards, Fort Bend, Frio, Galveston, Gillispie, Goliad, Gonzales, Grimes, Guadalupe, Hardin, Harris, Hays, Hidalgo, Houston, Jackson, Jasper, Jefferson, Jim Hogg, Jim Wells, Karnes, Kendall, Kenedy, Kerr, Kimble, Kinney, Klebeg, LaSalle, Lavaca, Liberty, Live Oak, McCulloch, McMullen, Mason, Matagorda, Maverick, Medina, Menard, Montgomery, Nacogdoches, Newton, Nueces, Orange, Pecos, Poka, Real, Refugio, Sabine, San Augustine, San Jacinto, San Patrico, Schleicher, Shelby, Starr, Sutton, Terrell, Trinity, Tyler, Uvalde, Val Verde, Victoria, Walker, Waller, Washington, Webb, Wharton, Willacy, Wilson, Zapata, Zavala.

If you reside in the local telephone area of:
    Houston 664-4664
All other areas in the above counties: 800-827-1000

    Veterans Administration Regional Office
    1400 N. Valley Mills Drive, Waco, TX 76799

If you reside in the local telephone area of:
    Waco 772-3060
Bowie County served by:
    Bldg. 65, Ft. Roots North
    Little Rock, AR 72215 800-827-1000
All other counties served by Waco: 800-827-1000

UTAH
Veterans Administration Regional Office
Federal Building
P.O. Box 11500
125 S. State St.
Salt Lake City, UT 84147

If you reside in the local telephone area of:
    Salt Lake City 524-5960
All other Utah areas: 800-827-1000

VERMONT
Veterans Administration Regional Office
White River Junction, VT 05009

If you reside in the local telephone area of:
    White River Junction 296-5177
All other Vermont areas: 800-827-1000

VIRGINIA
Counties of Arlington and Fairfax and the cities of Alexandria, Fairfax, and Falls Church:
> Veterans Administration Regional Office
> 941 N. Capitol Street, NE
> Washington, DC 20421

If you reside in the above Virginia counties or cities: (202)418-4343

> Veterans Administration Regional Office
> 210 Franklin Road, SW
> Roanoke, VA 24011

If you reside in the local telephone area of:
> Roanoke 982-6440
All other Virginia areas: 800-827-1000

WASHINGTON
Veterans Administration Regional Office
Federal Building
915-2nd Avenue
Seattle, WA 98174

If you reside in the local telephone area of:
> Seattle 624-7200
All other Washington areas: 800-827-1000

WEST VIRGINIA
Counties of Brooke, Hancock, Marshall and Ohio served by:
> Veterans Administration Regional Office
> 1000 Liberty Avenue
> Pittsburgh. PA 15222

If you reside in the above counties: 800-827-1000

Remaining counties in West Virginia served by:
> Veterans Administration Regional Office
> 640 Fourth Avenue
> Huntington, WV 25701

If you reside in the local telephone area of:
> Huntington 529-5720
All other West Virginia areas: 800-827-1000

WISCONSIN
Veterans Administration Regional Office
5000 W. National Avenue
Bldg. 6
Milwaukee, WI 53295

If you reside in the local telephone area of:
> Milwaukee 383-8680
All other Wisconsin areas: 800-827-1000

WYOMING
Veterans Administration Regional Office
2360 E. Pershing Boulevard
Cheyenne, WY 82001

If you reside in the local telephone area of:
     Cheyenne 778-7396
All other Wyoming areas: 800-827-1000

Information You Need to Apply

The following information is always required when you apply for
VA benefits. You may want to enter the information here so that
it is readily available when you need it.

Veteran's Name: _____

Military Serial No.: _____

VA File No.: _____

Date of Birth: _____

Branch of Service: _____

Dates of Service: _____

Rank: _____

Social Security No.: _____

LISTING

Veterans Administration National Cemeteries

All national cemeteries operated by the Veterans Administration are listed below. If you need information on future cemeteries planned for your area or on which state veterans cemeteries in your area have available burial space, contact your local VA Regional Office.

Some of the cemeteries listed no longer have available space for casket burial (except for eligible survivors of family members already entered); however, they may have space for cremated remains in garden niches or in a columbarium (a structure of vaults lined with recesses for urns). Call or write directly to the cemetery for specific information on the availability of space for casket burial or cremated remains.

State Veteran Cemeteries: Several states have set aside cemeteries with financial assistance from the VA for the burial of veterans. Since space availability and eligibility varies from state to state, contact your local VA Regional Office for information concerning the cemeteries within your state. State veteran cemeteries can often provide an additional choice of location for burial in those cases where the VA National cemeteries in a state are full or are too far a distance from the deceased veteran's family.

Arlington National Cemetery in Virginia is under the jurisdiction of the Department of the Army. Grave space in this cemetery is limited to specific categories of military personnel and veterans except for cremated remains which may be placed in the columbarium. The categories of individuals eligible for burial are listed earlier in this chapter in the discussion of "Eligibility for Burial in Arlington National Cemetery."

ALABAMA

Mobile National Cemetery
1202 Virginia St.
Mobile, AL 36604
(Call Barrancas NC, FL for information)

Fort Mitchell National Cemetery
553 Highway 165
Seale, AL 36875
Tel: (205) 855-4731

ALASKA

Ft. Richardson National Cemetery
P.O. Box 5 - 498
Ft. Richardson, AK 99505
Tel: (907) 384-7075

Sitka National Cemetery
P.O. Box 1065
Sitka, AK 99835
(Call Ft. Richardson NC, AK for information)

ARIZONA
National Memorial Cemetery
of Arizona
23029 N. Cave Creek Rd.
Phoenix, AZ 85024
Tel: (602) 379-4615

Prescott National Cemetery
VA Medical Center
Prescott, AZ 86301
Tel: (602) 379-4615

ARKANSAS
Fayetteville National Cemetery
700 Government Ave.
Fayetteville, AR 72701
Tel: (501) 444-5051

Fort Smith National Cemetery
522 Garland Ave. & S. 6th St.
Fort Smith, AR 72901
Tel: (501) 783-5345

Little Rock National Cemetery
2523 Confederate Blvd.
Little Rock, AR 72206
Tel: (501) 324-6401

CALIFORNIA
Fort Rosecrans Nat'l. Cemetery
Point Loma, P.O. Box 6237
San Diego, CA 92166
Tel: (619) 553-2084

Golden Gate National Cemetery
1300 Sneath Lane
San Bruno, CA 94066
Tel: (415) 589-7737

Los Angeles National Cemetery
950 S. Sepulveda Blvd.
Los Angeles, CA 90049
Tel: (310) 824-4494

Riverside National Cemetery
22495 Van Buren Blvd.
Riverside, CA 92518
Tel: (909) 653-8417

San Joaquin Valley Nat'l. Cemetery
32053 W. McCabe Rd.
Gustine, CA 95322
Tel: (209) 854-1040

San Francisco National Cemetery
P.O. Box 29012
Presidio of San Francisco
San Francisco, CA 94129
Tel: (415) 561-2008

COLORADO
Fort Logan National Cemetery
3698 S. Sheridan Blvd.
Denver, CO 80235
Tel: (303) 761-0117

Fort Lyon National Cemetery
Veterans Admin. Medical Center
Fort Lyon, CO 81038
Tel: (719) 384-3152, ext. 231

FLORIDA
Barrancas National Cemetery
Naval Air Station
Pensacola, FL 32508
Tel: (904) 452-3357

Bay Pines National Cemetery
P.O. Box 477
Bay Pines, FL 33504
Tel: (813) 398-9426

Florida National Cemetery
6502 SW 102nd Ave.
Bushnell, FL 33513
Tel: (904) 793-7740

St. Augustine National Cemetery
104 Marine St.
St. Augustine, FL 32084
(Call Florida NC, FL for
information)

GEORGIA
Marietta National Cemetery
500 Washington Ave.
Marietta, GA 30060
Tel: (404) 428-5631

HAWAII
National Memorial Cemetery
of the Pacific
2177 Puowaina Dr.
Honolulu, HI 96813
Tel: (808) 556-1430

ILLINOIS
Alton National Cemetery
600 Pearl St.
Alton, IL 62003
(Call Jefferson Barracks NC, MO for information)

Camp Butler National Cemetery
R.R. #1
Springfield, IL 62707
Tel: (217) 522-5764

Danville National Cemetery
1900 East Main St.
Danville, IL 61832
Tel: (217) 431-6550

Mound City National Cemetery
Junction-Highway 37 & 51
Mound City, IL 62963
(Call Jefferson Barracks NC, MO for information.)

Quincy National Cemetery
36th & Maine Sts.
Quincy, IL 62301
(Call Rock Island NC, IL for information)

Rock Island Arsenal
P.O. Box 787
Moline, IL 61265
Tel: (309) 782-2094

INDIANA
Crown Hill National Cemetery
700 W. 38th St.
Indianapolis, IN 46208
(Call Marion NC, IN for information)

Marion National Cemetery
Veterans Admin Medical Center
Marion, IN 46952
Tel: (317) 674-0284

New Albany National Cemetery
1943 Ekin Avenue
New Albany, IN 47150
(Call Zachary Taylor NC, KY for information.)

IOWA
Keokuk National Cemetery
1701 J Street
Keokuk, IA 52632
Tel: (319) 524-1304

KANSAS
Ft Leavenworth Nat'l. Cemetery
P.O. Box 1694
Leavenworth, KS 66027
(Call Leavenworth NC, KS for information.)

Fort Scott National Cemetery
P.O. Box 917
Ft. Scott, KS 66701
Tel: (316) 223-2840

Leavenworth National Cemetery
P.O. Box 1694
Leavenworth, KS 66048
Tel: (913) 758-4105

KENTUCKY
Camp Nelson National Cemetery
6980 Danville Rd.
Nickolasville, KY 40356
Tel: (606) 885-5727

Cave Hill Nat'l. Cemetery
701 Baxter Ave.
Louisville, KY 40204
(Call Zachary Taylor NC, KY for information)

Danville National Cemetery
277 North First St.
Danville, KY 40442
(Call Camp Nelson NC, KY for information)

Lebanon National Cemetery
20 Highway 208
Lebanon, KY 40033
Tel: (502) 893-3852

Lexington National Cemetery
833 West Main St.
Lexington, KY 40508
(Call Camp Nelson NC, KY for information)

Mill Springs National Cemetery
R.R. #2, Box 172
Nancy, KY 42544
Tel: (606) 885-5727

Zachary Taylor National Cemetery
4701 Brownsboro Road
Louisville, KY 40207
Tel: (502) 893-3852

LOUISIANA
Alexandria National Cemetery
209 Shamrock Ave.,
Pineville, LA 71360
Tel: (318) 449-1793

Baton Rouge Nat'l. Cemetery
220 North 19th St.
Baton Rouge, LA 70806
*(Call Port Hudson NC, LA
for information)*

Port Hudson National Cemetery
20978 Port Hickey Rd.
Zachary, LA 70791
Tel: (504) 654-3767

MAINE
Togus National Cemetery
VA Medical and Regional
Office Center
Togus, ME 04330
*(Call Massachusetts NC, MA
for information)*

MARYLAND
Annapolis Nat'l. Cemetery
800 West St.
Annapolis, MD 21401
*(Call Baltimore NC, MD
for information)*

Baltimore National Cemetery
5501 Frederick Ave.
Baltimore, MD 21228
Tel: (410) 644-9696

Loudon Park Nat'l. Cemetery
3445 Frederick Ave.
Baltimore, MD 21228
*(Call Baltimore NC, ND
for information)*

MASSACHUSETTS
Massachusetts National
Cemetery
Bourne, MA 02532
Tel: (508) 563-7113

MICHIGAN
Fort Custer National Cemetery
15501 Dickman Road
Augusta, MI 49012
Tel: (616) 731-4164

MINNESOTA
Fort Snelling National Cemetery
7601 34th Avenue, South
Minneapolis, MN 55450
Tel: (612) 726-1127

MISSISSIPPI
Biloxi National Cemetery
P.O.Box 4968
Biloxi, MS 39535
Tel: (601) 388-6668

Corinth National Cemetery
1551 Horton St.
Corinth, MS 38834
Tel: (901) 386-8311

Natchez National Cemetery
41 Cemetery Rd.
Natchez, MS 39120
Tel: (601) 445-4981

MISSOURI
Jefferson Barracks
National Cemetery
2900 Sheridan Rd.
St. Louis, MO 63125
Tel: (314) 260-8691

Jefferson City Nat'l. Cemetery
1024 East McCarty St.
Jefferson City, MO 65101
*(Call Jefferson Barracks NC,
MO for information)*

Springfield National Cemetery
1702 E. Seminole St.
Springfield, MO 65804
Tel: (417) 881-9499

NEBRASKA
Fort McPherson Nat'l Cemetery
HCO 1, Box 67
Maxwell, NE 69151
Tel: (308) 582-4433

NEW JERSEY
Beverly National Cemetery
R.D. 1, Bridgeboro Rd.
Beverly, NJ 08010
Tel: (609) 877-5460

Finn's Point Nat'l. Cemetery
R.F.D. #3, Fort Mott Rd.
Box 542
Salem, NJ 08079
*(Call Beverly NC, NJ
for information)*

New Jersey Veterans
Memorial Cemetery
R.R. #1, Provinceline Road
Tel: (609) 758-7250
*(This cemetery has a special
section for burial of Jewish
veterans.)*

NEW MEXICO
Fort Bayard National Cemetery
P.O. Box 189
Fort Bayard, NM 88036
*(Call Fort Bliss NC, TX
for information)*

Santa Fe National Cemetery
501 N. Guadalupe St.
Box 88, Santa Fe, NM 87504
Tel: (505) 988-6400

NEW YORK
Bath National Cemetery
VA Medical Center
Bath. NY 14810
Tel: (607) 776-2111, Ext. 1293

Calverton National Cemetery
210 Princeton Blvd.
Calverton, NY 11933
Tel: (516) 727-5410 or 5770

Cypress Hills Nat'l. Cemetery
625 Jamaica Ave.
Brooklyn, NY 11208
*(Call Long Island NC, NY
for information)*

Long Island Nat'l. Cemetery
Farmingdale, L.I., NY 11735
Tel: (516) 454-4949

Woodlawn National Cemetery
1825 Davis St.
Elmira, NY 14901
*(Call Bath NC, NY for
information)*

NORTH CAROLINA
New Bern National Cemetery
1711 National Ave.
New Bern, NC 28560
Tel: (919) 637-2912

Raleigh National Cemetery
501 Rock Quarry Rd.
Raleigh, NC 27610
Tel: (919) 832-0144

Salisbury National Cemetery
202 Government Rd.
Salisbury, NC 28144
Tel: (704) 636-2661

Wilmington National Cemetery
2011 Market St.
Wilmington, NC 28403
Tel: (919) 637-2912

OHIO
Dayton National Cemetery
VA Medical Center
4100 W. Third St.
Dayton, OH 45428
Tel: (513) 262-2115

OKLAHOMA
Fort Gibson Nat'l. Cemetery
Rt. 2, Box 47
Fort Gibson, OK 74434
Tel: (918) 478-2334

OREGON
Eagle Point National Cemetery
2763 Riley Road
Eagle Point, OR 97524
Tel: (503) 826-2511

Roseburg National Cemetery VA
Medical Center
Roseburg, OR 97470
(Call (503) 273-5250
for information)

Willamette Nat'l. Cemetery
11800 SE Mt. Scott Blvd.
P.O. Box 66147
Portland, OR 97266
Tel: (503) 273-5250

PENNSYLVANIA
Indiantown Gap Nat'l. Cemetery
R.R. 2, Box 484
Annville, PA 17003
Tel: (717) 865-5254

Philadelphia Nat'l. Cemetery
Haines Street & Limekiln Pike
Philadelphia, PA 19138
(Call Beverly NC, NJ
for information)

PUERTO RICO
Puerto Rico National Cemetery
P.O. Box 1298
Bayamon, PR 00961
Tel: (809) 785-7281

SOUTH CAROLINA
Beaufort National Cemetery
1601 Boundary St.
Beaufort, SC 29902
Tel: (803) 524-3925

Florence National Cemetery
803 E. National Cemetery Rd.
Florence, SC 29501
Tel: (803) 669-8783

SOUTH DAKOTA
Black Hills National Cemetery
P.O. Box 640
Sturgis, SD 57785
Tel: (605) 347-3830

Fort Meade Nat'l. Cemetery
VA Medical Center
Fort Meade, SD 57785
(Call Black Hills NC, SD
for information)

Hot Springs Nat'l. Cemetery
VA Medical Center
Hot Springs, SD 57747
Tel: (605) 347-3830

TENNESSEE
Chattanooga National Cemetery
1200 Bailey Ave.
Chattanooga, TN 37404
Tel: (615) 855-6590

Knoxville National Cemetery
939 Tyson Street, NW
Knoxville, TN 37917
Tel: (615) 461-7935

Memphis National Cemetery
3568 Townes Ave.
Memphis, TN 38122
Tel: (901) 386-8311

Mountain Home Nat'l. Cemetery
P.O. Box 8
Mountain Home, TN 37684
Tel: (615) 461-7935

Nashville National Cemetery
1420 Gallatin Road South
Madison, TN 37115
Tel: (615) 327-5360

TEXAS
Fort Bliss National Cemetery
P.O. Box 6342
Fort Bliss, TX 79906
Tel: (915) 564-0201

Ft. Sam Houston Nat'l. Cemetery
1520 Harry Wurzbach Rd.
San Antonio, TX 78209
Tel: (210) 820-3891

Houston National Cemetery
10410 Veterans Memorial Dr.
Houston, TX 77038
Tel: (713) 447-8686

Kerrville National Cemetery
VA Medical Center
3600 Memorial Blvd.
Kerrville, TX 78028
Tel: (210) 820-3891

San Antonio Nat'l. Cemetery
517 Paso Hondo St.
San Antonio, TX 78202
*(Call Fort Sam Houston NC, TX
for information)*

VIRGINIA

Alexandria Nat'l. Cemetery
1450 Wilkes St.
Alexandria, VA 22314
*(Call Culpeper NC, VA
for information)*

Balls Bluff Nat'l. Cemetery
Leesburg, VA 22075
*(Call Culpeper NC, VA
for information)*

City Point National Cemetery
10th Ave. and Davis St.
Hopewell, VA 23860
(Call Richmond NC, VA for information)

Cold Harbor Nat'l. Cemetery
Rt. 156 North
Mechanicsville, VA 23111
*(Call Richmond NC, VA
for information)*

Culpeper National Cemetery
305 U.S. Avenue
Culpeper, VA 22701
Tel: (540) 825-0027

Danville National Cemetery
721 Lee St.
Danville, VA 24541
*(Call Salisbury NC,
VA for information)*

Fort Harrison Nat'l. Cemetery
8620 Varina Road
Richmond, VA 23231
*(Call Richmond NC, VA
for information)*

Glendale National Cemetery
8301 Willis Church Rd.
Richmond, VA 23231
*(Call Richmond NC, VA
for information)*

Hampton National Cemetery
Cemetery Rd. at Marshall Ave.
Hampton, VA 23667
Tel: (804) 723-7104

Hampton National Cemetery
VA Medical Center
Hampton, VA 23667
*(Call Hampton NC at Cemetery
Rd. for information)*

Quantico National Cemetery
P.O. Box 10, Triangle, VA 22172
Tel: (703) 690-2217

Richmond National Cemetery
1701 Williamsburg Rd.
Richmond, VA 23231
Tel: (804) 222-1490

Seven Pines Nat'l. Cemetery
400 East Williamsburg Rd.
Sandston, VA 23150
*(Call Richmond NC, VA
for information)*

Staunton National Cemetery
901 Richmond Ave.
Staunton, VA 24401
*(Call Culpeper NC, VA
for information)*

Winchester National Cemetery
401 National Ave.
Winchester, VA 22601
(Call Culpeper NC, VA for
information)

WEST VIRGINIA
  Grafton National Cemetery
  431 Walnut St.,
  Grafton, WV 26354
  Tel: (304) 265-2044

  West Virginia Nat'l. Cemetery
  Route 2, P.O. Box 127
  Pruntytown, WV 26354
  Tel: (304) 265-2044

WISCONSIN
  Wood National Cemetery
  5000 W. Nat'l. Ave., Bldg. #1301
  Milwaukee, WI 53295
  Tel: (414) 382-5300

VETERANS WHO GAVE SO MUCH — INCLUDING THEIR LIVES — FOR OUR NATION . . .

World War I
  (1917-1918)
Participants **4,744,000**
Deaths in Service...**116,000**

World War II
  (9/16/40 thru 7/25/47)
Participants **16,535,000**
Deaths in Service...**406,000**

Korean Conflict
  (6/27/50 thru 1/31/55)
Participants **6,807,000**
Deaths in Service...**55,000**

Vietnam Era
  (8/5/64 thru 5/7/75)
Participants **9,200,000**
Deaths in Service...**109,000**

Persian Gulf War
  (Starting date is 8/2/90 thru date to be determined)
Participants **2,038,341**
Deaths in Service...**3,115**

Chapter 10

Special Services and Programs

What They Can Mean to You

Chapter Highlights

Special Services and Programs

Reaching out to the Nation

As you have seen, there are many government programs to assist older Americans. However, because the government does not have a big advertising budget, these programs often go unnoticed by the very people they were designed to help. Therefore, it becomes the task of the informed to spread the word about the government's work: which is one of the main reasons this book was written.

In addition to the many government programs discussed in earlier chapters, numerous other programs sponsored by government and private nonprofit organizations are reaching out to improve the lives of millions of elderly and handicapped Americans. Continuing this book's mandate — to keep you informed — this chapter describes some of these special programs and services.

It is my ultimate goal that you, the reader, will become a missionary . . . by spreading the word about what you read here, possibly improving the lives of others.

AREA AGENCIES ON AGING

Created in 1973 under the Older Americans Act, the Area Agencies on Aging address the specific needs and concerns of *all* Americans over 60. As the third member of the government's "aging network" — which also includes the federal Administration on Aging (AOA) and the state offices or commissions on aging (offices also exist for D.C. and the U.S. territories) — each of the 670 Area Agencies on Aging throughout the U.S. is responsible for a single city, county, or multicounty district.

Because the Area Agencies on Aging have different official names from locality to locality, you should contact your state's Office/Commission on Aging for the address and telephone number of the Agency that serves your community. A listing of these state offices follows this discussion.

Funded by the Older Americans Act, state and local governments, and private contributions, each Area Agency on Aging provides services — directly and indirectly — that are tailored to the needs of its particular community. Most Agency services are **indirect**; that is, the Agencies plan the services, then contract with organizations that can provide them — such as state and local government, area businesses, charities, and other nonprofit organizations. Thus, the Agencies develop a local system of social and nutritional support for elderly individuals. In addition, the Agencies act as **direct** sources of information about the referrals to the service they sponsor, and any other services available in their area.

Most services provided through your local Area Agency on Aging are **free**; others have a very minimal charge. To continue providing such services, the Area Agencies on Aging heartily welcome contributions from private or corporate donors.

While the specific services they provide vary from area to area, all Agencies on Aging provide:

■ **In-Home Services** — these may include:

— Home-delivered meals (known as "meals-on-wheels") which help older people maintain an adequate diet
— Homemaker and chore services, including light housekeeping, laundry, shopping, errands, and meal preparation
— In-home health and personal care
— Daily visits or phone calls to elderly persons who live alone
— Support services, like counseling and rehabilitation
— Respite care to relieve normal caregivers for short periods each day
— Home maintenance, repairs, and weatherization for those who are unable or cannot afford to take care of their homes.

- **Community Services** — these may include:
  - Multi-purpose Senior Centers
  - Adult day care
  - Communal meals
  - Adult protective services for elderly persons abused by others in their household
  - Legal aid and tax assistance
  - Counseling on available community services
  - Recreation and rehabilitation
  - Employment services, including job training and job search assistance

- **Access Services** — In addition to its role as clearinghouse for information and referrals in a community, the Agency may provide services like:
  - Transportation of older people to nutrition and meal sites, medical appointments, and shopping areas
  - Individual case management
  - Assistance finding housing alternatives in the community, such as "housemate" matching services
  - Outreach programs for needy Seniors who may be eligible for Supplemental Security Income, Medicaid, Food Stamps, and other programs designed to aid the elderly.

- **Services for Individuals in Long-Term Care Facilities** — these may include:
  - Individual counseling in the facility
  - Case work
  - Visitation
  - Escorts to activities outside the facility
  - Transportation of handicapped Seniors to services outside the facility
  - Ombudsman services to help ensure proper care of individuals in the facility, and to help resolve complaints about the facility or care received.

GET TO KNOW YOUR AREA AGENCY ON AGING

There is no way to adequately describe all the invaluable services and assistance provided by your Area Agency on Aging. The best way for you to learn about all your Area Agency has to offer is to call it, even if you don't need its help now. Above all, make sure to have your name put on the Agency's newsletter mailing list — this newsletter is one of the best sources of information about community services programs, and activities for the elderly, as well as a forum for advice and information directed to older people. Get to know your Area Agency on Aging now . . . **it is there to help you!**

Caregivers . . .

The Area Agencies on Aging are valuable sources of information for you as well as the older person you are caring for . . . take full advantage of the assistance they so willingly offer to caregivers of their parents or other Senior people.

LISTING

State Commissions and Offices on Aging

Correctly referred to as the State Units on Aging, the titles of these state organizations vary considerably. Most frequently, they are called commissions or offices. They were established with the passage of the Older Americans Act and are responsible at the state level for the administration and coordination of the many programs, services and assistance provided by this Act. The State Offices and Commissions on Aging work closely with the various local Area Agencies on Aging in their states. The Area Agencies on Aging are the offices that serve and assist you at the local level.

Call or write your state office or commission to find out which **Area Agency on Aging** serves your area, as well as to obtain information on any services or assistance provided at the state level for older Americans. Become familiar with the Area Agency that serves your community. If you feel that your own community does not provide certain needed services, or that inadequate services are being provided, you should promptly advise your state office.

ALABAMA
Commission on Aging
770 Washington Ave., Suite 470
Montgomery, AL 36130
Tel: (205) 242-5743
Toll Free: 800-243-5463

ALASKA
Older Alaskans Commission
P.O. Box 110209
Juneau, AK 99811
Tel: (907) 465-3250

AMERICAN SAMOA
Territorial Administration on
Aging, Office of the Governor
Pago Pago, AS 96799
Tel: 011 (684) 633-1252

ARIZONA
Aging & Adult Administration
1789 W. Jefferson St.
Phoenix, AZ 85007
Tel: (602) 542-4446
    (602) 255-3323 (TDD)

ARKANSAS
Division of Aging & Adult
Services
1417 Donaghey Plaza South
P.O. Box 1437/Slot 1412
Little Rock, AR 72203
Tel: (501) 682-2441

CALIFORNIA
  Department of Aging
  1600 K Street
  Sacramento, CA 95814
  Tel: (916) 322-3887
       (916) 323-8913 (TDD)

COLORADO
  Aging & Adult Services Div.
  Dept. of Social Services
  1575 Sherman Street, 4th Floor
  Denver, CO 80203
  Tel: (303) 866-3851

CONNECTICUT
  Elderly Services Division
  175 Main Street
  Hartford, CT 06106
  Tel: (203) 566-7772
  Toll Free 800-443-9946 (V/TDD)

DELAWARE
  Division on Aging
  Dept. of Health & Social
  Services/2nd Floor
  1901 DuPont Highway
  New Castle, DE 19720
  Tel: (302) 577-4791

DISTRICT OF COLUMBIA
  Office on Aging
  441 - 4th Street, NW
  9th Floor
  Washington, DC 20001
  Tel: (202) 724-5622

FLORIDA
  Dept. of Elder Affairs
  1317 Winewood Blvd., Rm. 317
  Tallahassee, FL 32399
  Tel: (904) 922-5297

GEORGIA
  Division of Aging Services
  2 Peachtree St., NW
  Rm 18.403
  Atlanta, GA 30303
  Tel: (404) 657-5258

GUAM
  Division of Senior Citizens
  Dept. of Public Health
  and Social Services
  Government of Guam
  P.O. Box 2816
  Agana, GU 96910
  Tel: 011 (671) 632-4141

HAWAII
  Executive Office on Aging
  Office of the Governor
  335 Merchant St., Rm. 241
  Honolulu, HI 96813
  Tel: (808) 586-0100

IDAHO
  Office on Aging
  Room 108-Statehouse
  Boise, ID 83720
  Tel: (208) 334-3833

ILLINOIS
  Dept on Aging
  421 E. Capitol Ave.
  Springfield, IL 62701
  Tel: (217) 785-3356

INDIANA
  Div. of Aging & Home Services
  402 W. Washington St.
  P.O. Box 7083
  Indianapolis, IN 46207
  Tel: (317) 232-7020
  Toll Free: 800-545-7763

IOWA
  Dept of Elder Affairs
  Suite 236, Jewett Bldg.
  914 Grand Ave.
  Des Moines, IA 50309
  Tel: (515) 281-5187

KANSAS
  Dept on Aging
  Docking State Office Bldg, 150-S
  915 Southwest Harrison St.
  Topeka, KS 66612
  Tel: (913) 296-4986

KENTUCKY
Division for Aging Services
Cabinet for Human Resources
275 E. Main Street
5th Floor, West
Frankfort, KY 40621
Tel: (502) 564-6930
    (502) 564-5497 (TDD)

LOUISIANA
Office of Elderly Affairs
4550 N. Boulevard
P.O. Box 80374
Baton Rouge, LA 70896
Tel: (504) 925-1700

MAINE
Bureau of Elderly and Adult
Services
35 Anthony Ave., Station 11
Augusta, ME 04333
Tel: (207) 624-5335

MARYLAND
Office on Aging
State Office Building
301 W. Preston St., Rm. 1004
Baltimore, MD 21201
Tel: (410) 225-1102
    (410) 383-7555 (TDD)

MASSACHUSETTS
Executive Office of
Elder Affairs
1 Ashburton Place, 5th Floor
Boston, MA 02108
Tel: (617) 727-7750
Toll Free: 800-882-2003
        800-872-0166 (TDD)

MICHIGAN
Office of Services to the Aging
611 W. Ottawa Street
Lansing, MI 48909
Tel: (517) 373-8230

MINNESOTA
Board on Aging
Human Services Building
444 Lafayette Road, 4th Floor
St. Paul, MN 55155
Tel: (612) 296-2770

MISSISSIPPI
Div. of Aging & Adult Services
750 N. State Street
Jackson, MS 39202
Tel: (601) 359-4929
Toll Free: 800-948-3090

MISSOURI
Division of Aging
615 Howerton Court
P.O. Box 1337
Jefferson City, MO 65102
Tel: (314) 751-3082

MONTANA
Office on Aging
48 N. Last Chance Gulch
P.O. Box 8005
Helena, MT 59620
Tel: (406) 444-5900
Toll Free: 800-332-2272

NEBRASKA
Dept on Aging
P.O. Box 95044
301 Centennial Mall-South
Lincoln, NE 68509
Tel: (402) 471-2306

NEVADA
Div. for Aging Services
Dept. of Human Resources
340 N. 11th St., Suite 114
Las Vegas, NV 89101
Tel: (702) 486-3545

NEW HAMPSHIRE
Division of Elderly &
Adult Services
State Office Park South
115 Pleasant Street
Annex Building No. 1
Concord, NH 03301
Tel: (603) 271-4680

NEW JERSEY
Division on Aging
Dept. of Community Affairs
101 South Broad Street CN807
Trenton, NJ 08625
Tel: (609) 984-3951
Toll Free: 800-792-8820

NEW MEXICO
State Agency on Aging
224 E. Palace Ave., 1st Fl.
La Villa Rivera Bldg.
Santa Fe, NM 87501
Tel: (505) 827-7640 (V/TDD)
Toll Free: 800-432-2080

NEW YORK
Office for the Aging
Agency Bldg. #2, ESP
Albany, NY 12223
Tel: (518) 474-5731 (V/TDD)
Toll Free: 800-342-9871

NORTH CAROLINA
Division of Aging
693 Palmer Dr.
Caller Box 29531
Raleigh, NC 27626
Tel: (919) 733-3983

NORTH DAKOTA
Aging Services
Dept. of Human Services
State Capitol Bldg.
P.O. Box 7070
Bismarck, ND 58507
Tel: (701) 328-2577
Toll Free: 800-755-8521

NORTHERN MARIANA ISLANDS
Office of Aging, Dept. of
Community & Cultural Affairs,
Civic Center—Susupe Saipan,
Northern Mariana Islands 96950
Tel: (607) 234-6011

OHIO
Department of Aging
50 W. Broad Street, 5th Floor
Columbus, OH 43215
Tel: (614) 466-1221
    (614) 466-6191 (TDD)
Toll Free: 800-282-1206

OKLAHOMA
Aging Services Division
312 NE 28th Street
P.O. Box 25352
Oklahoma City, OK 73125
Tel: (405) 521-2327
    (405) 521-2327 (TDD)

OREGON
Senior Services Division
500 Summer St., NE, 2nd Floor
Salem, OR 97310
Tel: (503) 945-5811
Toll Free: 800-232-3020

PENNSYLVANIA
Department of Aging
400 Market Street
Harrisburg, PA 17101
Toll Free: 800-783-7067

PUERTO RICO
Governors Office of Elderly
Affairs/Gericulture Commission
Box 11398
Santurce, PR 00910
Tel: (809) 722-2429

RHODE ISLAND
Dept. of Elderly Affairs
160 Pine Street
Providence, RI 02903
Tel: (401) 277-2858 (V/TDD)

SOUTH CAROLINA
Division on Aging
202 Arbor Lake Drive, Suite 301
Columbia, SC 29223
Tel: (803) 737-7500

SOUTH DAKOTA
Office of Adult Services & Aging
700 Governors Drive
Pierre, SD 57501
Tel: (605) 773-3656

TENNESSEE
Commission on Aging
Andrew Jackson Bldg.
500 Deaderick St., 9th Fl.
Nashville, TN 37243
Tel: (615) 741-2056

TEXAS
Department on Aging
P.O. Box 12786,
1949 IH 35 South
Austin, TX 78741
Tel: (512) 444-2727 (V/TDD)
Toll Free: 800-252-9240

TRUST TERRITORY OF THE PACIFIC
Office of Elderly Programs
Community Development Div.
Government of TTPI
Saipan, Mariana Islands 96950
Tel: (670) 9335 or 9336

UTAH
Division of Aging and Adult
Services
120 North 200 West
P.O. Box 45500
Salt Lake City, UT 84103
Toll Free: 800-606-0608

VERMONT
Dept. of Aging & Disabilities
103 S. Main Street
Waterbury, VT 05671
Tel: (802) 241-2400

VIRGINIA
Department for the Aging
700 E. Franklin St., 10th Floor
Richmond, VA 23219
Tel: (804) 225-2271 (V/TDD)

VIRGIN ISLANDS
Senior Citizen Affairs Div.
Dept. of Human Services
19 Estate Diamond
Fredericksted
St. Croix, VI 00840
Tel: (809) 772-0930

WASHINGTON
Aging & Adult Services
Administration, OB44A
12th and Jefferson Sts.
Olympia, WA 98504
Tel: (206) 586-3768
    (206) 753-4927 (TDD)

WEST VIRGINIA
Commission on Aging
Holly Grove—State Capitol
1900 Kanawha Blvd., East
Charleston, WV 25305
Tel: (304) 558-3317

WISCONSIN
Board on Aging and
    Long-Term Care
214 N. Hamilton Street
Madison, WI 53703
Tel: (608) 266-8944
Toll Free: 800-242-1060

WYOMING
Division on Aging
Hathaway Bldg., Room 139
2300 Capitol Ave.
Cheyenne, WY 82002
Tel: (307) 777-7986
Toll Free: 800-442-2766

ASSISTANCE FOR THE HANDICAPPED

Although this book was specifically written to inform older Americans about the many government assistance programs and benefits available to them, it was also intended to emphasize those programs available to our nation's handicapped, blind and disabled individuals. As noted in previous chapters, there are numerous federal programs that provide direct and often continuing assistance to disabled individuals. In review, these include:

- Social Security disability insurance benefits
- Supplemental Security Income (SSI) monthly payments
- Medicare and Medicaid, which can provide medical assistance
- Food Stamps to help provide a more nutritious diet
- Veterans' special programs for the disabled
- Various housing and employment programs that give preference to the handicapped
- Federal tax benefits

. . . and several other federal government programs described in Chapter 1 that greatly benefit handicapped people.

Because a large part of the federal funds for services for the handicapped are distributed to the states, which then determine how to spend the money and what programs they will provide, there are many more federal programs of assistance administered by the state. In addition, each state and its local governments provide other services that they finance from their own resources.

State and local programs change considerably from one year to the next — new ones begin and old ones are modified or dissolved. Consequently, it would be impossible to describe all the state and local programs that help the handicapped. Unfortunately, the job of locating the services and assistance for the handicapped in your area falls to you. However, many resources within your reach, such as your local Area Agency on Aging and Human Services Information office, government agencies and voluntary organizations, will help you find the services that you need. This discussion includes a listing of several helpful resources, as well as some special services provided by the government and nonprofit organizations which could add immeasurably to your life.

HELPING PEOPLE HELP THEMSELVES: VOCATIONAL/REHABILITATION AGENCIES

Using state revenues and matching federal funds, a State Vocational and Rehabilitation Agency fulfills its mandate to help the blind, deaf and handicapped become employable and retain their dignity, self-respect and independence. Through these agencies, most states also aid individuals whose handicaps are too severe for them to undertake any type of employment by providing "independent living training," a series of special programs to help them learn the skills they need to live as independently as possible.

Each agency provides a range of services and training according to the state's resources; the financial assistance the agencies provide can vary widely — even within a state. In states with sufficient resources, the agencies operate units which deal specifically with services for the blind, the deaf and those with communication disorders. The staffs of these units also act as consultants to regular vocational rehabilitation counselors throughout the state. In those states that do not have separate units for the blind or deaf, these services are provided through the agency's regular offices.

ELIGIBILITY

Before a disabled person can receive assistance, a rehabilitation counselor must review his/her case to determine whether employment is probable after rehabilitation. If the applicant's disabilities will prevent him/her from entering the labor market, the counselor determines whether the applicant should receive independent living training. State vocational and rehabilitation agencies charge no application fee nor do they charge for any service provided to applicants to determine eligibility for agency programs. However, once they are determined to be eligible, applicants may be asked to contribute to the cost of some services if they are financially able to do so. Individuals who cannot pay are never denied services.

After the agency counselor determines which services the individual should receive, the counselor and the handicapped person work together to plan a program designed specifically to meet that person's needs. Each counselor's goal is to help build upon an individual's **abilities** and the individual's potential existing skills **rather** than just trying to deemphasize the individual's **disabilities!**

During an individual's evaluation and participation in any rehabilitation program, the agency may provide a variety of services, such as:

- A medical examination (physical and/or psychological) to determine the extent of disability, suitability for employment and what medical help may be required;

- A vocational evaluation to identify skills and abilities, an appropriate occupation and the services necessary for the applicant to achieve his/her maximum potential;

- Counseling and guidance to help the individual meet reasonable expectations;

- Medical help to reduce or remove a disability and improve or restore job performance. This help may include medical, surgical, psychiatric, and/or hospital services. It may also include artificial limbs, braces, hearing aids and eyeglasses needed on the job;

- Vocational training at trade schools, rehabilitation centers or at home;

- Educational assistance, which may include payment of college tuition, fees and other educational expenses, if a college education is required to enable the individual to earn a livelihood;

- Financial assistance during the period of rehabilitation; this assistance includes room and board, transportation, and other necessary help;

- Referral and job placement services to help the individual secure suitable employment;

- On-the-job help, which may include paying expenses related to the job, such as purchasing occupational licenses, tools, equipment and supplies;

- Telecommunications, sensory and other aids and devices.

THESE PROGRAMS CAN CHANGE YOUR LIFE — SO APPLY NOW!

If you are blind, deaf, or handicapped it behooves you to take advantage of your state agency's invaluable programs. It costs you nothing to apply if you are determined to be ineligible for the agency's services. If you have any difficulty locating the State Vocational/Rehabilitation Agency regional office near you, contact the central office of the state agency (a listing is provided at the end of this section). They will set up your appointment with a rehabilitation counselor or, if necessary, arrange for the counselor to visit you at home, to help you apply and to conduct the eligibility evaluation.

NONPROFIT SOURCES OF ASSISTANCE

In addition to the various government programs for the disabled, blind, and hearing-impaired, numerous private organizations at the national, state and local level provide numerous services to the handicapped. These services include:

- products and aids
- information, publications, and recordings
- rehabilitation services
- financial assistance programs
- recreational and social activities.

Most of these nonprofit organizations are supported predominantly by contributions from their members and donations from individuals interested in their causes. Some organizations also receive federal and/or state grants which enable them to continue their work or to fund specific projects. However, most of these organizations rely solely on the generosity of individuals.

Without the assistance of these organizations and that of the hundreds of local volunteer groups throughout the country, many handicapped people would not be able to work or even live a full, meaningful life.

The following organizations provide assistance to the handicapped in America. Call or write to those of interest to you for further information on their services and membership.

ORGANIZATIONS THAT ASSIST THE PHYSICALLY OR MENTALLY DISABLED

Disabled American Veterans
807 Maine Avenue, SW
Washington, DC 20024
Tel: (202) 554-3501

National Foundation of Dentistry for the Handicapped
1600 Stout Street, Suite 1420
Denver, CO 80202
Tel: (303) 298-9650

The National Foundation of Dentistry for the Handicapped sponsors a special free program of dental care donated by volunteer dentists for needy elderly and handicapped persons. The Foundation currently operates in California (San Francisco Bay area only), Colorado, Illinois, Indiana Louisiana, Maryland, New Jersey, New York (upstate area only) Oregon, Pennsylvania, Rhode Island, with plans to expand to other states. Contact the Foundation for information on this program and its availability in your state, or for information on dental care and hygiene for the handicapped.

National Organization on Disability
910 - 16th St., NW, Suite 600
Washington, DC 20006
Tel: (202) 293-5960
     (202) 293-5968 TDD

National Rehabilitation Information Center (NARIC)
8455 Colesville Road, Suite 935
Silver Spring, MD 20910
Tel: (301) 588-9284
Toll Free: 800-346-2742

National Self-Help Clearinghouse
25 W. 43rd St.,
Room 620
New York, NY 10036
Tel: (212) 642-2944

National Spinal Cord Injury Association
600 West Cummings Park, Suite 2000
Woburn, MA 01801
Toll Free: 800-962-9629

Paralyzed Veterans of America
National Office, 801-18th Street, NW
Washington, DC 20006
Tel: (202) 872-1300
Toll Free: 800-424-8200

ORGANIZATIONS FOR THE BLIND
AND VISUALLY-IMPAIRED

American Council of the Blind
1155 15th St., NW, Suite 720
Washington, DC 20005
Tel: (202) 467-5081
Toll Free: 800-424-8666

American Foundation for the Blind, Inc.
15 West 16th Street
New York, NY 10011
Tel: (212) 620-2000
Toll Free: 800-232-5463

Association for the Education and Rehabilitation of the Blind and Visually Impaired
206 North Washington Street, Suite 320
Alexandria, VA 22314
Tel: (703) 548-1884

Lions Clubs International
300 22nd Street
Oak Brook, IL 60521
Tel: (708) 571-5466

National Association for the Visually Handicapped, Inc.
22 W. 21st Street
New York, NY 10010
Tel: (212) 889-3141

National Federation of the Blind
1800 Johnson Street
Baltimore, MD 21230
Tel: (410) 659-9314

National Society to Prevent Blindness
500 East Remington Road
Schaumburg, IL 60173
Tel: (708) 843-2020

Vision Foundation, Inc.
818 Mt. Auburn Street
Watertown, MA 02172
Tel: (617) 926-4232

The Vision Foundation was formed specifically for individuals — particularly the elderly — who are not blind, but who have vision impairments. Their mandate is to help the visually-impaired adjust to their impairments, obtain information, and meet locally with others who have similar problems.

ORGANIZATIONS FOR THE DEAF AND HEARING-IMPAIRED

Alexander Graham Bell Association for the Deaf
3417 Volta Place, NW
Washington, DC 20007
Tel: (202) 337-5220 (voice/TDD)

American Speech-Language-Hearing Association
10801 Rockville Pike
Rockville, MD 20852
Tel: (301) 897-5700 (voice/TDD)
Toll Free: 800-638-8255 (voice/TDD)

National Association of the Deaf
814 Thayer Avenue
Silver Spring, MD 20910
Tel: (301) 587-1788 (voice)
      (301) 587-1789 (TDD)

National Information Center on Deafness
Gallaudet University, 800 Florida Avenue, NE
Washington, DC 20002
Tel: (202) 651-5051 (voice)
      (202) 651-5052 (TDD)

Self-Help for Hard of Hearing People, Inc. (SHHH)
7800 Wisconsin Avenue
Bethesda, MD 20814
Tel: (301) 657-2248
      (301) 657-2249 (TDD)

Telecommunications for the Deaf, Inc. (TDI)
8719 Colesville Road, Rm. 300
Silver Spring, MD 20910
Tel: (301) 589-3006 (TDD)
      (301) 589-3786 (voice)

ORGANIZATIONS WHICH DISTRIBUTE RECORDINGS AND LARGE-PRINT MATERIALS FOR THE BLIND AND VISUALLY-IMPAIRED

Associated Services for the Blind
919 Walnut Street, 2nd Floor
Philadelphia, PA 19107
Tel: (215) 627-0600

Recording for the Blind, Inc.
20 Roszel Road
Princeton, NJ 08540
Tel: (609) 452-0606

American Printing House for the Blind
P.O. Box 6085
Louisville, KY 40206
Tel: (502) 895-2405

HELP FROM "MAN'S BEST FRIEND": CANINE COMPANIONS FOR THE ELDERLY, DEAF, AND HANDICAPPED

Most of us have watched blind men and women and their seeing-eye dogs on their way to work, a restaurant, a store, or a park. Thousands of these highly-trained animals — correctly known as **guide dogs** — ensure that their mistresses and masters get where they want to go, guiding them safely through traffic and around all sorts of obstacles that sighted people take for granted. In this way, guide dogs help blind individuals lead independent, active, and productive lives.

Recently, thanks to a small but growing nonprofit organization, **Canine Companions for Independence** (CCI), man's best friend is now helping sighted people whose handicaps, disabilities, deafness, or age makes them ideal candidates for the assistance of specially-trained dogs. CCI breeds, raises, and trains dogs to perform specific functions like helping maneuver or pull wheelchairs for the handicapped, or listening for noises and sounds and alerting their deaf masters/mistresses to possible danger. These are just a few of the numerous signaling and hearing, social and service activities performed by these remarkable animals.

CCI's investment of $8,000 per dog to prepare their canine companions to perform their particular tasks is almost completely met by the generosity of the public. The organization offers these dogs to those who need their services for a mere $125, which CCI charges not to help meet their costs so much as to ensure the sincerity of the requester and his/her ability to feed and care for the animal.

If you are interested in obtaining more information about CCI and the availability of canine companions (there is a waiting list), call or write to:

> Canine Companions for Independence
> P.O. Box 446
> Santa Rosa, CA 95402
> Tel: (707) 577-1700
> Toll Free: 800-767-2275

If you want information about how to obtain a guide dog for the blind, call or write to:

> Guide Dog Foundation for the Blind
> 371 East Jericho Turnpike
> Smithtown, NY 11787
> Tel: (516) 265-2121
> Toll Free: 800-548-4337

CLOSED-CAPTIONING SERVICE FOR THE HEARING IMPAIRED

Television is America's number one form of entertainment. But, for those who can't hear what is being said on TV, the pleasure of watching is greatly diminished . . . if not eliminated. For many of the over 21 million Americans with hearing impairments, over two million of whom are estimated to be profoundly deaf, TV programs would in the past have been frustratingly incomprehensible. Yet, today, hearing impaired people watch about as much TV as the rest of the population.

Thanks to a process called *closed captioning*, individuals with hearing impairments can now fully enjoy the entertainment offered by television. Closed captioning involves the translation of the audio portion of the TV broadcast into captions (or subtitles) which are then projected at the bottom of the TV screen or whatever location prevents them from obstructing the view of the action. Broadcast on a special frequency, these captions can only be seen when the viewer activates the caption decoding unit, or adapter, connected to the television set.

Because a decoder is required to receive closed captioning, TV channels can broadcast the same programs for everyone. Those who hear clearly do not have to be bothered by unnecessary captions, while the hearing impaired, by simply switching on their adapter and reading the closed captions, can understand all of what is happening on screen.

Established in 1979, the National Captioning Institute (NCI) has become the leading supplier of this valuable service for the hearing impaired. Each year, the number of viewers who use this service increases by thousands — resulting in an ever-growing demand for programs that are closed captioned. Currently, about 175 hours each week of closed captioned TV programming is broadcast by the major networks and PBS and about 275 hours on cable networks.

Over the years, NCI has not only improved the adapter — called the *TeleCaption 4000* — but has provided closed captions for almost every type of TV program, including movies, news, sports, educational, religious, and children's programming. NCI has also developed the technology to caption "live" programs as they take place. Such live closed captioned broadcasts include football games, the Emmy Awards, presidential speeches and press conferences, and the Olympics. In addition to closed captioning for ABC, CBS, NBC, and PBS, the Institute provides captioning for many independent producers, cable companies, syndicates, and home videos.

NCI underwrites the cost of closed captioning — approximately $2,500 for a one-hour program (approximately 30 hours of work) — with grants from the federal government, national advertisers, corporations, program sponsors, networks, and the NCI Caption Club, whose membership comprises hearing impaired individuals, their families and support organizations.

Most significant: captioning is **free.** There is no subscription charge. The only item for which the user must pay is the TeleCaption 4000 adapter, which costs about $200. The adapter can be easily hooked up to televisions, VCRs, cable TV hookups, and satellite receivers. The TeleCaption 4000 is available from Harris Communications (a distributor for NCI) by calling toll-free 800-825-6758 (V/TDD).

If you want more information on NCI's closed captioning, call or write to:

National Captioning Institute, Inc.
Public Relations
1900 Gallows Rd.
Vienna, VA 22182
Tel: (703) 917-7600 (voice or TDD)
Toll Free: 800-533-9673 (voice)
             800-321-8337 (TDD)

NATIONAL LIBRARY SERVICE FOR THE BLIND AND PHYSICALLY HANDICAPPED

Established by Congress in 1931 and greatly expanded in 1966 to include millions of additional participants, the National Library Service for the Blind and Physically Handicapped is still unknown to many blind and physically handicapped individuals for whom it was founded. This service, administered through the Library of Congress, publishes books and magazines in braille and on recorded discs and cassettes.

Eligible participants in the National Library program include anyone who cannot hold, handle, or see well enough to read conventional print materials because of a visual or physical handicap (such as paralysis, amputation, lack of muscle coordination, or prolonged weakness).

The reading materials are distributed through a national network of state and local libraries and sent to eligible participants, who can return them, postage-free, by mail. Also, any special equipment required to play the discs or cassettes (which are recorded at slower speeds than conventional records and tapes), or other devices like headphones, amplifiers, or playback machines for the mobility impaired, are loaned **indefinitely** to those who need them.

All kinds of books may be borrowed in braille and recorded formats — mysteries, bestsellers, poetry, religious materials, etc. — along with several popular magazines, including *Good Housekeeping*, *Sports Illustrated*, and *National Geographic*. The program also provides braille and large-print music scores and instructional cassettes for piano, organ, guitar, and other musical instruments.

Two twice-monthly publications — *Talking Book Topics*, in large print and on flexible disc, and *Braille Book Review*, in large print and braille — announce newly-released books and provide information on the library's various services.

If you want to join this program, request an application and the name of the participating library in your area by writing to:

> National Library Service for the
> Blind and Physically Handicapped
> Library of Congress
> Washington, DC 20542

FEDERAL INFORMATION RELAY SERVICE

In August 1986, an extremely helpful service for the deaf and hearing impaired began its operation: the Federal Information Relay Service. Funded by the Architectural and Transportation Barriers Compliance Board and provided by the Office of the Secretary's Telecommunications Center at the Department of the Treasury, the original one-year pilot project has become a permanent service with an ever-increasing user base. Over a year ago, administration of the program was transferred to the Government Services Administration (GSA). The Relay Service has one extremely important function: to provide communication between government offices without TDDs (Telecommunications Devices for the Deaf) and individuals who are hearing-impaired.

Anyone with a TDD can call the TDD Relay Service for help contacting any agency of the Executive, Legislative or Judicial branch of the federal government. Also, any federal employee without access to a TDD can contact a hearing-impaired individual who has a TDD via this service. The TDD Relay Service operator relays messages between the conversing parties by "translating" the speaking caller's words into TDD signals to the hearing-impaired, and vice versa. To use this service, you must have the telephone number of the office or individual you wish to contact; the TDD operator does not provide directory assistance.

The Relay Service operates from 8 a.m. to 8 p.m., Eastern Standard Time (EST), Monday through Friday, except holidays. The telephone numbers are:

Toll Free: 800-877-8339 (v/TDD)
(except Alaska and Hawaii)

Because so many individuals now use this service and the Relay Service staff is limited, you should follow these suggestions before placing your call:

- Have the telephone number of the agency/office/person you wish to contact ready. If necessary, use directory assistance or dial (800) 855-1155 (for TDD users only) to obtain the telephone number you need.

- When the call is made by the TDD Relay Service operator, hold your message until the other party is on the line.

- Limit your call to 15 minutes or less.

Telecommunications for the Deaf Relay Service: A special TDD and voice relay service has been recently activated by the Telecommunications for the Deaf organization. This outstanding service offers assistance in contacting private organizations or individuals who cannot be contacted by the Federal Information Relay Service. You may use the new service by calling toll-free 800-735-2258 (v/TDD).

FEDERAL GOVERNMENT TDD ASSISTANCE

Because they know how difficult it can be for individuals with hearing and speech impairments to contact government offices for assistance, many federal agencies maintain specific telephone numbers for persons who use a *Telecommunications Device for the Deaf*. These devices, referred to as TDDs, enable individuals who have hearing/speech impairments to communicate via telephone by typing a message on the device's keyboard. The message is transmitted over the telephone lines and displayed on the screen or printer of the receiving person's similar device. TDDs are the electronic machines that have largely replaced teletypewriters, called "TTYs" — the original communication devices used by individuals with hearing or speech impairments.

For a complete listing of federal TDD telephone numbers, contact the Telecommunications for the Deaf, Inc. which publishes an updated directory each year. The current directory contains over 30,000 TDD numbers of government offices and private organizations throughout the U.S. You can obtain a copy of this directory for a minimal cost by writing or calling:

Telecommunications for the Deaf, Inc.
8719 Colesville Road, Room 300, Silver Spring, MD 20910
Tel: (301) 589-3006 (TDD)
(301) 589-3786 (voice)

If you have the TDD telephone number of a federal government office and need help in placing your call or if you need any other operator assistance, dial the special toll-free TDD operator service number available for TDD users throughout the nation:

Toll Free: 800-855-1155

The operator can assist you in placing credit card calls, third number telephone calls, person-to-person calls and other operator-assisted calls.

LISTING

State Vocational and Rehabilitation Agencies

This listing identifies the various state government agencies that are responsible for coordinating and providing vocational rehabilitative services to physically, mentally and emotionally disabled individuals to make them as self-supporting and independent as possible through employment.

These vocational and rehabilitative programs may vary considerably, depending on the state's resources and the types of assistance they can offer. However, each state does have individualized programs directed to the elderly, the deaf, and the blind in addition to its programs for the disabled.

Although the major programs are designed to make individuals employable, many states also provide training and assistance to individuals who are unable to work because of their handicap. These programs help individuals learn skills that will enable them to take care of their daily needs by themselves.

Contact your state office for information on the various programs available. The state office will also provide the location of the office serving your local area so you can arrange an appointment with a vocational/rehabilitation counselor.

The use of V/TDD or TDD in this listing indicates the following:
    V/TDD = Answered by voice or Telecommunications
                 Device for the Deaf
    TDD   = Answered by Telecommunications Device for the ..
                 Deaf only.

ALABAMA
Div. of Rehabilitation Services
P.O. Box 11586
Montgomery, AL 36111
Tel: (205) 281-8780

ALASKA
Div. of Vocational Rehabilitation
Pouch F, MS 0581
Juneau, AK 99811
Tel: (907) 465-2814
        (907) 465-2440 (TDD)

AMERICAN SAMOA
Vocational Rehabilitation
Dept. of Human Resources
P.O. Box 3492
American Samoa Government
Pago Pago, AS 96799
Tel: (684) 633-2336

ARIZONA
Rehabilitation Services Admin.
1789 W. Jefferson
Phoenix, AZ 85007
Tel: (602) 542-3332
        (602) 542-6049 (v/TDD)

ARKANSAS
Div. of Services for the Blind
Dept of Human Services
411 Victory Street, P.O. Box 3237
Little Rock, AR 72203
Tel: (501) 324-9270

Rehabilitation Services Div.
P.O. Box 3781
Little Rock, AR 72203
Tel: (501) 682-6709
        (501) 682-6699 (TDD)

CALIFORNIA
Dept of Rehabilitation
830 K Street Mall
Sacramento, CA 95814
Tel: (916) 445-3971

COLORADO
Rehabilitation Services
Dept. of Social Services
1575 Sherman Street, 4th Fl.
Denver, CO 80203
Tel: (303) 866-2866 (v/TDD)

CONNECTICUT
State Dept of Education
Div. of Rehabilitation Services
10 Griffin Road, N
Windsor, CT 06095
Tel: (203) 298-2000

Board of Education and
Services for the Blind
170 Ridge Road
Wethersfield, CT 06109
Tel: (203) 566-5800

DELAWARE
Div. of Vocational Rehabilitation
Delaware Elwyn Inst., 4th Fl.
321 E. 11th Street
Wilmington, DE 19801
Tel: (302) 577-2851 (v/TDD)

Div. for the Visually Impaired
Dept of Health & Social Services
305 West 8th St.
Wilmington, DE 19801
Tel: (302) 421-5730

DISTRICT OF COLUMBIA
D.C. Rehabilitation Services Admin.
Dept of Human Services
605 G Street, NW, Rm. 1111
Washington, DC 20001
Tel: (202) 727-3227
        (202) 727-0981 (TDD)

FLORIDA
Div. of Vocational Rehabilitation
1709 "A" Mahan Drive
Tallahassee, FL 32399
Tel: (904) 488-6210
        (904) 488-2867 (v/TDD)

Division of Blind Services
Department of Education
2540 Exec. Center Circle
West Douglas Building
Tallahassee, FL 32399
Tel: (904) 488-1330 (v/TDD)

GEORGIA
Div. of Rehabilitation Services
Dept. of Human Services
878 Peachtree Street, NE, Rm. 706
Atlanta, GA 30309
Tel: (404) 894-6670
    (404) 894-8558 (V/TDD)

GUAM
Dept. Vocational Rehabilitation
Govt. of Guam
122 Harmon Plaza, Rm. B201
Harmon Industrial Park, Guam
96911
Tel: 011(671) 646-9468

HAWAII
Div. of Vocational Rehabilitation
and Services for the Blind
Dept. of Human Services
P.O. Box 339
Honolulu, HI 96809
Tel: (808) 586-5355

IDAHO
Div. of Vocational Rehabilitation
Len B. Jordan Bldg., Rm.150
650 W. State
Boise, ID 83720
Tel: (208) 334-3390
    (208) 334-2520 (v/TDD)

Idaho Comm. for the Blind
341 West Washington Street
Boise, ID 83702
Tel: (208)334-3220

ILLINOIS
Illinois Dept. of Rehabilitation Services
623 E. Adams Street
Springfield, IL 62794
Tel: (217) 785-0218
    (217) 782-5734 (TDD)

INDIANA
Dept. of Human Services
402 W. Washington St.
Indianapolis. IN 46207
Tel: (317) 232-6500
    (317) 232-1427 (TDD)

IOWA
Division of Vocational
Rehabilitation Services
510 E. 12th Street
Des Moines, IA 50319
Tel: (515) 281-4311 (V/TDD)

Commissioner for the Blind
524-4th Street
Des Moines, IA 50309
Tel: (515) 281-1333

KANSAS
Rehabilitation Services
Dept of Social & Rehab. Services
300 S.W. Oakley, 1st Fl.
Topeka, KS 66606
Tel: (913) 296-3911

KENTUCKY
Dept of Vocational Rehabilitation
Capital Plaza Tower
Frankfort, KY 40601
Tel: (502) 564-4566
Toll Free: 800-372-7172 (in KY)

Dept. for the Blind
427 Versailles Road
Frankfort, KY 40601
Tel: (502) 564-4754

LOUISIANA
Div. of Services Rehabilitation
Dept. of Social Services
P.O. Box 94371
Baton Rouge, LA 70804
Tel: (504) 342-2285
    (504) 342-2266 (v/TDD)

MAINE
Bureau of Rehabilitation Services
Dept. of Human Services
35 Anthony Avenue
Augusta, ME 04333
Tel: (207) 626-5300
Toll Free: 800-626-5321 (TDD)

MARIANA ISLANDS
Vocational Rehabilitation Div.
Commonwealth of Northern
Mariana Islands
P.O. Box 1521-CK
Saipan, Mariana Island 96950
Tel: 011 (670) 234-6538

MARYLAND
Div. of Vocational Rehabilitation
2301 Argonne Drive
Baltimore, MD 21218
Tel: (301) 554-3276
    (301) 554-3277 (TDD)

MASSACHUSETTS
Commission for the Blind
88 Kingston Street
Boston, MA 02111
Tel: (617) 727-5550
Toll Free: 800-392-6556 (TDD)
              800-392-6450 (V)

Rehabilitation Commission
27-43 Wormwood Street
Boston, MA 02210
Tel: (617) 727-2172
    (617) 727-9063 (TDD)

MICHIGAN
Bureau of Rehabilitation
& Disability Determination
P.O. Box 30010
Lansing, MI 48909
Tel: (517) 373-3390
    (517) 373-3979 (v/TDD)

Commissioner for the Blind
Dept of Labor
201 N. Washington Sq.
Lansing, MI 48909
Tel: (517) 373-2062
    (517) 373-4025 (v/TDD)

MINNESOTA
Div. of Rehabilitation Services
390 N. Robert St., 5th Fl.
St. Paul, MN 55101
Tel: (612) 296-1822
    (612) 296-3900 (TDD)

State Services for the Blind,
1745 University Ave.
St. Paul, MN 55104
Tel: (612) 642-0500
    (612) 642-0506 (v/TDD)

MISSISSIPPI
Vocational Rehabilitation Div.
P.O. Box 1698
Jackson, MS 39205
Tel: (601) 354-6825
    (601) 354-6830 (v/TDD)

Vocational Rehab. for the Blind
P.O. Box 4872
Jackson, MS 39215
Tel: (601) 354-6411

MISSOURI
State Dept. of Education
Div. of Vocational Rehab.
2401 E. McCarty
Jefferson City, MO 65101
Tel: (314) 751-3251 (V/TDD)

Bureau for the Blind
619 E. Capitol
Jefferson City, MO 65101
Tel: (314) 751-4249

MONTANA
Dept of Social & Rehabilitation
Services, Rehab. Services Div.
111 Sanders, P.O. Box 4210
Helena, MT 59604
Tel: (406) 444-2590 (V/TDD)

NEBRASKA
Div. of Rehabilitative Services
P.O. Box 94987
Lincoln, NE 68509
Tel: (402) 471-3649
    (402) 471-3659 (v/TDD)

Services for the Visually
Impaired
4600 Valley Road
Lincoln, NE 68510
Tel: (402) 471-2891
    (402) 471-3593 (v/TDD)

NEVADA
Rehabilitation Division
Dept. of Human Services
505 E. King St., Rm. 502
Carson City, NV 90710
Tel: (702) 687-4440 (V/TDD)

NEW HAMPSHIRE
Div. of Vocational Rehabilitation
State Dept. of Education
78 Regional Drive
Concord, NH 03301
Tel: (603) 271-3471 (V/TDD)

NEW JERSEY
Div. of Vocational Rehab. Services
Labor & Industry Bldg.
Trenton, NJ 08625
Tel: (609) 292-5987
    (609) 292-2919 (v/TDD)

Comm. for the Blind and
Visually Impaired
153 Halsey Street
P.O. Box 47017
Newark, NJ 07102
Tel: (201) 648-3333
    (201) 648-4559 (v/TDD)

NEW MEXICO
Div. of Vocational Rehabilitation
Dept. of Education
604 W. San Mateo
Santa Fe, NM 87503
Tel: (505) 827-3500 (v/TDD)

NEW YORK
New York State Education Dept.
Office of Vocational Rehab.
One Commerce Plaza, Rm. 1606
Albany, NY 12243
Tel: (518) 474-2714
    (518) 473-9333 (v/TDD)

State Dept. of Social Services
Comm. for the Blind & Visually
Handicapped
10 Eyck Office Bldg.
40 N. Pearl Street
Albany, NY 12243
Tel: (518) 473-1801

NORTH CAROLINA
Div. of Vocational Rehab.
P.O. Box 26053
Raleigh NC 27611
Tel: (919) 733-3364
    (919) 733-5920 (v/TDD)

Div. of Services for the Blind
Dept. of Human Resources
309 Ashe Avenue
Raleigh, NC 27606
Tel: (919) 733-9822
    (919) 733-5199

NORTH DAKOTA
Div. of Vocational Rehab.
State Capitol Bldg.
600 E. Boulevard Avenue
Bismarck, ND 58505
Tel: (701) 224-2907
    (701) 224-2699 (TDD)

OHIO
Rehabilitation Services Comm.
400 East Campus View Blvd.
Columbus, OH 43235
Tel: (614) 438-1210 (V/TDD)

OKLAHOMA
Div. of Rehabilitative Services
Dept of Human Services
P.O. Box 25352
Oklahoma City, OK 73125
Tel: (405) 424-6647
    (405) 424-2794 (v/TDD)

OREGON
Div. of Vocational Rehabilitation
Dept. of Human Resources
2045 Silverton Road, NE
Salem, OR 97310
Tel: (503)378-3850 (V/TDD)

Commission for the Blind
535 S.E. 12th Avenue
Portland, OR 97214
Tel: (503) 238-8380 (v/TDD)

PENNSYLVANIA
Office of Vocational Rehabilitation
1300 Labor and Industry Bldg.
7th & Forster Streets
Harrisburg, PA 17120
Tel: (717) 787-5244
    (717) 783-8917 (v/TDD)

Bureau of Blindness & Visual Services
Dept. of Public Welfare
1301 N. 7th Street
P.O. Box 2675
Harrisburg, PA 17105
Tel: (717) 787-6176
    (717) 787-6280 (v/TDD)

PUERTO RICO
Vocational Rehabilitation
Dept. of Social Services
P.O. Box 1118
Hato Rey, PR 00919
Tel: (809) 725-1792
    (809) 763-5237 (TDD)

RHODE ISLAND
Vocational Rehabilitation Services
40 Fountain Street
Providence, RI 02903
Tel: (401) 421-7005
    (401) 421-7016 (TDD)

Services for the Blind &
Visually Impaired
275 Westminster Street, 5th Fl.
Providence, RI 02903
Tel: (401) 277-2300
    (401) 277-3010 (v/TDD)

SOUTH CAROLINA
Vocational Rehabilitation Dept.
1410 Boston Ave.
P.O. Box 15
W. Columbia, SC 29171
Tel: (803) 734-4300
    (803) 734-5313 (v/TDD)

Commission for the Blind
1430 Confederate Ave.
Columbia, SC 29201
Tel: (803) 734-7522

SOUTH DAKOTA
Div. of Rehabilitative Services
700 Governors Drive
Pierre, SD 57501
Tel: (605) 773-3195
    (605) 773-4544 (TDD)

TENNESSEE
Rehabilitative Services
Dept. of Human Services
Citizens Plaza Building,
15th Floor
400 Deaderick Street
Nashville, TN 37248
Tel: (615) 741-2019
    (615) 741-5644 (v/TDD)

TEXAS
Texas Rehabilitation Comm.
4900 N. Lamar Blvd.
Austin, TX 78751
Tel: (512) 445-8100
Toll Free: 800-735-2988(voice)
        800-735-2989(TDD)

State Comm. for the Blind
4800 N. Lamar Blvd.
Austin, TX 78711
Tel: (512) 459-2500
    (512) 459-2608 (v/TDD)

UTAH
Div. of Rehabilitation Services
State Office of Education
250 E. 5th South
Salt Lake City, UT 84111
Tel: (801) 538-7530 (V/TDD)

Services for Visually
Handicapped
State Office of Education
309 E. 1st, South
Salt Lake City, UT 84111
Tel: (801) 533-9393

VERMONT
Vocational Rehabilitation Div.
Osgood Building,
Waterbury Complex
103 S. Main Street
Waterbury, VT 05671
Tel: (802) 241-2189 (V/TDD)

Div. for Blind & Visually
Impaired
Osgood Building,
Waterbury Complex
103 S. Main Street
Waterbury, VT 05676
Tel: (802) 241-2211

VIRGIN ISLANDS
Div. of Handicapped Services
Dept. of Human Services
Barbel Plaza South
St. Thomas, VI 00802
Tel: 011 (809) 774-0930

VIRGINIA
Dept. of Rehabilitative Services
4901 Fitzhugh Avenue
P.O. Box 11045
Richmond, VA 23230
Tel: (804) 367-0316
    (804) 367-0315 (V/TDD)

Dept. of Visually Handicapped
397 Azalea Avenue
Richmond, VA 23227
Tel: (804) 371-3140 (V/TDD)

WASHINGTON
Div. of Vocational
Rehabilitation
Dept. of Social & Health Services
OB 21-C
Olympia, WA 98504
Tel: (206) 753-0293
    (206) 753-5473 (V/TDD)

Dept. of Services for the Blind
521 East Legion
Olympia, WA 98501
Tel: (206) 586-1224
    (206) 721-6437 (TDD)

WEST VIRGINIA
Div. of Vocational Rehabilitation
State Board of Rehabilitation
State Capitol Complex
Charleston, WV 25305
Tel: (304) 766-4600
    (304) 766-4970 (V/TDD)

WISCONSIN
Div. of Vocational Rehabilitation
Dept. of Health & Social
Services
1 West Wilson, 8th Floor
Madison, WI 53707
Tel: (608) 266-5466
    (608) 266-9599 (V/TDD)

WYOMING
Div. of Vocational Rehabilita-
tion
Dept. of Employment
1 East Herschler Bldg.
Cheyenne, WY 82002
Tel: (307) 777-7385
    (307) 777-7389 (V/TDD)

JOB PROGRAMS FOR OLDER WORKERS

Three important government-subsidized programs provide nation-wide employment services and promote job opportunities for older workers: (1) the *Job Training Partnership Act (JTPA)*, (2) the *Senior Community Service Employment Program (SCSEP)* under Title V of the Older Americans Act, and (3) the State Employment Security Agencies' *Job Service* offices. In addition, *ACTION*— a federal agency, for volunteer services — sponsors two job programs that provide modest, tax-free stipends to low-income volunteers over 60: the *Foster Grandparent Program* and the *Senior Companion Program*. All of these programs are described below.

Many other employment services and programs for the elderly and handicapped are sponsored by state and local governments and private industry in your community. Because these programs vary considerably from state to state and within the state, you should contact your State Office on Aging, your local Area Agency on Aging, and/or your Human Services Information office for information on programs in your local area and in neighboring areas.

Some communities have government-supported Senior Employment Centers which provide training and locate employment for older workers. Be sure to contact these local organizations for assistance: *they are there to help you!*

JOB TRAINING PARTNERSHIP ACT (JTPA)

In 1983, JTPA replaced the Comprehensive Employment and Training Act (CETA), which had promoted public service employment of workers 55 and older. By contrast, JTPA emphasizes training and, because the federal government's role is primarily advisory, gives state government and private industry a much more active role in tailoring the program to meet regional needs.

JTPA offers many services, including (but not limited to) job development, remedial education, work experience, and follow-up services for workers placed in non-subsidized employment. In addition, JTPA's Employment and Training Assistance for Dislocated Workers program helps workers of all ages who lose or cannot obtain employment due to mass layoffs, natural disasters, high local unemployment, or federal actions like facility closings. Services provided to these individuals include training, retraining, job search assistance and placement, and relocation assistance.

Although JTPA is designed primarily to assist economically disadvantaged workers, the program also helps those who have encountered barriers to employment, i.e., older and handicapped workers, displaced homemakers, veterans, past offenders, and people who are not proficient in English.

Before 1986, income eligibility for JTPA was based on the combined income of the applicant's entire household. However, the 1986 "Family of One" ruling stated that only the applicant's income was to be considered when determining his/her eligibility. As a result, even if you were disqualified for JTPA programs *before* 1986, you may be eligible now, so it's important that you reapply.

For more information on how to qualify for and obtain JTPA assistance, contact your Area Agency on Aging or Human Services Information office. They will direct you to the nearest JTPA program office in your state. Or contact any Job Service Office (discussed later in this chapter).

SENIOR COMMUNITY SERVICE EMPLOYMENT PROGRAM (SCSEP)

SCSEP is administered at the federal level by the U.S. Department of Labor. It is designed to provide part-time jobs in community service for unemployed, low-income individuals 55 and older (with priority given to those 60 and older) who have poor employment prospects. To qualify for the program, applicants must have incomes that do not exceed 125 percent of the federal poverty level.

SCSEP has projects in all 50 states, the District of Columbia, Puerto Rico, and all U.S. territories. These projects are sponsored by state/territorial governments and the ten national organizations.

Participants in SCSEP work 20-25 hours per week at schools, hospitals, day care centers, fire prevention centers, programs for the handicapped, and conservation projects. By law, participants must be paid no less than the federal minimum wage, the state minimum wage, or the local prevailing rate of pay for similar employment — whichever is highest. In addition to wages, participants receive physical examinations, personal and job counseling training, and — sometimes — transportation to and from their place of employment.

If you are interested in SCSEP and want to find out whether you are eligible, contact your local Area Agency on Aging, Job Service office, or one of the national sponsors listed below.

Green Thumb, Inc.
SCSE Project
2000 N. 14th St.
Suite 800
Arlington, VA 22201
Tel: (703) 522-7272

National Council on the Aging
SCSE Project
409 Third Street, SW
Washington, DC 20024
Tel: (202) 479-1200

U.S. Forest Service
Human Resource Programs
P.O. Box 96090
Washington, DC 20009
Tel: (703) 235-8834

National Urban League, Inc.
SCSE Program
500 East 62nd Street
New York, NY 10021
Tel: (212) 310-9000

National Indian Council on Aging, Inc.
SCSE Program
6400 Uptown Blvd, NE,
Suite 510W
Albuquerque, NM 87110
Tel: (505) 888-3302

National Asian Pacific Center on Aging
Melbourne Tower, Suite 914
1511 Third Avenue
Seattle, WA 98101
Tel: (206) 624-1221

National Council of Senior Citizens
Senior Aides Program
1331 F Street, NW, 7th Floor
Washington, DC 20005
Tel: (202) 624-9507

The National Center on Black Aged, Inc.
SCSE Project
1424 K Street, NW, Suite 500
Washington, DC 20005
Tel: (202) 637-8400

**American Association of
Retired Persons**
SCSE Project
601 E Street, NW
Washington, DC 20049
Tel: (202) 434-2277

**Asociacion Nacional Pro
Personas Mayores**
SCSE Project
3325 Wilshire Blvd., Suite 800
Los Angeles, CA 90010
Tel: (213) 487-1922

JOB SERVICE

Funded by the U.S. Department of Labor's Employment and Training Administration and the state and local governments, the State Employment Security Agencies 2,000-plus Job Service offices provide employment services to all employable legal residents of the United States. Special assistance is given to the elderly and handicapped, people not proficient in English, veterans, past offenders, and first-time workers. These services — which are free — include:

- job development
- occupational testing
- labor market information
- employment counseling
- referrals to work and training programs
- help finding full-and part-time work.

To facilitate job placement, most Job Service offices maintain up-to-date listings of local openings. Applicants who require assistance above and beyond that provided by the Job Service offices are referred to community agencies who can help in areas like financial assistance, geriatric services, and vocational rehabilitation.

To use the services provided by this program contact the nearest Job Service office, noted in your telephone directory's "blue pages" listing of state government offices under "Employment Service" or "Employment Security Commission." If you have difficulty locating the Job Service office in your area, ask the telephone directory assistance operator for help.

FOSTER GRANDPARENT AND SENIOR COMPANION PROGRAMS

The American Council to Improve Our Neighborhoods (ACTION) sponsors two programs, the *Foster Grandparent Program* and the *Senior Companion Program*, both of which are open to anyone 60 or older who is physically able and willing to serve 20 hours per week and who meets certain income eligibility guidelines (these guidelines vary from state to state). Each participant in these programs receives a modest, tax-free stipend, a transportation allowance, hot meals while at work, accident insurance, and an annual physical examination. In addition, participants receive several hours of pre-service orientation and regular in-service training to help them in their work.

The Foster Grandparent Program gives participants the chance to provide companionship to physically, emotionally, and mentally handicapped children and to children who have been abused, neglected, come under the authority of the juvenile justice system, or have other special needs. Each Foster Grandparent is assigned to an individual child.

Senior Companion Program participants provide individualized care and assistance to other adults, primarily the frail elderly. These supportive services help prevent the inappropriate institutionalization of housebound persons. Senior companions play an integral part in the comprehensive care that allows housebound persons to continue independent living. Similarly, they prevent the *untimely* deinstitutionalization of elderly persons by facilitating their readjustment to life in the community.

If you are interested in either program, call or write to:

ACTION
Older American Volunteer Programs
1100 Vermont Avenue, NW, 6th Floor
Washington, DC 20525
Tel: (202) 606-4849
(202) 606-4853

TAX ASSISTANCE

The complexity of federal tax rules and allowances, deductions, credits and special provisions can make preparing your tax return difficult and often frustrating. For older Americans, tax preparation can be an even greater challenge because so many aspects of their lives affect their returns. For example, the receipt of Social Security and Railroad Retirement benefits, other pension incomes, decreased or lost earning power, sale of their home, increased medical and prescription drug costs, or the loss of a spouse can complicate tax preparation further.

The many changes of the Tax Reform Act of 1986 — the most significant new tax legislation since World War II — also affect Seniors' taxes considerably. In fact, the act's effect will be felt throughout the nation by both individuals and businesses for many years to come. The legislation, which many felt would simplify the process of taxation, turned out to be very complicated (879 pages of text). However, with the act, Congress did achieve its primary goal of providing a complete tax overhaul that created a more equitable system of taxation for the American people.

While certain long-standing tax advantages to the elderly were repealed or reduced, the act mandated increases in personal exemptions, to be phased in over a period of several years. In addition, the act increased the standard deduction for the elderly, reduced tax rates, and raised the maximum ceiling for non-taxable low incomes. With these changes, the 1986 Tax Reform Act exempted an estimated six million more low-income taxpayers — many of whom are elderly — from having to file any federal income tax forms at all.

IRS studies of older Americans' tax returns since the enactment of the Tax Reform Act indicate that nearly 50 percent of Seniors overpay their federal taxes. Consequently, it is imperative that you obtain the assistance and information you need to accurately prepare your tax forms. As an American you are only obliged to pay your fair share of taxes . . . and no more!

This discussion is not meant to be a line-by-line description of federal tax forms. Instead, I hope to introduce some general tax information you may not be aware of, to highlight certain tax provisions of particular interest to older individuals, and — most important — to direct you to **free** sources of tax information, publications, and assistance in preparing your tax forms.

INCREASE IN TAX BENEFITS FOR 1996

Taxpayers planning for 1996 will find larger standard deductions, personal exemptions, and earned income credits, plus wider tax brackets beginning at higher income levels. Under federal tax law, these amounts are indexed each year so that inflation does not erode these benefits or push taxpayers into higher tax brackets.

Among the 1996 changes:

■ Standard deduction for couples is $6,700; for singles, $4,000;

■ Each exemption on the tax return is $2,550 *except* when your adjusted gross income (AGI) exceeds $176,950 if married filing jointly ($147,450 if head of household; $117,950 if single; $88,475 if married filing separately). Your deduction for exemptions is reduced by 2% for each $2,500 ($1,250 if married and filing separately) or part of that amount by which your AGI is more than the amount based on your filing status. The additional standard deductions in 1996 for age and blindness is $800 for couples, $1,000 for singles.

The earned income credit (EIC) — a refundable tax break for low-income workers with a child — will be greater and will have a higher eligibility ceiling. A "qualifying child" includes a son, daughter, adopted child, grandchild, stepchild, or foster child age 18 or younger; full-time students may be age 23 or younger. There is no age limit for a child who is permanently and totally disabled. The maximum basic EIC in 1996 is $6,336 for a qualifying individual with one child, $8,890 for a taxpayer with two or more children, and $4,220 for a taxpayer with no children.

Beginning in 1996, you cannot claim the EIC if your investment income is over $2,350. Investment income includes taxable interest and dividends, tax-exempt interest, and net income from rents and royalties. Rents and royalties received in a trade or business are not investment income.

SPECIAL STATE AND LOCAL TAX PROVISIONS

Although the majority of states offer exemptions or provisions to older individuals — usually beginning at age 60 or 65 but sometime as early as age 55 — a vast number of Seniors are unaware of the special tax provisions available to them in their own states and counties. This is not surprising when one considers that so many of them overpay their federal taxes.

Special state and local tax relief provisions for Seniors often include complete exemptions of disability retired pay, military retired pay, civil service annuities, general income deductions for age or disability, partial or full exemptions for annuities under either the Survivor Benefit Plan or Retired Serviceman's Family Protection Plan, reduction of utilities taxes and most important, relief or reduction of real estate taxes, personal property taxes as well as, payment of vehicle decal fees. In addition, the elderly are often eligible for reduced state taxes due to property tax exemptions or deferrals until they sell their home or die.

Important! While such tax savings as described here may be available in your state, they are almost never automatically given to you. You must apply for them. When you request information on federal taxes, be certain to ask your state or local tax authorities about any special tax provisions for Seniors in your own state and county.

GENERAL TAX INFORMATION

Although you may be very knowledgeable about preparing your tax forms, you may still have questions about resolving a tax problem with the IRS, what to do when you can't pay your taxes on time, or how long to keep your tax records. The following section answers some of the questions older individuals ask the IRS most frequently.

Q. *How long should I keep my tax records?*
A. The statute of limitations for individuals' tax record preservation is usually three years from the date the return was due or filed, or two years from the date the tax was paid, whichever is later. However, it is highly recommended that certain records be kept indefinitely, such as real estate or investment information.

Q. *How do I amend my return?*

A. To amend a tax — once it has been filed — for changes to income, deductions or credits, complete and file Form 1040X *Amended U.S. Individual Income Tax Return* as soon as possible. Any local IRS office will help you complete the form. If there is no local office near you, you can get assistance by calling the toll-free IRS assistance number: 800-829-1040.

Q. *How can I get copies of my returns?*

A. To obtain copies of tax returns, submit IRS Form 4506, *Request for Copy of Tax Form.* The current charge for a copy of a return is $14.00.

Q. *How can I resolve tax problems with the IRS?*

A. The IRS maintains a nationwide program to assist taxpayers who have been unable to resolve difficult and persistent problems or complaints that have not been solved through normal IRS channels. If you have such a problem, write to the local IRS District Director or call the local IRS office and ask for the *Problem Resolution Assistance Office.* The toll-free IRS assistance number — 800-829-1040 — will also provide the address and telephone number of the resolution office serving your area.

Q. *What do I do if my husband/wife dies?*

A. When a taxpayer dies before filing a return, the taxpayer's spouse or personal representative must file a return and sign for the deceased person. Write "deceased" across the top of the return and after the deceased taxpayer's name. Also show the date of death in the name and address space of the return. A surviving spouse filing a joint return with the decedent can receive a refund without having to complete Form 1310, *Statement of Person Claiming Refund Due to a Deceased Taxpayer,* to claim the refund.

Q. *What do I do when I can't pay my taxes?*

A. The IRS advises taxpayers who are not able to pay their federal tax on time to file a tax return by the due date and pay as much as they can with the return. By filing on time, taxpayers avoid the penalty — 5 percent per month or part of a month — that applies to any tax due on a late return. Late payments are subject to interest and a penalty of half a percent per month or part of a month.

Taxpayers who cannot pay on time should either pay the balance when IRS sends the notice of taxes due or contact their local IRS office to discuss arrangements to pay the taxes owed. Under certain circumstances, the IRS may allow a taxpayer to pay by installments.

Q. *How do I appeal an IRS audit?*
A. If you find any discrepancies in an IRS audit of your tax filings, you have the right to appeal the audit. When the IRS completes your audit, it sends a notice describing proposed changes for you to make to your return and indicating your right to appeal within 30 days. The notice also outlines the appeal process. You have the right to disagree with the auditor at the time of the meeting and request an immediate meeting with the auditor's supervisor to resolve any discrepancies you have with the auditor's interpretations and decisions without having to go through the formal appeal process.

If the appeal process is completed and you are still dissatisfied with the audit decisions, you can take the matter directly to the U.S. Tax Court, U.S. Claims Court or a U.S. District Court.

Q. *How can I get more time to file my returns?*
A. To request an extension for filing your individual income tax returns, submit Form 4868, Automatic Extension of Time to File U.S. Individual Income Tax Return, to your IRS Service Center no later than April 15. If you do file for an extension, you must estimate any taxes due and pay them when you submit Form 4868. To estimate taxes due, review last year's tax returns and this year's records.

An extension filed on Form 4868 gives you until August 15 to file your actual tax return. When you do file your return, make sure to take credit for any payment made with Form 4868 (according to the instructions provided with form 1040 or 1040A). Do not use Form 1040 EZ or have the IRS figure your tax if you have filed for an extension.

INDIVIDUAL RETIREMENT ARRANGEMENTS (IRAs)

An individual retirement arrangement (IRA) is a personal savings plan that offers tax advantage to setting aside money for retirement. This means that individuals may be able to deduct their contributions to an IRA in whole or in part, depending on their circumstances.

Generally, amounts in an IRA, including earnings and gains, are not *taxed until distributed to the individual.*

Two common types of IRAs are an *Individual Retirement Account* which can be set up with any financial organization that satisfies the requirements of the Internal Revenue Code and an *Individual Retirement Annuity* which is set up by purchasing a special annuity contract from a life insurance company. Both are excellent ways to provide for your future security.

Anyone can set up an IRA if he/she has taxable compensation during the year and has not reached age $70^1/_2$ by the end of the year. Compensation includes wages, salaries, tips, commission fees, bonuses, and taxable alimony and separate maintenance payments. In addition, anyone who is covered by an employer-provided pension plan but whose adjusted gross income (AGI) falls below $25,000 ($40,000 for joint filers) may set up an IRA and receive a full deferral of taxation. Contributions are partially tax-deferred up to an AGI of $35,000 ($50,000 for joint filers). Individuals who are not allowed the full deferral can still make non-deductible contributions up to the annual allowable maximum. IRA investment earnings retain a tax-deferred status regardless of the tax treatment of new contributions.

Yearly contributions to IRAs are limited to 100% of an individual's compensation, or $2,000, whichever is less; a total of $2,250 is allowed for a "spousal IRA" if one spouse does not work. If both spouses work, each may open an IRA and may contribute up to $2,000, or 100% of their annual salaries and wages, whichever is less.

Individuals who retire but still work part-time regardless of their age may continue to contribute to an IRA, up to age $70^1/_2$; however, their contribution per year cannot exceed their compensation. Withdrawal of funds must begin by the year after an individual reaches age $70^1/_2$. The minimum withdrawals are based on the individual's life expectancy as estimated by the Internal Revenue Service. Individuals withdrawing contributions before the age of $59^1/_2$ will be penalized at the rate of 10% unless the individual becomes totally disabled, dies or makes withdrawals in the form of a life-time annuity.

TWO TAX RULES YOU SHOULD KNOW

Two very important tax rules affect a gain from the sale of your home and the amount of the interest deduction which may be taken for your home's mortgage. These rules are of considerable interest to most older home owners because of how they can affect tax liability if the homeowners sell their home or purchase a second home. Both rules are described here to make sure you are aware of their effect on the amount of taxes you may have to pay under the current law.

■ **Home Mortgage Interest Rule** — In 1987, Congress amended the rules that applied to the deduction of interest on debt secured by an individual's main home or second home.

These loans include a:

(1) Mortgage to buy your home;

(2) Second mortgage;

(3) Line of credit;

(4) Home equity loan.

In most cases, you will be able to deduct all of your home mortgage interest. Whether it is all deductible depends on the date you took out the mortgage, the amount of the mortgage, and your use of its proceeds.

If all of your mortgages fit into one or more of the following categories, you can deduct **all** of the interest on those mortgages. If one or more of your mortgages is not described below, get IRS Publication 936 to figure the amount of interest you can deduct.

• Mortgages you took out on or before October 13, 1987 (called "grandfathered debt").

• Mortgages you took out after October 13, 1987, to buy, build, or improve your home (called "home acquisition debt"), but only if these mortgages plus any grandfathered debt totaled $1 million or less throughout 1991.

• Mortgages you took out after October 13, 1987, other than to buy, build, or improve your home (called "home equity debt"), but only if these mortgages totaled $100,000 or less throughout 1991.

If you are married and file a separate return, the home acquisition debt limit is $500,000 and the home equity debt limit is $50,000.

Important: You cannot deduct this interest if you use the proceeds of the mortgage to receive tax-free income.

■ **One-Time $125,000 Tax Exclusion** — Individuals may exclude from their gross income some or all of their capital gains from the sale of their principal home if they meet certain age, owner-ship, and use tests at the time of the sale. The rule states that you may choose to exclude from your gross income $125,000 of capital gains ($62,500 if married but filing separately) on the sale or exchange of your principal home if:

(1) You were 55 or older on the date of the sale or exchange.

and

(2) You owned and lived in your principal home for at least three years out of the five-year period ending on the date of the sale or exchange — this does not have to be a continuous three year period.

and

(3) You or your spouse did not exclude a gain on the sale or exchange of a home after July 26, 1976.

If, after subtracting the allowed $125,000 maximum, a balance of capital gains remains, you can postpone crediting that balance amount towards your tax liability by using the money to purchase another residence.

This extremely popular tax break for people over 55 carries with it important advantages and disadvantages that are frequently misunderstood. The *advantages* are:

(1) Taxpayers who have become physically or mentally incapable of self-care, and who have entered a state-licensed facility for the care of the mentally or physically disabled qualify for the once-in-a-lifetime exemption if they owned and used a property as their principal residence for at least one year out of the five-year period.

(2) According to IRS interpretation of the law, in many cases, joint owners in the same property can both qualify for the $125,000 exemption. For example, a husband and wife as one joint owner, and the wife's mother as the other joint owner, can each exclude their share of the gain on the sale of property up to $125,000 which was attributable to their undivided interest in the property.

An important *disadvantage* is that federal law treats every married, home-owning couple as a single taxpaying unit. Consequently, any spouse who uses the exclusion, then divorces and remarries carries the $125,000 tax consequence which prohibits the new spouse from using the $125,000 tax exemption. This same situation applies to remarried widows/widowers who have already used the one-time exemption during the previous marriage.

Important: Before you divorce or remarry, make sure you fully understand the implications of this once-in-a-lifetime tax exclusion, particularly if your (future) spouse has not used his/her exclusion.

FREE TAX ASSISTANCE

Although most older taxpayers understand and prepare their own tax returns, or hire income tax preparers to do it for them, millions of the elderly can neither afford to pay someone to help them nor prepare their tax returns on their own. For these people, the IRS provides both a walk-in assistance service at local IRS offices and three programs of free assistance in preparing tax returns. These programs are: (1) *Community Outreach Tax Assistance*, (2) *Volunteer Income Tax Assistance*, and (3) *Tax Counseling for the Elderly*.

■ **Community Outreach Tax Assistance** — This program is designed for taxpayers who have a common occupation or tax concern. Aimed at groups like retirees, farmers and small business owners, the assistance is provided year-round by IRS employees or qualified volunteers. The program provides two types of help: (1) line-by-line aid for group income tax return preparation, and (2) tax information seminars on tax topics aimed at attendees.

- **Volunteer Income Tax Assistance (VITA)** — IRS trained volunteers help prepare basic tax returns for older, handicapped or non-English-speaking taxpayers. This help is provided at neighborhood centers, libraries, churches and shopping malls.

- **Tax Counseling for the Elderly (TCE)** — This program provides volunteer tax assistance to people 60 years of age or older, especially those who are disabled or have other special needs. The volunteers are associated with nonprofit organizations funded by IRS grants which pay the volunteers' mileage and other travel expenses as they visit TCE sites like libraries, retirement homes, neighborhood centers, churches and homes of the housebound.

The best known program under TCE is the Tax-*Aide* program which began in 1969 under the auspices of the American Association of Retired Persons (AARP). Tax-Aide has helped millions of older taxpayers prepare their annual federal and state tax returns. Through a cooperative agreement with the Internal Revenue Service, AARP recruits and trains the volunteers. According to the IRS, Tax-Aide volunteers provide extremely high-calibre assistance; recent surveys show that tax returns prepared with the help of Tax-Aide volunteers had an error rate of less than five percent.

For information on the locations and schedules of free tax assistance in your community, contact your local library, Area Agency on Aging, Human Services Information office or local IRS office.

Important: Volunteers are critically needed to expand all three of these vital programs. If you would like to become a volunteer, contact your local IRS office, use the toll-free IRS number — **800-829-1040** — or contact AARP's Tax-Aide office directly by calling or writing to:

Tax-Aide Program
AARP Program Department
601 E St., NW
Washington, DC 20049
Tel: (202) 434-6005

OTHER FREE TAX SERVICES

The IRS has two nation-wide information services which provide recorded tax information: *Tele-Tax* and *Tax Tips on Tape*.

■ *Tele-Tax* — This service provides recorded information via a toll-free telephone number. The service covers approximately 150 tax-related topics, including Topic Number 999 — which provides local information, like where to get Volunteer Income Tax Assistance and Tax Counseling for the Elderly in your neighborhood.

For further information on Tele-Tax — including instructions for using it, the list of topics it covers, and the recording number required to access each topic's recording — order Publication No. 1163, *Tele-Tax*, from the IRS, or contact your local library for a copy of the pamphlet.

■ *Tax Tips on Tape* — The IRS has produced several programs on tape, each about a tax subject of interest to a specific audience. Each year the programs will be broadcast nationwide on 240 Public Broadcasting System stations and a number of cable systems. Current segments focus on tax concerns and information for Older Americans, day care providers, workers who receive tips, farmers and fishermen, taxpayers overseas, taxpayers who move, and several other areas that may interest older taxpayers. While all programs are recorded in English, those of particular interest to the Spanish and Chinese-speaking communities were also produced in those languages.

Check your local TV listings for the dates, times, and channel of these *Tax Tips on Tape* broadcasts. Your local IRS office will also have copies of some of the programs, in limited quantities, on videocassette — as will some public libraries and community colleges.

OBTAINING FREE PUBLICATIONS

Each year the IRS prepares updated publications which can answer many of your tax questions and help you prepare your annual federal tax return. All of these publications are free and readily obtainable. The following sources provide both publications and federal tax forms.

■ **Local public libraries** — Your library generally maintains reference copies throughout the year of the most demanded publications and forms. You can photocopy any of the available forms or publications if the library does not have additional copies to give out.

■ **Local IRS offices** — These offices maintain, although sometimes in limited numbers, almost every publication and form that the IRS publishes.

- **IRS Forms and Publications Telephone Center** — The IRS maintains a nationwide toll-free telephone ordering center throughout the year. You can call **800-829-3676** to obtain any form currently available. Your publications arrive approximately 7 to 10 working days after you place your order. If you are not sure what publication will help you, the IRS telephone representative will help you select the correct publications or forms.

- **IRS mail-order distribution centers** — You can order through the mail any form or publication published by the IRS including advance orders for those which have not yet been released by writing to one of these three IRS Distribution Centers:

If you live in:
Alaska, Arizona, California, Colorado, Hawaii, Idaho, Kansas, Montana, New Mexico, Nevada, Oklahoma, Oregon, Utah, Washington, Wyoming:

Write to:

> Western Area Distribution Center
> IRS Forms
> Rancho Cordova, CA 95743-0001

If you live in:
Alabama, Arkansas, Illinois, Indiana, Iowa, Kentucky, Louisiana, Michigan, Minnesota, Mississippi, Missouri, Nebraska, North Dakota, Ohio, South Dakota, Tennessee, Texas, Wisconsin:

Write to:

> Central Area Distribution Center
> IRS Forms
> P.O. Box 8903
> Bloomington, IL 61702-8903

If you live in:
Connecticut, Delaware, District of Columbia, Florida, Georgia, Maine, Maryland, Massachusetts, New Hampshire, New Jersey, New York, North Carolina, Pennsylvania, Rhode Island, South Carolina, Vermont, Virginia, West Virginia:

Write to:

> Eastern Area Distribution Center
> IRS Forms
> P.O. Box 25866
> Richmond, VA 23261-5074

Individuals who live abroad may order forms from the Richmond, VA or Rancho Cordova, CA distribution center, whichever is closer.

In addition to the general tax information publication No. 17, "Your Federal Income Tax," there are several publications of particular interest to older individuals, including:

- Publication No. 1, "Your Rights as a Taxpayer"
- Publication No. 554, "Tax Information for Older Americans"
- Publication No. 524, "Credit for the Elderly or the Disabled"
- Publication No. 505, "Tax Withholding and Estimated Tax"
- Publication No. 575, "Pension and Annuity Income"
- Publication No. 915, "Social Security Benefits and Equivalent Railroad Retirement Benefits"
- Publication No. 225, "Farmer's Tax Guide"
- Publication No. 590, "Individual Retirement Arrangements"
- Publication No. 910, "Guide to Free Tax Service."

The IRS plans to publish an annual review of the major tax laws enacted by Congress in the preceding year. It is advisable that you request this important review — Publication No. 933, "Major Tax Law Changes," every March or April. It can be invaluable in clarifying changes that may affect your federal tax liability and filing.

IRS TELEPHONE ASSISTANCE SERVICE

A readily accessible means of assistance to help answer your questions on the new tax laws or to help prepare your federal tax return is provided by the Internal Revenue Service. During the entire year, the IRS maintains a toll-free telephone assistance service throughout the nation specifically to answer tax questions and help individuals prepare their returns. However, you should be aware that even if the IRS telephone assistant responds erroneously to your tax questions, you are responsible for the accuracy of your return and payment of the correct tax amount.

It is advisable to record the date, time, name of the IRS representative who responds to your tax questions and the response, in case there is a discrepancy in your tax return which was based on the response you received from the IRS telephone assistant.

All individuals, **except** those who live in an area where a local IRS office is available to answer tax questions from the public, should call the following toll-free number:

800-829-1040.

Anyone who does not have a tax question, but only wants to order tax forms and publications, should call:

800-829-3676.

Individuals who are deaf or hearing impaired **and** have access to TDD equipment should call the following toll-free number for assistance:

800-829-4059*

*This TDD number can be used throughout the U.S. including Alaska, Hawaii, U.S. Virgin Islands, and Puerto Rico.

LEGAL ASSISTANCE FOR THE ELDERLY

The elderly often have legal problems unique to them. Because of the complexity of the frequently-changing government programs they depend on, often compounded by their generally lower incomes, many Seniors find it difficult to obtain the competent legal assistance younger people take for granted.

Several typical disputes and issues plague the elderly — some of which often occur simultaneously — and lead them to seek legal advice. These include:

- questions on financial, nutritional, and health assistance from government programs like Social Security, Supplemental Security Income, Medicare, Medicaid, and Food Stamps
- disagreement with the government over public pensions from the Veterans Administration, Railroad Retirement, and Civil Service
- handling of private — often limited — pensions
- drawing up wills and trusts
- landlord-tenant disputes
- elderly abuse
- consumer problems with essential items like hearing aids, eyeglasses, health products, and insurance
- guardianship

- involuntary commitment to an institution
- property tax assessments and tax exemptions
- age discrimination
- probate.

Knowing they can obtain good legal services and professional legal representation is absolutely critical to Seniors' well-being. Without adequate legal help, many lose their entitled benefits and, in some cases, their independence — sometimes unjustly.

Unfortunately, as the nation's elderly population grows — along with its need for legal aid — the availability of and access to free or low-cost legal services lags behind. However, many private volunteer attorneys and paralegals (non-lawyers trained to provide legal assistance), the American Bar Association and state Bar Associations, nonprofit organizations interested in the elderly, plus funding from federal programs (Social Services Block Grant, the Older Americans Act, and the Legal Services Corporation) have joined to provide affordable or free legal assistance — albeit limited — in every community in the nation. Locating this assistance, on the other hand, often requires a considerable and determined effort.

This discussion is intended to help make your search for assistance a little easier. It provides information about the various legal aid programs for the elderly throughout the nation. It also clarifies major legal issues that concern older individuals.

When you apply for benefits and assistance of any kind, it is absolutely necessary that you provide pertinent documentation — be it birth certificate, marriage license, divorce decree, or death certificate of a spouse. Because these documents often get lost over the years, a listing of the State Vital Records and Statistics Offices is provided at the end of this discussion. These offices will help you obtain certified copies of the documents you need. If you cannot locate any of these documents, do not wait until you need them. Contact your state office **now** to replace those that are missing.

FREE AND LOW-COST LEGAL ASSISTANCE

Some communities have sufficient legal aid services to cover most of the elderly population's needs, while others have barely enough to meet demands. However, the following sources of free or low-cost legal aid generally operate in all communities. If you have trouble finding one of these sources, contact your local Area Agency on Aging or Human Services Information Center for help.

LEGAL AID AND LEGAL SERVICES OFFICES

Almost every community has these offices to help people who cannot afford private lawyers and who meet financial eligibility requirements. Each office is usually staffed by lawyers, paralegals, and law students. **All services are free**, although the types of services available may vary considerably from office to office. However, all offices usually handle landlord-tenant disputes, utilities, Social Security, welfare, unemployment, and family issues.

LEGAL CLINICS

Located in many communities, these clinics help individuals with simple legal matters, like preparing a will. Although the clinics usually charge a fee, they cost much less than a standard law practice because their volume and use of paralegal assistants help them keep down client expenses.

REDUCED-FEE LAWYER REFERRAL SERVICE

Through private law practices in the community, the elderly can obtain discounted services on almost all legal matters. Often, the lawyer's rate is based entirely on the elderly client's ability to pay. More and more communities are undertaking such referral services because of their success in other communities.

VOLUNTEER LAWYER PROJECTS

These invaluable projects provide legal assistance to low-income elderly. Lawyers volunteer their time and expertise in anything from drawing up wills to settling problems with government benefits from Supplemental Security Income, Medicaid, etc. Many volunteer lawyer projects are assisted by the Legal Counsel for the Elderly (LCE) in Washington, DC, a publicly and privately funded nonprofit organization sponsored by the American Association of Retired Persons. As the national support center for volunteer lawyer projects, LCE continually develops new projects throughout the country.

The assistance these projects offer to the elderly is not only **completely free** but constitutes some of the best legal assistance you can receive, because LCE gives the projects' network of lawyers additional training and support in handling legal problems common to the elderly. Many volunteer lawyers also offer protective services for Seniors who are incapable of managing their own financial affairs.

RETIRED LAWYERS' NO-COST COUNSEL

Many communities with a large population of retired lawyers offer monthly free legal programs for the elderly. The retired attorneys volunteer to conduct group seminars on legal topics of interest to Seniors. In many cases, the retired lawyers also provide advice and assistance on an individual basis. Your local Area Agency on Aging can tell you whether your community has such a service and, if so, direct you to it.

SMALL CLAIMS COURTS

All states (except Tennessee and Virginia — Virginia has currently a pilot program operating in Fairfax County) operate Small Claims Courts — or "People's Courts"—which enable individuals to resolve minor disputes without having to hire a lawyer. Generally, the costs of filing is only a few dollars. Information about how to file a claim — a simple procedure — can be obtained from your county clerk. Most Small Claims Courts limit their cases to those involving claims under $500. However, some courts hear disputes involving claims up to $5,000.

DISPUTE RESOLUTION CENTERS

Dispute Resolution Centers (DRC) help people resolve disputes out of court. Sponsored by local judicial systems and (generally) funded entirely by private foundations and organizations, there are over 600 DRCs in 46 states. DRC cases involve a wide array of problems, such as age discrimination, consumer issues, harassment, evictions, and neighborhood disagreements. The DRC's mediation services are usually provided for free and do not involve a court trial — which gives them an advantage over a Small Claims Court.

LEGAL CONCERNS OF THE ELDERLY

While the elderly have as wide a range of legal concerns as any other group — actually wider — they are all affected by certain issues unique to them.

WILLS AND TRUSTS

Wills: While most people recognize the importance of having a will, only three out of ten Americans actually prepare wills before they die. Often the idea of drawing up a will seems morbid to them — or they feel they don't have enough property to make a will worthwhile. As a result, the vast majority die *intestate* (without a will), leaving their homes, property, and personal belongings to be distributed by the state.

A will is an effective legal tool for providing explicit instructions on how property should be distributed and/or used after a person dies. In most cases, a will also minimizes death taxes and legal and probate expenses, and enables the individual to name an executor to be responsible for carrying out the will's instructions.

Because a will is one of the most important documents you will ever sign, it should be drawn up by a lawyer and witnessed to ensure its legality. Some states consider handwritten ("holographic") or oral wills invalid; in any case, such wills are easily disputed in court.

Even if your total property — home, finances, etc.—doesn't seem to amount to much, a will can ensure that items of much greater value — that is, sentimental value — are left to the persons to whom they would mean the most.

Trusts: A trust involves the transfer of property to a *trustee*, who then invests in and manages it for the benefit of the trust's beneficiaries. This property transfer does not constitute a sale. The beneficiaries are selected by the *grantor*— the person creating the trust. A trustee can be a family member, friend, bank, or trust company; in almost every case, the trustee is paid for this service.

Trusts are not just tools for the extremely wealthy. Many older individuals concerned about dying before their dependents (e.g., handicapped children) use trusts as a way to provide for those dependents when there is no one else to care for them — or when they don't want to burden family or friends. If you consider preparing a trust of this nature, be certain to enlist the aid of a lawyer who is experienced in preparing such trusts. The requirements of state law in such matters can make them very complicated. To find a suitable lawyer, contact your local Lawyer Referral Service.

LIVING WILLS: THE "RIGHT TO DIE"

A Living Will is a signed, dated, witnessed document which lets you state your wishes about the use of life-sustaining procedures during a terminal illness. Living Wills are discussed in detail in Chapter 8, "Dying, Death and Funerals."

POWER OF ATTORNEY

Power of Attorney is a legal device which permits an individual (the "principal") to give another person (the "attorney-in-fact") the authority to act on the principal's behalf The attorney-in-fact is authorized to handle banking and real estate, to incur expenses, pay bills, and handle a wide variety of legal affairs. Power of attorney is valid for a stated period of time — that is, for as long as the principal is mentally competent. If the principal dies, or becomes comatose or mentally incompetent, the power of attorney expires immediately. To provide for the latter two occurrences, the principal should authorize a *Durable Power of Attorney.* A Power of Attorney can also be limited to a specific matter, that is, you can assign power of attorney in handling a certain business matter — this power of attorney would not extend to any other affairs.

DURABLE POWER OF ATTORNEY

A Durable Power of Attorney is assigned and operates just like a Power of Attorney, except this authorization remains valid after the principal becomes comatose or mentally incompetent. Every state now has statutes recognizing Durable Powers of Attorney.

Of utmost importance: a Durable Power of Attorney can make· health care decisions on behalf of the principal if he/she becomes incompetent. This makes a Durable Power of Attorney an important alternative to guardianship, conservatorship, and trusteeship.

GUARDIANSHIP

Guardianship — also called *conservatorship* — is a legal mechanism used by the court to declare a person incompetent and appoint a guardian to that person. The court transfers responsibility for managing financial affairs, living arrangements, and medical care decisions to the guardian. Every state has different laws regarding guardianship.

Unfortunately, guardianship has become the target of abuse by family members who use it to gain control of a person's assets. Consequently, most states are developing new laws to protect people who need help with their daily living requirements but who do not deserve a declaration of incompetency or the assignment of a guardian.

Contact your local Area Agency on Aging for information about guardianship. Often, the Agency can provide the assistance the elderly person needs to live independently without a guardian.

AGE DISCRIMINATION IN EMPLOYMENT

All older workers should be aware of the Age Discrimination in Employment Act, which no longer puts a ceiling on the age of the persons it protects (formerly, it only covered workers under the age of 70). The Act guarantees certain rights to older workers and offers considerable protection against all forms of discriminatory employment practices in areas such as discharges, hiring, promotion, demotion, benefits, and compensation.

If you feel you have been discriminated against in employment because of your age, file a charge with your local Equal Employment Opportunity Commission (EEOC)—or at the EEOC's Washington, DC headquarters — within 180 days after the adverse action took place. After you file the charge, you have 300 days to actually file suit.

To get more information about how to file a charge, contact any EEOC office, or call the EEOC's toll-free telephone number:
800-669-4000

Important! Because of the EEOC's failure to process age discrimination claims in time to meet the statute of limitations for such suits, Congress passed legislation giving Seniors 15 additional months to pursue their age discrimination claims. Any individual whose claims were caught in EEOC's backlog and had the statute of limitations time period expire because of it should **immediately** resubmit their age discrimination claim.

ELDERLY ABUSE

Although it is one of America's best kept secrets, abuse of the elderly is a serious and widespread problem, touching people in every walk of life. Recently, the House Subcommittee on Health and Long-Term Care reported that an estimated 1.5 million elderly Americans are abused each year — either physically, mentally or financially. This means that about 1 of every 20 older Americans may fall prey to elder abuse each year. More conservative estimates from law enforcement agencies and other civic groups range from 500,000 to 1,000,000 victims annually. The biggest problem in obtaining more accurate figures is that these unfortunate victims are reluctant to report or even admit they are abused for fear of retaliation in the form of further abuse, abandonment, or institutionalization.

For those who are abused by families or other caregivers, there is finally help available. Many communities now have Adult Protective offices within their Social Services Departments or attached to their police departments; others have community-based task forces which interact to attack the root of the problem; still others are developing emergency relief homes for the abused until they can be resettled elsewhere or stabilize their home situations so they can return without fear of further abuse. In addition, most Area Agencies on Aging are taking an active role in promoting community awareness of the problem and providing programs to help the victims. If you are such a victim, it is absolutely essential that you contact your local Area Agency on Aging or Human Services Information office. It will handle your call confidentially and contact the organization in your community which can help you.

In addition, there are two outstanding organizations that provide assistance to America's abused elderly. Contact them for further information about the assistance they provide:

National Coalition Against
Domestic Violence
P.O. Box 34103
Washington, DC 20043
Tel: (202) 638-6388

National Organization for
Victim Assistance
1757 Park Road, NW
Washington, DC 20010
Tel: (202) 232-6682

A final word to victims of abuse: Do not blame yourself, feel embarrassed, ashamed, or make excuses for the abuser's mistreatment of you. Realize that the abuser needs help. If he or she abuses you, he/she may someday extend that abuse to others. Seek help now while you are still capable of doing so. In so doing, you may also help your abuser.

CONSUMER PROBLEMS

There is probably nothing more exasperating than discovering that something you bought is defective, was misrepresented by the sales person, or that a promised service is not delivered. However, before you seek legal assistance or file a claim in Small Claims Court, try to resolve your problem or complaint yourself, even if it takes considerable effort. Here are three steps to take:

- Contact the seller and explain the problem. (It may be resolved immediately.)

- If the seller doesn't resolve your problem, contact the company's owner or headquarters. Many companies have corporate customer service offices to answer questions and help resolve consumer complaints.

- If your problem is still unresolved, contact your State Consumer Protection Office for assistance. (A listing of these offices is provided at the end of this discussion.)

If, after taking these steps, you are still dissatisfied, you may wish to investigate some of the sources described below. Only if you exhaust all other channels should you take legal action.

Older individuals frequently order through the mail; therefore you should be aware of your legal rights when shopping by mail.

You have the right to:

- Have mail order purchases shipped when promised, or to cancel for full refund. If no shipping date is stated, your right to cancel begins 30 days after your order and payment are received or your account is charged by the company.

- Get a full refund — because of shipping delay — within seven working days (or one billing cycle) after seller receives your request to cancel.

- Obtain a copy of any offered warranty before you buy.

- Refuse a delivery of damaged or spoiled items.

- Consider unordered merchandise a gift and be free of pressure to return it or to pay for it.

SOURCES OF CONSUMER HELP AND INFORMATION

Several organizations and government offices may be able to help you resolve your consumer problems or give you helpful information. Also remember the help your local or state Consumer Protection Office can provide.

Better Business Bureau (BBBs)

There are currently over 170 BBBs throughout the country. They are nonprofit organizations sponsored by private local businesses to provide considerable general information on products or services, background information on local businesses and organizations, and records of a company's complaint-handling performance. Many BBBs will contact a firm on your behalf when you have a complaint or problem which has not been resolved. In addition, some bureaus offer a form of dispute resolution — when it is requested. Check your telephone directory for the BBB in your area.

Private Consumer Groups

Many private consumer organizations throughout the nation will often help individual consumers with complaints or provide information that can be useful in resolving complaints. Contact your state or local consumer protection office to find out whether there is such a group in your community.

One of the oldest, most important consumer organizations is the National Consumer League (NCL). Founded in 1899, the NCL covers such diverse areas as home health care, life-care communities, drugs, home energy, and investments. The NCL's main objective is to establish and maintain health and safety protections and to promote fairness at the marketplace and workplace. Contact the NCL at:

National Consumers League
1701 K Street, NW, Suite 120
Washington, DC 20006
Tel: (202) 835-3323

The following organizations offer assistance in two areas of particular concern to older individuals:

■ Solicitations and Contributions

There are two bureaus that provide general information and advice on organizations or charities that solicit contributions. They also compile reports on the activities of specific organizations. You can order up to three reports at a time by sending a self-addressed, stamped business-sized envelope to:

National Charities Information Bureau
19 Union Square West, 6th Floor
New York, NY 10003 (reports are free)

Philanthropic Advisory Service
Council of Better Business Bureaus, Inc.
4200 Wilson Blvd., Suite 800
Arlington, VA 22203 (charges a $1.00 handling fee).

■ When You Buy a "Lemon"

For years, if your new car turned out to be a "lemon," you had no recourse except to complain to the dealer or manufacturer or take them to court. Today, all that has changed. Forty-four states and the District of Columbia now have "Lemon Laws." These laws state that any new car with serious problems that cannot be fixed in a reasonable time can be returned to the dealer for an exchange or full refund. For further information on your state's lemon law, contact your local or State Consumer Protection Office. In addition, the *Center for Auto Safety*, a private nonprofit organization will send you **free** information describing every state's lemon law. Send your request with a self-addressed, stamped envelope to:

> Center for Auto Safety
> 2001 S Street, NW, Suite 410
> Washington, DC 20009
> Tel: (202) 328-7700

TRADE ASSOCIATIONS AND THIRD-PARTY DISPUTE RESOLUTION PROGRAMS

Almost 40,000 trade and professional associations in the U.S. represent a broad range of interests. Some of these associations have established third-party dispute resolution programs to handle consumer complaints not resolved at the point of purchase. Check with your local library for the book *National Trade Professional Associations of the United States* which describes the associations and their consumer functions. Your state Consumer Protection Office can also help you locate the trade association for your particular problem.

LOCAL MEDIA PROGRAMS

Many local newspapers and radio and television stations offer services such as consumer *Action Lines* or *Hot Lines* that frequently resolve consumer problems. However, be aware that because their time is limited, they handle only the most severe problems or businesses with multiple complaints. Contact your local library or check your local newspaper and radio and television stations to determine whether they operate such a service in your area.

MAIL FRAUD OR MISREPRESENTATION

To ask about mail order sales or report mail fraud or misrepresentation, contact your local Postmaster, Postal Inspector or the Chief Postal Inspector at:

> Chief Postal Inspector
> P. O. Box 96096
> Washington, DC 20066-6096
> Tel: (202) 636-2300

MAIL ORDER PROBLEMS

To register complaints or obtain information about mail order sales, contact your local or State Consumer Protection office or contact:

> The Direct Marketing Association (DMA)
> 1111 - 19th Street, NW, Suite 1100
> Washington, DC 20036
> Tel: (202) 955-5030

Upon written request, DMA's Mail Preference Service will also remove your name from most direct marketing mailing lists. To have your name and address removed from national mail marketing lists, contact:

> Mail Preference Service
> Direct Marketing Association
> P.O. Box 9008
> Farmingdale, NY 11735

To have your name removed from telephone marketing lists, contact:

> Telephone Preference Service
> Direct Marketing Association
> P.O. Box 9014
> Farmingdale, NY 11735

OCCUPATIONAL AND PROFESSIONAL LICENSING BOARDS

Over 1,500 state agencies license or register members of hundreds of professions and services, such as doctors, lawyers, auto repair shops, plumbers and electricians. In addition to their other duties, these boards often help resolve consumer complaints. They will also take disciplinary action against an offender when necessary. To locate the local office of an occupational or professional licensing board, check your local telephone directory under the headings of "Licensing Boards" or "Professional Associations," or look for the name of the individual agency. If there is no local office, contact your State Consumer Protection Office.

State Vital Records and Statistics Offices

Individual records of births, deaths, marriages and divorces are not maintained by the Federal government. They are kept in each state's vital statistics office, or, for very old records, in one of the city, county or local offices that has jurisdiction in the area where the event occurred. If you need a certified copy of one of these documents, visit or write the appropriate office to obtain it.

Charges for each copy of the document vary from state to state and payment must be submitted with your request. Remittances should be made in the form of money order or certified check. If a search by the state cannot locate the document you request, the payments are generally not refunded. The costs for one certified copy of a birth or death certificate are shown in this listing. Costs for additional copies are usually the same as for the first certified copy; however, some states charge less for additional copies ordered at the same time. Call the telephone numbers provided to verify costs or to obtain additional information.

In general, the state offices shown here maintain only information on births and deaths. Since records of marriages or divorces are maintained in the city, county or other local office which issued the marriage license or granted the divorce, you should contact the appropriate office for assistance. The state offices will direct you to the proper office if they do not maintain records of marriages and divorces.

Most of the states require the following information to fulfill your request for copies of birth or death certificates:

- Full name, sex and race of the person whose record is being requested
- Parents' names, including maiden name of mother
- The month, day and year of birth or death and the city, county or town where it occurred

- Your relationship to the individual and why you need the document.

Either print or type your request to ensure complete legibility. Furnishing all of the facts that the state requires will enable efficient processing and a prompt reply to your request.

Cost of Copy:

ALABAMA

Department of Public Health
Bureau of Vital Statistics
Center for Health Statistics
434 Monroe St., Rm 215
Montgomery, AL 36130
Tel: (205) 242-5033

Birth: $5.00   Death: $5.00
(Fee for special searches where date of event is unknown is $5.00 per hour.)

ALASKA

Dept. of Health & Social Services
Bureau of Vital Statistics
P.O. Box H-02G
Juneau, AK 99811
Tel: (907) 465-3391

Birth: $7.00   Death: $7.00

AMERICAN SAMOA

Registrar of Vital Statistics
Vital Statistics Section
Government of American Samoa
Pago Pago, AS 96799
Tel: 011 (684) 633-1222, Ext. 214

Birth: $2.00   Death: $2.00

ARIZONA

Arizona Dept. of Health Services
Vital Records Section
P.O. Box 3887
Phoenix, AZ 85030
Tel: (602) 542-1080

Birth: $8.00   Death: $5.00

ARKANSAS

Arkansas Department of Health
Division of Vital Records
4815 West Markham, Slot 44
Little Rock, AR 72201
Tel: (501) 661-2336

Birth: $5.00   Death: $4.00

Cost of Copy:

CALIFORNIA
Department of Health Services
Office of the State Registrar of
Vital Statistics
410 N Street
Sacramento, CA 95814
Tel: (910) 445-2684

Birth: $11.00   Death: $7.00

COLORADO
Colorado Department of Health
Vital Records Section
4210 East 11th Ave., Rm 100
Denver, CO 80220
Tel: (303) 320-8474

Birth: $6.00   Death: $6.00
(A Priority Service is available
which costs $10.00.)

CONNECTICUT
Department of Health
Vital Records Section
150 Washington Street
Hartford, CT 06106
Tel: (203) 566-2334

Birth: $5.00   Death: $5.00

DELAWARE
Office of Vital Statistics
Robbins Building
P.O. Box 637
Dover, DE 19903
Tel: (302) 736-4721

Birth: $5.00   Death: $5.00

DISTRICT OF COLUMBIA
Vital Records Branch
425-I Street N.W., Room 3009
Washington, DC 20001
Tel: (202) 727-9281

Birth: $8.00   Death: $8.00

FLORIDA
Department of Health and
Rehabilitative Services
Office of Vital Statistics
1217 Pearl St.
Jacksonville, FL 32202
Tel: (904) 359-6900

Birth: $8.00   Death: $4.00
(If year of event is unknown there
is also a search fee of $2.00 per
year.)

Cost of Copy:

GEORGIA
Georgia Department of Human
Resources, Vital Records Unit
Room 217-H
47 Trinity Avenue, S.W.
Atlanta, GA 30334
Tel: (404) 656-4900

Birth: $3.00   Death: $3.00

GUAM
Office of Vital Statistics
Department of Public Health and
Social Services
Government of Guam
P.O. Box 2816
Agana, GU 96910
Tel: (671) 734-7292

Birth: $5.00   Death: $5.00

HAWAII
Vital Records Section
State Department of Health
P.O. Box 3378
Honolulu, HI 96801
Tel: (808) 548-5819

Birth: $2.00   Death: $2.00

IDAHO
Department of Health & Welfare
Bureau of Vital Statistics,
450 W. State St., State House Mail
Boise, ID 83720
Tel: (208) 334-5988

Birth: $8.00   Death: $8.00

ILLINOIS
Illinois Department of Health
Division of Vital Records
605 West Jefferson Street
Springfield, IL 62702
Tel: (217) 782-6553

Birth: $15.00   Death: $15.00

INDIANA
Indiana State Board of Health
Division of Vital Records
1330 West Michigan St., Rm 111
P.O. Box 1964
Indianapolis, IN 46206
Tel: (317) 633-0274

Birth: $6.00   Death: $4.00

Cost of Copy:

IOWA
    Iowa Department of Public Health   Birth: $6.00   Death: $6.00
    Vital Records Section
    321 E. 12th Street
    Des Moines, IA 50319
    Tel: (515) 281-5871

KANSAS
    Dept. of Health & Environment   Birth: $6.00   Death: $6.00
    Office of Vital Statistics
    900 S.W. Jackson Street
    Topeka, KS 66612
    Tel: (913) 296-1400

KENTUCKY
    Department for Health Services   Birth: $5.00   Death: $4.00
    Office of Vital Statistics
    275 East Main Street
    Frankfort, KY 40621
    Tel: (502) 564-4212

LOUISIANA
    Vital Records Registry   Birth: $8.00   Death: $5.00
    Office of Public Health
    325 Loyola Ave.
    New Orleans, LA 70112
    Tel: (504) 568-2561

MAINE
    Office of Vital Records   Birth: $5.00   Death: $5.00
    State House, Station 11
    221 State Street
    Augusta, ME 04333
    Tel: (207) 289-3184

MARYLAND
    Dept. of Health & Mental Hygiene   Birth: $4.00   Death: $4.00
    Division of Vital Records
    4201 Patterson Ave.
    P.O. Box 68760
    Baltimore, MD 21215
    Tel: (301) 225-5988

Cost of Copy:

MASSACHUSETTS
Department of Public Health   Birth: $6.00   Death: $6.00
Registry of Vital Records & Statistics
150 Tremont Street, Room B-3
Boston, MA 02111
Tel: (617) 727-2816

MICHIGAN
Michigan Department of Public Health   Birth: $10.00*   Death: $10.00
Office of the State Registrar &   *(Special fee for Senior Citizens,
Center for Health Statistics   65 years or older, is $2.00 for
P.O. Box 30195   the first copy and $3.00 for
3423 N. Logan Street   each additional copy ordered
Lansing, MI 48909   at the same time.)
Tel: (517) 335-8655

MINNESOTA
Minnesota Department of Health   Birth: $11.00   Death: $8.00
Vital Records Section
717 Delaware Street, SE
P.O. Box 9441
Minneapolis, MN 55440
Tel: (612) 623-5121

MISSISSIPPI
Mississippi State Board of Health   Birth: $11.00   Death: $5.00
Vital Records
2423 N. State St.
Jackson, MS 39216
Tel: (601) 960-7981

MISSOURI
Department of Health   Birth: $4.00   Death: $4.00
Bureau of Vital Records
1730 E. Elm.
P.O. Box 570
Jefferson City, MO 65102
Tel: (314) 751-6376

MONTANA
Department of Health   Birth: $5.00   Death: $5.00
Bureau of Records & Statistics
Capital Station
Helena, MT 59620
Tel: (406) 444-2614

Cost of Copy:

NEBRASKA
  Department of Health   Birth: $6.00   Death: $5.00
  Bureau of Vital Statistics
  301 Centennial Mall South
  P.O. Box 95007
  Lincoln, NE 68509
  Tel: (402) 471-2871

NEVADA
  Office of Vital Statistics   Birth: $7.00   Death: $7.00
  505 East King St., Rm 102
  Carson City, NV 89710
  Tel: (702) 885-4480

NEW HAMPSHIRE
  Bureau of Vital Records   Birth: $3.00   Death: $3.00
  Health & Human Services Building
  6 Hazen Drive
  Concord, NH 03301
  Tel: (603) 271-4654

NEW JERSEY
  Department of Health   Birth: $4.00   Death: $4.00
  Bureau of Vital Statistics   (If year of event is unknown there
  S. Warren and Market Sts. CN-370   is also a search fee of $1.00 per
  Trenton, NJ 08625   year searched.)
  Tel: (609) 292-4087

*For records from May 1848 to May 1878, write or call the following for
fee schedules:*
  Archives & History Bureau
  State Library Division
  State Department of Education
  Trenton, NJ 08625
  Tel: (609) 292-6260

NEW MEXICO
  Vital Statistics Bureau   Birth: $10.00   Death: $5.00
  New Mexico Health Services Division
  1190 St. Francis Drive
  Santa Fe, NM 87503
  Tel: (505) 827-2338

Cost of Copy:

NEW YORK (except New York City)
State Department of Health   Birth: $15.00   Death: $15.00
Bureau of Vital Records
Empire State Plaza
Tower Bldg.
Albany, NY 12237
Tel: (518) 474-3075

NEW YORK CITY
New York City Department of Health Birth: $5.00   Death: $5.00
Bureau of Vital Records   (If year of event is unknown there
125 Worth St., Rm 133   is also a search fee of $1.00 per
New York, NY 10013   year searched.)
Tel: (212) 619-4530

NORTH CAROLINA
Department of Human Resources   Birth: $5.00   Death: $5.00
Division of Health Service
Vital Records Branch
225 N. McDowell St.
P.O. Box 27687
Raleigh, NC 27611
Tel: (919) 733-3526

NORTH DAKOTA
State Department of Health   Birth: $7.00   Death: $5.00
Division of Vital Records
600 East Boulevard
Bismarck, ND 58505
Tel: (701) 224-2360

OHIO
Ohio Department of Health   Birth: $7.00   Death: $7.00
Office of Vital Statistics
65 South Front Street, Room G-20
Columbus, OHIO 43266
Tel: (614) 466-2531

OKLAHOMA
Vital Records Section   Birth: $5.00   Death: $5.00
State Department of Health
1000 Northeast 10th Street
P.O. Box 53551
Oklahoma City, OK 73152
Tel: (405) 271-4040

Cost of Copy:

OREGON
   Department of Human Resources   Birth: $8.00   Death: $8.00
   Health Division, Vital Records Section
   P.O. Box 116
   Portland, OR 97207
   Tel: (503) 229-5710

PENNSYLVANIA
   Department of Health   Birth: $4.00   Death: $3.00
   Division of Vital Records
   101 South Mercer Street
   P.O. Box 1528
   New Castle, PA 16103
   Tel: (412) 656-3147

PUERTO RICO
   Department of Health   Birth: $2.00   Death: $2.00
   Demographic Registry Area   (Requires a postal money order,
   Box No. 11854   payable to the Secretary of the
   San Juan, PR 00910   Treasury, with request of copies.)
   Tel: (809) 728-7980

RHODE ISLAND
   Department of Health   Birth: $5.00   Death: $5.00
   Division of Vital Statistics
   3 Capital Hill, Rm 101
   Providence, RI 02908
   Tel: (401) 277-2811

SOUTH CAROLINA
   Dept. of Health & Environmental   Birth: $6.00   Death: $6.00
   Control, Office of Vital Records &
   Public Health Statistics
   2600 Bull Street
   Columbia, SC 29201
   Tel: (803) 734-4830

SOUTH DAKOTA
   Department of Health   Birth: $5.00   Death: $5.00
   Vital Records Section
   523 East Capitol
   Pierre, SD 57501
   Tel: (605) 773-3355

Cost of Copy:

TENNESSEE
Tennessee Vital Records   Birth: $10.00   Death $5.00
Department of Health and   (For those born before 1950)
Environment   Birth: $5.00   Death $5.00
Cordell Hull Building   (For those born after 1950)
Nashville, TN 37219
Tel: (615) 741-1763

TEXAS
Texas Department of Health   Birth: $8.00   Death: $8.00
Bureau of Vital Statistics
1100 West 49th Street
Austin, TX 78756
Tel: (512) 458-7451

UTAH
Utah Department of Health   Birth: $11.00   Death: $8.00
Bureau of Vital Records
288 North 1460 West
P.O. Box 16700
Salt Lake City, UT 84116
Tel: (801) 538-6105

VERMONT
Vermont Department of Health   Birth: $5.00   Death: $5.00
Vital Records Section
P.O. Box 70
60 Main Street
Burlington, VT 05402
Tel: (802) 863-7275

VIRGINIA
Department of Health   Birth: $5.00   Death: $5.00
Division of Vital Records
James Madison Building
P.O. Box 1000
Richmond, VA 23208
Tel: (804) 786-6228

VIRGIN ISLANDS
Bureau of Vital Statistics   Birth: $10.00   Death: $10.00
Department of Health
P.O. Box 520 C'sted.
St. Croix, VI 00820
Tel: 011 (809) 773-4050

                               Cost of Copy:

WASHINGTON
  Dept. of Social & Health Services   Birth: $11.00   Death: $11.00
  Vital Records
  1112 S. Quince
  P.O. Box 9709, ET-11
  Olympia, WA 98504
  Tel: (206) 753-5936
  Toll Free: 800-331-0680
              (In-state)
              800-551-0562
              (Out-of-state)

WEST VIRGINIA
  Department of Health   Birth: $5.00   Death: $5.00
  Division of Vital Records
  State Capital Complex Bldg., Rm 516
  Charleston, WV 25305
  Tel: (304) 348-2931

WISCONSIN
  Bureau of Health Statistics   Birth: $8.00   Death: $5.00
  Division of Vital Records
  1 West Wilson Street
  P.O. Box 309
  Madison, WI 53701
  Tel: (608) 266-1371

WYOMING
  Vital Records Services   Birth: $5.00   Death: $3.00
  Hathaway Building
  Cheyenne, WY 82002
  Tel: (307) 777-7591

LISTING

State Consumer Protection Offices

In addition to the state office, consumer protection offices are frequently maintained by county, city or local governments. These offices administer the various consumer laws designed to prevent business misrepresentations and assist the public in resolving their complaints. They also provide informational publications, educational materials and various helpful community services.

Generally, consumer problems or complaints are handled by the **local** consumer protection office rather than the state office. If you have a problem with a company which either failed to respond or provided an unsatisfactory response, you should promptly call or write the nearest local consumer protection office, stating all facts necessary for an understanding of your complaint. When your problem or complaint has resulted from a purchase transaction in a state other than your own, you should contact that state's consumer protection office for assistance. To identify the office that can provide the type of consumer assistance you need, call or write the State Consumer Protection Offices in this listing.

Most consumer protection offices require that complaints be submitted in writing before they will take any action. To facilitate handling your complaint, you should enclose with your letter copies of:

(1) pertinent sales slips

(2) sales documents, including any warranties, guarantees, etc.

(3) all correspondence with the retailer or manufacturer involved

(4) your notes or memoranda of any verbal communications you had with individuals involved in the complaint; maintain all originals in a safe place.

ALABAMA
Consumer Protection Division
Office of Attorney General
11 South Union Street
Montgomery, AL 36130
Tel: (205) 242-7334
Toll Free: 800-392-5658
(Alabama only)

ALASKA
Consumer Protection Section
Office of Consumer Protection
has been closed.

AMERICAN SAMOA
Consumer Protection Bureau
P.O. Box 7
Pago Pago, AS 96799
Tel: 011 (684) 633-4163

ARIZONA
Financial Fraud Division
Office of Attorney General
1275 W. Washington Street
Phoenix, AZ 85007
Tel: (602) 542-3702 (fraud only)
Toll Free: 800-352-8431
(Arizona only)

ARKANSAS
Consumer Protection Division
Office of Attorney General
200 Tower Bldg. 323 Center St.
Little Rock, AR 72201
Tel: (501) 682-2007 (voice/TDD)
Toll Free: 800-482-8982
(voice/TDD in Arkansas)

CALIFORNIA
California Department of
Consumer Affairs
400 R Street, Ste. 1040
Sacramento, CA 95814
Tel: (916) 445-0660
(complaint assistance)
(916) 445-1254
(consumer information)
(916) 522-1700 (TDD)
Toll Free: 800-344-9940
(California only)

COLORADO
Consumer Protection Unit
Office of Attorney General
110 16th St., 10th Floor
Denver, CO 80202
Tel: (303) 620-4500

CONNECTICUT
Dept of Consumer Protection
State Office Building
165 Capitol Avenue
Hartford, CT 06106
Tel: (203) 566-4999
Toll Free: 800-842-2649
(Connecticut only)

DELAWARE
Division of Consumer Affairs
Dept of Community Affairs
820 N. French St., 4th Floor
Wilmington, DE 19801
Tel: (302) 577-3250

DISTRICT OF COLUMBIA
Department of Consumer and
Regulatory Affairs
614 H Street, N.W.
Washington, DC 20001
Tel: (202) 727-7000

FLORIDA
Dept. of Agriculture and
Consumer Services
Div. of Consumer Services
218 Mayo Building
Tallahassee, FL 32399
Tel: (904) 488-2226
Toll Free: 800-342-2176 (TDD)
(Florida only)
800-327-3382
(Florida only)

GEORGIA
Governor's Office of Consumer
Affairs
2 Martin Luther King Jr. Dr., S.E.
Plaza Level—East Tower
Atlanta, GA 30334
Tel: (404) 656-3790
Toll Free: 800-869-1123
(Georgia only)

HAWAII
Office of Consumer Protection
Department of Commerce and
Consumer Affairs
828 Font St. Mall
P.O. Box 3767
Honolulu, HI 96812
Tel: (808) 586-2630
Admin. and legal/Hawaii only)
(808) 587-3222
(Complaints/Hawaii only)

IDAHO
Office of Attorney General
State Capitol
Boise, ID 83720
Tel: (208) 334-2424
Toll Free: 800-432-3545
(Idaho only)

ILLINOIS
Governor's Office of Citizens
Assistance
222 S. College
Springfield, IL 62706
Tel: (217) 782-0244
Toll Free: 800-642-3112
(Illinois only)

INDIANA
Consumer Protection Division
Office of Attorney General
219 State House
Indianapolis, IN 46204
Tel: (317) 232-6330
Toll Free: 800-382-5516
(Indiana Only)

IOWA
Iowa Citizens'
Aide/Ombudsman
1300 E. Walnut St.
Capitol Complex
Des Moines, IA 50319
Tel: (515) 281-5926
(515) 242-5065
Toll Free: 800-358-5510
(Iowa only)

KANSAS
Consumer Protection Division,
Office of Attorney General
301 W. 10th
Topeka, KS 66612
Tel: (913) 296-3751
Toll Free: 800-432-2310
(Kansas only)

KENTUCKY
Consumer Protection Division
Office of Attorney General
209 Saint Clair Street
Frankfort, KY 40601
Tel: (502) 564-2200
Toll Free: 800-432-9257
(Kentucky only)

LOUISIANA
Consumer Protection Section
Office of Attorney General
State Capitol Building
P.O. Box 94005
Baton Rouge, LA 70804
Tel: (504) 342-7373

MAINE
Bureau of Consumer Credit
Protection
State House Station No. 35
Augusta, ME 04333
Tel: (207) 582-8718

MARYLAND
Consumer/Investor Affairs
Consumer Protection Division
Office of Attorney General
200 St. Paul Place
Baltimore, MD 21202
Tel: (301) 528-8662
(301) 576-6372
(voice/TDD in Baltimore area)
Toll Free: (800) 969-5766

MASSACHUSETTS
  Consumer Protection Division
  Dept. of Attorney General
  131 Tremont Street
  Boston, MA 02111
  Tel: (617) 727-8400
        (Information and referral only)

MICHIGAN
  Consumer Protection Division
  Office of Attorney General
  P. O. Box 30213
  Lansing, MI 48909
  Tel: (517) 373-1140

MINNESOTA
  Office of Consumer Services
  Office of Attorney General
  117 University Avenue
  St. Paul, MN 55155
  Tel: (612) 296-2331

MISSISSIPPI
  Consumer Protection Division
  Office of Attorney General
  P.O. Box 22947
  Jackson, MS 39225
  Tel: (601) 354-6018

MISSOURI
  Office of the Attorney General
  Consumer Complaints
  P.O. Box 899
  Jefferson City, MO 65102
  Tel: (314) 751-3321
  Toll Free: 800-392-8222
            (Missouri only)

MONTANA
  Consumer Affairs Unit
  Department of Commerce
  1424 Ninth Avenue
  Helena, MT 59620
  Tel: (406) 444-4312

NEBRASKA
  Consumer Protection Division
  Department of Justice
  2115 State Capitol
  P.O. Box 98920
  Lincoln, NE 68509
  Tel: (402) 471-2682

NEVADA
  Department of Commerce
  State Mail Room Complex
  Las Vegas, NV 89158
  Tel: (702) 486-7355
  Toll Free: 800-992-0900
            (Nevada only)

NEW HAMPSHIRE
  Consumer Protection and
  Antitrust Division
  Office of Attorney General
  State House Annex
  25 Capitol St.
  Concord, NH 03301
  Tel: (603) 271-3641

NEW JERSEY
  Division of Consumer Affairs
  Dept. of Law & Public Safety
  P.O. Box 45027
  Newark, NJ 07101
  Tel: (201) 648-4010

  Dept. of Public Advocate
  CN850, Justice Complex
  Trenton, NJ 08625
  Tel: (609) 292-7087
      (New Jersey only)
  Toll Free: 800-792-8600

NEW MEXICO
  Consumer & Economic
  Crime Division
  Office of Attorney General
  P.O. Drawer 1508
  Santa Fe, NM 87504
  Tel: (505) 827-6060
  Toll Free: 800-432-2070
            (New Mexico only)

NEW YORK
N.Y. State Consumer
Protection Board
99 Washington Avenue
Albany, NY 12210
Tel: (518) 474-8583

NORTH CAROLINA
Consumer Protection Section
Office of Attorney General
Dept. of Justice Building
P.O. Box 629
Raleigh, NC 27602
Tel: (919) 733-7741

NORTH DAKOTA
Consumer Fraud Division
Office of Attorney General
600 E. Boulevard Ave.
Bismarck, ND 58505
Tel: (701) 244-2210
Toll Free: 800-472-2600
          (North Dakota only)

OHIO
Consumer Frauds and
Crimes Section
Office of Attorney General
30 E. Broad Street
State Office Tower, 25th Fl.
Columbus, OH 43266
Tel: (614) 466-4986
     (614) 466-1393 (TDD)
Toll Free: 800-282-0515
          (Ohio only)

OKLAHOMA
Consumer Affairs
Office of Attorney General
420 W. Main, Suite 550
Oklahoma City, OK 73102
Tel: (405) 521-4274

OREGON
Financial Fraud Section
Department of Justice
Justice Building
Salem, OR 97310
Tel: (503) 378-4320

PENNSYLVANIA
Bureau of Consumer Protection
Office of Attorney General
Strawberry Square, 14th Fl.
Harrisburg, PA 17120
Tel: (717) 787-9707
Toll Free: 800-441-2555
          (PA only)

PUERTO RICO
Dept. of Consumer Affairs
Minillas Station,
P.O. Box 41059
Santurce, PR 00940
Tel: (809) 721-0940

RHODE ISLAND
Consumer Protection Division
Department of Attorney General
72 Pine Street
Providence, RI 02903
Tel: (401) 277-2104
     (401) 274-4400, ext. 354
     (Voice/TDD)
Toll Free: 800-852-7776
          (RI only)

SOUTH CAROLINA
Dept. of Consumer Affairs
P.O. Box 5757
Columbia, SC 29250
Tel: (803) 734-9452
     (803) 734-9455 (TDD)
Toll Free: 800-922-1594
          (South Carolina only)

SOUTH DAKOTA
Division of Consumer Affairs
Office of Attorney General
500 E. Capitol
Pierre, SD 57501
Tel: (605) 773-4400
Toll Free: 800-592-1865
          (South Dakota only)

TENNESSEE
Division of Consumer Affairs
Dept. of Commerce & Insurance
500 James Robertson Pky.
5th Floor
Nashville, TN 37243
Tel: (615) 741-4737
Toll Free: 800-342-8385
        (Tennessee only)

TEXAS
Consumer Protection Division
Office of Attorney General
Capitol Station, P.O. Box 12548
Austin, TX 78711
Tel: (512) 463-2070

UTAH
Division of Consumer Protection
Dept. of Business Regulation
P.O. Box 45802
Salt Lake City, UT 84145
Tel: (801) 530-6601

VERMONT
Public Protection Division
Office of Attorney General
109 State Street
Montpelier, VT 05609
Tel: (802) 828-3171

VIRGIN ISLANDS
Dept. of Consumer Affairs
Property & Procurement Bldg.
Subbase #1, Rm 205
St. Thomas, VI 00802
Tel: (809) 774-3130

VIRGINIA
Division of Consumer Counsel
Office of Attorney General
Supreme Court Building
101 N. Eighth Street
Richmond, VA 23219
Tel: (804) 786-2116
Toll Free: 800-451-1525
        (VA only)

WASHINGTON
Consumer and Business
Fair Practices Division
Office of Attorney General
111 Olympia Ave, NE
Olympia, WA 98501
Tel: (206) 753-6210

WEST VIRGINIA
Consumer Protection Division
Office of Attorney General
812 Quarrier Street, 6th Fl.
Charleston, WV 25301
Tel: (304) 348-8986
Toll Free: 800-368-8808
        (W. Virginia only)

WISCONSIN
Office of Consumer Protection
Department of Justice
801 W. Badger Rd.
Madison, WI 53708
Tel: (608) 266-9836
Toll Free: 800-422-7128
        (Wisconsin only)

WYOMING
Office of Attorney General
123 State Capitol Building
Cheyenne, WY 82002
Tel: (307) 777-7874

GOLDEN AGE PASSPORT

For those who enjoy using our federal parks and recreation areas, the government has authorized a special pass especially for you. This lifetime entrance permit is called, appropriately, the "Golden Age Passport," and is available to any citizen or permanent resident of the United States age 62 or older for a one-time fee of *only* $10.

This passport allows free entrance to federal parks, monuments, and recreation areas which have entrance charges, and gives you a 50 percent discount on federal use fees for facilities and services like camping, boat launching, cave tours, parking and many others. However, it does not cover fees charged by private concessionaires.

One of the nicest features of the Golden Age Passport is that it covers the permit holder in a private vehicle and any companions traveling in that vehicle. If you enter a park or recreation area by another means of transportation, the passport admits you (the permit holder), your spouse, children and parents.

The Golden Age Passport can be obtained in person from most federally-operated recreation areas by simply requesting it and showing some proof of age, such as your driver's license, birth certificate or Medicare card.

This passport can be obtained at any of the following locations:

- Forest Services supervisor's offices
- Most Forest Service ranger station offices
- National Park Service areas where entrance fees are charged
- Bureau of Land Management state and district offices
- The Tennessee Valley Authority's *Land Between the Lakes* and all recreation areas that charge fees
- All Fish and Wildlife Service regional offices and National Wildlife Refuges where Land and Water Conservation Fund use fees are in effect
- The Bureau of Reclamation-Hoover Dam.

"Golden Access Passports" for Blind and Disabled Persons — A special permit called the Golden Access Passport is available *free* to citizens or permanent residents of any age who are eligible to receive disability or blindness benefits under federal law. This passport provides the same features and special provisions as the Golden Age Passport and is obtained in the same way; however, individuals requesting this passport must present a medical certification of their blindness or permanent disability.

PRESIDENTIAL GREETINGS PROGRAM

One of the most pleasant surprises someone could receive on a birthday or wedding anniversary is a special greeting of congratulations from the President of the United States. Almost every President has personally acknowledged important events in the lives of certain individuals, but under President Eisenhower a special program for the nation's elderly came into effect, when he began sending congratulations to individuals on their 100th birthday. Due to the increased longevity of our present population, former President Reagan's greeting program recognized far more celebrants than did earlier administrations. President Reagan sent over 12,500 greetings each year to those 100 years of age and older. President Bush continued the program with just as many greetings to Senior Americans.

President Clinton has expanded considerably the Presidential Greetings program and now honors those celebrating their 80th — or subsequent — birthday; those celebrating wedding anniversaries of 50 years or more; the birth of a child; acknowledgement of Boy Scout and Girl Scout awards; Bar Mitzvahs and Bat Mitzvahs; and sympathy cards for the loss of a loved one.

Staffed entirely by volunteers, of whom the majority are Senior Citizens themselves, the Presidential Greetings office sends over a half-million congratulations each year — bringing special joy to many Senior Citizens. If you are interested in obtaining a Presidential Greeting for someone who is celebrating one of the important events indicated, write at least **30 days in advance** to:

> Greetings Office, Rm. 39
> The White House
> Washington, DC 20500

Always include the following information in your request:

- full name, or names, of the celebrant(s)
- date of the event
- age of the individual for a birthday, or number of years of marriage for a wedding anniversary.
- full address to which the greetings should be sent and the name of the person to whom they should be sent — especially if the greetings are to be presented at the time of a celebration.

It is important that the information in your request be written clearly so the greetings are properly prepared and sent to the correct address.

YOUR FEDERAL GOVERNMENT AT WORK...
RECENT CHANGES

The following 1996 Congressional Acts and other changes will affect many of you:

- *Enactment of New Farm Bill:* With the signing in April by President Clinton of the 1996 farm bill, past subsidy programs for our nation's 1.8 million farmers have been replaced by a new system which provides guaranteed but gradually declining payments to farmers over the next seven years. The bill also contains several other provisions which include the elimination of government controls over what farmers can plant or what fields they must leave idle, the reauthorization for two years of the food stamp program, authorization of a $300 million economic development fund for rural America, and an end to the current special tax on dairy producers.

- *1996 Law Prohibits Taxing Former Residents' Pensions:* In January, a federal law was enacted which prohibits states from imposing taxes on pensions of retirees who have moved and are no longer residents of that state. In particular, the bill affects two states— New York and California—since they received millions of dollars in annual revenue by taxing the pensions of retirees who moved out of their states to reside in states with little or no income tax.

- *Speeding up FDA's Approval of New Anti-Cancer Drugs:* In March 1996, President Clinton announced that the Food and Drug Administration (FDA) will speed up the approval of new anti-cancer drugs by using the same rules that have accelerated the approval of anti-AIDS drugs. Under these rules, an anti-cancer drug may be given early FDA approval to be marketed—despite the lack of conclusive evidence of the effectiveness of the drug—if the drug has been shown to work in reducing tumors. In addition, the FDA will accelerate the approval of certain drugs that have been approved for market in other countries. These new initiatives will allow many patients with life-threatening illnesses to obtain access to potentially helpful drugs that have been denied in the past.

- *President Signs Line-Item Veto Law:* After finally concluding a debate that has been going on for decades, the 2nd session of the 104th Congress approved giving the President a "line-item" veto. In

April, President Clinton signed the veto power into law. Beginning in January 1997, the new law gives the President the power to strike out those spending items to which he objects in an appropriations bill. The law primarily affects only discretionary spending bills. It will not affect the majority of federal spending for existing entitlement programs such as Social Security and Medicare or other items that were specifically expended by Congress.

- *FDA Approves Use of Ultrasound in Diagnosing Breast Cancer:* The Food and Drug Administration (FDA) has recently approved using ultrasound equipment in determining whether lumps in women's breasts are benign or cancerous. The FDA reported that with this approval we may be able to reduce by almost 40 percent the number of women (currently at approximately 700,000 per year) who undergo biopsy surgery of breast lumps. Ultrasound machines use high-frequency sound waves that are sent through the body's tissue to form images from the echoes created by the sound waves. Hopefully, many doctors will soon rely on ultrasound equipment as a primary diagnostic procedure over that of biopsy surgery.

- *Congress Approves Increase in Earnings Limit for Social Security Recipients:* In late March 1996, Congress finally passed legislation that would allow individuals age 65 to 69 to continue working without fear of losing their Social Security benefits. Under the new law which is retroactive to January 1996, the earnings limit would rise from the current $11,520 to $30,000 by 2002. Only earnings are counted towards the limit; pensions, dividends and interest do not count. It is estimated that over a million individuals will benefit from the new limit of $12,500 in 1996. The law does not affect the earnings limit for retirees age 62 to 64. Their current limit is $8,280 before losing any Social Security benefits.

Federal Holidays

In the majority of our states the following holidays are observed with the closing of federal, state and county government offices, banks, post offices and libraries. **Plan ahead and do not schedule your visits or telephone inquiries to them during these days.** It is also advisable not to contact government offices during their busiest times, which are generally Mondays, any day following a holiday, and the first of each month. You will receive more attention and help, as well as not having to spend considerable time waiting for assistance, if you schedule around these times.

News Year's Day	January 1
Martin Luther King, Jr. Day	3rd Monday in January
Washington's Birthday	3rd Monday in February
(also known as Presidents' Day)	
Memorial Day	Last Monday in May
Independence Day	July 4
Labor Day	1st Monday in September
Columbus Day	2nd Monday in October
Veterans Day	November 11
Thanksgiving Day	4th Thursday in November
Christmas Eve[*]	December 24
Christmas Day	December 25

[*] Even though Christmas Eve is not considered a federal holiday, you will find that a half day is generally celebrated, or at least, that most office staffs are curtailed to a minimum throughout the day. Consider Christmas Eve as a time not to schedule visits or telephone inquiries.

Chapter 11

Making Life a Little Better

Help For Everyone

Chapter Highlights

Making Life a Little Better

Help for Everyone

Now that you've read about the myriad government and private programs, benefits and entitlements designed to help the elderly, it's time to reflect on other aspects of life that touch almost every older individual in a personal way. This chapter discusses such things as visiting the seriously or critically ill, special educational/travel programs for Seniors, vacationing (including a listing of State Offices of Tourism), the opportunities offered by your local Senior Center, the many activities and services of the public library, Seniors and the political process, saving money through Senior discounts, and the many organizations formed especially for older Americans.

No matter who you are, there should be something in this chapter to interest you, and possibly enrich your life.

SENIOR DISCOUNTS . . . A WORLD OF SAVINGS

Each year, vast numbers of Senior Citizens throw hundreds of dollars away **and don't even know it.** This waste continues year after year because these Seniors don't take advantage of one of the best means of money-saving available to them: *Senior Citizen discounts.*

Of course, many Senior Citizens do take advantage of these savings — which can equate to price reductions ranging anywhere from 5 to 50 percent — but many, many more do not. This apparent lack of interest perplexes the many merchants and community leaders who sponsor reduced prices and discounted admissions for use of community services and facilities. Just a few years ago, even the nationwide "Silver Pages" program — promoted by the Area Agencies on Aging — had to be discontinued by its sponsor due to lack of market interest. The program offered those 60 and older a chance to save on a wide range of goods and services listed in their local *Silver Pages* directory.

Senior Citizen discounts are often advertised inconspicuously . . . if at all; they are not automatically given. Therefore, it may take you a little effort and trial and error to obtain these valuable savings. However, the "trouble" will be worth it, because these discounts can save you hundreds of dollars each year:

Some Senior discounts available in most every community are:

- Half-fares on public transport system buses, subways (metros), and commuter trains;

- Waiver of monthly service fees on checking accounts, including free checks and — often — traveler's checks;

- Discounts for adult classes at local high schools, colleges, universities, and technical schools. Some schools also provide discount meals for Seniors;

- Discounted admissions to public and private recreational facilities, such as swimming pools, golf courses, and tennis courts;

- Discounted movie tickets for almost all showings. Often, Seniors get even greater discounts at morning or afternoon showings;

- Senior discount days at many local stores, including grocery stores;

- Reduced ticket prices at most museums, galleries, and performing arts centers;

- Discounts from businesses that sell goods and services, such as television repair, furnace and plumbing services, etc.

- 10-15% discounts on prescription drugs (including generics) at many drug stores. These drug stores often offer additional advisory services to Seniors;

- Members' savings for Seniors who belong to many local organizations or national affiliates, such as reduced rates for hotels, car rentals, and other goods and services;

- "Early Bird" specials at local restaurants geared towards Seniors whose schedules are flexible enough to let them eat earlier than the "9-to-5" population;

- Discount rates for gas and electricity (check with your local utilities to see if they offer such a discount to elderly households);

- Phone company discounts to Seniors and/or housebound individuals for local telephone service. If your local phone company doesn't offer such a service, be sure to express your concern to the company, the local authorities, and/or your local Area Agency on Aging.

SPECIAL TIPS ON SENIOR DISCOUNTS

To limit the recipients to Senior Citizens, many organizations and merchants apply some rules or restrictions on their Senior discounts. The best way to ensure that you can benefit from these discounts is to follow these tips:

- Always carry a photo I.D. that gives your birthday (for example, a driver's license). If you don't drive, your state's Motor Vehicle Department will issue you a "Resident's Identification Card" at a minimal cost — or, sometimes, for free to Senior Citizens. These cards are just as valid as driver's licenses as a form of identification.

- Because most discounts are not given automatically, **always ask** if a Senior discount is available wherever you shop or eat. Sometimes, businesses without official discount programs will give you a Senior discount anyway *if you ask for it*.

- Always request your Senior discount before you buy, make reservations, or eat. Many merchants, hotels, and restaurants will not deduct the discount amount after they've drawn up the bill.

- If you find that a certain merchant or organization doesn't offer Senior discounts, be sure to mention this to the manager or owner in a friendly way. Remind them that a discount program is one of the best ways to ensure patronage, because Seniors always give preference to businesses that offer such discounts, even if only five or 10 percent. You may be surprised to find a Senior discount offered the next time you visit.

BEGIN SAVING MONEY TODAY!

Senior Citizen discounts can equate to thousands of dollars in savings over the years . . . money you can use to help meet the high costs of housing, food, and medical care, as well as the pleasures in life that you can't always afford. If you haven't done so already, why not

start taking advantage of the many Senior discounts in your community? Also, spread the word about the discounts you find to other
Seniors who could use the savings.

Before you buy anything in the future, **ask whether a discount
is available to you.** Remember, most businesses, organizations, restaurants, and public services want your patronage; this is why they offer
Senior discounts. Just ask, and the door to a world of savings will be
opened to you.

ORGANIZATIONS FOR SENIORS . . .
THE BENEFITS OF BELONGING

A book on benefits and assistance for older individuals would not
be complete without a discussion of the many national organizations
formed by and for older individuals. Without their dedicated advocacy on behalf of the elderly and their united efforts to sensitize Congress,
state legislatures, and local governments to the needs of older Americans, many of the benefits the elderly have won in recent years
would never have happened.

The joint advocacy of the Senior organizations has helped reduce
Senior poverty from 35 percent in the late 1950s to less than half that
amount today. Many programs that benefit the elderly — Medicare,
Supplemental Security Income, Food Stamps, Medicaid, the Age Discrimination in Employment Act, and the vital Older Americans Act,
as well as many housing, transportation, and job programs for the
elderly — are also, in great part, the result of this united front.

Yet, as you all know, there is still much left to be done to bridge
the gap between what Senior Citizens need and the programs and services
actually available to them. The reality is, despite the improved outlook,
many Seniors have too little money, unsatisfactory housing, and inadequate health care — particularly long-term care in nursing homes or
at home. These are the issues facing today's Senior organizations.

While they all perform roles in improving the lives of the nation's
older individuals, each Senior organization has its own mandate,
methodology, and membership. The mandates of these organizations are loosely categorized below:

- *Quality of Life* — Membership in these organizations is directed towards professionals and other groups involved in all issues that affect the quality of life of older individuals. They serve as national resources for information, training, advocacy, and research on aging.

  Examples: National Council on the Aging; National Alliance of Senior Citizens.

- *Cause Advocacy* — These organizations are coalitions of individuals and other organizations formed to advocate specific causes, like the protection and improvement of Social Security and other elderly programs.

  Examples: National Committee to Preserve Social Security and Medicare; Save Our Security.

- *Human Rights and Anti-Discrimination* — While not always formed solely to benefit Senior Citizens, these organizations often sponsor and maintain specific elderly programs — like housing projects — to enable Seniors to live in dignity and independence.

  Examples: B'nai B'rith International; Gray Panthers.

- *Special Interests* — These organizations are directed towards particular groups of elderly individuals.

  Examples: National Association of Retired Federal Employees; National Caucus and Center on Black Aged.

- *Service-Oriented* — Perhaps the most well-known category, these organizations direct their membership at individual Seniors by offering — for very low annual dues — myriad services and group benefits at reduced rates. They also keep their members informed about government and other programs of assistance available to them.

  Examples: American Association of Retired Persons; Mature Outlook.

WHY JOIN? —
WHAT SENIOR ORGANIZATIONS CAN DO FOR YOU

There are four main reasons to join a national Senior organization:

1. You will become part of the growing, increasingly powerful network of Seniors that forms the "united front" of Senior organizations to lobby Congress and state and local government on behalf of Seniors' needs and rights.

2. You can enjoy many activities sponsored by the organization's local and affiliated groups in your area. These activities enable you to associate with other members who have similar interests and concerns.

3. You will receive the magazine, newsletter, and other publications put out by your organization. These contain information about government programs, elderly benefits, and other important information directed at older Americans.

4. If offered by your organization, you will be able to benefit from savings programs, services, and discounted items, supplies, and medications.

Veterans — Don't forget all the fine veterans' organizations listed in Chapter 9, "Veterans Entitlements".

LISTING

Organizations and Associations

Again and again this book has mentioned numerous national organizations which provide the elderly with assistance in health, welfare, insurance, housing, and many other areas. Each organization is worthy of far greater recognition than is possible in this short discussion. Therefore, do not hesitate to contact any or all of them for information about their objectives and membership.

The following listing provides the names and addresses of the organizations mentioned above, as well as other fine groups dedicated to improving the lives of America's Senior Citizens.

AMERICAN ASSOCIATION OF RETIRED PERSONS (AARP)

601 E St., NW; Washington, DC 20049
Tel: (202) 434-2277

World's largest nonprofit non-partisan organization dedicated to (1) enhancing the quality of life for older persons, (2) promoting dignity and purpose for older persons, (3) providing leadership in determining the role and place of older persons in society, and (4) improving the image of aging. Runs community volunteer programs. Represents the interest of older citizens at all levels of government. Offers benefits and services including free publications, mail-order pharmacy service, group health insurance, reports on legislative developments, discounts on books, automobile club, travel service, and investment programs. Publications include the monthly *AARP News Bulletin* and bimonthly *Modern Maturity*. **Dues:** $8.00 per year, $20.00 for 3 years.

B'NAI B'RITH INTERNATIONAL

1640 Rhode Island Ave., NW; Washington, DC 20036
Tel: (202) 857-6580

Serving Jews and non-Jews, B'nai B'rith stresses the purest principles of philanthropy, honor, and patriotism, and supports the arts and sciences. Members visit and care for the sick, rescue victims of persecution, and provide for, protect, and assist the poor, aged, widowed, and orphaned. B'nai B'rith sponsors many special programs for the elderly. Through its

Senior Citizens Housing Committee, B'nai B'rith builds and operates Senior Citizen housing projects throughout the U.S. which provide comfortable, affordable housing for lower-income elderly of all races and religions. **Dues:** Varies according to district.

CATHOLIC GOLDEN AGE (CGA)

430 Pennsylvania Avenue; Scranton, PA 18503
Tel: (717) 342-3294 or Toll Free: 800-233-4697

Unites its members behind issues of major concerns to Catholics — such as respect for life, human rights, world peace, elimination of poverty and hunger — and to Senior Citizens — such as health care costs, Social Security benefits, and housing. Benefits and services include life, health, and Medicare Supplemental insurance, pharmacy service, eye-wear discounts, group travel and pilgrimages, and discounts on car rentals, hotels, motels, and interstate moving costs. CGA provides legislative information, companionship through its local chapters, and Masses, Novenas, and prayers for its members. It publishes the quarterly *CGA World.* **Dues:** $7.00 per year.

GRAY PANTHERS

1424 - 16th St., NW, Suite 602; Washington, DC 20036
Tel: (202) 466-3132

Activist group founded to promote changes in laws and attitudes which discriminate against persons based on their age. The Gray Panthers lobby to protect Social Security, guarantee decent housing and health care, and eliminate age discrimination. Publications include books, manuals, and a bimonthly newsletter, *The Network.* **Dues:** $15.00 per year.

MATURE OUTLOOK, INC.

6001 N. Clark Street; Chicago, IL 60660
Toll Free: 800-336-6330

Formerly the National Association of Mature People. Mature Outlook — in association with Sears — directs most of its efforts at providing cost-saving services and products. Services and benefits include free publications on topics pertinent to Seniors' welfare, the bimonthly *Mature Outlook,* and a bimonthly newsletter, Allstate insurance programs, mail-order pharmacy service, optical discounts, travel programs, motor club, hotel, motel, and car rental discounts, coupons for Sears products, special loan rates through Allstate Enterprises, and several investment programs. **Dues:** $9.95 per year.

NATIONAL ALLIANCE OF SENIOR CITIZENS, INC. (NASC)

1700 - 18th Street, NW, Suite 401; Washington, DC 20009
Tel: (202) 986-0117

Nonprofit nationwide lobby for the Senior community. Its primary concern is for the income, health, and personal security of the elderly. Benefits and services include a prescription drug service, vitamin and health care products service, car rental and lodging discounts, automobile and travel clubs, group health and life insurance, investment program, and discount book buying service. Publications include the bimonthly *Our Age* and the monthly *The Senior Guardian*. **Dues:** $10.00 per year.

NATIONAL ASSOCIATION FOR THE HISPANIC ELDERLY (ASOCIACION NACIONAL PRO PERSONAS MAYORES)

3325 Wilshire Blvd., Suite 800; Los Angeles, CA 90010
Tel: (213) 487-1922

Nonprofit organization established to serve older Mexican Americans, Puerto Ricans, Cubans, Central and South Americans, and Spaniards. The National Association is committed to promoting coalitions throughout the nation to improve the well-being of older Hispanics and other low-income elderly. Its main efforts include *Project Ayuda* — an employment program for low-income Seniors — training and technical assistance on aging for community groups and professionals, and the National Hispanic Research Center. Its media center produces and disseminates bilingual information through many audio and visual media. Publications include a quarterly legislative bulletin and the quarterly *Our Heritage*. **Dues:** $5.00 per year for Seniors.

NATIONAL ASSOCIATION OF RETIRED FEDERAL EMPLOYEES (NARFE)

1533 New Hampshire Ave., NW; Washington, DC 20036
Tel: (202) 234-0832

Spokesman for federal annuitants. Its primary objective is to protect the interests of all persons qualified under the federal government's Civil Service Retirement and Disability system. NARFE lobbies to maintain retirement benefits for retired federal workers and their dependents and to ensure that they keep pace with inflation. Its monthly magazine *Retirement Life* keeps its members informed about legislative proposals of special interest. NARFE's network of 1,650 local chapters throughout the U.S. and its territories provide focal points for recreational, social, informative, and community activities. **Dues:** $15.00 per year.

NATIONAL CAUCUS AND CENTER ON BLACK AGED, INC. (NCBA)

1424 K Street. NW, Suite 500; Washington, DC 20005
Tel: (202) 637-8400

Nonprofit organization dedicated to improving the economic status and quality of life of older persons, particularly the black elderly. Operates a national social service network for the black elderly. Benefits and services include group rates for life, hospitalization and accident insurance, Medicare Supplemental Insurance, mail order services for prescription drugs, vitamins, and health care products, discounts on travel, lodging, and car rental, and consumer buying group. Publishes a quarterly newsletter, *Golden Page.* **Dues:** $7.00 per year.

NATIONAL COMMITTEE TO PRESERVE SOCIAL SECURITY AND MEDICARE

2000 K Street, NW, Suite 800; Washington, DC 20006
Tel: (202) 822-9459

Founded to preserve and protect the integrity of the Social Security and Medicare programs and to build a widespread Senior membership to support the Committee's lobbying activities. Publishes a monthly newsletter, *Saving Social Security* which alerts its members to congressional action on these vital programs. **Dues:** $10.00 minimum contribution.

NATIONAL COUNCIL OF SENIOR CITIZENS (NCSC)

1331 F St., NW; Washington, DC 20004
Tel: (202) 347-8800

Lobby for state and federal legislation to benefit the elderly. Administers programs to promote shelter and home energy, safety, education, health care, and employment for older Americans. Benefits include group health insurance to supplement Medicare, discount prescription drugs, travel service, automobile insurance, and hotel and motel discounts. Publications include special reports and the monthly *Senior Citizen News,* while the "NCSC Legislative Hotline" provides weekly phone summaries of Congressional activities of interest to Seniors, forthcoming committee hearings, and other legislative information. **Dues:** $12.00 per year.

NATIONAL COUNCIL ON THE AGING, INC. (NCOA)

409 Third St., SW; Washington, D.C. 20024
Tel: (202) 479-1200

Committed to giving a national focus to the needs and concerns of older people. National Council activities include lobbying and advocacy, professional affiliates, national conferences, media campaigns, job training and placement for low-income elderly, public opinion polls, the nation's largest library on aging, publications like the bimonthly *Perspective on Aging* and the quarterly *Current Literature on Aging,* and education, arts, and humanities programs. The National Council developed pilot programs for the Foster Grandparent Program, Meals on Wheels, and the national congregate meals program. **Dues:** $30.00 for retirees.

NATIONAL INDIAN COUNCIL ON AGING, INC. (NICOA)

6400 Uptown Blvd., NE, Suite 510W; Albuquerque, NM 87110
Tel: (505) 888-3302

Founded to provide improved comprehensive services to elderly Native Americans and Native Alaskans in accordance with the recommendations for remedial action formulated at the 1976 and 1978 National Indian Conferences on Aging. The Council also serves as a national clearinghouse for issues affecting the Indian and Alaskan Native elderly. **Dues:** $10.00 for individual membership.

OLDER WOMEN'S LEAGUE (OWL)

666-11th St., NW, Suite 700; Washington, DC 20001
Tel: (202) 783-6686

Works to provide mutual support for its members, to achieve economic and social equity for its constituents, and to improve the image and status of middle aged and older women. Major OWL efforts include lobbying to protect Social Security benefits, to correct inequities in the system pension rights, and to provide access to affordable health insurance, caregiver support services, and jobs for older women. Publications include *OWL Observer* (published 10 times per year), *Wingspan* manuals on midlife planning, *Gray Papers* of research on women's issues, and other status reports, pamphlets, and brochures. **Dues:** $15.00 per year.

SAVE OUR SECURITY COALITION (S.O.S.)

1201-16th Street, NW
Washington, DC 20036
Tel: (202) 822-7848

Nonprofit organization dedicated to protecting and improving Old Age and Survivors' benefits, Disability Insurance, Medicare and Medicaid. Unemployment benefits, and Supplemental Security Income, S.O.S. has an extensive research and education program and publishes several pamphlets and booklets on major issues of concern to the elderly. **Dues:** $10.00 contribution.

SENIOR CENTERS . . . PROVIDING MANY PLEASURABLE ACTIVITIES

For years now, Senior Centers have offered individuals over 60 a special place for recreation, social activities and companionship with other people their age. Many elderly once believed that Senior Centers were only for the very old and disabled or that they were nothing but elderly "day-care centers." But just one visit to their local Senior Center changed their beliefs when they discovered that most Senior Centers offer so many activities and programs that it requires lots of stamina to participate in them all. The truth is, Senior Centers are full of vitality.

As an alternative to staying home, alone and inactive, Senior Centers provide outstanding places to meet others and become socially involved without feeling uncomfortable or unwanted. Many individuals have made good friends at their centers.

Most Senior Center programs, activities and services vary according to the Center's size and available funds. Centers can generally be categorized into two types:

1. **Multiservice/Meal Centers** — usually have a full-time professional staff and host the largest variety of recreation and social activities, as well as providing lunch for free or at a nominal cost;

2. **Senior Centers** — provide many activities but are limited because of accommodations or funding and may not have a full-time professional staff. These centers do not usually serve lunch.

In addition, hundreds of community clubs cater to older individuals but don't have a permanent location. These clubs frequently form their own Senior Centers, especially in communities where a center is not available or readily accessible.

To impress upon you the variety of interesting programs and activities available through your local Senior Center, the following sampling lists those offered by the majority of centers; remember this is just a **sampling;** many centers offer an even greater variety of events and activities:

- international festivals with costumes and ethnic foods
- movies
- dances

- table games such as bingo and ping-pong
- lessons in arts and crafts like sewing, painting, ceramics and photography
- field trips to theaters and museums
- foreign language instruction classes
- special breakfasts and pot-luck dinners
- voter assistance and registration
- tax preparation assistance
- tetanus and influenza immunizations
- health counseling for high blood pressure, diabetes and arthritis
- diet and exercise classes
- visiting dieticians who help in meal planning
- bridge tournaments
- information and referral to local in-home services
- assistance with food stamp applications and Medicare claim forms
- local job registry
- discussion groups of all sorts.

If you have never visited a Senior Center in your community, **now is the time.** Contact your local Area Agency on Aging or Human Services Information staff to find out the location of the Senior Center nearest to you so you can start participating. Once you become a regular participant, your Senior Center will provide some of your most pleasurable experiences.

YOUR LIBRARY AND ITS SERVICES . . . THEY DON'T COST ANYTHING

If you have not visited a public library in several years, you would be amazed at how the library has changed and at the information, activities and programs it now offers. What is more, all these many diverse offerings are free.

Today's public libraries are much more than lenders of books and magazines or reference book centers. They have expanded their scope, offering a myriad of multi-media materials, artistic, literary and informational programs, and other activities, that they have become one of our nation's most important cultural centers. With over 15,200 public libraries and branches serving the American people, there should be at least one library easily accessible to you.

Not all library systems can afford to provide all the same services as others. However, even the smallest community libraries usually offer an impressive variety of materials and programs. Probably no other place offers as many free resources as your local public library. In addition to being a resource center for information and programs on hobbies, businesses or professions, most public libraries offer:

- videotapes, records and compact discs — many libraries have the equipment necessary to play them; some libraries even loan this equipment;

- InfoTrac II computer information systems which help find magazine articles (The program's information is updated monthly.);

- personal computers and typewriters to use at the library;

- film programs for adults and children;

- talking books and braille books;

- large print books and materials;

- reading machines that enlarge printed materials and microfiche;

- foreign language books, and books, records and tapes that teach foreign languages to English-speakers and that teach English to foreigners;

- reading machines that transform printed text into a computer-generated voice (availability of these systems is limited because of their cost);

- Telecommunication Devices for the Deaf (TDDs) and other phone services for the hearing impaired;

- telecaption adapters for the deaf;

- special activities and programs, such as storytelling, book discussion groups, emergency first aid lessons, CPR classes, lessons in arts and crafts, plant clinics, adult literacy programs, tax preparation assistance, voter registration and recitals;

- current consumer, medical, legal, and government publications on many topics of concern to older people.

In addition, most libraries offer special services for older individuals, the handicapped, and the housebound, including:

- **Bookmobile service** — delivery of a large selection of best sellers and in-demand books to people who live or meet in institutions like Senior residences. You can make selections from the Bookmobile's stock, or make special requests for books which are then delivered upon the Bookmobile's next visit.

- *Special center deliveries* — delivery of books and other materials for patrons of nursing homes, Senior nutrition centers, etc. When desired, a collection of books can be left at the facility for others to share. Requests for books and information are taken at each delivery and filled upon the return visit.

- **Home delivery** — delivery to people confined to their residences. The individual requests library materials, which are then delivered to the home.

One of the library's most important features — particularly for older persons — is its telephone information service. Every day, librarians find the answers to numerous questions on anything from how to spell a word to the details of some local legislation. And, when your question cannot be answered immediately, the librarian will call you back when the information has been found.

Because librarians are happy to respond via telephone, older people, whether housebound or handicapped, can still get the answers to critical questions — like "Who are my Congressmen?" — and obtain important information on local support groups, voter registration, consumer advocates, corporate consumer contacts . . . and many more.

Why not do yourself a favor by visiting your nearest public library? You will never regret getting back to the public library, and your life will be enriched by the many services it offers you.

VISITING THE SERIOUSLY ILL . . . IT MEANS SO MUCH TO THEM!

One of the most important times to show others that you care for them is when you visit or call them during a prolonged or serious illness. Naturally, when someone is hospitalized or ill for a short period of time, your visit is appreciated. However, the importance of your attention increases as the confinement lengthens. As days turn into weeks, knowing that others really care becomes extremely significant to the patient.

Many of us are not certain what we should do when we visit friends and loved ones who are seriously ill and hospitalized or confined to their homes or a nursing home. The following suggestions should help you prepare for these important visits.

- Call — **do not visit** — when you have a bad cold or flu. You don't want to expose someone whose own resistance is already lowered by illness.

- Plan your visit to coincide with scheduled or appropriate visiting hours. When visiting a private home, **always** let the family or patient know ahead of time when you are planning to visit. Even a call on the morning of your anticipated visit will be appreciated and could preclude an untimely arrival.

- Don't worry about bringing a gift. Your presence is worth more than any trinket. However, if bringing something makes you feel more comfortable, make it a small item such as a magazine, a toilet article like a favorite soap or lotion, or — if the patient's diet allows — a home-baked item or a few pieces of fresh fruit.

- If you arrive at the patient's room to find the door closed (or the bed drapes pulled), check with a nurse or the family **before** knocking or entering the room.

- Never cry or show distress over a patient's condition while visiting. Make an excuse to leave the room temporarily — like having to use the bathroom — if you have difficulty controlling your emotions.

- If the patient wants to talk about his/her illness, be a good listener, but change the subject as soon as possible to prevent it from becoming the major topic of conversation. Discuss everyday items like neighbors, pets, projects you are working on, or interesting items in the news.

- Completely **avoid** talking about other people's illnesses, deaths, or unfortunate mishaps. Always discuss items that can lift the patient's spirits — not those that might depress him/her.

- If there is another patient or visitor in the room, be thoughtful and acknowledge that person, but direct your attention to the person you are visiting.

- **Don't overstay your visit!** Unless you are asked by the family or nurse to stay longer for a particular reason, or if you have come a long distance and are unable to visit again soon, leave within 30 minutes to an hour. If you must wait for someone to drive you home, wait outside the patient's room to avoid imposing on the patient.

- Leave as warmly as you came, with a **smile** and a short farewell that lets the patient know you will return. Do not commit yourself to returning on a specific day or time unless you are certain you can make it.

WHEN THE PATIENT IS IN AN INTENSIVE CARE UNIT

In view of the critical condition of a patient in an Intensive Care Unit, the following thoughts about visiting such a patient may be helpful to you and to the patient.

- Hospitals usually have rules limiting visitors of patients in intensive care units to members of the immediate family. However, if there are no close family members and you are very special to the patient, you may be considered an appropriate visitor.

- Since visiting hours are very restrictive, inquire ahead of time about when you will be permitted to visit so as to schedule your visit appropriately. When you arrive, check with the nurse on duty to ensure that any care being given is not interrupted.

- Do not bring any gifts unless asked to do so by the nurse. In some cases, you may be permitted to bring a family picture to display near the patient.

- Regardless of the number of tubes or special machines and monitor screens present, direct your full attention to the patient.

- A patient on a ventilating machine should not try to speak. Talk to him/her in a normal voice, but do not expect any verbal response. Unless diminished hearing is a problem for the patient, he/she can hear you.

- Touch the patient's hands or forehead, if possible, to provide additional comfort and possibly ease the patient's efforts to respond to you.

- If an alarm on one of the monitors sounds, do not panic or run from the room — a nurse will be there shortly. Many times, the alarms do not indicate that anything serious is happening to the patient.

- A family spokesperson should be selected to call the unit for updates on the patient's condition and relay information to others so the nurses can spend as much time as possible caring for the patient.

- Generally, your visiting time should be very short — only 10 or 15 minutes — unless the nurse allows you to remain longer.

- Leave when it is time, with a **brief** assurance to the patient that you are close by and will be there whenever needed.

Always Remember: Your visit to a seriously or critically ill friend can be immensely uplifting and important for him or her, and will also give you the satisfaction of knowing you saw your friend one more time. Do not delay! Visit your sick friends as soon as possible . . . it will mean so much to them.

Just in case you would like to call . . .

(All telephone numbers are in area code 202)
The White House..456-1414
President William Jefferson Clinton.........................456-1414
Vice President Al Gore, Jr..456-2326
Chief of Staff Leon Panetta......................................456-6797
U.S. Senate Information..224-3121
U.S. House of Representatives Information 225-3121

EXPRESSING YOUR OPINION . . .
IT CAN MAKE A DIFFERENCE

Although many of you may think your opinion doesn't matter much, be aware that, to most people how you feel — particularly about issues concerning the elderly — is extremely important. There isn't a single politician — federal, state, or local — who doesn't take into consideration what the elderly think, what their needs are, and what programs will be able to help them. For, as every politician knows, when it comes time to vote, the first ones at the polls are America's Senior Citizens. Even in elections with low voter turnout, Seniors go to the polls in record numbers. In fact, surveys of recent elections show that older Americans account for nearly half of all voters!

There are many ways you can express your opinion about legislation, the inadequacy or lack of services and assistance, or injustices that prevail in our system. Two of the most effective outlets for voicing your opinion are to: (1) **Vote** in every national, state, and local election; (2) **Write** directly to your Senators and Representatives in Congress and to the Congressional committees and subcommittees responsible for drafting and presenting bills to the Senate and House floors. At the end of this discussion information is given on how to obtain complete listings of all House and Senate committees to which you should address letters concerning current or proposed legislation.

VOTING

Older Americans are probably better informed about voting than any other group of U.S. citizens. However, the following information may help reinforce your knowledge, or bring to light some new information.

■ You must be a resident of the state in which you register to vote. If you move to another state or local registration area (for example, if you move in or out of an incorporated city, county, township, or village), you must register again at your new location.

■ Federal law prohibits states and localities from enforcing residency requirements of more than 30 days to prevent new residents from voting in federal elections. However, the states and localities can enforce these requirements for state and local elections. Therefore, if you have just moved to an area, be sure you've lived there long enough before trying to vote in state and/or local elections.

■ While you can register throughout the year, some states require you to register a certain number of days before the actual election to give them time to process your paperwork. This period can range from 10 to 30 days. The only states which allow people to register up to and on election day are Maine, Minnesota, and Wisconsin. No registration is required in North Dakota.

■ In addition to Guam and Puerto Rico, some states allow registration by mail; these are:

Alaska	Nebraska
California	New Jersey
Connecticut	New York
Delaware	Ohio
District of Columbia	Oregon
Hawaii	Pennsylvania
Idaho	South Carolina
Iowa	South Dakota
Kansas	Tennessee
Kentucky	Texas
Maine	Utah
Maryland	Washington
Minnesota	West Virginia
Montana	Wisconsin

Mail-in registrations must be postmarked by the date set by each state. In some cases, they must be witnessed and notarized. Usually, states which don't allow mail-in registration will make special exceptions for members of the armed forces and other individuals employed outside the U.S. (and their families, if residing with them), and for those physically unable to register in person. Almost every state has a program to register housebound citizens at home.

■ **Absentee Ballots** — Every state has laws that permit their residents to vote by mail if they know they will be away from home on election day due to unavoidable circumstances (work-related travel, family emergency, hospital stay, etc.); because voting is considered a privilege and not an absolute right, most states do not allow absentee voting by people who are just going on vacation. As with registration, members of the armed forces and other individuals employed outside the U.S. (and their families, if residing with them) can vote by mail.

You can obtain voting and registration information year-round from your public library, local board of elections office, local Area Agency on Aging, Human Services Information office, and the League of Women Voters. The last group is a non-partisan organization of women and men whose sole purpose is to promote U.S. citizens' political responsibility through active and informed participation in the electoral process. The League is particularly active in providing information about registration requirements and locations, helping voters obtain absentee ballots, and disseminating other voting information for your state or the state to which you're moving.

Remember, even if you are housebound or out of the country, as an American you have a responsibility to vote. Your vote **does** make a difference. You will find that help is readily available to ensure that you can register and vote.

WRITING TO CONGRESS

Because most of us don't have a regular correspondence with members of Congress or the Senate, when the time does come that we want to express our opinions, we may find the task more difficult than anticipated. It's not always easy to decide what a letter should include to make it get the attention of the Congressman/woman, Senator, or Committee, let alone what it must say to inspire them to act.

However, it's not really hard to write an effective letter if you keep in mind the following guidelines:

■ Always use the correct form of address:

for Senators:	**for Representatives:**
Honorable (name)	Honorable (name)
United States Senate	U.S. House of Representatives
Washington, DC 20510	Washington, DC 20515
Dear Senator (name):	Dear Representative (name):
	or
	Dear Mr./Mrs./Ms. (name):

■ Make your letter as specific and brief as possible.

■ If you are discussing a particular bill, be sure to include the bill's number, or, if you don't know the number, the name of its author or sponsor.

- Identify the aspects of the bill you don't like — or those you do — and explain why. Don't just generalize "I don't like the bill." In most cases, Congress or the Senate will amend a bill to eliminate portions they can identify as objectionable or controversial.

- Share your own perspective on the bill in a constructive way. Discuss its potential effect on yourself and/or others. Include any personal expertise you have on the subject. You'd be surprised how often citizens provide Representatives/Senators and Committees with new, important or unconsidered information.

- Be sure to include your name, address, and telephone number. This will enable the Representative/Senator or his/her staff to contact you if they want to discuss your letter further.

While the main reason people write to their Representatives and Senators is to discuss specific legislative matters, your letter can also request aid in satisfactorily resolving difficulties you have had with federal agencies. Representatives, Senators, and their staffs take particular pride in being able to help resolve an elderly constituent's problems with Social Security, disability payments, Supplemental Security Income, Medicare, Medicaid, VA claims, federal pensions, IRS tax problems, or in other critical areas. Do not hesitate to contact your Representative and/or Senator about these problems: he or she **will** help.

When you write to any committee concerning proposed legislation, you may address your letter to the committee chairman or any member of the committee (be sure the person you write to is currently a member). If one of your state's senators or representatives is a member of the committee, it is better to write to him/her rather than the committee chairman, because as your elected representative, he/she has a vested interest in your concerns. To obtain complete listings of the various House and Senate committees and subcommittees, call or write to:

For Senate Committees:
Office of the Secretary
U.S. Senate
U.S. Capitol Bldg., Rm. S-312
Washington, D.C. 20510
Tel: (202) 224-2115

For House Committees:
Office of the Clerk
U.S. House of Representatives
The Capitol
Washington, D.C. 20515
Tel: (202) 225-7000

You don't have to be an outstanding letter writer to express your opinion. As long as your letter is legible and follows the few guidelines mentioned here, it will be well-received. When you express your opinion in this way, you are taking an active part in the nation's political process. Your letter could make a tremendous difference, not only to you, but to many other Americans.

ELDERHOSTEL . . .
THE JOYS OF LEARNING IN LATER LIFE

If you want an opportunity to participate in something intellectually stimulating, challenging, interesting and above all, enjoyable, you should seriously consider the Elderhostel program. Since its inception in 1975, this unique educational program has been extremely successful in attracting thousands of participants each year. To many, it has been a most pleasurable learning experience and an ideal travel opportunity.

Elderhostel is an educational program for adults 60 or older. Others may participate if they are at least 50 years old and are accompanying eligible participants. Elderhostel allows individuals to take up to three non-credit courses in a wide variety of liberal arts and sciences subjects. You do not have to have a diploma from any school, nor have prior knowledge or training for any of the courses. Even though the courses are taught on an adult level, the instructors assume that the students have had no previous in-depth exposure to the subjects. Every Elderhostel program is designed for individuals with various educational backgrounds.

Elderhostel provides inexpensive academic programs, generally a week or more in duration, at over 1,000 colleges, universities and other educational facilities in the United States, Canada and several countries overseas. Its participants are housed on campus in the dormitories of the host institutions while attending the programs. Participants eat together in the campus dining facilities and have access to all cultural, educational and recreational resources of the institution. Practically all necessities are provided for the participant — plus the opportunity to make new friends and have a great time while sampling college life.

Costs are low, running with a few exceptions $275 for a one-week program in the United States and $295 in Canada. This fee covers tuition, room and board, use of the campus facilities and — often — several extra-curricular activities. A number of scholarships — or "hostelships" — are available for those who cannot afford the costs of participating in an Elderhostel; however, these hostelships are limited to programs within the United States and Canada. The cost of the overseas programs are also reasonable and offer participants an outstanding opportunity to travel abroad and learn about their host country.

Elderhostel catalogs are available at most libraries. However, you can obtain additional information about this program, its scholarships, and free copies of the catalogs by writing to:

> ELDERHOSTEL, INC.
> 75 Federal Street
> Boston, MA 02110

VACATIONING...PLANNING AHEAD

After months or even years of looking forward to the quintessential vacation, how many of us have found that anticipation has far exceeded the actual event? In fact, for many, that longed-for vacation turned into one of the biggest disasters of their lives!

Except for natural disasters, political upheavals, and labor actions, most of the events that turned a potentially glorious vacation into a nightmare could have been avoided...by planning ahead. After the months of economizing and saving, shouldn't you make the necessary effort to ensure that your vacation is a wise investment?

Although many of you have many years of planning truly great vacations under your belts, this discussion offers some additional suggestions which may help you in your planning.

TRAVEL AT HOME

Learn about Where You're Going: Obtain as much information as you can about the state(s) and areas you plan to visit. This information is available from each state's Office of Tourism (a listing of State Offices of Tourism follows this discussion). You will be amazed at the amount of information you'll be "bombarded" with once you make your request, including schedules of events and lists of sights that charge no admission. Be sure to request this information well in advance of your trip so you can use it when you draw up your itinerary.

Medical Alert Identification: If you have a medical condition or allergy of critical significance in an emergency, be sure to wear a Medical Alert necklace or bracelet and carry a Medical Alert Card at all times. On vacation, you will be away from your own doctors and others who are familiar with your condition.

If you don't belong to an organization that provides Medical Alert items, contact the *Medic Alert Foundation International.* Basic membership in the foundation costs only $35 for life, and includes a stainless steel emblem, wallet card, and hotline service. An annual fee of $15 is charged for updating your medical information. To join, call or write to the foundation at:

Medic Alert Foundation International
P.O. Box 1009
Turlock, CA 95381
Tel: Toll Free 800-432-5378

Sudden Illnesses: Although you can't plan ahead for any sudden illness or medical problem you may experience on vacation, you can prepare for such an eventuality by contacting the *American Academy of Family Physicians* (AAFP). The Academy will send you a list of family doctors — members of the AAFP — in the state(s) in which you will be traveling. Contact them as early as you can for this listing at:

American Academy of Family Physicians
8880 Ward Parkway
Kansas City, MO 64114
Tel: (816) 333-9700

Medications: If you require medication, bring an ample supply with you as well as a new or refillable prescription in case you need more.
Dental Checkup: Before you go on vacation, be sure you have a dental

checkup. Too many vacations are ruined by toothaches, irritations from dental plates, or loss of fillings that were loose before the trip.

Travelers Checks: To avoid loss or theft, carry as little cash as you can when you travel. Instead, keep your funds in the form of travelers checks, which can be cashed easily wherever you go as long as you carry proper identification. If the checks are lost or stolen, they can be replaced easily and on short notice — sometimes the same day; for this reason, you should always keep a list of the travelers check numbers separate from the checks. **Never endorse the checks before you use them.** (When you travel abroad, you should never take U.S. dollars in cash. Carry travelers checks and convert them to the local currency as you need it rather than in a lump sum.)

Traveling by Car: If you plan to travel in your own car, have it fully serviced before you leave. If you haven't had the oil changed in the last 3,000 miles, or a tune-up in the last 10,000 miles, make sure these are done before you depart. Have all fluids, and the cooling and electrical systems checked, and check the tires for wear and tear. If the treads aren't very deep, it is time to buy new ones **before** you undertake a lot of driving.

If you don't already belong, you may want to join a motor vehicle club like the American Automobile Association (AAA) or one of the clubs sponsored by any Senior Organizations to which you may belong. These clubs offer 24-hour roadside assistance and towing — which can be a godsend if your car breaks down on an unfamiliar road. You can become an immediate member of the AAA by calling one of its local affiliates listed in your telephone directory. No matter which club you join, membership could pay for itself the first time your car breaks down far from a service station and needs to be towed. You should also check your own car insurance policy to see if and under what circumstances it covers towing. If you don't have towing coverage, it usually costs very little to add it to your policy.

If you travel by rental car, find out what kind of service coverage the rental company provides. Remember, however, if you own a car, your own insurance coverage almost always covers any rental vehicle you may drive. You seldom need to pay extra for the rental company's insurance. If you are planning to rent a car, check with your insurance company to see what kind of coverage your policy provides for rental cars.

Travel by Train, Bus, or Plane: If you aren't driving, making sure you book your transportation reservations as far in advance as you can. For air travel, making reservations 30 days in advance can often save you up to 50 percent on the cost of your ticket; however, in other cases, booking less than seven days ahead can give you the same savings. Therefore, it is critical that you **shop around.** Air travel is a highly competitive business. Comparison shopping between all the airlines that fly to your destination often reveals that you can get a significantly lower fare than the first one quoted to you.

You can often save even more money and time — and make your reservations more easily — by booking your trip with a travel agent. *Most agents are paid by the airlines, so their services are free to you* (or they may charge very nominal service fees). Travel agents have a computer database of information about every commercial airline's destinations, schedules, and fares, and they can get you discount fares that you can't get yourself.

If you travel a lot, be sure to join the airline's frequent flyer club. You'd be amazed how quickly — sometimes by taking only one long flight — you can earn enough frequent flyer points to get your next airline ticket — plus discount coupons for major hotel and car rental chains — for free!

Your Itinerary: Before you leave on vacation, be sure to give a friend, relative, and/or neighbor your detailed travel schedule, including names, addresses and telephone numbers of hotels, motels, or people you will visit, as well as the issuers and numbers of your travelers checks and airline tickets (if you travel overseas, also include your passport number, and the date and place it was issued) . This way, if an emergency arises while you're away, you can be easily contacted.

TRAVEL ABROAD

In addition to the suggestions above, which also apply to travel outside the U.S., some additional tips may help you when you travel overseas:

Learn about Where You're Going: To obtain information about your destination(s), contact the tourist authorities for those countries (these tourist authorities are often headquartered in New York City and Los Angeles; call directory assistance in those cities — area code + 555-1212 — for their numbers), and visit travel agents, bookstores, and public libraries. Knowing about the culture, people, and history of the countries you visit will make your trip more meaningful.

Passports: Apply at least six (6) months in advance for your passport. You can apply at one of the State Department's regional Passport Agencies (or at the central Passport Office on 19th Street, NW, in Washington, DC Tel: (202) 647-0518), or at one of the several thousand federal or state courthouses or U.S. Post Offices authorized to accept passport applications. The current fee for a ten-year passport is $65.00; for renewals, the fee is $55.00.

It generally takes 2 to 4 weeks from the date of application to obtain a passport. However, people who must travel on extremely short notice (e.g., in an emergency), the passport office can expedite your application within a matter of days. Contact the office for more information.

Visas: Many countries require visitors to obtain visas which permit entry into the country for a specified purpose and period of time. You should apply for a visa as soon as you can. You should contact the embassy or consulate of the country you plan to visit to obtain information about the country's visa requirements:

Emergency Assistance: If a problem or emergency such as an illness, death or loss of a passport occurs while you are travelling outside the U.S., the American Citizens Service in Washington, D.C. is available to assist you on a 24-hour basis. Always carry the following address and telephone number with you on your trips outside the U.S.

American Citizens Service
U.S. Department of State
2201 C Street, NW, Room 4811
Washington, DC 20520
Tel: (202) 647-5225

This Center also provides several services to American citizens when they travel in problem areas. Before departing, ask the Center to send you information about their assistance for travelers in those foreign countries.

Special Brochure for Senior Citizens: *Travel Tips for Senior Citizens,* prepared by the State Department, contains most of the information you need about traveling overseas. It can be obtained **free** from the American Citizens Service.

Health and Trip Cancellation Insurance: Medicare and many private insurance policies do not pay for medical services received outside the U.S. Several companies and organizations provide temporary health insurance for travelers overseas. In addition, these companies provide trip cancellation insurance, which reimburses your investment in a trip that you must postpone or cancel due to illness or other emergency (trip cancellation insurance does not cover changes of mind). For information about temporary health insurance and trip cancellation insurance, check with any local insurance agent, travel agent, or contact either of the following:

Travel Assistance International
1133 15th Street, NW, Suite 400
Washington, DC 20005
Toll Free: 800-821-2828

Access America, Inc.
P.O. Box 90315
Richmond, VA 23286
Toll Free: 800-284-8300

Vaccinations: Make sure you get any necessary vaccinations early and double check to see if any of your earlier vaccinations' protection have lapsed. To determine which vaccinations you need for the countries you plan to visit, contact your local Department of Health.

CONSUMER TIPS FOR AIRLINE TRAVEL

Here are some tips from the U.S. Office of Consumer Affairs concerning the purchase of airline tickets and other aspects of airline travel that could prove helpful to you when planning your vacations.

- Travel agents are sources of information about fares, schedules and baggage limits, as well as local businesses that can issue airline tickets and boarding passes. In addition, travel agencies sometimes purchase discount seats to popular destinations. So check with travel agents, even if the airlines are sold out.

- When making your airline reservation, always ask about fees or penalties for changing or cancelling a reservation or a paid ticket. There might be a variety of ticket prices, with varying penalties and conditions. Choose one that best fits your needs. In general, the less expensive the fare, the more restrictions it is likely to include. So, if price is important to you, book early and make sure your plans will not change.

- Read the disclosure statement on the back of your ticket. It explains your rights and responsibilities as a passenger, as well as the airline's liability for overbooking seats or for losing or damaging luggage. However, not all passenger rights are included on the back of an airline ticket; some are incorporated by reference. Travelers wanting more information should ask the airline for a copy of its "Conditions of Carriage."

- When flights are overbooked, airlines must ask for volunteers to give up their reservations in exchange for compensation of the airline's choosing. If you volunteer, be sure to get any compensation agreements in writing.

- If you are "bumped" or involuntarily reassigned to a later flight, the airline must provide a written statement of your rights and entitled compensation. The complete rules for compensation are available at all airport ticket counters and boarding locations.

LISTING

State Offices of Tourism

Before you plan your next vacation in the United States, be sure to take advantage of the many services provided by the State Offices of Tourism shown in the following listing. You can obtain brochures, maps, park listings, directories, and information on special festivals, events, tours and more by simply writing or calling any of these offices. The assistance and information they provide is **free**. In several states, you can call toll-free. Unless indicated otherwise, the toll-free numbers shown operate nationwide.

Most states send the information in a week or two. However, some of them do take longer, so contact them well in advance of your trip.

ALABAMA
Bureau of Tourism and Travel
401 Adams Ave.
Montgomery, AL 36104
Tel: (334) 242-4169
Toll Free: 800-252-2262

ALASKA
Alaska Division of Tourism
Pouch E 101
Juneau, AK 99811
Tel: (907) 465-2010

ARIZONA
Arizona Office of Tourism
2702 N. 3rd St., Suite 4015
Phoenix. AZ 85003
Toll Free: 800-842-8257

ARKANSAS
Department of Parks and Tourism
One Capitol Mall
Little Rock, AR 72201
Tel: (501) 682-7777
Toll Free: 800-828-8974

CALIFORNIA
California Department. of
Commerce
Office of Tourism
P.O. Box 1499
Sacramento, CA 95812
Tel: (916) 322-1396
Toll Free: 800-862-2543

COLORADO
Colorado Tourism Board
1625 Broadway, Suite 1700
Denver, CO 80202
Tel: (303) 592-5510T
Toll Free: 800-433-2656

CONNECTICUT
Connecticut Department of
Economic Development
865 Brook Street
Rocky Hill, CT 06067
Tel: (860) 258-4290
Toll Free: 800-282-6863

DELAWARE
Delaware Tourism Office
P.O. Box 1401
99 Kings Highway
Dover, DE 19903
Tel: (302) 739-4271
Toll Free: 800-441-8846

DISTRICT OF COLUMBIA
Washington, DC Convention
and Visitors Association
1212 New York Ave, N.W., Suite 600
Washington, DC 20005
Tel: (202) 789-7000

FLORIDA
Florida Division of Tourism
126 W. Van Buren
Tallahassee, FL 32399
Tel: (904) 487-1462

GEORGIA
Georgia Department of Industry
and Trade
Tourism Office
P.O. Box 1776
Atlanta, GA 30301
Tel: (404) 656-3590
Toll Free 800-847-4842

HAWAII
Hawaii Visitors Bureau
2270 Kalakaua Ave., Suite 1108
Honolulu, HI 96815
Tel: (808) 923-1811

IDAHO
Idaho Travel Council
700 W. State Street
Boise, ID 83720
Tel: (208) 334-2470
Toll Free: 800-635-7820

ILLINOIS
Illinois Bureau of Travel
100 W. Randolph St.
Suite 3-400
Chicago, IL 60601
Toll Free: 800-226-6632

INDIANA
Tourism Development Division
Indiana Department. of
Commerce
One North Capitol, Suite 700
Indianapolis, IN 46204-2243
Tel: (317) 232-8860
Toll Free: 800-289-6646

IOWA
Iowa Development
Commission
Tourism Office
200 E. Grand Avenue
Des Moines, IA 50309
Tel: (515) 242-4705
Toll Free: 800-345-4692

KANSAS
Department. of Economic
Development
400 S.W. 8th Street, Suite 500
Topeka, KS 66603
Tel: (913) 296-2009
Toll Free: 800-252-6727

KENTUCKY
Kentucky Department of
Travel Development
Tourism Cabinet
Capital Plaza Tower, 22nd Fl.
Frankfort, KY 40601
Tel: (502) 564-4930
Toll Free: 800-225-8747

LOUISIANA
Office of Tourism
P.O. Box 94291
Baton Rouge, LA 70804
Tel: (504) 342-8119
Toll Free: 800-633-6970

MAINE
Maine Tourism Info Services
The Main Publicity Bureau, Inc.
P.O. Box 7300
Hallowell, ME 04347
Tel: (207) 289-6070
Toll Free: 800-533-9595

MARYLAND
State of Maryland.
Office of Tourism
217 E. Redwood St., 9th Fl.
Baltimore, MD 21202
Tel: (301) 333-6611
Toll Free: 800-543-1036

MASSACHUSETTS
Massachusetts Division of
Tourism, Department of
Commerce and Development
100 Cambridge Street,13th Fl.
Boston, MA 02202
Tel: (617) 727-3201
Toll Free: 800-447-6277

MICHIGAN
Travel Bureau, Michigan
Department of Commerce
P.O. Box 30226
Lansing, MI 48909
Tel: (517) 373-0670
Toll Free: 800-543-2937

MINNESOTA
Minnesota Tourism Division
375 Jackson Street. Rm. 250
St. Paul, MN 55101
Tel: (612) 296-5029
Toll Free: 800-657-3700

MISSISSIPPI
Mississippi Division of
Tourism Development
P.O. Box 1705
Ocean Springs, MS 39566
Tel: (601) 359-3297
Toll Free: 800-927-6378

MISSOURI
Missouri Div. of Tourism
Truman State Office Bldg.
P.O. Box 1055
Jefferson City, MO 65102
Tel: (314) 751-4133
Toll Free: 800-877-1234

MONTANA
Travel Montana
Department of Commerce
1424 Ninth Avenue
Helena, MT 59620
Tel: (406) 444-2654
Toll Free: 800-541-1447

NEBRASKA
Department. of Economic
Development
Div. of Travel & Tourism
301 Centennial Mall South
P.O. Box 94666
Lincoln, NE 68509
Tel: (402) 471-3796
Toll Free: 800-228-4307

NEVADA
Nevada Commission on Tourism
Capitol Complex
600 E. Williams, #207
Carson City, NV 89710
Tel: (702) 885-4322
Toll Free: 800-638-2328

NEW HAMPSHIRE
State of New Hampshire
Office of Vacation Travel
P.O. Box 856
Concord, NH 03302
Tel: (603) 271-2666
Toll Free: 800-386-4664

NEW JERSEY
Div. of Travel and Tourism
Department of Commerce and
Economic Development, CN 826
Trenton, NJ 08626
Tel: (609) 292-2470
Toll Free: 800-537-7397

NEW MEXICO
Economic Dev. & Tourism
Department.
1100 Saint Francis Drive
Santa Fe, NM 87503
Tel: (505) 827-0291
Toll Free: 800-545-2040

NEW YORK
Department of Economic
Development, Division of
Tourism
One Commerce Plaza
Albany, NY 12245
Tel: (518) 474-4116
Toll Free: 800-225-5697

NORTH CAROLINA
Division of Travel & Tourism
Department of Commerce
430 N. Salisbury Street
Raleigh, NC 27611
Tel: (919) 733-4171
Toll Free: 800-847-4862

NORTH DAKOTA
North Dakota Tourism Promotion
Liberty Memorial Bldg.
604 E. Boulevard
Bismarck, ND 58505
Tel: (701) 224-2525
Toll Free: 800-437-2077

OHIO
Department of Development
Office of Travel & Tourism
P.O. Box 1001
Columbus, OH 43266
Tel: (614) 462-4992
Toll Free: 800-282-5393

OKLAHOMA
Tourism & Recreation Department.
500 Will Rogers Building
Oklahoma City, OK 73105
Toll Free: 800-652-6552

OREGON
Oregon Tourism Commission
775 Summer St., NE
Salem, OR 97310
Tel: (503) 378-3451
Toll Free: 800-547-7842

PENNSYLVANIA
Division of Tourism
453 Forum Bldg.
Harrisburg, PA 17120
Tel: (717) 787-5453
Toll Free: 800-847-4872

RHODE ISLAND
Department. of Economic
Development
7 Jackson Walkway
Providence, RI 02903
Tel: (401) 277-2601
Toll Free: 800-556-2484

SOUTH CAROLINA
South Carolina Div. of Tourism
1205 Pendleton St., Suite 106
Columbia, SC 29201
Tel: (803) 734-0135

SOUTH DAKOTA
South Dakota Tourism
711 Wells Ave.
Pierre, SD 57501
Tel: (605) 773-3301
Toll Free: 800-732-5682

TENNESSEE
Tennessee Tourist Development
P.O. Box 23170
Nashville, TN 37202
Tel: (615) 741-2158

TEXAS
Texas Tourist Dev. Agency
P.O. Box 12728
Austin, TX 78711
Tel: (512) 462-9191
Toll Free: 800-888-8839

UTAH
Utah Tourism & Recreation
Information
Council Hall
300 N. State St.
Salt Lake City, UT 84114
Tel: (801) 538-1467

VERMONT
Agency of Development and
Community Affairs,
Travel Div.
134 State Street
Montpelier, VT 05602
Tel: (802) 828-3236
Toll Free: 800-837-6668

VIRGINIA
Division of Tourism
202 N. Ninth Street, Suite 500
Richmond; VA 23219
Tel: (804) 786-4484
Toll Free: 800-847-4882

WASHINGTON
Department of Trade and
Economic Development
Tourism Development Div.
101 General Admin. Bldg.
Olympia, WA 98504
Tel: (206) 753-5600
Toll Free: 800-544-1800

WEST VIRGINIA
Department of Commerce
Tourism Division
State Capital Charleston, WV
25305
Tel: (304) 348-2766
Toll Free: 800-225-5982

WISCONSIN
Wisconsin Department. of
Development
Division of Tourism
P.O. Box 7606
Madison, WI 53707
Tel: (608) 266-2161
Toll Free: 800-372-2737
*(If calling from Wisconsin
and bordering states; all
others call (608) 266-2161.)*
800-432-8747
*(Nationwide for ordering infor-
mation package)*

WYOMING
Wyoming Travel Commission
I-25 at College Drive
Cheyenne, WY 82002
Tel: (307) 777-7777
Toll Free: 800-225-5996

Toll Free Telephone Numbers for Airline & Hotel/Motel Reservations

This listing contains the toll-free telephone numbers of the major airlines and most of the larger chains of hotels and motels operating in the U.S. Since *almost all* of them offer Senior discounts, be sure to ask what the discount is and if it is the lowest price obtainable for your reservation.

Airlines

Alaska	800-426-0333	Northwest	800-225-2525
American	800-443-7300	Southwest	800-435-9792
America West	800-235-9292	TWA	800-221-2000
Continental	800-525-0280	United	800-241-6522
Delta	800-221-1212	USAir	800-428-4322

Hotels & Motels

Best Western Motels	800-528-1234
Clarion Motels	800-252-7466
Comfort Inns	800-228-5150
Courtyard by Marriot	800-321-2211
Days Inn	800-325-2525
Econo-Travel Lodges & Motels	800-446-6900
Embassy Suites	800-362-2779
Friendship Inns	800-453-4511
Hampton Inns	800-426-7866
Hilton Inns	800-445-8667
Holiday Inns	800-465-4329
Howard Johnson's (HoJo's)	800-654-2000
Hyatt Hotels	800-233-1234
Loews Hotels	800-235-6397
Marriott Hotels	800-228-9290
Master Host/Red Carpet & Scottish Inns	800-251-1962
Quality Inns	800-228-5151
Radisson Hotels	800-333-3333
Ramada Inns	800-272-6232
Red Lion Hotels & Inns	800-547-8010
Red Roof Inns	800-843-7663
Renaissance Hotels & Resorts	800-228-9898
Rodeway Inns	800-228-2000
Sheraton Hotels & Motor Inns	800-325-3535
Super 8	800-800-8000
Travelodge	800-255-3050
Westin Hotels & Resorts	800-228-3000

Chapter 12

Your Pharmacist, Medications and Generic Drugs

What They Can Mean to You

Chapter Highlights

The generic drug scare is over! After a thorough investigation of thousands of drugs, the FDA has proclaimed the safety and effectiveness of generic drugs. Read the latest generic drug update on page 527 for more information.

Your Pharmacist, Medications And Generic Drugs

What They Can Mean to You

As we age, many of us may experience multiple or chronic illnesses requiring the prescription of various drugs to control them. According to the National Center for Health Statistics, our elderly consume 25 percent of all prescription drugs and take an average of 13 prescription drugs each year. Add to this the over-the-counter medications regularly taken, such as aspirin for arthritic pain, and the figure is astounding. Many elderly individuals spend so much each month on medications that they must cut back on other necessities, such as food and home energy, creating even more problems for their health.

It is vital for your well-being to learn about the medications you take and how you can save on their costs. This chapter deals with this aspect of your health care and, in particular, with generic equivalent drugs that can save you hundreds of dollars or more each year — money that you need to meet other necessities of life.

WHAT ARE GENERIC DRUGS?

When a new drug is developed, the manufacturer gives it a name for marketing purposes, which is referred to as its "brand name". Generally, each brand name drug is protected by patent and supplied by only one pharmaceutical company. In addition, each drug has a second name which is descriptive of its chemical composition, grouping or class. This other name is the "generic name" of the drug. Simply stated, all drugs have two names: one under which they are registered and sold to the public — the "brand name" and one which is descriptive of its chemical nature — the "generic name."

For example, Bayer is a well-known brand name for the generic product aspirin, just as the antibiotic Achromycin is a brand name for the generic drug tetracycline. The major difference between them is that generic drugs are usually cheaper in price — in some cases the savings can be as much as 50 percent.

Not all drugs are available as generic drugs. However, generic drug alternatives are available throughout the country for approximately 25 percent of all prescription drugs and almost 50 percent of the most frequently prescribed brand name drugs. The reason many brand name drugs are still not available generically is that a manufacturer who patents a particular drug has patent protection for at least 17 years in order to recoup the high cost of research and development. This protection encourages the pharmaceutical companies to conduct research on potential new medications and eventually develop them for the public's benefit.

When a patent expires on a brand name drug, or if there was no original patent, other manufacturers may be approved by the Food and Drug Administration to produce a generic equivalent. When approved, the manufacturer may sell the drug under a different brand name or under the drug's generic name. Surprisingly, almost 90 percent of all generic drugs are made by the major pharmaceutical companies, and in many cases, by the same ones who developed the brand name drugs.

The Food and Drug Administration evaluates both brand name and generic drugs for safety and effectiveness. When the generic drugs behave comparably in the body to their brand name counterpart, we refer to them as **generic equivalent** drugs. Generic equivalent drugs comprise more than 80 percent of the generic drug market today and they can be safely substituted for the brand name drugs.

Of utmost importance is that every available generic drug on the market today must comply with the same strict requirements established by the Food and Drug Administration for brand name drugs. In addition, all approved therapeutically equivalent generics must be identical to their brand name drugs in that they (1) contain the same active ingredients; (2) are identical in strength, dosage form and method of administration, oral or injection; (3) are used generally for the same illnesses; (4) have the same precautions, warnings and other instructions on the label; (5) are bioequivalent, which means they release the same amount of drug into the body at the same rate and affect the body in the same way as the equivalent brand name drug. Consequently, approved generic drugs are as safe and effective as the brand name drugs.

DRUG PRODUCT SELECTION LAW

Each state now has its own version of a law that permits generic drug substitution by pharmacists when filling your prescription unless your doctor designates on your prescription form that a specific brand name drug is required. It is advisable that you discuss the possibility of using available generic drugs with your physician and request that the prescription is written to allow your pharmacist to substitute whenever possible.

The intent of this law, which has taken many years to be enacted throughout the country, is to give the consumer the opportunity to save money on prescribed drugs. It is a very beneficial law, especially to those of our older population who may have limited incomes and take several medications on a continuing basis.

UNDERSTANDING YOUR PRESCRIPTION

When your doctor issues you a prescription, it is to your benefit to understand what it says. Check it over **before** leaving the doctor's office and ask any questions you need to understand your prescribed medication. Look for the following:

- If the prescription is not legible, ask the doctor to clarify it. This way both you and your pharmacist will be sure it will be filled properly

- The first word the doctor will write is the name of the drug being prescribed. If the doctor has indicated a brand name, ask if a generic equivalent can be used instead and, if so, ask the doctor to write on the prescription that a substitution may be made.

- The next thing the doctor will write is whether the medications to be in the form of capsules, tablets, suppositories, cream or liquid, followed by the strength of the dosage, usually expressed in milligrams (mg), grams (g), ounces (oz).

- Next will be the amount of medication to be given by the pharmacist each time your prescription is filled — for example 20 capsules or 10 fluid ounces. If the doctor does not specify how many times the prescription may be refilled, ask that it be added so that the doctor doesn't have to be called when you need a refill.

- Lastly, the prescription will specify how many times a day your medication should be taken. Although these directions are frequently expressed by abbreviations of Latin words, your pharmacist will translate them on the container label so they may be readily understood. One of the most common abbreviations is: "t.i.d." (Latin words *ter in die),* which means "three times a day."

If the medication needs to be taken right away, ask your doctor to give you two prescriptions: one to be filled immediately at any nearby local pharmacy and the other at your regular pharmacy or mail order pharmacy service.

CHOOSING YOUR PHARMACIST AND PHARMACY

Choosing a pharmacist is almost as important as choosing a doctor. Since prices vary considerably from one pharmacy to another, price comparison is an important consideration in making your selection.

The ideal selection would be a helpful pharmacist who offers you both the lowest price and the best service. Naturally, your selection will also depend on what services are provided by a pharmacy and whether or not their pharmacists offer assistance and information about your medications willingly.

For those in rural areas, selection may be limited. However, with mail order pharmacy services, you now have a choice, especially for those medications you use regularly for long-term conditions such as arthritis, high blood pressure and digestive disorders. Many of the organizations and associations described in this book have reliable pharmaceutical services for their members.

The following questions should be kept in mind when selecting a pharmacist:

- Is the pharmacist responsive to your questions about your medications? Does he appear to be helpful or indifferent to your concerns? These questions are essential to determine if you will be able to communicate with him effectively.

- Does the pharmacy provide 24-hour emergency service? If not, is it at least open at convenient hours?

- Is delivery service provided when it is not possible for you to pick up your medications?

- If you are considering using a mail order service, find out who pays the postage for the mailing of medications, when the payment for your order is expected and how long it takes to process the order.

- Does the pharmacy provide Senior Citizen discounts — if so, how much? You will find that most pharmacies are competitive and vary in the amounts they offer and the services they provide to Senior Citizens.

- Does the pharmacist readily substitute generic drugs for brand name drugs?

- Does the pharmacy maintain a large inventory of generic drugs or is it limited in those it can provide? Many pharmacies do not maintain large inventories of generic drugs. However, most mail order services and chain pharmacies are able to maintain larger inventories because of their wide distribution.

- Since many private health insurance programs and Medicaid (unlike Medicare) usually cover costs of prescription drugs, inquire whether the pharmacy accepts payment for your medications from the insurance company or from Medicaid.

- Does the pharmacist maintain a file on all the prescriptions he fills for you? If so, is the profile reviewed **each time** you receive a new medication to check for possible problems or adverse reactions with other medications you may currently be using? This is a new service for most pharmacies that is receiving considerable attention because of its value to the consumer.

PROPER USE OF YOUR MEDICATIONS

Medications can heal, reduce pain and inflammation, prevent infection, control sugar and enzyme levels and contribute in numerous ways to your total well-being and longevity. However, interactions of certain medications with other prescribed drugs, over-the-counter medications such as aspirin or antacids, certain foods, alcohol and even smoking can seriously affect the way they behave in your body.

According to the Food and Drug Administration, almost half of the more than 1.5 billion medications prescribed annually in this country are used improperly by the patient. Since older people may experience several illnesses which require different medications at the same time, it is important to become as knowledgeable as possible about your medications and their proper use. Consider carefully these recommendations concerning your use of medications:

- Learn as much as you can from either your doctor or pharmacist about every medication prescribed for you. The following questions will be helpful to ask about each new prescription or medication you are currently taking:

  — What is the drug and what is it supposed to do?

  — When should it be taken (morning, mid-day or night)?

  — How much should be taken each time, how many times each day and for how long?

  — Should the prescription be taken with water, milk or food? Before or after a meal?

  — Should driving or other activities be avoided while taking it?

  — Should alcohol of any type be avoided while taking it?

  — Are there any medications that shouldn't be taken while taking this particular one? Inquire about aspirin, Tylenol, ibuprofen, laxatives, antacids or any other over-the-counter medication you maybe taking.

  — Are there any possible side effects that should be known? If so, what can be done to alleviate them?

  — Are there any special storing instructions?

- Follow the prescribed dosage and schedule carefully. Do not take an extra dosage to "catch-up" on one that you missed without first consulting your doctor or pharmacist.

- **Never** take another person's prescribed medication regardless of how similar your symptoms are to theirs. This is critical because people **do** react differently — often adversely — to the same medication.

- When your doctor prescribes a new medication, make sure you inform him of all medications you are currently taking — both prescribed and over-the-counter.

- Immediately call your doctor when you notice any unusual reaction or problem you may experience with certain medications, such as indigestion, dizziness, unusual heart palpitations, sleeplessness, loss of appetite, rashes, diarrhea, etc.

- Throw away all old or expired medications. If you are uncertain about a medication, contact your pharmacist to see if it is still effective or should be discarded.

KEEPING A RECORD OF YOUR MEDICATIONS

If you are taking several medications regularly, keep a record of all the prescribed drugs you are taking. Prepare it so it can be used as a check-list throughout the week. Use a notepad or something that can be carried with you during the day to help you remember the times you are to take each medication. In addition, you may want to obtain some type of pill container which separates your medications by times of day they should be taken.

DRY MOUTH (XEROSTOMIA) AND MEDICATIONS . . . A FREQUENT SIDE EFFECT

Of the various side effects which may result from taking medicines, one of the most frequent is dry-mouth, medically termed Xerostomia. Some 300 to 400 commonly used drugs, obtained either via prescription or over-the-counter, can cause extreme dryness of the mouth. The degree of its severity varies greatly among individuals, but principally it consists of a continual dryness or burning sensation in the mouth. Some medications, such as antihistamines, can cause some dryness in the mouth, but that is not Xerostomia. The effects of Xerostomia on the tissues of the mouth are more severe and may cause great discomfort.

Because it is usually essential that you continue your medication, you should be aware of this possible side effect and know what you can do to help alleviate it. Although there is no known treatment, there are several things you can do to control the dryness and protect your teeth and the tissues of the mouth from any related damage. The National Institute of Dental Research recommends the following:

- Brush your teeth frequently each day, using a toothpaste that contains fluoride. Ask your dentist if you should use a topical fluoride on a daily basis.
- Try to avoid foods that are sticky and contain sugar. Brush immediately after eating any of these foods.
- Have your teeth cleaned by your dentist at least three times a year and have him treat all cavities immediately.
- Chew sugarless gum since it will help produce more saliva. If you have dentures, make sure the chewing does not create any discomfort or irritation.
- Take frequent sips of water or sugarless soft drinks. It will be helpful to pause while speaking to sip some type of liquid. In addition, drink frequently while eating to help swallowing.
- Slowly suck on sugarless mints or hard candies.
- Keep a glass of water by your bed to alleviate dryness during the night or when you waken.
- Avoid coffee, tea and soft drinks that contain caffeine, as well as tobacco, alcohol, spicy, salty and highly acidic foods.
- Ask your doctor or pharmacist about any artificial saliva products that you can use to help lubricate the mouth.

DRUG HEADLINES

The following news items on the development of new medications and the use of prescribed and over-the-counter drugs will affect the health and well-being of millions of Americans — of which you are probably one. Of particular importance to Seniors is the first item on the past few month's investigation of the safety and effectiveness of generic drugs. Please pass the information on to others who may not have read or heard about these news items.

- **_Generic Drug Scare!_** Those who have been afraid to take any form of generic drug after learning of the scandal that rocked the generic drug industry and the Food and Drug Administration (FDA) can now relax and continue to use generic drugs without fear. The FDA announced that after examining more than 2,500 samples of generic products and their brand-name equivalents, there was nothing wrong with the drugs themselves. The investigation, which involved several thousand individual tests, found fewer problem drugs — only 1.1 percent did not conform to production quality specifications — than usually uncovered by FDA random reviews of brand-name or generic drugs. The FDA concluded that currently marketed prescription generic drugs are both **safe and effective.** (Over-the-counter generics were not investigated because their safety and effectiveness were **never** in question.)

- **_FDA Approval of New Stomach Ulcer Therapy!_** In early April 1996, the Food and Drug Administration (FDA) approved a two-drug (Prilosec and Biaxin) combination therapy to help cure stomach ulcers and actually prevent them from reoccurring. The approval allows Astra Merck, Inc. to sell its ulcer drug Prilosec in combination with Abbot Laboratories' antibiotic Biaxin. Over the past several years, research has shown that a bacterium called Helicobacter pylori is the major cause of stomach ulcers. The combination of these two drugs not only heals the ulcer but in a vast number of cases actually eradicates the bacteria. For further information about this revolutionary treatment, contact your physician.

- **_America's Other Drug Problem!_** A recent Department of Health and Human Services (DHHS) study revealed that mismedication of older adults was so severely widespread that it could be termed "the nation's other drug problem." According to DHHS statistics, while adults age 60 and over comprise only 17% of the U.S. population, they account for 39% of all hospitalizations, and 51% of deaths from drug reactions. Every year, more than 240,000 elderly people are hospitalized for adverse reactions to prescription or over-the-counter drug. Drug-induced falls produce about 32,000 older consumer deaths each year.

Much of this problem could be prevented, if older people, their families, and their doctors discussed their medicines before, during, and after using them. Regardless of your age, be sure to read the section in this chapter on proper use of medications... it could save your life.

■ *FDA Approves Drug to Dissolve Blood Clots:* The FDA approved a new drug — Anistreplase — that will quickly dissolve the blood clots which can cause permanent damage to an individual following a heart attack. Two other clot-dissolving drugs — Alteplase (TPA) and Streptokinase — were previously approved by the FDA; however, the advantage of Anistreplase is that it can be administered in five minutes or less while the other two require continuous administration for one to three hours. The drug will be marketed under the brand name *Eminase* by its manufacturer, Smith Kline Beecham.

A WORD OF CAUTION!

Always keep nitroglycerin tablets — used for angina or heart attacks — in the bottle they came in or in an airtight container. Don't use fancy pillboxes or containers that are not airtight! Nitroglycerin tablets lose their effectiveness rapidly when exposed to the air.

LISTING

Frequently Prescribed Drugs And Their Generic Equivalents

This listing contains some of the **most frequently** prescribed brand name drugs that are available generically in most large pharmacies and mail-order pharmacy services. Many of the small or rural pharmacies only maintain a stock of those that are prescribed on a regular basis in their area.

If you are taking any of the brand name drugs shown here, be sure to ask your pharmacist or pharmacy service (1) if they have the generic equivalent available and (2) whether a substitution can be made to your prescription by the pharmacist or whether your doctor must approve it. Remember that all 50 states now have laws allowing generic substitutions on your prescription for brand name drugs, but that these laws do **vary** in the regulations and rules governing these substitutions.

Since approved generic drugs may differ in color, taste, tablet shape, inert ingredients and packaging from their comparable brand name drugs, do not expect the generic forms to look or taste like their brand name equivalents. Ask your pharmacist to label your medication's container in print large enough to read and easily identify the drug it contains.

As explained earlier in this chapter, any opportunity you have of using generic drugs in place of the brand name drugs can save you money. **Always ask** whether your prescribed medication is available generically even if it isn't shown in this listing, since there are many other less common drugs which have available generic equivalents.

BRAND NAME	GENERIC NAME
A	
Achromycin V	Tetracycline HCL
Actifed	Triprolidine HCL/ Pseudoephedrine HCL
Aldactazide	Spironolactone with Hydrochlorothiazide
Aldactone	Spironolactone
Aldomet	Methyldopa
Alupent	Metaproterenol Sulfate
Amcill	Ampicillin
Amphicol	Chloramphenicol
Amphylline	Aminophylline
Amoxil	Amoxicillin
Antepar	Piperazine Citrate
Antivert	Meclizine HCL
Anturane	Sulfinpyrazone
Apresazide	Hydralazine Hydrochlorothiazide
Apresoline	Hydralazine Hydrochlorothiazide
Aristocort	Triamcinolone
Arlidin	Nylidrin HCL
Artane	Trihexyphenidyl
Asendin	Amoxapine
Atarax	Hydroxyzine HCL
Ativan	Lorazepam
Azo Gantrisin	Azo-Sulfisoxazole
Azulfidine	Sulfasalazine
B	
Bactocil	Oxacillin Sodium
Bactrim	Trimethoprim Sulfamethoxazole
Bancap	Acetaminophen/Butalbital
Benadryl	Diphenhydramine HCL
Benemid	Probenecid

BRAND NAME	GENERIC NAME
Bentyl	Dicyclomine
Blocadren	Timolol Maleate
Brethine	Terbutaline
Butazolidin	Phenylbutazone
C	
Calan SR	Verapamil HCL
Cardizem	Diltiazem
Catapres	Clonidine HCL
Centrax	Prazepam
Choledyl	Oxtriphylline
Chloromycetin	Chloramphenicol
Cleocin	Clindamycin HCL
Clinoril	Sulindac
Cloxapen	Cloxacillin Sodium
Cogentin	Benztropine Mesylate
Colace	Docusate Sodium
Colbenemid	Probenecid with Colchicine
Combid	Prochlorperazine with Isopropamide
Combipres	Chlorthalidone/Clonidine HCL
Compazine	Prochlorperazine
Coumadin	Warfarin Sodium
Cyclospasmol	Cyclandelate
Cytomel	Liothyronine
D	
Dalmane	Flurazepam HCL
Danocrine	Danazol
Darvocet-N	Propoxyphene Napsylate with Acetaminophen
Darvon	Propoxyphene
Decadron	Dexamethasone
Decapryn	Doxylamine Succinate

BRAND NAME	GENERIC NAME
Deltasone	Prednisone
Demerol	Meperidine HCL
Desoxyn	Methamphetamine HCL
Desyrel	Trazodone HCL
Dexedrine	Dextroamphetamine Sulfate
Diabinese	Chlorpropamide
Diamox	Acetazolamide
Dimetapp	Bromophen TD
Diprosone	Betamethasone Dipropionate
Ditropan	Oxybutynin Chloride
Diucardin	Hydroflumethiazide
Diupres	Chlorothiazide with Reserpine
Diuril	Chlorothiazide
Donnatal	Belladonna Alkaloids with PB
Drixoral	Brompheniramine
Dyazide	Hydrochlorothiazide/Triamterene
E	
E.E.S.	Erythromycin Ethyl Succinate
Elavil	Amitriptyline HCL
Elixophyllin Elixir	Theophylline
Empirin Compound with Codeine	Aspirin with Codeine
E-Mycin	Erythromycin
Endep	Amitriptyline Hydrochloride
Enduron	Methyclothiazide
Equanil	Meprobamate
Erythrocin Stearate	Erythromycin Stearate
Esidrix	Hydrochlorothiazide
Eskalith	Lithium

BRAND NAME	GENERIC NAME
F	
Feosol	Ferrous Sulfate
Fiorinal	APC with Butalbital
Flagyl	Metronidazole
Flexeril	Cyclobenzaprine HCL
Furadantin	Nitrofurantoin
G	
Gantanol	Sulfamethoxazole
Gantrisin	Sulfisoxazole
Garamycin	Gentamicin Sulfate
H	
Haldol	Haloperidol
Hydergine	Ergoloid Mesylate
Hydrodiuril	Hydrochlorothiazide
Hydropres	Hydrochlorothiazide with Reserpine
Hygroton	Chlorthalidone
I	
Inderal	Propranolol HCL
Indocin	Indomethacin
Ismelin	Guanethidine Monosulfate
Isoptin	Verapamil HCL
Isordil	Isosorbide Dinitrate
Isordil Sublingual	Isosorbide Dinitrate Sublingual
Isordil Tembid	Isosorbide Dinitrate T.D.
K	
Kay-Ciel	Potassium Chloride
Keflex	Cephalexin
Kenacort	Triamcinolone
Kenalog Cream	Triamcinolone Cream
K-Lor Powder	Potassium Powder

BRAND NAME	GENERIC NAME
K-Lyte (Orange)	Eff Potassium
Kwell	Lindane
L	
Lanoxin	Digoxin
Larotid	Amoxicillin
Lasix	Furosemide
Ledercillin VK	Penicillin VK
Librax	Chlordiazepoxide Clidinium Br
Librium	Chlordiazepoxide HCL
Lomotil	Diphenoxylate HCL with Atropine Sulfate
Loniten	Minoxidil
Ludiomil	Maprotiline HCL
M	
Mandelamine	Methanamine Mandelate
Marax	Hydroxyzine, Ephed. and Theophylline
Medrol	Methylprednisolone
Megace	Megestrol Acetate
Mellaril	Thioridazine HCL
Miltown	Meprobamate
Motrin	Ibuprofen
Mycolog	Nystatin
Mycostatin	Nystatin
Mysoline	Primidone
N	
Naldecon	Phenylpropanolamine
Nalfon	Fenoprofen
Naqua	Tricolormethiazide
Navane	Thiothixene
Nembutal Sodium	Sodium Pentobarbital
Neotrizine	Trisulfapyrimidines

BRAND NAME	GENERIC NAME
Nicolar	Niacin
Nitrobid	Nitroglycerine T.D.
Nitrospan	Nitroglycerine LA
Norpace	Disopyramide
Norpramin	Desipramine HCL
O	
Omnipen	Ampicillin
Oretic	Hydrochlorothiazide
Orinase	Tolbutamide
Ornade	CPM/Phenylpropanolamine
P	
Panmycin	Tetracycline
Parafon Forte	Chlorzoxazone with Acetaminophen
Pavabid	Papaverine T.D.
PBZ	Triplennamine
Pentids	Penicillin G Potassium
Pen-Vee K	Penicillin V-K
Percocet	Acetaminophen/Oxycodone HCL
Periactin	Cyproheptadine HCL
Peritrate	Pentaerythritol Tetranitrate
Persantine	Dipyridamole
Phenergan	Promethazine HCL
Plegine	Phendimetrazine Tartrate
Polaramine	Dexchlorpheniramine
Polycillin	Ampicillin
Premarin	Conjugated Estrogens
Prinicipen	Ampicillin
Pro-Banthine	Propantheline Bromide
Procan-SR	Procainamide-SR
Procardia	Nifedipine

BRAND NAME	GENERIC NAME
Proloprim	Trimethoprim
Pronestyl	Procainamide HCL
Provera	Medroxyprogesterone
Q	
Quinaglute Dura-Tabs	Quinidine Gluconate SR
Quinamm	Quinine
Quinora	Quinidine Sulfate
R	
Raudixin	Rauwolfia Serpentina
Redisol	Cyanocobalamin
Reglan	Metoclopramide
Restoril	Temazepam
Ritalin	Methylphenidate HCL
Robaxin	Methocarbamol
Rondec	Carbinoxamine Pseudoephedrine
Rufen	Ibuprofen
S	
Salutensin	Hydroflumethiazide with Reserpine
Seconal Sodium	Secobarbital Sodium
Seldane	Terfenadine
Septra DS	Trimethoprim Sulfamethoxazole
Ser-Ap-Es	H.H.R. Compound
Serax	Oxazepam
Serpasil	Reserpine
Sinequan	Doxepin
Slow K	Pottassium Chloride
Soma	Carisoprodol
Sorbitrate	Isosorbide Dinitrate
Stelazine	Trifluoperazine HCL
Sumycin	Tetracycline

BRAND NAME	GENERIC NAME
Synthroid	Levothyroxine Sodium
T	
Tegretol	Carbamazepine
Temaril	TrimeprazineTartrate
Tenuate Dospan	Diethylproplon TD
Tepanil	Diethylproplon TD
Terramycin	Oxytetracycline HCL
Tetracyn	Tetracycline
Theo Dur	Theophylline SR
Thorazine	Chlorpromazine HCL
Thyroid Armour	Thyroid U.S.P.
Trimpex	Trimethoprim
Tofranil	Imipramine HCL
Tolinase	Tolazamide
Trinsicon	Hematinic with Intrinsic Factor
Tylox	Acetaminophen/Oxycodone HCL
Tuss-Ornade	Phenylpropanolamine/Caramiph
Tylenol with Codeine	Acetaminophen with Codeine
U-Z	
Urecholine	Bethanecol
Valisone	Betamethasone Valerate
Valium	Diazepam
Vasodilan	Isoxsuprine
V-Cillin-K	Penicillin V Potassium
Veetids	Penicillin V-K
Vibramycin	Doxycycline
Vistaril	Hydroxyzine Pamoate
Wygesic	Acetaminophen/Propoxyphene HCL
Zyloprim	Allopurinol

Guidelines for a Long and Healthy Life

According to the National Institute on Aging, your chances of living a longer, healthier life increase when you:

- *Eat a well balanced diet.* Your diet should include all the essential nutrients — vitamins, minerals, proteins, fats and carbohydrates, particularly complex carbohydrates like fruits, vegetables, and whole grains (also good sources of dietary fiber). Your need for fat is much better served by eating monounsaturates, like olive oil — avoid saturated fats like palm oil, coconut oil and butter. Also limit your intake of sugar and sodium in processed foods and in the form of table sugar and table salt.

- *Do some form of exercise regularly.* The medical community agrees that just 20 minutes three times a week of proper exercise will keep you fit. However, before beginning any exercise program, check with your doctor about what type of exercise would be best for you.

- *Get enough sleep.*

- *Don't smoke.*

- *If possible, don't drink.* If you must drink, do so only in moderation.

- *Avoid exposure to sun and cold.* Too much sun can cause skin cancer and sunstroke. Too much cold puts a great strain on the heart.

- *Have regular medical checkups.* Always see your doctor immediately if you suspect you have a physical or medical problem, and follow his/her advice.

- *Keep active.* In addition to regular exercise, try to keep busy through work, recreation and other activities.

- *Allow time each day to rest and relax.*

- *Make safety a habit.* Always hold on to railings when climbing stairs and ramps; and always wear your seatbelt.

- *Maintain a positive attitude towards life.* Keeping fit and living long really can be a matter of mind over matter.

FROM THE ORIGINAL PUBLISHER ...

In my eighty-plus years, of which almost 50 have been in publishing, helping bring this book to the American public has been a highlight of my career. It gives me the greatest amount of personal satisfaction to know I have played a part in helping other Seniors get the knowledge and help so many of them need.

Considering the many complex, often confusing federal and state organizations involved in the many programs and services for the elderly, it is not surprising that Seniors have difficulty getting the information they need. Ken Skala has created a remarkably informative book for Seniors and their families. It is one of the most complete, unique compilations of vital information available today.

There is practically no aspect of life during the "golden years" that Mr. Skala has not touched on in his book. It shows the full extent of his expertise and deep concern for the welfare of Seniors. I sincerely believe that *American Guidance for Seniors* will help everyone who reads it.

... **Lee E. Sharff**

. . . More About
American Guidance for Seniors

"*American Guidance* fulfills the promise of its title. . . . More than just a reference book, it is a practical guide for daily use by Seniors, their families, and younger people responsible for the well-being of older folks. In short, an invaluable source of information across the whole spectrum of issues vital to our growing population of Seniors."
— *Retirement Life*, published by the
National Association of Retired Federal Employees

"The *best* self-help book on the market . . . a *treasure chest* of information at your fingertips! And you don't have to be a Senior to take advantage of its rich resources. This book should be in every home in America."
— North American Bookdealers Exchange

"The print is large, the information is clear, and the list of possible benefits, organizations, and agencies often overlooked is comprehensive."
— Jean Dietz, *The Boston Globe*

"*American Guidance for Seniors* deserves a permanent place on everyone's library shelf."
— Terry Savage, *Chicago Sun-Times*

"Skala's 550-page book explains complex programs for the elderly in simple terms."
— Bill Kaufman, *New York Newsday*

"Absolutely one of the best sources of vital information available concerning the needs and problems of our rapidly expanding Senior population. All retirees should own this book."
— Sol Gordon, Col. USAF (Ret.), Publisher,
The Retired Military Almanac

★　★　★　★

Selected to be transcribed into braille and recorded form by the National Library Service. *American Guidance for Seniors* is available free of charge to the nation's blind and physically handicapped people unable to read ordinary print in a conventional manner. Contact the Library of Congress, National Library Service for the Blind and Physically Handicapped, Washington, DC 20542.